Essentials of Employment Law
10th edition
David Lewis and Malcolm Sargeant

David Lewis is Professor of Employment Law at Middlesex University and Programme Leader for the MA in Human Resource Management and Employment Law. Apart from teaching on a range of degree courses and being a regular contributor to specialist commercial seminars, he has considerable experience as a consultant. He is a member of the editorial committee of the *Industrial Law Journal* and was appointed an ACAS arbitrator in 1999.

Malcolm Sargeant is Professor of Labour Law at Middlesex University. He has written widely on employment law subjects, especially on issues related to transfers of undertakings, discrimination in employment and age discrimination. Prior to becoming an academic he was personnel manager of a large financial services company and director of a recruitment and management consultancy. He teaches Discrimination Law and Employment Law at Middlesex University.

The Chartered Institute of Personnel and Development is the leading publisher of books and reports for personnel and training professionals, students, and all those concerned with the effective management and development of people at work. For details of all our titles, please contact the publishing department:
tel: 020-8612 6204
e-mail publish@cipd.co.uk
The catalogue of all CIPD titles can be viewed on the CIPD website:
www.cipd.co.uk/bookstore

Essentials of Employment Law
10th edition

David Lewis and Malcolm Sargeant

Chartered Institute of Personnel and Development

This edition first published 2009

First edition published 1983
Second edition published 1986
Third edition published 1990
Fourth edition published 1994
Fifth edition published 1997
Sixth edition published 2000
Seventh edition published 2002
Eighth edition published 2004
Ninth edition published 2007

Typeset by Fakenham Photosetting Ltd
Printed in Spain by Graphycems

British Library Cataloguing in Publication Data
A catalogue record of this book is available from the British Library

ISBN 978 1 84398 231 9

The views expressed in this publication are the authors' own and may not necessarily reflect those of
the CIPD.

The CIPD has made every effort to trace and acknowledge copyright-holders. If any source has been
overlooked, CIPD Enterprises Ltd would be pleased to redress this in future editions.

Chartered Institute of Personnel and Development, CIPD House,
151 The Broadway, London, SW19 1JQ

Tel: 020 8612 6200
E-mail: cipd@cipd.co.uk
Website: www.cipd.co.uk
Incorporated by Royal Charter.
Registered Charity No. 1079797

Contents

Abbreviations

AC Appeal Cases
ACAS Advisory, Arbitration and Conciliation Service
ACOP Approved Code of Practice
All ER All England Law Reports
AMRA Access to Medical Records Act 1988
CA Court of Appeal
CAC Central Arbitration Committee
Ch Chancery Division
CMLR Common Market Law Reports
CO Certification Officer
COSHH Control of Substances Hazardous to Health Regulations 2002
CRE Commission for Racial Equality
CRTUPEA Regulations Collective Redundancies and Transfers of Undertakings (Protection of Employment) (Amendment) Regulations 1999
DDA Disability Discrimination Act 1995
DDAA Disability Discrimination Act 1995 (Amendment) Regulations 2003
DPA Data Protection Act 1998
EA Employment Act 2002
EADR Regulations Employment Act 2002 (Dispute Regulations) Regulations 2004
EAT Employment Appeal Tribunal
EC European Community
ECA European Communities Act 1972
ECHR European Court of Human Rights
ECJ European Court of Justice
ECR European Court Reports
EESO Regs Employment Equality (Sexual Orientation) Regulations 2003
EOC Equal Opportunities Commission

EPA Equal Pay Act 1970
ERA Employment Rights Act 1996
ERel Act Employment Relations Act 1999
ETA Employment Tribunals Act 1996
EU European Union
EWC Expected Week of Confinement
EWC Directive European Works Council Directive 1997
GOQ Genuine Occupational Qualification
HASAWA Health and Safety at Work Act 1974
HRA Human Rights Act 1998
HSC Health and Safety Commission
HSCE Health and Safety (Consultation with Employees) Regulations 1996
HSE Health and Safety Executive
ICR Industrial Cases Reports
IRLB Industrial Relations Law Bulletin
IRLR Industrial Relations Law Reports
LBPIC Regulations Telecommunications (Lawful Business Practice) (Interception of Communications) Regulations 2000
LWTL Lawtel
MHSW Regulations Management of Health and Safety at Work Regulations 1999
MLP Maternity Leave Period
MPL Maternity and Parental Leave, etc Regulations 1999
MPP Maternity Pay Period
NMW National Minimum Wage
PPE Personal Protective Equipment
PTW Regulations Part-time Workers (Prevention of Less Favourable Treatment) Regulations 2000
QB Queen's Bench
RB Regulations Employment Equality (Religion or Belief) Regulations 2003
RIDDOR Reporting of Injuries,

Diseases and Dangerous
Occurrences Regulations 1995
RIP Regulation of Investigatory Powers
Act 2000
RRA Race Regulations Act 1976
RTOST Regulations Right to Time off
for Study or Training Regulations
2001
SDA Sex Discrimination Act 1975
SI Statutory Instrument
SMP Statutory Maternity Pay
SNB Special Negotiating Body
SRSC Regulations Safety
Representatives and Safety
Committee Regulations 1977
SSCBA Social Security and Benefits
Act 1992

SSP Statutory Sick Pay
TICE Regulations Transitional
Information and Consultation of
Employees Regulations 1999
Transfer Regulations Transfer of
Undertakings (Protection of
Employment) Regulations 1981
TUC Trades Union Congress
TULRCA Trade Union and Labour
Relations (Consolidation) Act 1992
TURERA Trade Union Reform and
Employment Rights Act 1993
WLR Weekly Law Reports
WT Working Time
WT Regulations Working Time
Regulations 1998

List of cases cited

A v Chief Constable of West Yorkshire Police (2004) IRLR 574
Abbey Life Assurance Co Ltd v Tansell (2000) IRLR 387
Abadeh v British Telecommunications plc (2001) IRLR 23
Abdoulaye v Renault (1999) IRLR 811
Abernethy v Mott, Hay and Anderson (1974) IRLR 213
ABP v TGWU (1989) IRLR 399
Abrahams v Performing Rights Society (1995) IRLR 486
Abrahamsson v Andersson and Fogelqvist (2000) IRLR 732
ACAS v UKAPE (1980) IRLR 124
Adams v British Airways (1996) IRLR 574
Adams v Lancashire County Council (1996) IRLR 154 199
Adamson v B&L Cleaning Ltd (1995) IRLR 193
Adeneler v Ellinikos Organismos Galaktos Case C-212/04 (2006) IRLR 716
Addison v Ashby (2003) IRLR 211
Adi (UK) Ltd v Willer (2001) IRLR 542
Adin v Sedco Forex International (1997) IRLR 280
Affleck v Newcastle Mind (1999) IRLR 405
Ahmad v Inner London Education Authority (1977) ICR 490
Ahmed v United Kingdom (1999) IRLR 188
Airbus Ltd v Webb (2008) IRLR 309
Air Canada v Lee (1978) IRLR 392
Airlie v City of Edinburgh District Council (1996) IRLR 516
Alabaster v Barclays Bank (No.2) (2005) IRLR 576
Alamo Group (Europe) Ltd v Tucker (2003) IRLR 266
Alboni v Ind Coope Retail Ltd (1998) IRLR 131
Alcan Extrusions v Yates (1996) IRLR 327
Aldridge v British Telecom (1990) IRLR 10
Alexander v Bridgen Ltd (2006) IRLR 422
Alexander v STC Ltd (1991) IRLR 286
Ali v Christian Salvesen Food Services Ltd (1997) IRLR 17
Alidair Ltd v Taylor (1978) IRLR 82
Allan Janes LLP v Johal (2006) IRLR 599
Allders International v Parkins (1981) IRLR 68
Allen v Amalgamated Construction Ltd (2000) IRLR 119
Allen v GMB (2008) IRLR 690
Allonby v Accrington and Rossendale Collage (2001) IRLR 364
Allonby v Accrington and Rossendale College (2004) IRLR 224
Alonso v Osakidetza-Servicio (2007) IRLR 911
Amicus v Macmillan Publishers Ltd (2007) IRLR 378
Amicus v Macmillan Publishers Ltd (2007) IRLR 885
Amministrazione delle Finanze v Simmenthal Case 106/77 (1978) ECR 629
Anglian Homes Ltd v Kelly (2004) IRLR 793

Annandale Engineering v Samson (1994) IRLR 59
Anyanwu v South Bank University (2001) IRLR 305
APAC v Kirwin (1978) IRLR 318
Aparau v Iceland Frozen Foods (1996) IRLR 119
Archibald v Fife Council (2004) IRLR 651
Arie Botzen and others v Rotterdamsche Droogdok Maatschappij BV (1986) 2 CMLR 50 ECJ
Armour v Skeen (1977) IRLR 310
Armstrong v Newcastle NHS Trust (2006) IRLR 124
Armstrong v Walter Scott Motors Ltd (2003) EAT 766/02
Artisan Press v Strawley (1986) IRLR 126
Ashley v Ministry of Defence (1984) IRLR 57
ASLEF v Brady (2006) IRLR 76
Aspden v Webbs Poultry Group (1996) IRLR 521
Attorney-General v Blake (2001) IRLR 37
AUT v Newcastle University (1987) ICR 317
Avon County Council v Howlett (1993) 1 All ER 1073
Avon and Somerset Police Authority v Emery (1981) ICR 229
Awotana v South Tyneside NHS Trust (2005) IRLR 958
Azmi v Kirklees B.C. (2007) IRLR 484

B v BAA (2005) IRLR 927
Babula v Waltham Forest College (2007) IRLR 346
BAC v Austin (1978) IRLR 332
Bacica v Muir (2006) IRLR 35
Bailey v Home Office (2005) IRLR 369
Bainbridge v Circuit Foil UK Ltd (1997) IRLR 305
Bakers' Union v Clark's of Hove Ltd (1978) IRLR 366
Balamoody v UKCC (2002) IRLR 288
Balfour Kilpatrick Ltd v Acheson (2003) IRLR 683
Bank of Credit and Commerce International SA v Ali (No.3) (1999) IRLR 508
Barber v RJB Mining (UK) Ltd (1999) IRLR 308
Barclays Bank v Kapur (1991) IRLR 136
Barnsley M.B.C. v Prest (1996) ICR 85
Barretts & Baird Ltd v IPCS (1987) IRLR 3
Barton v Investec Ltd (2003) IRLR 332
Bass Leisure v Thomas (1994) IRLR 104
Baxter v Harland & Wolff (1990) IRLR 516
BBC v Souster (2001) IRLR 150
BCCI v Ali (No.3) (1999) IRLR 508
Beneviste v University of Southampton (1989) IRLR 122
Benson v Secretary of State (2003) IRLR 748
Benton v Sanderson Kayser (1989) IRLR 299
Berg and Busschers v Besselsen (1988) IRLR 255
Betts v Brintel Helicopters (1997) IRLR 361
Bevan Ashford v Malin (1995) IRLR 360
Birch and Humber v University of Liverpool (1985) IRLR 165
Bliss v South East Thames Regional Health Authority (1988) IRLR 308

Byrne v BOC Ltd (1992) IRLR 505
Byrne v City of Birmingham D.C. (1987) IRLR 191
Byrne Brothers (Formwork) Ltd v Baird (2002) IRLR 96

Cable & Wireless v Muscat (2006) IRLR 355
Cadman v Health and Safety Executive (2006) IRLR 969
Cadoux v Central Regional Council (1986) IRLR 131
Calder v Finlay (1989) IRLR 55
Calder v Rowntree Mackintosh (1993) IRLR 212
Caledonia Bureau Investment & Property v Caffrey (1998) IRLR 110
Caledonian Mining Ltd v Bassett (1987) IRLR 165   1
Cambridge and District Co-op v Ruse (1993) IRLR 156
Camden and Islington NHS Trust v Kennedy (1996) IRLR 381
Camelot v Centaur Communications (1998) IRLR 81
Camellia Tanker Ltd v ITWF (1976) IRLR 183
Canary Wharf Management v Vedebi (2006) IRLR 416
Canniffe v East Riding Council (2000) IRLR 555
Cantor Fitzgerald v Bird (2002) IRLR 867
Cantor Fitzgerald International v Callaghan (1999) IRLR 234
Capek v Lincolnshire County Council (2000) IRLR 590
Capita Health Solutions Ld v McLean (2008) IRLR 595
Capper Pass Ltd v Lowton (1976) IRLR 366
Cardiff Women's Aid v Hartup (1994) IRLR 390
Carlson v Post Office (1981) IRLR 158
Carmichael v National Power plc (2000) IRLR 43
Carrington v Helix Ltd (1990) IRLR 6
Cartwright v Clancey Ltd (1983) IRLR 355
Caruana v Manchester Airport plc (1996) IRLR 378
Catamaran Cruisers v Williams (1994) IRLR 386
Cavanagh v Ulster Weaving Co Ltd (1959) 2 All ER 745
Cawley v South Wales Electricity Board (1985) IRLR 89
CCSU v Minister for the Civil Service (1985) ICR 374
CCSU v United Kingdom (1987) EHRR 269
Centrum voor Gelijkheid van Kansen en Racismebestrijding v Frima Feryn (2008)
IRLR 732
Cerberus Ltd v Rowley (2001) IRLR 160
Cereal Packaging Ltd v Lyncock (1998) IRLR 510
Chacón Navas v Eurest Colectividades SA Case C-13/05 (2006) IRLR 706
Chapman v Letheby & Christopher Ltd (1981) IRLR 440
Chattopadhyay v Headmaster of Holloway School (1981) IRLR 487
Chief Adjudication Officer v Rhodes (1999) IRLR 103
Chief Constable of Lincolnshire Police v Stubbs (1999) IRLR 81
Chief Constable of West Yorkshire v A (2000) IRLR 465
Chief Constable of West Yorkshire v Khan (2001) IRLR 830
Christie v Haith Ltd (2003) IRLR 670
Churchill v Yeates Ltd (1983) IRLR 187
Claridge v Rowney Ltd (2008) IRLR 672
Clark v BET plc (1997) IRLR 348

McNicol v Balfour Beatty Rail Maintenance Ltd (2002) IRLR 711
Meade v Haringey L.B.C. (1979) ICR 494
Meade-Hill v British Council (1995) IRLR 478
Mears v Safecar Security Ltd (1982) IRLR 501
Mennell v Newell & Wright Ltd (1997) IRLR 519
Merckx v Ford Motor Co. Belgium SA (1996) IRLR 467
Messenger News Group v NGA (1984) IRLR 397
Methuen v Cow Industrial Polymers (1980) IRLR 289
Metropolitan Borough of Solihull v NUT (1985) IRLR 211
Mid-Staffordshire General Hospitals NHS Trust v Cambridge (2003) IRLR 566
Middlebrook Mushrooms Ltd v TGWU (1993) IRLR 232
Middlesborough B.C. v TGWU (2002) IRLR 332
Mihlenstedt v Barclays Bank (1989) IRLR 522
Mikkelsen case [*Foreningen af Arbejdsledere i Danmark v A/S Dansmols Inventar*] (1985) ECR 2639
Miklaszewicz v Stolt Offshore Ltd (2002) IRLR 344
Millar v Inland Revenue Commissioners (2006) IRLR 112
Millbrook Furnishing Ltd v McIntosh (1981) IRLR 309
Ministry of Defence v Cannock (1994) IRLR 509
Ministry of Defence v Crook (1982) IRLR 488
Ministry of Defence v Hay (2008) IRLR 928
Ministry of Defence v Meredith (1995) IRLR 539
Mirror Group Ltd v Gunning (1986) IRLR 27
Modern Injection Moulds Ltd v Price (1976) IRLR 172
Monk Staff Association v Certification Officer and ASTMS (1980) IRLR 431
Montgomery v Johnson Underwood Ltd (2001) IRLR 269
Moonsar v Fiveways Express Transport (2005) IRLR 9
Moore v Duport Furniture (1982) IRLR 31
Morgan v West Glamorgan County Council (1995) IRLR 68
Morgans v Alpha Plus Ltd (2005) IRLR 234
Morris v Secretary of State (1985) IRLR 297
Morris v Walsh Western UK Ltd (1997) IRLR 562
Morris Angel v Hollande (1993) IRLR 169
Morrison v ATGWU (1989) IRLR 361
Morrow v Safeway Stores (2002) IRLR 9
Morse v Wiltshire County Council (1998) IRLR 352
Moss v McLachlan (1985) IRLR 76
Motherwell Railway Club v McQueen (1989) ICR 419
Motorola Ltd v (1) Davidson and (2) Melville Craig Group Ltd (2001) IRLR 4
Mowlem Northern Ltd v Watson (1990) IRLR 500
Moyhing v Barts NHS Trust (2006) IRLR 860
MSF v Refuge Assurance plc (2002) IRLR 324
Mugford v Midland Bank plc (1997) IRLR 208
Murco Petroleum Ltd v Forge (1987) IRLR 50
Murphy v Bord Telecom Eireann (1988) IRLR 267
Murray v Foyle Meats Ltd (1999) IRLR 562

NAAFI v Varley (1976) IRLR 408

Preface to the 10th edition

As expected, there have been many changes to employment law since the previous edition was published. In addition to the Employment Act 2008, which removed the statutory disputes procedures, one of the most important pieces of legislation on the horizon is a new Equality Act. This will replace a number of statutes and regulations and is likely to come into effect during the next two to three years. We briefly summarise the anticipated contents of the Equality Bill in Chapter 6 but the Bill itself has not been published at the time of going to press. We hope to put new developments on the accompanying website to keep the reader informed.

In addition to updating the material in the light of legislative changes and court decisions, this edition has reorganised the chapters on discrimination law. Finally, the authors would like to acknowledge the support of their families in producing this work and especially welcome Karen into the fold.

David Lewis
Malcolm Sargeant
April 2009

CHAPTER 1

The Sources and Institutions of Employment Law

OVERVIEW

This chapter will introduce you to both the way in which employment law is made and the institutions that develop, supervise and enforce it. We start with the distinction between civil and criminal law and a basic introduction to the legal system in England and Wales. Employment law is created by primary and secondary legislation which is then interpreted by the courts, especially by employment tribunals and the Employment Appeal Tribunal. They are influenced by Codes of Practice and, importantly, by EU law and the decisions of the European Court of Justice. Finally, we look at those organisations set up by Parliament to regulate industrial relations and dispute resolution.

CIVIL AND CRIMINAL LAW

Criminal law is concerned with offences against the state and, apart from private prosecutions, it is the state which enforces this branch of the law. The sanctions typically imposed on convicted persons are fines and/or imprisonment. Civil law deals with the situations where a private person who has suffered harm brings an action against (ie sues) the person who committed the wrongful act which caused the harm. Normally the purpose of suing is to recover damages or compensation. Criminal and civil matters are normally dealt with in separate courts which have their own distinct procedures.

In this book we shall be concentrating largely on civil law but we shall be describing the criminal law insofar as it imposes duties in relation to health and safety and restricts the activities of pickets. In employment law the two most important civil actions are those based on the law of contract and the law of tort (delict in Scotland). The essential feature of a contract is a binding agreement in which an offer by one person (for example, an employer) is accepted by someone else (for example, a person seeking work). This involves an exchange of promises. Thus, in a contract of employment there is a promise to pay wages in exchange for a promise to be available for work. As we shall see later, the parties to a contract are not entirely free to negotiate their own terms because Parliament imposes certain restrictions and minimum requirements. The law of tort (delict) places a duty on everyone not to behave in a way that is likely to cause harm to others, and in the employment field the tort of negligence has been applied so as to impose a duty on employers to take reasonable care of their employees during the course of their employment. Various torts have also been created by the judiciary in order to impose legal liability for industrial action – for example, the tort of interfering with trade or business – but Parliament has intervened to provide immunities in certain circumstances (see Chapter 19).

LEGISLATION AND CODES OF PRACTICE

In England and Wales the most important source of law governing industrial relations is legislation enacted by Parliament. Often the government will precede legislation by issuing Green Papers or White Papers. Traditionally the Green Paper is a consultative document and the White Paper is a statement of the government's policy and intentions, although this distinction does not always seem to be adhered to. The government will announce its legislative programme for the forthcoming session in the Queen's Speech. A Bill is then introduced into the House of Commons (sometimes this process can begin in the House of Lords) and is examined at a number of sessions (readings) in both the House of Commons and the House of Lords. The agreed Bill becomes an Act (or statute) when it receives the Royal Assent. It is then referred to (cited) by its name and year, which constitutes its 'short title' (eg Employment Rights Act 1996).

The provisions of an Act may not be brought into operation immediately, for the government may wish to implement it in stages. Nevertheless, once the procedure is completed, the legislation is valid. The main provisions of a statute are to be found in its numbered sections, whereas administrative details, repeals and amendments of previous legislation tend to be contained in the schedules at the back. Statutes sometimes give the relevant Secretary of State the power to make rules (regulations) to supplement those laid down in the Act itself. These regulations, which are normally subject to parliamentary approval, are referred to as statutory instruments (SI) and this process of making law is known as delegated or subordinate legislation. Statutory instruments are cited by their name, year and number (eg the Transfer of Undertakings (Protection of Employment) Regulations 2006, SI No.246).

CODES OF PRACTICE

Legislation sometimes allows for an appropriate Minister or a statutory body to issue Codes of Practice. The primary function of these codes is to educate managers and workers by publicising the practices and procedures which the government believes are conducive to good industrial relations. Under section 199 of the Trade Union and Labour Relations (Consolidation) Act 1992 (TULRCA 1992) the Advisory, Conciliation and Arbitration Service (ACAS) has a general power to issue codes 'containing such practical guidance as [ACAS] thinks fit for the purpose of promoting the improvement of industrial relations'. Following representations by interested parties ACAS submits a draft code to the Secretary of State for approval before it is laid before Parliament. At the time of writing, ACAS Codes of Practice exist on the following topics: *Disciplinary and Grievance Procedures*; *Disclosure of Information to Trade Unions for Collective Bargaining Purposes*; and *Time Off for Trade Union Duties and Activities*. By virtue of section 14 of the Equality Act 2006, the Commission for Equal and Human Rights (CEHR) can issue codes of the same standing as those of ACAS and section 16 of the Health and Safety at Work Act 1974 (HASAWA 1974) gives the Health and Safety Executive (HSE) the power to approve Codes of Practice provided it obtains the consent of the Secretary of State on each occasion. The Information Commissioner also has powers to produce Codes of Practice for data controllers. Finally, sections 203–6 TULRCA 1992 entitle the Secretary of State to issue codes, but before publishing a draft he or she is obliged to consult ACAS. However, no such duty exists if a code is merely being revised to bring it into conformity with subsequent statutory provisions.[1] Although emerging by different means, all these codes have the same legal standing – ie nobody can be sued or prosecuted for breaching a code – but in any proceedings before a tribunal, court (if the code was issued under TULRCA 1992 or HASAWA 1974) or the Central Arbitration Committee (CAC) a failure to adhere to a recommendation 'shall be taken into account'.[2]

COMMON LAW AND THE COURT HIERARCHY

The feature which distinguishes the English legal system from non-common-law systems is that in this country judicial decisions have been built up to form a series of binding precedents. This is known as the case-law approach. In practice this means that tribunals and judges are bound by the decisions of judges in higher courts. Thus employment tribunals, which are at the bottom of the English court hierarchy, are required to follow the decisions of the Employment Appeal Tribunal (EAT or Appeal Tribunal), the Court of Appeal and the Appeal Committee of the House of Lords, although they are not bound by other employment tribunal decisions. The Employment Appeal Tribunal is bound by the decisions of the Court of Appeal and the House of Lords and normally follows its own previous decisions. The Court of Appeal has a civil and criminal division and, while both are bound by the House of Lords' decisions, only the civil division is constrained by its own previous decisions. The House of Lords has stated that it will regard its own earlier decisions as binding unless in the circumstances of a particular case it is thought just to depart from them. In addition all English and Scottish courts must follow the decisions of the European Court of Justice (ECJ). When a court or tribunal needs clarification of European Union law in order to make a decision, it will refer the matter to the ECJ under Article 234 of the EC Treaty.

What constitutes the binding element of a judicial decision is for a judge or tribunal in a subsequent case to determine. Theoretically what has to be followed is the legal principle or principles which are relied on in reaching the decision in the earlier case. In practice judges and tribunals have a certain amount of discretion, for they can take a broad or narrow view of the principles which are binding upon them. If they do not like the principles that have emerged, they can refuse to apply them so long as they are prepared to conclude that the facts of the case before them are sufficiently different from the facts in the previous decision. Not surprisingly, this technique is known as 'distinguishing'. Thus, while it is correct to argue that the doctrine of precedent imports an element of certainty, it is wrong to assume that there is no scope for innovation in the lower courts. In addition to interpreting the law, the judiciary can and does make law.

THE COURT HIERARCHY

The court structure in England and Wales is shown in diagrammatic form in Figure 1 (below).

Figure 1 Court structure in England and Wales

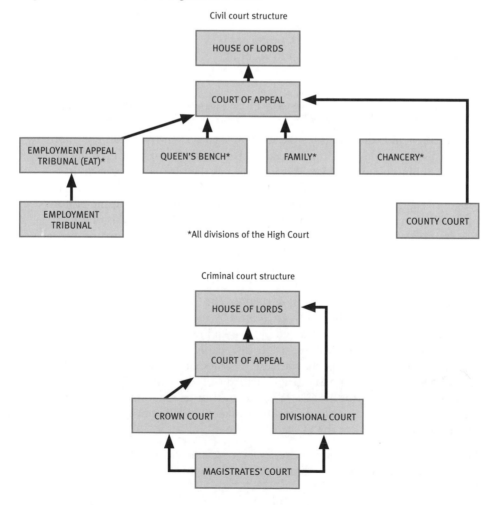

Most proceedings involving individual employment rights are commenced at employment tribunals and appeals against an employment tribunal decision can normally be heard by the EAT only if there has been an error of law. An error of law occurs when a tribunal has misdirected itself as to the applicable law, when there is no evidence to support a particular finding of fact, or when the tribunal has reached a perverse conclusion, ie one which cannot be justified on the evidence presented.[3] Further appeals can be made on a point of law to the Court of Appeal and the House of Lords, but only if permission is granted by either the body which made the decision or the court which would hear the appeal. Other civil actions can be started in the County Court or High Court. Appeals on a point of law against a decision made by either court can be lodged with the Court of Appeal and, if permission is granted, further appeal lies to the House of Lords. There is also a 'leapfrog procedure' which enables an appeal against a decision of the High Court to go directly to the House of Lords so long as all the parties involved give their consent.

Criminal proceedings are normally commenced in magistrates' courts – for example, if pickets are charged with obstructing police officers in the execution of their duty. The defence can launch an appeal on fact which goes to the Crown Court, but it is also possible for either party to appeal on a point of law to the Divisional Court of the Queen's Bench and then on to the House of Lords. Prosecutions for serious offences – for example, under section 33 of HASAWA 1974 – are dealt with in the Crown Court, and appeals on a point of law go to the Court of Appeal and the House of Lords in the usual way.

EUROPEAN UNION LAW

The United Kingdom joined the European Economic Community in 1973. Since then there have been a number of Treaties by which the Member States have agreed to develop the scope of the law of the European Union (EU). Article 249 of the EC Treaty (previously Article 189 EC) allows the EU to introduce different types of legislation, the most important ones being regulations and Directives.

CASE STUDY

In the case of *Mangold v Helm*[4] the Munich Labour Court referred questions to the ECJ about whether the German law on fixed-term working was compatible with Community law on age discrimination. Although the implementation date for the age provisions of Directive 2000/78 was December 2003, Member States were allowed to delay implementation until December 2006 'to take account of particular conditions'.

In a decision which has significant ramifications, the ECJ held that national courts must guarantee the full effectiveness of the general principle of non-discrimination by setting aside any provision of national law which conflicts with Community law even where the period prescribed for transposition has not expired.

Regulations tend to be of a broad nature and are directly applicable in all Member States. Most EU legislation that affects employment law is introduced, however, in the form of directives. Directives are legislative instruments that require a Member State to translate (transpose) the contents of the directive into national law. Member States are usually given a period of two to three years to carry this out.

If a Member State fails to transpose a Directive, a citizen may, in certain circumstances, rely on the EU law rather than on existing national laws. The Directive is then said to have direct effect. This can be the result of the Member State's either failing to transpose the Directive or inadequately transposing it. Direct effect is, however, usually only vertically effective – ie it can only be relied upon against the state or 'emanations' of the state.[5] This concept of direct effect has proved an important tool in the enforcement of Community law, especially with respect to Article 141 EC (previously Article 119 EC) on equal pay.

Early cases in the European Court of Justice established the supremacy of Community law over national law.[6] National courts also have an obligation to interpret national law so that it gives effect to EU law.[7] This means that national legislation should be interpreted in a way that is consistent with the objects of the Treaty, the provisions of any relevant Directives and the rulings of the European Court of Justice.[8] In relation to the interpretation of Directives, this principle applies whether the national legislation came after or preceded the particular Directive.[9]

It is the European Communities Act 1972 (ECA 1972) which gives effect to the UK's membership of the EU. First, section 2(1) enables directly effective EU obligations to be enforced as free-standing rights. Thus in *McCarthys Ltd v Smith*[10] Article 141 EC on equal pay was applied following a reference to the European Court of Justice. Second, section 2(2) facilitates the introduction of subordinate legislation to achieve compliance with EU obligations – eg the Fixed-term Employees (Prevention of Less Favourable Treatment) Regulations 2002.[11] Articles 226 EC and 228 EC (previously 169 and 171 EC) enable the European Commission to take steps to ensure that the UK complies with its obligations to give effect to Directives.[12] In addition, an individual may be able to obtain damages as a result of a Member State's failure to carry out its obligations under European Union law.[13]

THE KEY INSTITUTIONS

EMPLOYMENT TRIBUNALS

Industrial tribunals were first established under the Industrial Training Act 1964 but their jurisdiction has been greatly extended. Their name was changed to 'employment tribunals' by section 1 of the Employment Rights (Dispute Resolution) Act 1998. In this book they will always be referred to by this new name, even though many of the cases cited will refer to them as industrial tribunals.

The Employment Tribunal Service was established in 1997 to provide administrative and organisational support for employment tribunals and the Employment Appeal Tribunal. There are 25 local tribunal offices in England and Scotland. The President of these tribunals is a barrister or solicitor of seven years' standing who is appointed by the Lord Chancellor for a five-year term. Normally tribunal cases are heard by legally qualified chairpersons and two other people who are known as lay members.[14] Tribunal appointments are for five years initially, and whereas the chairpersons are appointed by the Lord Chancellor and are subject to the same qualification requirements as the President, the lay members are appointed by the Secretary of State. They are drawn from two panels; one is formed as a result of nominations made by employer organisations, and the other consists of nominees from organisations of workers. Since 1999 the government has also advertised in the press so that individuals may nominate themselves for one of the panels. However, while lay members are expected to have an understanding of workplace practices and how people work together, they are not supposed to act as representatives of their nominating organisations.

Representation at hearings

Hearings at employment tribunals are relatively informal.[15] The parties may represent themselves or be represented by a legal practitioner, a trade union official, a representative from an employers' association or any other person. In practice, employers tend to be legally represented more often than employees, one reason being the unavailability of legal aid at present. (Applicants may be able to obtain advice and assistance in preparing their case under the legal aid scheme.) Human resource managers should give very serious thought to the question of representation, because the manager who understands how the shop floor operates and is familiar with the types of argument that may be raised during the disciplinary process may prove more effective than a lawyer from outside.

Apart from appeals against improvement or prohibition notices issued under HASAWA 1974, costs are not normally awarded unless either party (or their representative) is deemed to have acted vexatiously, abusively, disruptively, or otherwise unreasonably, or the bringing or conducting of the proceedings was misconceived.[16]

Challenging tribunal decisions

Tribunal decisions can be challenged either by review or by appeal. The power of review, which enables the whole or part of a case to be re-heard and set aside or vary the original decision, may be exercised only on one of the following grounds:

- the decision was wrongly made as a result of error on the part of tribunal staff
- a party did not receive notice of the proceedings
- the decision was made in the absence of a person entitled to be heard

- new evidence has become available since the making of the decision and its existence could not have been reasonably known of or foreseen
- the interests of justice require a review.[17]

An appeal to the Employment Appeal Tribunal can only be made on a point of law and must be lodged within 42 days.[18]

THE EMPLOYMENT APPEAL TRIBUNAL (EAT)

The EAT, which was established in 1976, is serviced by Employment Tribunal Service offices in London and Edinburgh. It can sit anywhere in England, Wales or Scotland and consists of High Court judges nominated by the Lord Chancellor (one of whom serves as President) and a panel of lay members who are appointed on the joint recommendation of the Lord Chancellor and the Secretary of State. This panel consists of nominees from employers' and workers' organisations. Appeals are heard by a judge and either two or four lay persons, all of whom have equal voting rights. However, a judge can sit alone where the appeal arises from proceedings before an employment tribunal consisting of the chair alone.

Parties can be represented by whomsoever they please, and costs will be awarded only where the proceedings are deemed to have been unnecessary, improper, or vexatious or where there has been unreasonable conduct in bringing or conducting the proceedings.[19] Finally, the Appeal Tribunal may adjourn proceedings where there is a reasonable prospect of a conciliated settlement being reached.[20]

THE ADVISORY, CONCILIATION AND ARBITRATION SERVICE (ACAS)

ACAS has been in existence since 1974. Its work is directed by a council consisting of a chairperson and between nine and 15 members appointed by the Secretary of State. Three or four members are appointed after consultation with trade unions, the same number following consultation with employers' organisations, and the remainder are independent. The Service is divided into 11 regions which perform most of the day-to-day work – for example, handling direct enquiries from the public. Although ACAS is financed by the government, section 247(3) TULRCA 1992 states that it shall not be 'subject to directions of any kind from any Minister of the Crown as to the manner in which it is to exercise its functions'.

ACAS has the general duty of promoting the improvement of industrial relations, in particular by exercising its functions in relation to the settlement of trade disputes.[21] It also has specific functions which merit separate consideration.

Advice

ACAS may, on request or on its own initiative, provide employers, their associations, workers and trade unions with advice on any matter concerned with or affecting industrial relations.[22] In practice the forms of advice range from telephone inquiries to in-depth projects, diagnostic surveys and training exercises.

Conciliation

Where a trade dispute exists or is likely to arise, ACAS may, on request or of its own volition, offer assistance to the parties with a view to bringing about a settlement. This may be achieved by conciliation or other means – for example, the appointment of an independent person to render assistance. Before attempting to conciliate in collective trade disputes, ACAS is required to 'have regard to the desirability of encouraging the parties to a dispute to use any appropriate agreed procedures'.[23] According to its Annual Report for 2007/8, 640 collective cases were completed and conciliation was successful in 603 of these.

In addition to collective matters, ACAS has the task of conciliating in employment tribunal cases. When a complaint is presented to an employment tribunal, a copy of it is sent to a conciliation officer who has the duty to promote a settlement without the matter having to go to a hearing. Conciliation officers can intervene if requested to do so by the parties or where they believe they could act with a reasonable prospect of success. At the instigation of either party the officer may act before a complaint has been presented in respect of a matter which could be the subject of tribunal proceedings (for the conciliation officer's particular duty in unfair dismissal cases, see Chapter 15). So as not to undermine the conciliation process it is stipulated that anything communicated to an officer in connection with the performance of his or her functions shall not be admissible in evidence in any proceedings before an employment tribunal without the consent of the person who communicated it.

The ACAS Annual Report for 2007/8 reveals that 58,513 (26%) of the 227,782 employment tribunal claims were for equal pay, and 43,231 (19%) were for unfair dismissal. 67,968 individual conciliation cases were cleared. Of these, 42% were settled, 33% were withdrawn and 25% went to tribunal.

Arbitration

At the request of one party but with the consent of all the parties to a collective dispute (or potential dispute), ACAS may appoint an arbitrator or arbitration panel from outside the Service or refer the matter to be heard by the Central Arbitration Committee (CAC). In performing this function ACAS is obliged to consider whether the dispute could be resolved by conciliation, and arbitration is not to be offered unless agreed procedures for the negotiation and settlement of disputes have been exhausted (save where there is a special reason which justifies arbitration as an alternative to those procedures).[24] CAC awards can be published only with the consent of all parties involved.

In addition, ACAS operates a voluntary arbitration scheme which provides an alternative to employment tribunals for the resolution of disputes over unfair dismissal. Where the parties agree to use the scheme, they must waive the rights they would otherwise have in relation to an unfair dismissal claim. Arbitrators are appointed from the ACAS Arbitration Panel, and hearings, which are held in private, are intended to be relatively speedy, cost-efficient and non-legalistic. The parties can reach an agreement settling their dispute at any stage. However, where an arbitrator makes an award the parties cannot appeal on a point of law except where the Human Rights Act 1998 or EC law is relevant.[25]

Inquiry

ACAS may inquire into any question relating to industrial relations generally, in a particular industry or in a particular undertaking. Any advice or findings that emerge may be published so long as the views of all concerned parties have been taken into account.[26]

Other duties

Apart from the general power to issue codes of practice, ACAS has an important conciliation role to play in statutory recognition claims and in those situations where a recognised union has lodged a complaint that an employer has failed to disclose information which it requires for collective bargaining purposes (see Chapter 18).

THE CENTRAL ARBITRATION COMMITTEE (CAC)

The CAC consists of a chairperson, deputy chairpersons and other members, all of whom are appointed by the Secretary of State after consultation with ACAS. The members must have experience as employer or worker representatives, while the deputy chairpersons tend to be lawyers or academic experts in industrial relations. Like ACAS, the CAC is not subject to directions from a Minister. Apart from receiving requests to arbitrate directly from parties to a dispute, the CAC receives arbitration requests from ACAS (see above). Additionally, the CAC is required to make determinations under sections 183–5 TULRCA 1992 (dealing with complaints arising from a failure to disclose information). CAC awards are published and take effect as part of the contracts of employees covered by the award. Unless it can be shown that the CAC exceeded its jurisdiction,[27] breached the rules of natural justice or committed an error of law,[28] no court can overturn its decisions.

The CAC is also required to resolve disputes under the Transnational Information and Consultation of Employees Regulations 1999,[29] and the Annual Report 2007/8 reveals that seven applications were received in this period. The Employment Relations Act 1999 (ERel Act) added an important new role in relation to the recognition and de-recognition of trade unions. The CAC receives the application for recognition and supervises the process, including the holding of a ballot amongst the affected employees, leading to a decision on whether recognition or de-recognition should be granted (see Chapter 18). It is required to establish a panel consisting of an independent chair and an experienced representative of employers and an experienced representative of workers to fulfil these functions. In dealing with these cases the Act requires the CAC to have regard to the object of encouraging and promoting fair and efficient practices in the workplace (so far as is consistent with its other obligations). According to the CAC Annual Report for 2007/8, trade unions submitted 64 applications for statutory recognition, and eight complaints about disclosure of information were received.

THE CERTIFICATION OFFICER

The Certification Officer is also appointed by the Secretary of State after consultation with ACAS and is required to produce an annual report for them. He or she is responsible for maintaining a list of trade unions and employers' associations and, if an application is submitted, has to determine whether or not a listed union qualifies for a certificate of independence. The Certification Officer also handles:

- disputes which arise from trade union amalgamations and mergers and the administration of political funds

- complaints that the provisions of Chapter IV TULRCA 1992, concerning trade union elections, have been infringed and can determine the procedure to be followed on any application or complaint received[30]

- complaints by a member of breach of a trade union's own rules relating to a union office, disciplinary proceedings, ballots (on any issue other than industrial action) and the constitution and proceedings of the executive committee or of any decision-making meeting.[31]

In relation to all these jurisdictions an appeal can only be lodged if a point of law is involved.

Under the Trade Union and Labour Relations (Consolidation) Act 1992, the Certification Officer can direct a trade union to produce documents relating to its financial affairs. Where there appears to have been impropriety, the Certification Officer can appoint inspectors to investigate.[32]

The Information Commissioner

This officer replaced the Data Protection Commissioner. The Information Commissioner has a number of general duties, including the preparation and dissemination of codes of practice for guidance.[33]

KEY LEARNING POINTS

- The most important source of law governing industrial relations is legislation enacted by Parliament.

- Legislation sometimes allows for a Minister or a statutory body to issue Codes of Practice.

- The most relevant Codes of Practice for employment law are issued by ACAS, the CEHR, the Information Commissioner and the Secretary of State.

- The case-law approach of the courts means that they are bound by the decisions of judges in higher courts.

- National courts must follow the decisions and guidance given by the European Court of Justice.

- European laws take precedence and are directly effective against the state or emanations of the state, if not transposed correctly.

- Employment tribunals are specialist bodies, whose decisions can be appealed against, on points of law, to the Employment Appeal Tribunal.

- ACAS has the general duty of improving industrial relations and provides advice, individual and collective conciliation and arbitration services.

- The Central Arbitration Committee deals with complaints about failure to disclose information for the purposes of collective bargaining.

- The Central Arbitration Committee also has an important role to play in the procedure for the statutory recognition of trade unions.

- The Certification Officer maintains lists of employers' associations and trade unions and issues certificates of independence.

Reinforce your understanding of this chapter by visiting www.cipd.co.uk/sss for activities, questions, weblinks and additional case studies

REFERENCES

1   See section 205 TULRCA 1992

2   Section 207A TULRCA 1992 provides for tribunal awards to be adjusted in certain circumstances where there has been a failure to comply with a Code.

3   *British Telecom v Sheridan* (1990) IRLR 27

4   (2006) IRLR 143

5   See *Marshall v Southampton and South West Hampshire Area Health Authority* Case 152/85 (1986) IRLR 140

6   See *Amministrazione delle Finanze v Simmenthal* Case 106/77 (1978) ECR 629

7   See *Litster v Forth Dry Dock Engineering Co Ltd* (1989) IRLR 161

8   *Pickstone v Freemans plc* (1988) IRLR 357

9   See *Marleasing SA v Comercial Internacional de Alimentacion SA* Case 106/89 (1990) ECR 4135

10 (1980) IRLR 208

11 SI 2002/2034

12 See *Commission v UK* (1994) IRLR 292

13 See Cases 46/93 and 48/93 *Brasserie du Pêcheur SA v Federal Republic of Germany* and *R v Secretary of State for Transport ex parte Factortame* (1996) ECR 1029

14 Certain claims can be heard by a chair sitting alone.

15 On tribunal practice and procedures see specialist texts.

16 Rule 40 Schedule 1 Employment Tribunal (Constitution and Rules of Procedure) Regulations 2004 SI No.1861

17 Rule 34 (see note 15)

18 Rule 3 Employment Appeal Tribunal Rules 1993 SI No.2854

19 Rule 34A Employment Appeal Tribunal Rules 1993 SI No.2854

20 Rule 36 (see note 15)

21 Section 209 TULRCA 1992

22 Section 213 TULRCA 1992

23 Section 210(3) TULRCA 1992

24 See section 212(3) TULRCA 1992

25 See ACAS Arbitration Scheme (Great Britain) Order 2004 SI No.753 and *The ACAS arbitration scheme for the resolution of unfair dismissal disputes: a guide to the scheme.*

26 See section 214 TULRCA 1992

27 See *R v CAC ex parte Hy-Mac Ltd* (1979) IRLR 461

28 See *R v CAC (on the application of the BBC)* (2003) IRLR 460

29 SI No.3323

30 See section 256 TULRCA 1992

31 Section 108A TULRCA 1992

32 See sections 37A–E TULRCA 1992

33 See section 51 Data Protection Act 1998

CHAPTER 2

Formation of the Contract of Employment (1): The sources of contractual terms

OVERVIEW

This chapter and the next one are concerned with the contract of employment and how it comes into existence. We consider the influences that contribute to establishing the contents of the contract. Express terms agreed between the employer and the employee, or the employee's representatives, normally take precedence over all other terms. There is a statutory requirement for the employer to issue written particulars of employment to new employees within two months of their start date. These particulars are considered in detail here, as is the effect of collective agreements, workforce agreements, works rules, and custom and practice.

CONTRACTS OF EMPLOYMENT

Apart from those of apprentices and merchant seamen, who can only be employed under written deeds and articles respectively, contracts of employment may be oral or in writing.[1] A contract of employment is like any other contract in the sense that it is subject to the general principles of law. In theory this means that the parties are free to negotiate the terms and conditions that suit them so long as they remain within the constraints imposed by statute and the common law.[2] In practice the majority of the workforce do not negotiate on an individual basis. An important proportion are engaged on such terms and conditions as are laid down in currently operative collective agreements. However, these agreements are confined to the minority of employers because about two thirds of workplaces in the UK do not have any employees covered by collective agreements.

ILLEGAL CONTRACTS

One aspect of the common law which has been relied on, particularly in unfair dismissal cases, is the principle that courts will not enforce an illegal contract.[3] Thus, if employees receive additional payments which are not taxed, they may be debarred from exercising statutory rights on the ground that they were not employed under valid contracts of employment. However, an occasional payment by an employer to an employee without deduction of tax does not render the contract of employment unenforceable.[4]

Where illegality is alleged, the burden of proof is on the party making the allegation to show that the contract had been entered into with the object of committing an illegal act or had been performed with that objective. If the contract was unlawful at formation or the intention was to perform it unlawfully then the contract will be unenforceable. However, if at the time of formation the contract was perfectly lawful and it was intended to be performed lawfully, the effect of some act of illegal performance is not automatically to make the contract unenforceable. If the contract is performed illegally and the person seeking to enforce it takes part in the illegality, that may render the contract unenforceable at his or her instigation. Yet not every illegal act participated in by the enforcer will have that effect. Where the enforcer has to rely on his or her own illegal action then the court will not assist. However, if he or she does not have to do so, the question is whether the method of performance and the degree of participation in the illegality is such as to make the contract illegal.[5] Thus in *Hewcastle Catering v Ahmed* [6] the employee's involvement in a VAT fraud devised by the employer, and from which only the employer benefited, did not preclude a claim of unfair dismissal. According to the Court of Appeal, the general principle that a contract is unenforceable on grounds of illegality applies if in all the circumstances the court would appear to encourage illegal conduct. However, the defence of illegality will not succeed where the employer's conduct in participating in the illegal contract is so reprehensible in comparison with that of the employee that it would be wrong to allow the employer to rely on its being unenforceable. Subsequently, it has been accepted that if a contract has the effect of depriving HM Revenue and Customs of tax to which it is entitled, this does not necessarily make it unlawful: 'There must be some form of misrepresentation, some attempt to conceal the true facts of the relationship, before the contract is rendered illegal.'[7]

Although a contract of employment can be entered into quite informally, because of the consequences of having an employee on the books (see Chapter 4) a considerable degree of formality is desirable. Indeed, if practical as well as legal difficulties are to be avoided, great care should be taken to ensure that all the relevant terms and conditions are understood at the time employment commences.

EXPRESS TERMS AND STATUTORY STATEMENTS

Express terms are those which are expressly stated to form part of the contract and they are binding irrespective of whether they differ from those contained in a job advertisement.[8] Apart from statutorily implied terms, which cannot be undermined, express terms normally take precedence over all other sources, ie common law implied terms and custom and practice. Not later than two months after the start of employment of a person whose employment continues for a month or more, the employer must supply written particulars of key terms of employment.[9] Indeed, in *Lange v Schünemann GmbH* [10] the European Court of Justice indicated that Article 2(1) of Directive 91/53 (on proof of the employment relationship) obliged an employer to notify an employee of any term which must be considered an essential element of the contract. The reasoning behind this is clear: if employees receive written statements of the main terms of employment, disputes over the nature and scope of their contracts will be minimised.

STATEMENT OF PARTICULARS

The following information must be given to employees individually, although in relation to the matters mentioned in 6, 7, 9 and 15 below it is sufficient to make the information reasonably accessible to them by means of a document to which they are referred.[11]

1 *The identity of the parties*
Sometimes the identity of the employer can be in dispute – eg where people are 'hired out' to other organisations[12] or where the employer consists of a management committee running a charity.[13]

2 *The date on which the employee's period of continuous employment began (taking into account any employment with a previous employer which counts towards that period)*
Section 211 ERA 1996 defines the meaning of 'continuous employment' (see Chapter 16). It begins with the day that a person starts work for an organisation but periods spent taking part in a strike do not count towards length of service.[14] The period of continuous employment is important because certain statutory rights are associated with length of service, for example, the right not to be unfairly dismissed and the right to redundancy payments. Section 218 ERA 1996 preserves continuity of employment in certain circumstances, as do the Transfer of Undertakings (Protection of Employment) Regulations 2006[15] (Transfer Regulations). If continuity is not preserved, for whatever reason, qualified employees are entitled to redundancy payments from their previous employer. According to Regulation 4(1) of the Transfer Regulations, where there is a transfer of an undertaking (or part of an undertaking), employees who are transferred are to be treated as if they had originally made contracts with the transferee employer. (On the scope of the Transfer Regulations see Chapter 16.)

3 *The scale or rate of remuneration, or the method of calculating remuneration, and the intervals at which remuneration is paid*
The word 'remuneration' is not defined in the statute and ought to be regarded as including all financial benefits (see Chapter 5 on the National Minimum Wage Act 1998).

4 *Any terms and conditions relating to hours of work and normal working hours*
The concept of normal working hours is crucial, so in order to avoid confusion, employers should specify whether or not overtime is mandatory – ie forms part of the normal working hours. Care is especially needed when considering annualised hours contracts, where it may still be advisable to

define the working week for the purpose of calculating holiday entitlement and any overtime payments owed to people who leave during the working year. The courts or tribunals will not necessarily be prepared to fill gaps left by agreements that are not comprehensive. In *Ali v Christian Salvesen*[16] the Court of Appeal concluded that the parties to a collective agreement, which was expressly incorporated into a contract of employment, might deliberately have omitted provisions dealing with termination of employment during the calculation period on the grounds that it was too complicated or too controversial to include. Working hours are usually a matter for the parties to determine, but see Chapter 10 on the impact of the Working Time Regulations.[17]

5   *Any terms and conditions relating to holidays and holiday pay*
Employees are entitled to be paid if holidays are taken in accordance with the terms of their employment during their period of notice.[18] According to the EAT, the daily rate of pay for the purposes of accrued holiday entitlement should be calculated by dividing the annual salary by the number of working days.[19] Those employees protected by the Working Time Regulations are entitled to 5.6 weeks' paid holiday per leave year (Regulation 13). The leave year can be the subject of agreement or, if there is no such agreement, it will commence on the day employment began and each subsequent anniversary thereafter (see Chapter 10).

6   *Any terms and conditions relating to incapacity for work due to sickness or injury*
This includes any provision for sick pay (see Chapter 5).

7   *Any terms and conditions relating to pensions and pension schemes*

8   *A note stating whether a contracting-out certificate is in force*
This book does not generally address the complex issues of pension entitlement. However, it should be noted that where it is a contractual term that employees are entitled to benefits under a pension scheme, employers must discharge their functions under such a scheme in good faith and, so far as it is within their power, procure the benefits to which the employees are entitled.[20]

9   *The length of notice which the employee is entitled to receive and is obliged to give*
See Chapter 11.

10 *The title of the job or a brief description of the employee's work*
If, in the interests of flexibility, a job description is widely drawn, it should be pointed out to employees that the ambit of their contractual obligations may be wider than the particular duties upon which they are normally engaged.[21]

11 *Where the employment is temporary, the period for which it is expected to continue or, if it is for a fixed term, the date when it is to end*
On fixed-term contracts see Chapter 4.

12 *The place of work or, if the employee is required or permitted to work at various places, an indication of the employer's address*

If an employee works in a number of different countries, the place of work has been defined by the European Court of Justice as the place where the employee habitually carries out his or her work.[22]

13 *Any collective agreements which directly affect the terms and conditions of employment, including, where the employer is not a party, the person by whom they were made*
Such agreements can be incorporated into a contract of employment (see below) and may even be transferred to a new employer by the Transfer Regulations.[23]

14 *Where the employee is required to work outside the UK for more than a month*
The period of work outside the UK, the currency in which payment will be made, any additional pay and benefits to be provided by reason of the work being outside the UK, any terms and conditions relating to the employee's return to the UK.
The Posted Workers Directive[24] provides added protection for people working in a Member State other than that in which they normally work. Any rules in force concerning terms and conditions of employment, as a result of law, regulation, administrative provision or by collective agreements in the state to which the employee is posted are to be guaranteed. These rules can include maximum work periods; rest periods; paid holidays; minimum rates of pay (although not supplementary occupational pensions); conditions for hiring out temporary workers; health and safety; protective measures for pregnant women and those that have recently given birth; and equal treatment between men and women.

15 *Any disciplinary rules applicable to the employee and any procedure applicable to the taking of disciplinary decisions (including dismissal) relating to the employee* [25]

16 *The name or description of the person to whom employees can apply if they are dissatisfied with any disciplinary decision or seek to redress a grievance*

The statement must indicate the manner in which any such application should be made.

17 *Any further steps consequent upon an application expressing dissatisfaction over a disciplinary decision (including dismissal) or grievance*
Two points should be noted here. First, although ERA 1996 does not state that employers must have disciplinary rules, the Code of Practice on Disciplinary and Grievance Procedures emphasises their desirability (see Chapter 13). Second, rules, disciplinary decisions (including dismissals), grievances and procedures relating to health and safety at work are exempted because separate rules and procedures are thought to be appropriate in this area and should be referred to in the information provided by employers under section 2 HASAWA 1974 (see Chapter 9).

If there are no particulars to be entered under any of the above headings, that fact must be mentioned in the written statement. It should also be noted that information relating to items 8, 11, 13, 14 and 16 may be given in instalments within the two-month period. The other items must be dealt with in a single document called a 'principal statement'. The information required can be supplied in the form of a written statement, a contract of employment or a letter or engagement.[26]

Changes cannot be made to a contract of employment without the consent of the employee, but where there is a change in any of the details required by section 1, written notification must be given to the employee within one month.[27] The nature of the changes must be set out in full, although the employer may refer to other documents for the same matters and in the same manner as for the original provision of particulars. There is no provision for the changes to be notified in instalments.

THE STATUS OF THE STATEMENT OF PARTICULARS

It is important to understand that the statement issued does not constitute a contract or even conclusive evidence of its terms, but is merely the employer's version of what has been agreed.[28] Indeed, in *Robertson v British Gas*[29] the Court of Appeal decided that a statutory statement could not even be used as an aid to the interpretation of the contract. If agreement has not been reached in a key area, management may choose to include in that statement what it considers to be reasonable arrangements. Technically the statement will be inaccurate (because the terms were on offer rather than agreed at the time they were issued) but if the employee accepts the arrangements or acquiesces in them – ie by not challenging them – the employer's proposals may be deemed to have contractual effect. However, the EAT has suggested that a distinction might be drawn between a matter which has immediate practical application and one which does not. In *Jones v Associated Tunnelling Co.*[30] it was thought that it would be asking too much of ordinary employees to require them to object to erroneous statements of terms which had no immediate practical impact on them. The law does not oblige employees to sign the written particulars or even acknowledge their receipt, but if they confirm that what has been issued is an accurate summary of the main employment terms, the particulars may be treated by the courts as having contractual status.[31]

'Mandatory' and 'non-mandatory' terms

Where an employee is given a complete but incorrect statement – ie some of the particulars are wrong in that they do not reproduce what was agreed between the parties – the employee can complain to an employment tribunal, which has the power to confirm, amend or replace the particulars. If there is no written statement or an incomplete one is issued, the tribunal must determine what the missing particulars are.[32] According to the Court of Appeal,[33] the particulars required under 1, 2, 3, 9 and 10 above are 'mandatory' terms in that actual particulars must be given under those headings. On the other hand, the particulars required under 4–7 were viewed as 'non-mandatory' in the sense that no particulars need to be inserted if none has been agreed. As regards 'non-mandatory' terms, the Court of Appeal held that an employment tribunal could not invent a term if nothing had been agreed by the parties. However, where a 'mandatory' term was omitted from a statement a tribunal would probably have to infer one. When the tribunal has decided what particulars should have been included, the employer is deemed to have provided the employee with a statement containing those particulars.[34] The sanction on an employer who fails to supply a suitable statement is that, in any of the proceedings listed in Schedule 5 EA 2002, a tribunal is obliged to make or increase an award by a minimum of two weeks' pay (or a maximum of four weeks' pay if that is considered just and equitable).[35]

COLLECTIVE AGREEMENTS

Terms may be derived from collective agreements as well as being individually negotiated. Such agreements tend to be classed as being of either a procedural or a substantive nature. A procedural agreement aims to govern the relationship between the signatories (employers and trade unions) by establishing methods of handling disputes, whereas a substantive agreement is intended to regulate the terms and conditions of employment of those who are covered by it. Like any other agreement, collective agreements will be construed by giving meaning to the words used in the factual context known to the parties at the time.[36] It is possible to conclude a collective agreement which is legally enforceable, although this is not normally the wish of either party. By what mechanism then do individual employees derive the legal right to claim the terms and conditions which have been negotiated on their behalf? The answer lies in the process of incorporation, for by this device collectively agreed terms become legally binding as part of the individual contract of employment.[37] The simplest way of ensuring that substantive terms are incorporated into an employee's contract is by an express provision to this effect. Thus, workers may be employed on the basis of 'terms and conditions of employment which are covered by existing collective agreements negotiated and agreed with specific trade unions or unions recognised ... for collective bargaining purposes'.[38] Commonly, collective agreements will be expressly incorporated because they are referred to in a section 1 ERA 1996 statement of particulars.

In relation to the matters specified above, section 2 ERA 1996 permits employers to refer to 'some other document which is reasonably accessible', and this document may be a copy of the currently operative collective agreement. Equally, it is possible for terms to be incorporated from a collective agreement by implication or custom and practice, although this is less desirable because of the uncertainties involved.[39] Implied incorporation occurs when employees have specific knowledge of the collective agreement and there is conduct which demonstrates that they accept the agreement and are willing to work under it. While this might be relatively straightforward in the case of union members, difficulties can arise in establishing the legal position of non-members. If such employees have habitually accepted and abided by the terms negotiated by the union, an implication arises that they will be bound by future agreements. However, if at any stage non-members declare that they are no longer willing to be bound by such agreements, that implication is no longer valid.[40]

NO-STRIKE CLAUSES AND COLLECTIVE AGREEMENTS

It is not always easy to decide which terms of a collective agreement are appropriate for incorporation into an individual contract of employment. Substantive terms are relatively straightforward (eg wages, hours, etc) but procedural requirements may also be binding as a result of an express obligation or the employer's implied duty to act in good faith.[41] Particular difficulties have been experienced in relation to no-strike clauses. An undertaking by the union not to call a strike before relevant procedures have been exhausted imposes an obligation on the union alone, but the following clause is clearly capable of being incorporated into individual contracts of employment: 'Employees will not engage in a strike or other industrial action until the grievance procedure has been exhausted.' The situation has been clarified by section 180 TULRCA 1992 which provides that no-strike clauses are binding only if the collective agreement:

- is in writing and contains a provision stating that the clause may be incorporated into a contract of employment

- is reasonably accessible to the employees concerned

- is concluded by an independent trade union and the individual contract of employment expressly or impliedly incorporates the no-strike clause.

Such clauses can be useful in drawing an employee's attention to the illegality of industrial action but strictly speaking they are unnecessary because most forms of industrial action are likely to breach an obligation imposed on all employees by the common law – ie the duty not to impede the employer's business (see Chapter 3).

CASE STUDY

Christopher Keeley's contract of employment consisted of a written statement of employment terms which incorporated by reference the employer's staff handbook. Under the heading *Employee benefits and rights* there was a section on redundancy which dealt with certain procedural aspects. It also contained provisions giving those made redundant the right to time off to look for alternative work and the right to appeal against dismissal. Under the heading *Compensation* it provided that 'Those employees with two or more years' continuous service are entitled to receive an enhanced redundancy payment from the company, which is paid tax-free to a limit of £30,000. Details will be discussed during both collective and individual consultation.'

Following his dismissal on grounds of redundancy Mr Keeley claimed that he was contractually entitled to receive an enhanced redundancy payment. His claim was rejected in the High Court but allowed on appeal. According to the Court of Appeal, the fundamental starting point is the wording of the provision itself and the aptness of the provision in its own right to be a contractual term. The importance of the provision to the overall bargain is also highly relevant. A provision which is part of the employee's remuneration package may still be apt for construction as a term of the contract even if couched in terms of explanation or expressed in discretionary terms.[42]

WORKFORCE AGREEMENTS

The Working Time Regulations 1998 and the Maternity and Parental Leave Regulations 1999 are examples of where it is possible for 'relevant' agreements to be reached which enable employers to agree variations to the Regulations directly with their employees or with their representatives. These 'relevant' agreements can be reached via a process of bargaining. Where there are no collective agreements, employers can reach workforce agreements with their employees or their representatives. For example, Regulation 23 of the Working Time Regulations allows a workforce agreement to modify or exclude Regulation 4(3) concerning the reference period for calculating the 48-hour average, Regulations 6(1) to (3) and (7) concerning night work, Regulation 10(1) concerning the entitlement to an 11-hour break in each 24 hours, Regulations 11(1) and (2) concerning a weekly or fortnightly break, Regulation 12(1) concerning rest breaks, provided certain conditions are met. These conditions are contained in Schedule 1. An agreement is a workforce agreement where:

● it is in writing

● it has effect for a specified period not exceeding five years

● it applies to all the relevant members of a workforce or all the relevant members who belong to a particular group

● it is signed by the representatives of the group[43]

● copies of the agreement are readily available for reading prior to the signing.

WORKS RULES AND POLICY GUIDANCE

The essential difference between collective agreements and works rules lies not so much in their subject matter but in the fact that the contents of the latter are unilaterally determined by the employer. While both can be expressly or impliedly incorporated into individual contracts of employment (using the mechanisms described above), works rules offer one great advantage to the employer: whereas a collective agreement can be altered only with the consent of the parties to it, management can lawfully change the content of works rules at any time. A refusal to adhere to the revised rules would amount to a breach of contract (ie a failure to obey lawful and reasonable orders) even if there had been no advance warning or consultation with the employees affected. Thus a contractual term to the effect that employees must abide by 'the currently operative works rules' affords management the maximum degree of flexibility.[44]

There may be rules that constitute employer guidance or policy and are therefore not appropriate as contractual terms. Such a situation might arise when the employer is setting out practice and procedures rather than conferring rights on individuals. This occurred in *Wandsworth London Borough Council v D'Silva*[45] where changes to a code of practice on staff sickness were made by the employer without consultation with employees or their representatives.

The EAT held that these changes amounted to alterations to a code of good practice rather than an attempt to unilaterally alter the contract of employment. However, the dismissal of an employee for failing to comply with revised works rules or policy guidance will not necessarily be fair because it will depend on what an employment tribunal regards as being 'reasonable in all the circumstances' (see Chapter 13).

CUSTOM AND PRACTICE

In the days when written contracts of employment were less common and written statements of particulars were not required by statute, custom and practice played an important part in helping to identify the contractual terms. Today custom and practice is not such an important source of law, although it may still be invoked occasionally to fill gaps in the employment relationship. To do so, a custom or practice must be definite, reasonable and generally applied in the area or trade in question. If these criteria are met, the fact that the particular employee against whom the custom is applied is ignorant of its existence appears to be of no consequence.[46] In determining whether a policy drawn up unilaterally by management has become a term of the employee's contract on the grounds that it is an established custom and practice, all the circumstances have to be taken into account. Amongst the most important circumstances are whether the policy has been drawn to the attention of employees by management or has been followed without exception for a substantial period.[47]

The major drawback of custom and practice is its uncertain legal effect and therefore its unreliability. After what period of time can it be said that a non-union member who has always worked in accordance with current collective agreements is bound to accept future agreements? If a custom and practice is useful to management, it is logical that efforts should be made to convert it into an express term of the contract. This may not always be possible, either because of the imprecise nature of the custom or because unions might oppose such a move as being contrary to the interests of their members. It almost goes without saying that a union will be in a better position to modify a custom or practice if it has not become embodied in a contract of employment. Finally, it should be noted that there may still be a place for custom and practice as an aid to interpreting a contractual term that is truly ambiguous.[48]

TERMS IMPLIED BY STATUTE AND REGULATIONS

There are a number of examples of statutes and regulations implying terms into contracts of employment:

1 *Terms and conditions awarded by the CAC*
   Under section 185 TULRCA 1992 (on disclosure of information) these terms operate as part of the contract of employment of each worker affected. However, the terms and conditions imposed may be superseded or varied by a

collective agreement between the employer and the union 'for the time being representing the employee' or an express or implied agreement between the employer and the employee so far as that agreement effects an improvement in the terms and conditions awarded by the CAC.

2 *The equality clause*
This is inserted by virtue of section 1 of the Equal Pay Act 1970 (EPA 1970), as amended.

3 *The National Minimum Wage Act 1998*
This allows the Secretary of State to make provision for determining the hourly rate to be paid. Section 2(3) allows provision to be made with respect to when a person is to be treated as working and when he or she is not.

4 *The Working Time Regulations*
These provide for maximum hours to be worked in various situations and occupations (see Chapter 10).

TERMS IMPLIED BY THE COMMON LAW

There are two distinct types of common-law implied terms. First, where there is a gap in the contract of employment it is possible to imply a term if a court can be persuaded that it is necessary to do so in the circumstances of the particular case (implied terms of fact). Second, there are terms which are regarded by the courts as being inherent in all contracts of employment (implied terms of law). The next chapter will examine the major obligations which are automatically imposed on the parties to a contract of employment.

It is a basic principle that a contractual term can be implied only if it is consistent with the express terms of the contract. However, despite the increased use of written contracts and statements, it is not unusual for the parties to discover that they have failed to provide for a particular contingency. If there is a dispute over something which is not expressly dealt with in the contract of employment, a court or tribunal may be asked to insert a term to cover the point at issue. The party wishing to rely on an implied term must satisfy a court either that such a term was so obvious that the parties did not think it necessary to state it expressly (the 'officious bystander' test) or that such a term was necessary to give 'business efficacy' to the relationship.[49]

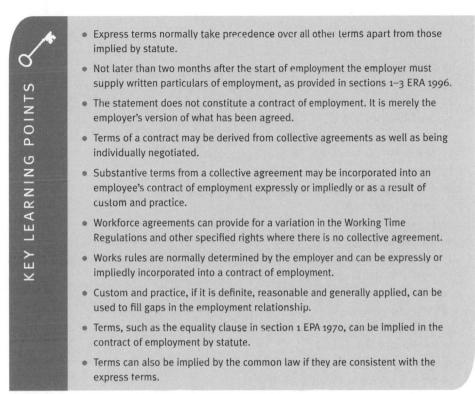

KEY LEARNING POINTS

- Express terms normally take precedence over all other terms apart from those implied by statute.
- Not later than two months after the start of employment the employer must supply written particulars of employment, as provided in sections 1–3 ERA 1996.
- The statement does not constitute a contract of employment. It is merely the employer's version of what has been agreed.
- Terms of a contract may be derived from collective agreements as well as being individually negotiated.
- Substantive terms from a collective agreement may be incorporated into an employee's contract of employment expressly or impliedly or as a result of custom and practice.
- Workforce agreements can provide for a variation in the Working Time Regulations and other specified rights where there is no collective agreement.
- Works rules are normally determined by the employer and can be expressly or impliedly incorporated into a contract of employment.
- Custom and practice, if it is definite, reasonable and generally applied, can be used to fill gaps in the employment relationship.
- Terms, such as the equality clause in section 1 EPA 1970, can be implied in the contract of employment by statute.
- Terms can also be implied by the common law if they are consistent with the express terms.

Reinforce your understanding of this chapter by visiting www.cipd.co.uk/sss for activities, questions, weblinks and additional case studies

REFERENCES

1 On apprenticeship contracts see *Flett v Matheson* (2006) IRLR 277
2 On the relevance of the Unfair Contract Terms Act 1977 see *Commerzbank AG v Keen* (2007) IRLR 132
3 Although tribunal jurisdiction in anti-discrimination cases may not depend on the existence of an enforceable contract of employment; see *Vakante v Governors of Stanhope School (No.2)* (2005) ICR 231
4 See *Annandale Engineering v Samson* (1994) IRLR 59
5 See *Colen v Cebrian Ltd* (2004) IRLR 210 and *Blue Chip Ltd v Helbawi* (2009) IRLR 128
6 (1991) IRLR 473
7 *Enfield Technical Services Ltd v Payne* (2008) IRLR 500
8 See *Deeley v British Rail Engineering Ltd* (1980) IRLR 147
9 Sections 1–2 ERA 1996
10 (2001) IRLR 244
11 See sections 2(2) and (3) ERA 1996
12 For a discussion of this see *Secretary of State v Bearman* (1998) IRLR 431
13 See *Affleck v Newcastle Mind* (1999) IRLR 405
14 Sections 215 and 216 ERA 1996
15 SI 2006/246

16   (1997) IRLR 17

17   SI 1998/1833

18   See section 88(1)(d) ERA 1996

19   See *Leisure Leagues Ltd v Maconnachie* (2002) IRLR 600

20   See *Mihlenstedt v Barclays Bank* (1989) IRLR 522

21   See *Glitz v Watford Electrical* (1978) IRLR 89

22   See *Rutten v Cross Medical Ltd* (1997) IRLR 249

23   See *Werhof v Freeway Traffic Systems GmbH & Co.* (2006) IRLR 400

24   Directive 96/71

25   Section 3(1) ERA 1996

26   Section 7A ERA 1996

27   See section 4 ERA 1996

28   See *Systems Floors (UK) Ltd v Daniel* (1981) IRLR 475

29   (1983) IRLR 302

30   (1981) IRLR 477; see also *Aparau v Iceland Frozen Foods* (1996) IRLR 119

31   See *Gascol Conversions v Mercer* (1974) IRLR 155

32   Section 11 ERA 1996

33   *Eagland v British Telecom plc* (1992) IRLR 323

34   Section 12(2) ERA 1996

35   Section 38(5) EA 2002 deals with exceptional circumstances

36   See *Adams v British Airways* (1996) IRLR 574

37   See *Gibbons v Associated British Ports* (1985) IRLR 376

38   See *Airlie v City of Edinburgh District Council* (1996) IRLR 516

39   See *Hamilton v Futura Floors* (1990) IRLR 478 and *Henry v LGTS Ltd* (2002) IRLR 472

40   See *Singh v British Steel* (1974) IRLR 478

41   See *Lakshmi v Mid Cheshire Hospitals NHS Trust* (2008) IRLR 956

42   *Keeley v Fosroc Ltd* (2006) IRLR 961. On the enforceability of a recognition agreement
     see *NCB v NUM* (1986) IRLR 439

43   There are provisions which allow employers with fewer than 20 employees to have the
     majority of those employees sign in order for a workforce agreement to come into being.

44   See *Cadoux v Central Regional Council* (1986) IRLR 131

45   (1998) IRLR 193

46   See *Sagar v Ridehalgh* (1931) Ch 310

47   See *Quinn v Calder* (1996) IRLR 126

48   See *Dunlop Tyres Ltd v Blows* (2001) IRLR 629 on the interpretation of an ambiguous
     collective agreement

49   See *United Bank v Akhtar* (1989) IRLR 507

CHAPTER 3

Formation of the Contract of Employment (2): Implied terms of law

OVERVIEW

In the previous chapter we looked at the different ways in which contractual terms may come into existence and observed that certain terms could be implied into all contracts of employment. Here we examine the major obligations imposed on both employers and employees by law. Some of these are based on long-established common law principles, while others (such as those connected with unfair dismissal) are of relatively recent origin, having emerged as a result of legislative intervention.

DUTIES OF THE EMPLOYER

TO PAY WAGES

This is the most basic obligation of employers and is normally dealt with by an express term. In certain circumstances, however, the law does not leave the parties entirely free to determine the amount of remuneration payable – eg in the application of the national minimum wage or if an equality clause operates. Pay issues are considered in Chapter 5.

TO PROVIDE WORK

Employers are generally not obliged to provide work, and most employees who receive their full contractual remuneration cannot complain if they are left idle. Nevertheless, in certain circumstances the failure to provide work may amount to a breach of contract.

If a person's earnings depend upon work being provided

Employees who are paid by results or commission or who receive shift premiums must be given the opportunity to work because the payment of basic wages alone would deprive them of a substantial part of what they had bargained for – the opportunity to earn more.

Where the lack of work could lead to a loss of publicity or affect the reputation of an employee

Indeed, in one tribunal case it was held that the higher a person is in the management structure, the more important it is for work to be given when it is available.[1]

Where an employee needs to practise in order to preserve his or her skills

The Court of Appeal has suggested that such employees should be given the opportunity of performing work.[2] This is linked to the issue of 'garden leave' (see below), which is the practice of continuing to pay an employee for a period, but not allowing him or her to work during that time. It has sometimes been used to prevent a valuable employee from leaving and immediately taking up employment with a competitor. A problem arises when such a period without work has a detrimental affect on an employee's skills. In *William Hill Organisation Ltd v Tucker*[3] the Court of Appeal held that the employer had an obligation to provide work when the work was available. This was partly because of the need to practise and partly because there was a contractual obligation on the employee to 'work those hours necessary to carry out his duties in a full and professional manner'. The High Court has subsequently held that the right to work is subject to the qualification that the employee has not, as a result of some prior breach of duty, demonstrated in a serious way that he or she is not ready or willing to work. Thus in *SG&R Valuation Service v Boudrais*[4] the employer was granted an interim injunction which had the effect that the defendants had to remain on 'garden leave' for the rest of their notice periods.

TO CO-OPERATE WITH THE EMPLOYEE

Originally this duty amounted to little more than an obligation not to impede employees in the performance of their contracts. However, one of the effects of the unfair dismissal provisions has been that the courts have displayed a greater willingness to accept that employers have a positive duty to ensure that the purposes of the contract are achieved. Thus it has frequently been stated that employers must not destroy the mutual trust and confidence upon which co-operation is built without reasonable and proper cause.[5] However, the House of Lords has ruled that such a term is concerned with preserving the continuing employment relationship and does not apply to the way that the relationship is terminated.[6] There are also limits as to how positive this obligation should be. In *University of Nottingham v Eyett*,[7] for example, a failure by an employer to warn an employee, who was proposing to exercise important rights in connection with pension benefits, that the way the employee was proposing to exercise those rights was not the most financially advantageous was not seen as breaching a duty of mutual trust and confidence. Each case depends on its particular set of facts, but some examples of situations in which employers have been held to be in breach of this implied term are:

- changing the terms of a transferred employee's bridging loan to his or her detriment[8]

- the operation by an employer of a business in a dishonest and corrupt manner which damaged an innocent employee's reputation.[9] However, the employee may only be able to claim damages if he or she can show that the damage to reputation actually caused financial loss[10]

- an employer's discretion under a mobility clause being exercised in a way that made it impossible for the employee to comply with a contractual obligation to move[11]

- a failure to investigate a genuine safety grievance[12]

- employees not being afforded a reasonable opportunity to obtain redress of a grievance[13]

- a false accusation of theft on the basis of flimsy evidence[14]

- reprimanding an employee in public[15]

- the persistent attempt by an employer to vary an employee's conditions of service[16]

- without reasonable cause, denying the employee the opportunity given to everyone else of signing a revised contract with enhanced redundancy payments[17]

- a serious failure over a period of time to make reasonable adjustments to accommodate a disabled person[18]

- failing to notify an employee on maternity leave of a vacancy for which she would have applied had she been aware of it.[19]

This duty should also inhibit employers from issuing unjustified warnings which are designed not to improve performance but to dishearten employees and drive them out.[20]

The House of Lords has also accepted that in certain circumstances it will be necessary to imply an obligation on the employer to take reasonable steps to bring a contractual term to the employee's attention. Such a duty will arise when:

- the contractual terms have not been negotiated with individuals but result from collective bargaining or are otherwise incorporated by reference

- a particular term makes available to employees a valuable right contingent upon action being taken by them to avail themselves of its benefit

- employees cannot in all the circumstances reasonably be expected to be aware of the term unless it is drawn to their attention.[21]

Although employers should provide sufficient information to enable employees to understand the choices available to them, the Court of Appeal has ruled that they do not have to ensure that the information was actually communicated. All the employer has to do is to take reasonable steps to inform the employees about their rights.[22]

TO TAKE REASONABLE CARE OF THE EMPLOYEE

In addition to this duty implied by law, there are a number of key statutes in the area of health and safety. We shall be looking at the legislation in Chapter 9, although it is important to note at this stage that a person who is injured in the course of employment in a factory may be able to bring an action for damages based either on the common law duty or breach of statute or other regulations. 'In the course of employment' means the claimant was doing something that he or she was employed to do, or something reasonably incidental to those things. In *Chief Adjudication Officer v Rhodes*,[23] an employee of the Benefits Agency was assaulted at her home, when off sick from work, by a neighbour whom she had reported for suspected fraud. The Court of Appeal decided that although the incident arose out of her employment it did not take place in the course of that employment.

Recognising that employers cannot guarantee that no employees will be injured at work, the standard of care which the law demands is that which 'an ordinary prudent employer would take in all the circumstances'.[24] Generally speaking, if a job has risks to health and safety which are not common knowledge but about which an employer knows or ought to know, and against which she or he cannot guard by taking precautions, then the employer should tell anyone to whom employment is offered what those risks are if, on the information then available, knowledge of those risks would be likely to affect the decision of a sensible prospective employee about accepting the offer.[25] Thus the common law accepts that employers should be held liable only if they fail to safeguard against something which was reasonably foreseeable.[26] In terms of damages, the House of Lords held in *Corr v IBC Ltd*[27] that it is the foreseeability of the risk of physical injury that is important. In this case depression was a direct and foreseeable consequence of the accident and suicide was the direct result of the depression.

It should also be observed that the general duty of care does not extend to taking all reasonable steps to protect the economic welfare of employees, whether by insuring them against special risks known to the employer or by advising them of those risks so that they can obtain appropriate cover.

Employers' single personal duty of care to each employee

Employers are entitled to follow recognised practices in their industry, unless the practices are obviously unsafe, but must make arrangements to ensure that they keep abreast of current developments – for example, by joining an employers' association. Once an employer knows of a source of danger, or could have been expected to know of it, it is necessary to take all reasonable steps to protect employees from risks which have hitherto been unforeseeable.[28] The duty is to assess the likelihood of injury and to weigh the risk against the cost and inconvenience of taking effective precautions to eliminate it. Employers owe a single personal duty of care to each of their employees, having proper regard to the employee's skill and experience, etc. Thus even if the employer delegates this duty to another person who is reasonably believed to be competent to perform it, the employer will remain personally liable for injuries to an employee caused by that other person's negligence.[29] Similarly, where an employee's labour is subcontracted, the employer's duty of care is still owed.[30]

Having considered some general issues, it may be useful to subdivide this duty into the following headings:

Safe premises

The case of *Latimer v AEC Ltd*[31] provides a suitable illustration of what is required of employers in this connection. Owing to exceptionally heavy rainfall, a factory was flooded. A layer of oil and grease was left on the floor which the employers attempted to cover with sawdust. However, this was not spread across all of the factory floor and an employee slipped in an area that was uncovered. It was held by the House of Lords that the employers had taken reasonable precautions and they could not be expected to close down their factory in order to avoid what was a fairly small risk of injury.[32] Subsequently it has been acknowledged that in certain circumstances UK-based employers may have to satisfy themselves as to the safety of overseas sites. According to the Court of Appeal, the employer's duty to take all reasonable steps to ensure the safety of employees applies whether the premises where the employee is required to work are occupied by the employer or by a third party.[33]

Safe plant, equipment and tools

If employers know that a tool or a piece of machinery could be a source of danger, it is incumbent upon them to take reasonable precautions to safeguard employees. Where tools or equipment are purchased from a reputable supplier and employers have no reason to suspect that they are defective, they cannot be held liable at common law. If in these circumstances an employee were to sustain an injury as a result of a defect, in order to recover damages he or she would be obliged to sue the person responsible, such as the supplier or manufacturer, under the general law of negligence.

Safe system of work

Under this heading are included all the matters which relate to the manner in which the work is performed: job design, working methods, the provision of protective clothing, training and supervision. Indeed, it is now accepted that employers have a duty not to cause their employees psychological damage by the volume or character of the work that they are required to perform.[34] However, the Court of Appeal has ruled that unless an employer knows of some particular problem or vulnerability, it is usually entitled to assume that the employee can withstand normal pressures of the job. According to this court, there are no occupations which should be regarded as intrinsically dangerous to mental health.[35] Equally contentious is the view that if the only reasonable way of safeguarding the employee would be to demote or dismiss, an employer will not be in breach of the duty of care in allowing a willing employee to continue in the job. However, in *Coxall v Goodyear Ltd*[36] it was held that the employer was under a duty either to take the claimant off the job or, as a matter of last resort, to dismiss. If safety rules and procedures exist, employees must be informed of their content, and if safety clothing or equipment is required, it must be readily available.[37] Clearly, the more dangerous the task or workplace situation, the greater is the need for precautions to be taken – but how far must an employer go to ensure that safety devices are properly used?

In *Crouch v British Rail Engineering*[38] the Court of Appeal decided that where an employee is regularly performing tasks which involve a reasonably foreseeable risk to the eyes, the employer has the duty actually to put goggles into the employee's hands. Similarly, employees who are likely to do a great deal of typing should be told that they must take breaks and rest pauses.[39] In *Pape v Cumbria County Council*[40] the High Court ruled that an employer has a duty to warn cleaners of the dangers of handling chemicals with unprotected hands and to instruct them on the need to wear gloves at all times. The circumstances that have to be considered in ascertaining the extent of the duty of care include: the risk of injury; the gravity of any injury which might result; the difficulty of providing protective equipment or clothing; the availability of that equipment or clothing and the distance the worker might have to go to fetch it; the frequency of occasions on which the employee is likely to need the protective equipment or clothing; and the experience and degree of skill to be expected of the employee. Bearing in mind both this common law duty and the obligations imposed by legislation (see Chapter 9), managers would be advised to ensure that an unreasonable refusal to follow safety rules or procedures is classed as a breach of discipline which could ultimately lead to dismissal for misconduct.

CASE STUDY

Mark Hone was a licensed house manager for five years before he collapsed and never returned to work. He had complained that he did not have adequate support and that he was regularly working 90 hours a week. As a result of a meeting, the operations manager accepted that an assistant manager should be appointed, but apart from some occasional relief no help was provided.

Mr Hone sought damages on the basis that he had suffered psychological injury caused by the stress of being required to work excessive hours without proper support. In upholding an award of £21,840, the Court of Appeal confirmed that the correct test for deciding whether psychological injury was reasonably foreseeable was that: 'The indications of impending harm to health arising from stress at work must be plain enough for any reasonable employer to realise that he should do something about it.'[41]

Competent and safe colleagues

Employers are required to take reasonable steps to ensure that employees do not behave in such a fashion that they are a source of danger to others. This means that employers must engage competent staff, or train recruits to a safe-worker level, must instruct their employees in safe working methods, and must then provide adequate supervision to check that these methods are being adhered to. Practical jokers cannot be tolerated, and if they do not respond to warnings, their employment should be terminated in accordance with disciplinary procedures.

TO PROVIDE REFERENCES

In *Spring v Guardian Assurance plc*[42] the complainant argued that a reference provided by a former employer was a malicious falsehood and/or a negligent misstatement and/or a breach of an implied term in the contract of employment that any reference would be compiled with all reasonable care. The House of Lords concluded that an employer has a duty to take reasonable care in compiling a reference by ensuring the accuracy of the information upon which it was based. The duty is to provide a reference which is in substance true, accurate and fair, and this will usually involve making a reasonable enquiry into the factual basis of any statements made.[43] The provider of a reference must not give an impression that is unfair or misleading overall, even if the component parts of the reference are accurate.[44] Clearly this can mean the inclusion of matters not in the employee's favour as well as those that are.

DUTIES OF THE EMPLOYEE

TO CO-OPERATE WITH THE EMPLOYER

We are concerned here with the duty to obey lawful and reasonable orders and the duty not to impede the employer's business. In this context the obligation to carry out lawful orders has two distinct aspects. First, it means that employees are not required to comply with an order if to do so would break the law – for example, by producing false accounts. Second, it also means that employees are not obliged to accept orders which fall outside the scope of the contract. This is consistent with the view that (at least in theory) the terms of a contract cannot be varied unilaterally (see Chapter 11). However, the EAT has suggested that there can be an implied term that an employee may be obliged to perform duties that are different from those expressly required by the contract or to perform them at a different place. Nevertheless, it is likely to be legitimate to find an implied obligation to undertake a duty which is outside the express terms only where: the circumstances are exceptional; the requirement is plainly justified; the work is suitable; the employee suffers no detriment in terms of contractual benefits and status; and the change is temporary.[45] Additionally, as we shall discover later (Chapter 13), the law of unfair dismissal does not prevent employees from being fairly dismissed for refusing to follow instructions which may be outside their contractual obligations.[46]

As regards the duty not to impede the employer's business, it is clear that going on strike breaches a fundamental term of the contract because the essence of the employment relationship is that the employee is ready and willing to work in exchange for remuneration. However, is there a duty on employees not to engage in industrial action which falls short of a strike? In the leading case of the *Secretary of State v ASLEF*,[47] which involved a work to rule on the railways, the Court of Appeal gave different reasons for reaching the conclusion that such a duty exists. Lord Justice Roskill thought that there is an implied term that employees ought not to obey lawful instructions in such a way as to disrupt the employer's business. Lord Justice Buckley extended the notion of fidelity (see below) and proclaimed that 'the employee must serve the employer faithfully with a view to promoting those commercial interests for which he is employed'. Lord Denning chose to focus attention on motive – ie the wilfulness of the disruption caused – and his formulation leads to the conclusion that all forms of industrial action are likely to be unlawful. The High Court has also ruled that it is a professional obligation on teachers to co-operate in running schools and that the failure to cover for absent colleagues amounts to a breach of contract.[48] (On the options open to an employer where an employee only partly performs the contract, see Chapter 11.)

FIDELITY

Employees must avoid putting themselves in a position whereby their own interests conflict with the duty they owe their employer or an employer to whom they have been seconded.[49] Thus employees must not accept any reward for their work other than from their employer, for example, a gift or secret commission. There is no implied obligation on employees to disclose their own misconduct, and whether there is a duty to report the misconduct of fellow employees depends on the individual contract of employment and the circumstances.[50] However, the Court of Appeal has suggested that senior employees have a duty to disclose both their own wrongdoing and that of others.[51] There are two particular aspects of the duty of fidelity which we must now consider: the obligation not to compete with the employer, and the obligation not to disclose confidential information.

The obligation not to compete with the employer

Generally the spare-time activities of employees are no business of the employer, although an injunction may be granted to prevent employees from working for competitors during their spare time if it can be shown that the employer's business would be seriously damaged. However, in *Nova Plastics Ltd v Froggatt*[52] the EAT rejected the argument that there is a general implication that any work for a competitor should be regarded as being a breach of trust or a failure to give loyal service. It should be noted that the intention to set up in competition with the employer is not in itself a breach of the implied duty of loyalty, although there is a line over which the employee must not go.[53] The renting and equipping of premises in an employee's spare time and the arranging of financial backing to set up in competition may be construed as a breach of an implied duty of fidelity.[54] If the employer has reasonable grounds for believing that the employee has committed or is about to commit some wrongful act, dismissal may be justified (see Chapter 13).[55]

Restraint clauses

Normally, ex-employees are entitled to make use of the skills and knowledge which they have acquired and are allowed to compete with a former employer provided they do not rely on confidential information (see below). However, this is not the position if there is an express clause in the contract of employment which restrains competition by employees when they leave.[56] Such restraint clauses (restrictive covenants) will be enforced by the courts only if they provide protection against something more than competition alone, if they are shown to be reasonable in the circumstances, and if they are not contrary to the public interest.[57] A clause stopping an ex-employee ever dealing with any of the plaintiff's customers with whom he or she dealt might be unreasonable, but one restricting contact with customers dealt with during the previous six months might be acceptable.[58] The reasonableness of the restraint is to be assessed as at the date the contract was made.[59] According to the Court of Appeal, the employer must establish that the nature of the employment was such as to expose the employee to the kind of information capable of protection beyond the duration of the contract.[60] Non-competition clauses in a contract may be reasonable to protect the employer's proprietary interests in the customer connections that have been built up by the departing employees, although non-solicitation clauses should not be too broad. It would be an unreasonable restraint of trade to stop employees or ex-employees soliciting even the most junior of employees.[61]

'Garden leave'

What about the enforcement of 'garden leave' clauses – ie clauses which provide that during the period of notice an employee is not obliged to work but will receive full pay and meanwhile must not work for anyone else? Such clauses will not be enforced if it appears that the business for which the employee wishes to work before the notice expires has nothing to do with the employer's business. On the other hand, where the period during which the employee is not required to work is not excessive and there is a risk of damage to the employer's business, it may be appropriate to restrain the employee from taking other employment during the notice period, either under a specific clause or as a breach of duty of fidelity.[62] However, the wrongful dismissal of an employee will prevent the employer from relying on a restrictive covenant.[63] Finally, one effect of Regulation 4 of the Transfer Regulations (see Chapter 16) is that the transferee may benefit from a restrictive covenant in contracts of employment made with the transferor. Thus an employee may be restrained from doing or seeking to do business with anyone who had dealt with the transferor during the period stipulated in the original contract.[64]

The obligation not to disclose confidential information

The following principles have been enunciated by the Court of Appeal.[65] First, an individual's obligations are to be determined by the contract of employment and, in the absence of any express term, the employee's obligations in respect of the use and disclosure of information are the subject of implied terms. Second, while the individual remains in employment the obligations are included in the implied term which imposes a duty of fidelity on the employee. The extent of this duty varies according to the nature of the contract and would be broken if an employee copied a list of the employer's customers for use after the employment ended, or deliberately memorised such a list.[66] Third, the implied term which imposes an obligation on the employee as to his or her conduct after the employment has terminated is more restricted than that imposed by the duty of fidelity. The obligation not to use or disclose information might cover secret processes of manufacture or designs, or any other information of a sufficiently high degree of confidentiality as to amount to a trade secret.[67] However, this obligation does not extend to information which is only 'confidential' in the sense that any unauthorised disclosure to a third party while the employment subsisted would be a breach of the duty of fidelity. Fourth, in order to determine whether any particular item of information falls within the implied term thus preventing its use or disclosure after the employment has ceased, it is necessary to consider all the circumstances of the case. Amongst the matters to which attention must be paid are:

- the nature of the employment – a high obligation of confidentiality might be imposed if the employment was such that confidential material was habitually handled

- the nature of the information – in deciding whether there is a legitimate trade secret to be protected, a distinction needs to be made between information which can be legitimately regarded as the property of the employer and the skill, know-how and general knowledge which can be regarded as the property of the employee. According to the courts, 'objective knowledge' is the employer's property and 'subjective knowledge' belongs to the employee[68]

- whether the employer impressed on the employee the confidentiality of the information – however, an employer cannot prevent the use or disclosure of information merely by telling the employee that it is confidential.

In practice it can be very difficult to differentiate between use and abuse of the knowledge which an ex-employee possesses – for example, of the former employer's customers. Thus employers should be advised to draft express restraint clauses which set precise limits on the future employment of key workers. Such clauses must be carefully worded, for it is a court's duty to give effect to covenants as they are expressed rather than to correct errors or remedy omissions.[69] Because breaches are relatively easy to identify, enforcing such clauses should be a fairly simple process. Indeed, the mere presence of a restraint clause can be valuable as a reminder to the employee that disclosure of confidential information will not be condoned. The employer who relies solely on the implied term is at a serious disadvantage, because an employee can be stopped from disclosing confidential information only when the employer has proved that such information has already been divulged. Only then will an aggrieved employer have a remedy against a third party to whom the employee has passed trade secrets or confidential information.[70]

Two further points must be considered. First, in an appropriate case a court has power to grant injunctions against ex-employees to restrain them from fulfilling contracts already concluded with third parties.[71] Second, although the Data Protection Act 1998 imposes additional constraints on an employee's ability to disclose information, the Public Interest Disclosure Act 1998 protects workers who make certain disclosures in the public interest (see below).

TO TAKE REASONABLE CARE

Employees must exercise reasonable skill and care in the performance of their contracts.[72] If they do not do so, apart from any disciplinary action that may be taken against them, there is an implied duty to indemnify the employer in respect of the consequences of their negligence.[73] Thus, if by virtue of the doctrine of vicarious liability (see Chapter 4) an employer is required to pay damages to an injured third party, in theory the amount paid out could be recovered by suing the negligent employee. In practice, such embarrassing litigation is avoided because it is the employer's insurance company that actually pays the damages.

PUBLIC INTEREST DISCLOSURES

The purpose of the Public Interest Disclosure Act 1998, which primarily amended the ERA 1996, is to protect individuals who make certain disclosures of information in the public interest. Section 43A ERA 1996 defines a 'protected disclosure' as a qualifying disclosure which is made to the persons mentioned in sections 43C–43H ERA 1996 (below). Section 43B(1) defines a 'qualifying disclosure' as one which a worker *reasonably believes*[74] tends to show one or more of the following: (a) a criminal offence; (b) a failure to comply with any legal obligation;[75] (c) a miscarriage of justice; (d) danger to the health and safety of any individual (ie not necessarily a worker); (e) damage to the environment; or (f) the deliberate concealment of information tending to expose any of the matters listed above. Four general points about these categories should be noted. Firstly, they are not restricted to confidential information. Secondly, there is no requirement for any link between the matter disclosed and the worker's employment. Thirdly, the matter disclosed may have occurred in the past, be currently occurring, or be likely to occur. Fourthly, the statute does not protect actions which are directed at establishing or confirming the reasonableness of a belief.[76]

Section 43C(1) ERA 1996 protects workers who make qualifying disclosures *in good faith* to their employer or to another person who is responsible for the matter disclosed. It would seem that the burden is on the employer to show that the claimant lacked good faith and, if an ulterior motive was the dominant purpose for making the disclosure, protection will not be afforded.[77]

According to section 43C(2) ERA 1996, workers are to be treated as having made disclosures to their employer if they follow a procedure which the employer has authorised, even if the disclosure has been made to someone else such as an independent person or organisation. Section 43D ERA 1996 enables workers to seek legal advice about their concerns and to reveal to their adviser the issues about which a disclosure may be made. Under these circumstances, section 43B(4) ERA 1996 provides that the legal adviser is bound by professional privilege and cannot make a protected disclosure.

Section 43E ERA 1996 protects workers in government-appointed organisations if they make a disclosure in good faith to a Minister of the Crown rather than to their legal employer. Section 43F(1) ERA 1996 protects workers who make disclosures in good faith to a person prescribed for the purpose by the Secretary of State.[78] However, the worker must reasonably believe (a) that the matter falls within the remit of the prescribed person, and (b) that the information and any allegation contained in it are substantially true.

Section 43G ERA 1996 enables workers to make a protected disclosure in other limited circumstances. In order to be protected, workers must:

- act in good faith
- reasonably believe that the information and any allegation contained in it are substantially true
- not act for personal gain (according to section 43L(2) ERA 1996, in determining whether a person has acted for personal gain, a reward payable under any enactment will be disregarded)
- have already disclosed substantially the same information to the employer or to a person prescribed under section 43F ERA 1996, unless they reasonably believe that they would be subject to a detriment for doing so, or that the employer would conceal or destroy the evidence if alerted
- act reasonably. For these purposes regard shall be had, in particular, to:
  - the identity of the person to whom the disclosure is made (for example, disclosure to an MP may be reasonable whereas disclosure to the media may not be)
  - the seriousness of the matter
  - whether there is a continuing failure or one likely to recur
  - whether the disclosure is made in breach of a duty of confidentiality owed by the employer to another person
  - any action the employer (or prescribed person) has taken or might have been expected to take in relation to a previous disclosure
  - whether the worker has complied with any procedure authorised by the employer for making a disclosure.

Section 43H ERA 1996 deals with disclosures about exceptionally serious wrongdoing. Again, in order to be protected:

- workers must act in good faith
- they must reasonably believe that the information and any allegation contained in it are substantially true
- they must not act for personal gain
- the relevant failure must be of an exceptionally serious nature

- in all the circumstances it must be reasonable to make the disclosure. In this respect particular regard will be had to the identity of the person to whom the disclosure is made.

Section 43J ERA 1996 prevents employers from generally contracting out of the provisions in Part IVA. In particular, it deals with 'gagging clauses' by invalidating a worker's agreement (whether contained in a contract or settlement of legal proceedings) not to make a protected disclosure.

Section 43K(1) ERA 1996 is designed to enable everyone who works to benefit from Part IVA, irrespective of whether they fall within the section 230 ERA 1996 definition of 'employee' or 'worker'. Thus for these purposes the definition of 'worker' is extended to include certain agency workers; certain workers who would not otherwise be covered because they are not obliged to carry out all of their duties personally; NHS practitioners such as GPs, certain dentists, pharmacists and opticians; and certain trainees.[79] Section 43K(2) ERA 1996 extends the definition of 'employer' accordingly.

Section 47B(1) ERA 1996 gives workers the right not to be subjected to any detriment for making a protected disclosure.[80] For these purposes, the extended meaning of 'worker' in section 43K applies and it is made clear that 'detriment' covers both actions and a deliberate failure to act.[81] Thus the following would be covered: discipline or dismissal, or being denied a pay rise or facilities that would otherwise be provided.

In addition, workers who have been dismissed for making a protected disclosure and are not qualified to claim unfair dismissal under Part X of the ERA 1996 (the general unfair dismissal provisions) can bring a claim under section 47B ERA 1996. The obvious example here is a worker who does not have a contract of employment. Section 48(1A) ERA 1996 enables a worker to complain to an employment tribunal that section 47B has been infringed, and compensation for injury to feelings is available.[82]

DISCLOSURE AND DISMISSAL

Section 103A ERA 1996 makes it automatically unfair to dismiss employees on the grounds that they have (at any time)[83] made a protected disclosure. No qualifying period of service is required.[84] Similarly, section 105(6A) ERA 1996 makes it unfair to select employees for redundancy if the reason for doing so is that they have made a protected disclosure. Finally, it should be noted that there is no limit on the compensation that can be awarded by an employment tribunal if section 103A ERA 1996 applies.

THE LAW GOVERNING INVENTIONS AND COPYRIGHT

According to section 39(1) of the Patents Act 1977, an invention belongs to an employer if:

- it was made in the course of the employee's normal duties or those specifically assigned to him or her, and the circumstances in either case were such that an invention might reasonably be expected to result from the carrying out of those duties, or

- it was made in the course of the employee's duties and at the time of making the invention, because of the nature of the duties and the particular responsibilities arising from them, there was a special obligation to further the interests of the employer's undertaking.

In all other circumstances the invention belongs to the employee notwithstanding any contractual term to the contrary. This section was considered in *Reiss Engineering v Harris*[85] where the Patents Court held that, for these purposes, employees' 'normal duties' are those which they are actually employed to do. Section 39(1)(a) was interpreted as referring to an invention which achieves or contributes to achieving whatever was the aim or object to which the employee's efforts in carrying out his or her duties were directed – ie an invention similar to that made but not necessarily the precise invention as that actually made. The extent and nature of the 'special obligation' in section 39(1)(b) will depend on the status of the employee and the attendant responsibilities and duties of that status.

Even if the invention belongs to the employer, an employee can apply to the Patents Court or Controller of Patents for an award of compensation. This may be granted if the patent is of outstanding benefit (in money or money's worth) to the employer and it is just to make an award. The burden of proof lies on the employee to show that the employer has derived benefit from the patented invention. Where inventions belong to employees and their interests have been assigned to the employer, they are still entitled to seek compensation if they can show that the financial benefit they have derived is inadequate in relation to the benefit derived by the employer from the patent and it is just that additional compensation should be paid. However, no compensation can be paid if, at the time the invention is made, there is in force a 'relevant collective agreement' (an agreement between a trade union to which the employee belongs and the employer or an association to which the employer belongs) which provides for the payment of compensation for inventions made by the employee. It is expected that collective agreements will improve upon the statutory rights, yet there appears to be nothing to prevent employers and unions from negotiating less favourable compensation schemes.

According to section 11 of the Copyright, Designs and Patents Act 1988, where a literary, dramatic, musical or artistic work is made by an employee in the course of employment, the employer is the first owner of any copyright, subject to any agreement to the contrary.

KEY LEARNING POINTS

- The law regards employers and employees as having certain obligations to each other. These obligations arise out of long-established common law principles and more recent statutory intervention in the employment relationship.

- The duties of the employer include:

- paying wages if an employee is available for work and not making unlawful deductions

- providing work in circumstances where a lack of work will affect an employee's earnings, reputation or skills

- co-operating with the employee and preserving the mutual trust and confidence upon which this co-operation depends

- taking reasonable care of the employee by providing a safe working environment and safe working practices

- taking reasonable care with regard to references.

- The duties of the employee include:

- co-operating with the employer and obeying lawful and reasonable instructions

- not damaging the employer's business by competing with the employer in breach of a duty of fidelity

- not disclosing certain confidential information to competitors

- taking reasonable care and exercising reasonable skills in the performance of his or her contract.

Reinforce your understanding of this chapter by visiting www.cipd.co.uk/sss for activities, questions, weblinks and additional case studies

REFERENCES

1 *Bosworth v A Jowett* (1977) IRLR 341

2 *Langston v AUEW* (1974) ICR 180

3 (1998) IRLR 313

4 (2008) IRLR 770

5 See *Hilton v Shiner Ltd* (2001) IRLR 727

6 See *Johnson v Unisys Ltd* (2002) IRLR 271 and *Eastwood v Magnox plc* (2004) IRLR 733

7 (1999) IRLR 87. See also *Crossley v Faithful & Gould Ltd* (2004) IRLR 377

8 *French v Barclays Bank* (1998) IRLR 647

9 *Malik v Bank of Credit and Commerce* (1997) IRLR 462

10 See *Bank of Credit and Commerce International SA v Ali (No.3)* (1999) IRLR 508

11 *United Bank v Akhtar* (1989) IRLR 507

12 *BAC v Austin* (1978) IRLR 332

13 *Goold Ltd v McConnell* (1995) IRLR 516

14 *Robinson v Crompton Parkinson* (1978) IRLR 61

15 *Morrow v Safeway Stores* (2002) IRLR 9

16 *Woods v WM Car Services* (1982) IRLR 413

17 See *Transco plc v O'Brien* (2002) IRLR 444

18 See *Greenhof v Barnsley M.B.C.* (2006) IRLR 98

19 See *Visa v Paul* (2004) IRLR 42

20 *Walker v J Wedgewood Ltd* (1978) IRLR 105

21 See *Scally v Southern Health Board* (1991) IRLR 522

22 See *Ibekwe v LGTS Ltd* (2003) IRLR 697

23 (1999) IRLR 103

24 *Paris v Stepney B.C.* (1951) AC 376

25 See *White v Holbrook Ltd* (1985) IRLR 215

26 See *Hewett v Brown Ltd* (1992) ICR 530 on the duty owed to the employee's family

27 (2008) ICR 372

28 See *Baxter v Harland & Wolff* (1990) IRLR 516

29 See *McDermid v Nash Dredging* (1987) IRLR 334

30 On dual vicarious liability for borrowed employees see *Viasystems v Thermal Transfer Ltd* (2005) IRLR 953

31 (1953) AC 643

32 See also *Smith v Scot Bowyers Ltd* (1986) IRLR 315

33 See *Cook v Square D Ltd* (1992) IRLR 34

34 See *Walker v Northumberland County Council* (1995) IRLR 35 and *Dickins v O2 plc* (2009) IRLR 58

35 *Sutherland v Hatton* (2002) IRLR 263. See also *Hartmann v South Essex NHS Trust* (2005) IRLR 293

36 *Coxall v Goodyear Great Britain Ltd* (2002) IRLR 742

37 See *Pentney v Anglian Water Authority* (1983) ICR 463

38 (1988) IRLR 404

39 See *Pickford v Imperial Chemical Industries* (1996) IRLR 622

40 (1991) IRLR 404

41 *Hone v Six Continents Retail Ltd* (2006) IRLR 49. See also *Intel Corporation Ltd v Daw* (2007) IRLR 355

42 (1994) IRLR 460

43 See *Cox v Sun Alliance Ltd* (2001) IRLR 448

44 See *Kidd v AXA Equity* (2000) IRLR 301

45 *Luke v Stoke on Trent City Council* (2007) IRLR 305

46 See *Farrant v The Woodroffe School* (1998) IRLR 176

47 (1972) QB 443

48 See *Sim v Rotherham M.B.C.* (1986) IRLR 391

49 *MacMillan Inc v Bishopsgate Investment Trust plc* (1993) IRLR 393

50 See *Sybron Corporation v Rochem Ltd* (1983) IRLR 253

51 See *Item Software v Fassihi* (2004) IRLR 928

52 (1982) IRLR 146

53 See *Helmet Systems Ltd v Tannard* (2007) IRLR 126

54 See *Lancashire Fires Ltd v S A Lyons & Co. Ltd* (1997) IRLR 113

55 See *Laughton v Bapp Industrial Ltd* (1986) IRLR 245 and *Adamson v B&L Cleaning Ltd* (1995) IRLR 193

56 On injunctions to prevent economic losses see *UBS Ltd v Vestra LLP* (2008) IRLR 965

57 See *TFS Derivatives Ltd v Morgan* (2005) IRLR 246

58 See *Dentmaster (UK) Ltd v Kent* (1997) IRLR 636

59 See *Allan Janes LLP v Johal* (2006) IRLR 599

60 See *Thomas v Farr Plc* (2007) IRLR 419

61 See *Dawnay, Day & Co. v de Bracconier d'Alphen* (1997) IRLR 285

62 See *Eurobrokers Ltd v Rabey* (1995) IRLR 206 and *Credit Suisse Ltd v Armstrong* (1996) IRLR 450

63 See *Cantor Fitzgerald International v Callaghan* (1999) IRLR 234 and *Rock Refrigeration Ltd v Jones* (1996) IRLR 675

64 See *Morris Angel v Hollande* (1993) IRLR 169

65 See *Faccenda Chicken Ltd v Fowler* (1986) IRLR 69

66 See *Crowson Fabrics Ltd v Rider* (2008) IRLR 288 and *PennWell Publishing Ltd v Ornstien and others* (2007) IRLR 700

67 See *Lancashire Fires Ltd v S A Lyons & Co Ltd* (note 54)

68 See *S B J Stephenson Ltd v Mandy* (2000) IRLR 233

69 See *WAC Ltd v Whillock* (1990) IRLR 23; on the possibility of severing unlawful clauses and enforcing the remainder see *Marshall v NM Financial Management* (1996) IRLR 20

70 See *Sun Printers Ltd v Westminster Press Ltd* (1982) IRLR 92

71 See *PSM International v McKechnie* (1992) IRLR 279

72 See also section 7 HASAWA 1974 (Chapter 9)

73 See *Janata Bank v Ahmed* (1981) IRLR 457

74 See *Babula v Waltham Forest College* (2007) IRLR 346

75 See *Hibbins v Hester Way Neighbourhood Project* (2009) IRLR 198

76 See *Bolton School v Evans* (2006) IRLR 500

77 See *Street v Derbyshire Unemployed Worker Centre* (2004) IRLR 687

78 See The Public Interest Disclosure (Prescribed Persons) Order 1999 SI 1549

79 See *Croke v Hydro Aluminium Worcester Ltd* (2007) ICR 1303

80 See *Woodward v Abbey National plc* (2006) IRLR 677 on post-dismissal detriment

81 See *Cumbria County Council v Carlisle-Morgan* (2007) IRLR 314 on the vicarious liability of employers for detriment caused by others

82 See *Virgo Fidelis School v Boyle* (2004) IRLR 268

83 See *Miklaszewicz v Stolt Offshore Ltd* (2002) IRLR 344

84 On the burden of proof see *Kuzel v Roche Ltd* (2008) IRLR 530

85 (1985) IRLR 232

CHAPTER 4

Recruitment and Selection

OVERVIEW

In this chapter we raise some of the issues that will have to be considered by the human resources department. Firstly, is it preferable to hire employed or self-employed persons? Secondly, what are the possible implications of outsourcing the work to be done? Thirdly, if employees are engaged, should they have indefinite, fixed-term, part-time or some other form of contract of employment? Fourthly, what are the issues concerned with employing workers on a temporary basis? Lastly, is it necessary to impose a probationary period on new recruits? The latter part of the chapter deals with some of the regulatory constraints which impinge upon the process of recruitment and selection, including rules concerning rehabilitated offenders and migrant workers. The law relating to the employment of disabled persons and to sex, race and age discrimination is dealt with in Chapters 6 and 7.

EMPLOYMENT STATUS

Before recruiting or selecting an individual, one of the first important decisions to be reached is what sort of contract he or she is to be hired under:

- Is it to be a contract of service (ie an employee) or a contract for services (ie an independent contractor)?

- Is it to be a fixed-term or an open-ended contract?

- Is it to be a full-time or a part-time contract?

- Would it be better to use the services of an employment agency and take on a temporary agency worker?

Although some statutes apply to all of these categories of worker – for example, the Sex Discrimination Act 1975 – some do not, and some categories of workers are provided with special protection. Examples include:

- Employees gain the benefit of a number of statutory rights, such as protection with regard to unfair dismissal, the right to maternity and parental leave

- Employees are subject to the unwritten general obligations implied into all contracts of employment (see Chapter 3).

- When employees, rather than self-employed persons, are engaged, employers are required by statute to deduct tax under Schedule E as well as social security contributions. In addition, employers are obliged to pay employers' National Insurance contributions and to insure against personal injury claims brought by employees.

Perhaps the most significant difference at common law is that the doctrine of vicarious liability applies to employees but not to the self-employed, although in exceptional circumstances employers will be liable for the tortious acts of their independent contractors – for example, if they authorise the commission of the wrongful act or have a responsibility which cannot, by law, be delegated to someone else.

The essence of the doctrine of vicarious liability is that employers are held liable to third parties for the civil wrongs committed by employees in the course of their employment. Determining what is 'in the course of employment' has caused immense difficulties over the years but the position today appears to be as follows. Employees act 'in the course of employment' where they carry out acts which are authorised by the employer. Similarly, where their actions are so closely connected with the employment as to be incidental to it, although prohibited and unauthorised by the employer, employees act 'in the course of employment'.[1] Thus in *Lister v Hedley Hall Ltd*[2] the employers were held vicariously liable for a warden who sexually abused the claimants while they were in his care. However, if an employee's action is so outside the scope of employment as to be not something the employee was employed to do, then the employer is not liable

Before an employer can be held vicariously liable, some nexus has to be established between the employee's wrongful act and the circumstances of employment. Thus a contractor engaged to clean offices (including telephones) was not vicariously liable when one of the contractor's employees dishonestly used the phones for his own purposes.[3] Employees remain personally liable for their own acts and theoretically may be required to reimburse the employer for any damages paid out as a result of their failure to take care (see Chapter 3). It should also be noted that in some cases the criminal law regards an employee's act as being that of the employer, in which case the latter will be responsible for the wrongs committed by the former.

Additionally, a company might be liable as a substitute employer for the negligence of employees not directly employed by it if it can be shown that the substitute employer had sufficient power of control and supervision properly to be regarded as the effective employer at the critical time.[4]

DISTINGUISHING EMPLOYEES FROM OTHER TYPES OF WORKER

Given all the consequences of having an employee on the books, is it always possible to discern whether a contract is a contract of service or a contract for services? Unfortunately, the answer is no. The courts have ruled that the intention of the parties cannot be the sole determinant of contractual status; otherwise, it would be too easy to contract out of employment protection legislation. It is the operation of the contract in practice that is crucial, rather than its appearance. Thus in *Hall v Lorimer*[5] the Court of Appeal considered the position of a person who gave up his employment to pursue the same occupation on a freelance basis. The person concerned carried out all his tasks at the employers' premises using equipment provided by the employers. The Court held that there was no single path to deciding whether the contracts under which a person worked were contracts of service or contracts for services. One had to stand back from the detail and take an informed and considered view of the whole picture. In this case the crucial factor was that the individual worked for a number of different employers.

Although the element of control is important, it may not be decisive in the case of skilled workers who decide for themselves how their work should be done. In such cases the question is broadened to 'Whose business is it?'[6] The fact that workers pay their own tax and National Insurance cannot be conclusive in determining employment status[7] and the cases show that people who perform work at home may be classed as employees so long as there is an element of continuing mutual contractual obligation.[8] In *Carmichael*,[9] the House of Lords held that the applicant's case 'founders on the rock of the absence of mutuality'. The case was about whether two tour guides were employees under contracts of employment and therefore entitled to a written statement of particulars of the terms of their employment (see Chapter 2). An important issue was that there was no requirement for the employer to provide work or for the individual to carry out that work. The Court heard that there were a number of occasions when the applicants had declined offers of work and ruled that there was an 'irreducible minimum of mutual obligation' that was necessary to create a contract of service. There had to be an obligation to provide work and an obligation to perform that work in return for a wage or some form of remuneration. However, the EAT has subsequently commented that a lack of any mutual obligations when no work is being performed is of little significance when determining the status of the individual when work is performed.[10]

Of crucial importance is whether one person working for another is required to perform his or her service in person or not. In *Express and Echo Publications v Tanton*,[11] a contract allowed a worker to provide a substitute if he was not available. This prevented the worker from being treated as an employee because the obligation to do the work in person was, according to the Court of Appeal, an 'irreducible minimum'. However, this was held not to apply to gymnasts working for a local authority who were able to provide substitutes for any shift that they were unable to work.[12] The difference in approach resulted from the fact that the local authority paid the substitutes directly and that the gymnasts could only be replaced by others on the Council's approved list.

Unless the relationship is dependent solely upon the true construction of a written contract, whether a person is engaged under a contract of employment is a question of fact for a court or tribunal to determine.[13]

OUTSOURCING

Increasingly employers are choosing to outsource parts or all of their non-core activities. Outsourcing can mean an arrangement whereby a contractor supplies staff who will be under the supervision of the hirer, or it can mean the outsourcing of the complete activity, so that the hirer is concerned only with the outcomes rather than with the means of achieving them. Activities that are commonly outsourced include catering and the cleaning of premises.

When an organisation decides on outsourcing an activity it must also decide what is to happen to its current employees who work in the part to be contracted out. It also has an obligation to inform and consult those employees at the earliest opportunity. There may not be a need for redundancies because the employees currently working in the part to be transferred may be protected by the Transfer of Undertakings (Protection of Employment) Regulations 2006[14] (these Regulations will be further considered in Chapter 16). Their contracts of employment are likely to transfer with the outsourcing contract. The contractor will become their employer and be liable for any debts arising out of the employment relationship. It will be as if they signed their original contract of employment with the new contractor and any outstanding claims from employees, whether they concern contractual or other obligations arising from the contract of employment, will transfer. For example, where two employees had an outstanding claim for sex discrimination at the time of the transfer, the claim was transferred to the contractor who was faced with the need to settle a dispute in which it had not taken part.[15]

Examples of outsourcing situations where the Transfer Regulations have been held to apply include the contracting out of a local authority refuse collection and cleansing work,[16] a contract to deliver Audi and Volkswagen cars around the country,[17] and the transfer of a security contract.[18] It has not always been clear when the Transfer Regulations apply (see Chapter 16) and there has been considerable litigation over the meaning of a transfer of an undertaking or business.

FIXED-TERM OR INDEFINITE CONTRACT?

Assuming that a decision has been taken that the organisation will engage employees itself, another matter for consideration is whether to hire for a fixed term or for an indefinite period. Concern that employers might abuse the use of fixed-term contracts was one of the motivations behind the EU Directive on Fixed-Term Work.[19] The aims of the Directive were twofold. Firstly, it aimed to improve the quality of fixed-term work by ensuring the application of the principle of non-discrimination. Secondly, it aimed to establish a framework to prevent abuse arising from the use of successive fixed-term contracts. The Directive was implemented in the United Kingdom by the Fixed-term Employees (Prevention of Less Favourable Treatment) Regulations 2002.[20]

The main features of the Regulations are:

- Fixed-term employees should not be treated less favourably than comparable permanent employees with respect to their terms and conditions of employment, unless there is an objective reason to justify the treatment.[21]

- Fixed-term employees should be able to compare their terms and conditions with permanent employees who do the same or similar work for the same employer if they think that they are being treated less favourably.[22]

- The use of successive fixed-term contracts should be limited. This was effected by setting a maximum period of four years for such successive contracts unless there are objectively justifiable reasons for their renewal. This four-year period is calculated on the basis of continuous service.

According to the European Court of Justice,[23] objective reasons must mean precise and concrete circumstances which justify the use of successive fixed-term contracts. The Court held that a rule which allowed gaps of more than 20 days to break continuity so that a new fixed-term contract need not be justified was contrary to the Directive. This is a problem for the United Kingdom because the rules normally only require a week's break to end continuity (see Chapter 16). In relation to pay, the ECJ has ruled that unequal treatment must be justified by precise and concrete factors in the specific context in which it occurs and on the basis of objective and transparent criteria. This is to ensure that there is a genuine need and that the unequal treatment is appropriate for achieving the objective pursued and is necessary for that purpose.[24]

If an employee considers that he or she has been treated less favourably than a comparable permanent employee, then he or she may request a written statement from the employer giving the reasons for the treatment. The employee is entitled to the statement within 21 days of the request and the statement is admissible as evidence in any subsequent tribunal proceedings.

 CASE STUDY

Department for Work and Pensions v Webley[25]

Atasha Webley worked as an administrative officer at Leyton Job Centre from 4 February 2002 to 17 January 2003. She was employed on a series of short, fixed-term contracts. Her letter of engagement had specified that she was employed on a short-term temporary and non-permanent basis. This was because the employer had a policy of terminating temporary employees after 51 weeks' service.

Mrs Webley brought a complaint under the Fixed-term Employees Regulations that the termination of her contract amounted to less favourable treatment compared to comparable permanent employees. Thus the question was whether the non-renewal of a fixed-term contract, amounting to dismissal, was capable of being less favourable treatment.

The Court of Appeal held that the ending of a fixed-term contract by the effluxion of time could not constitute less favourable treatment when compared to a permanent employee. If fixed-term contracts of employment were lawful, then the ending of those contracts must also be lawful.

An employee may present a complaint to an employment tribunal that he or she has received less favourable treatment. It will be for the employer to identify the reason for the less favourable treatment. If the employment tribunal finds that such treatment has taken place, it may make a recommendation for action by the employer and award compensation to the employee.[26] Employers will have to be aware of these legal requirements when deciding whether to employ individuals on a permanent or a fixed-term contract. It should also be noted that the expiry of a fixed-term contract without its renewal on the same terms amounts to a dismissal in law (see Chapter 12).

PART-TIME OR FULL-TIME?

In deciding whether to employ full-time or part-time staff, account will have to be taken of the Part-time Workers (Prevention of Less Favourable Treatment) Regulations[27] (PTW Regulations) which give effect to a European Council Directive.[28] The purpose of the Regulations is to give part-time workers the right not to be treated less favourably than comparable full-time workers, as regards the terms of the contract, or be subjected to some detriment by any act or failure to act.[29] This right applies only if the treatment is on the grounds that a worker is a part-timer and that the treatment cannot be justified on objective grounds. However, the EAT has indicated that the part-time nature of the worker's status does not have to be the sole reason for discrimination. Indeed, the fact that not all part-timers are adversely treated does not mean that those who are cannot bring proceedings if being part-time is a reason for their less favourable treatment.[30]

PART-TIME WORKERS AND COMPARABLE FULL-TIME WORKERS

The principle of non-discrimination applies to 'workers'. This has a wider meaning than 'employees', and the definition given in the PTW Regulations[31] is identical to that in section 230(3) ERA 1996.

Regulation 2 PTW Regulations has a similar definition of both full-time and part-time workers. They are individuals who are paid wholly or in part by reference to the amount of time worked and who are, in relation to other workers employed under the same type of contract, defined as full-time or part-time.

Comparable full-timers, in relation to part-timers, are individuals who are:

- employed by the same employer under the same sort of contract[32]
- engaged in the same or broadly similar work, having regard, where relevant, to whether they have similar levels of qualifications, skills and experience[33]
- based at the same establishment or, if there is no full-time comparator at the same establishment, at a different one.[34]

According to Regulation 2(4) PTW Regulations, the moment for deciding whether an individual is a full-time comparator is the time when the alleged less favourable treatment takes place. This is a very demanding test for establishing whether an individual's job can be used as a comparator on which to base a claim of discrimination. If there is not a full-timer who meets the criteria, it will not be possible to make a claim for discrimination based upon the PTW Regulations. For example, in a business where all the management staff are full-time and all the operatives are low-paid part-timers, it is unlikely that the PTW Regulations would be of any help to the part-time workers.

In *Matthews v Kent and Medway Fire Authority*,[35] some 12,000 'retained' firefighters brought claims under the PTW Regulations that they were being less favourably treated than full-time firefighters. They complained that they did not receive a number of benefits which their full-time colleagues had. These included not being in the Firemen's Pension Scheme, a lack of pay for additional responsibilities and a less favourable sick pay scheme. The House of Lords held that the retained firemen worked under the same sort of contract within the meaning of Regulation 2. Even though the full-time firefighters had a fuller and wider job, it was important to look at the work they were both engaged in to decide whether it was the same work or, importantly, whether it was broadly similar work.

There are a limited number of exceptions to these strict rules on comparators. These are:

● workers who become part-time. If a full-time worker varies or terminates his or her contract in order to work fewer hours each week and thus become a part-timer, it is permissible to assume that there is a full-time comparator employed on the same terms as applied before the variation or termination.[36]

● full-time workers who return to work for the same employer after an absence of less than 12 months but are then required to work fewer hours per week. This is conditional upon the returning individual working in the same job, or at the same level, as that in which he or she worked before the break. In such a situation it is possible to assume that there is a full-time comparator employed on the same terms and conditions as applied to the individual before the break in employment.[37]

LESS FAVOURABLE TREATMENT

In determining whether a part-timer has been discriminated against, the pro rata principle applies, unless it is inappropriate.[38] This means that a part-time worker is entitled to receive pay or any other benefit in proportion to the number of weekly hours that he or she works in comparison with a comparable full-time worker.[39] The one exception to this concerns overtime. Not paying overtime rates to a part-time worker until he or she has worked hours at least comparable to the basic working hours of the comparable full-time worker will not be regarded as less favourable treatment.

In the government's guidance accompanying the PTW Regulations the following are examples given as arising from the application of the principle of non-discrimination:

- Previous or current part-time status should not of itself constitute a barrier to promotion.

- Part-time workers should receive the same hourly rate as full-time workers.

- Part-time workers should receive the same hourly rate of overtime pay as full-time workers, once they have worked more than normal full-time hours.

- Part-time workers should be able to participate in profit-sharing or share option schemes available to full-time workers.

- Employers should not discriminate between part-time workers and full-time workers over access to pension schemes.

- Employers should not exclude part-timers from training simply because they work part-time.

- In selection for redundancy, part-time workers must not be treated less favourably than full-time workers.

DETRIMENT AND DISMISSAL

There is a distinction in the protection offered by the Regulations between employees and workers. Dismissal of employees, for any of the reasons listed below, will be regarded as an unfair dismissal in accordance with Part X of the ERA 1996 (see Chapter 13).[40] Regulation 6(1) PTW Regulations entitles a worker who considers that he or she has been treated less favourably to request in writing a statement giving particulars of the reasons for the treatment.[41] The worker is entitled to receive this statement within 21 days of the request. The written statement is admissible as evidence in any future proceedings and a tribunal may draw its own inferences if the statement is not provided or if it is 'evasive or equivocal'.[42]

Workers (which includes employees) have the right not to be subjected to a detriment by any act, or any deliberate failure to act, by the employer on the grounds that the employer believes that the worker has (or intends in due course to have):

- brought proceedings against the employer under the PTW Regulations

- requested from the employer a written statement of reasons under Regulation 6

- given evidence or information in connection with any proceedings brought by any worker

- done anything else under the PTW Regulations in relation to the employer or any other person

- alleged that the employer has infringed the Regulations

- refused, or proposes to refuse, to give up any rights held under the PTW Regulations.

COMPLAINTS TO EMPLOYMENT TRIBUNALS

A worker who believes that he or she has suffered less favourable treatment or other detriment in accordance with the Regulations may complain to an employment tribunal.[43] The complaint must be made within a period of three months from the date of treatment or detriment, although a longer period will be allowed if the tribunal finds it just and equitable to do so.[44] The options open to the employment tribunal are to:[45]

- make a declaration of the rights of the complainant in respect of the complaint

- order the employer to pay compensation to the complainant. Compensation does not include injury to the complainant's feelings and the complainant has a duty to mitigate his or her losses[46]

- recommend that the employer takes action to obviate or reduce the adverse effect on the complainant of any matter to which the complaint relates. The tribunal may specify a reasonable period during which this action should be taken. If the employer fails to follow the recommendation, without justification, the tribunal may increase the amount of compensation to be paid to the complainant.[47]

SHOULD TEMPORARY EMPLOYEES OR AGENCY STAFF BE HIRED?

In deciding whether to employ on a temporary or 'permanent' basis (see Chapter 11 on notice provisions), it should be noted that temporary staff have exactly the same statutory rights as other employees so long as they possess any necessary qualifying period of service. The only two exceptions to this proposition arise where an individual is employed on a temporary basis as a replacement for a woman on maternity leave or to replace someone absent from work under the statutory provisions relating to medical suspension (see Chapters 8 and 5 respectively).

Occasionally an organisation may ask an agency to provide staff, and if the worker engaged by the client organisation is under a personal obligation to perform the work, a contract of employment may exist. The exact relationship between the client and the individual supplied by the agency is a question of fact for an employment tribunal to decide. We will look firstly at issues relating to the relationship between the individual and the agency and secondly at the relationship, if any, between the individual and the client.

The case of *McMeechan v Secretary of State for Employment*[48] concerned a temporary worker who completed a series of individual assignments through an employment agency. He was given a job sheet and a standard written statement of terms and conditions for each assignment. The statement specified that he was providing services as a self-employed worker and was not operating under a contract of service, although the agency did deduct tax and National Insurance contributions. When the agency became insolvent, the individual made a claim to the Secretary of State for wages owed. The claim was refused because, it was argued, the individual was not an employee of the insolvent company. The Court of Appeal considered *Wickens v Champion Employment*,[49] which involved an attempt to show that all temporary staff of an agency were working under contracts of employment. This failed, according to the Court, because the relationship between the agency and the temporary staff lacked the essential elements of continuity and care by the employer that are characteristics of a contract of service.

The question for the Court in *McMeechan's* case was whether the individual assignment could amount to a contract of service or not. The arguments for there being a contract for services were that there was an express statement that the individual was self-employed and that the worker had freedom to work for a particular client on a self-employed basis. On the side of there being a contract of service were the power of the agency to dismiss for misconduct, the power to bring any assignment to an end, the establishment of a grievance procedure and the stipulation of an hourly rate of pay, which in turn was subject to deductions for unsatisfactory timekeeping, work, attitude or misconduct. The Court concluded that despite the label put on it by the parties, there was a contract of service between the temporary worker and the agency. The courts will therefore consider all aspects of the relationship in deciding whether the agency worker has a contract of employment or not.[50]

MUTUALITY OF OBLIGATION AND CONTROL

The second question is whether there can be an employment relationship between the individual, supplied on a temporary basis by an employment agency, and the client employer. In *Montgomery v Johnson Underwood Ltd*[51] a woman was placed by an agency with a client company and remained there for two years. Eventually the company asked the agency to terminate the assignment. As a result the individual made a complaint of unfair dismissal naming both the client company and the agency as her employer. The Employment Appeal Tribunal found that the agency had exercised little or no 'control, direction or supervision' over the individual during the assignment, and this proved crucial. There had to be the essential elements of mutuality of obligation and control.

The Court of Appeal relied upon *Carmichael*[52] to decide that 'mutuality of obligation' and 'control' are the minimum legal requirements for the existence of a contract of employment. Three conditions have to be fulfilled. These are that:

- the individual agrees, in return for wages or other remuneration, that he or she will provide his or her own work and skill in performance of some duty for the employer (mutuality of obligation)

- he or she agrees, expressly or impliedly, to be subject to the other's control in the performance of the duties (control)

- the other provisions of the contract are consistent with those of a contract of service.

Whether there exists a mutuality of obligation and the necessary level of control is a matter for the employment tribunal to decide. In this case the lack of control by the agency meant that the individual could not be regarded as an employee of that agency. However, an employer–employee relationship was established with the client in *Motorola Ltd v Davidson*.[53] This case concerned a long-term agency worker who, eventually, was suspended by the client company after a disciplinary hearing. This led to the client terminating the individual's assignment. The EAT held that once the individual was at the client's site, he was largely subject to the same control as if he had been an ordinary full-time employee. It was the client who decided 'the thing to be done, the way in which it shall be done, the means to be employed in doing it, the time when and the place where it shall be done'.[54]

CASE STUDY

Dacas v Brook Street Bureau (UK) Ltd[55]

Patricia Dacas worked as a cleaner for Brook Street Bureau. She had a contract with Brook Street which stated that her 'temporary worker agreement' would not give rise to a contract of employment between her and the agency.

For a number of years she was assigned to the same client of Brook Street, namely Wandsworth Borough Council. She was assigned exclusively to work at a Council-run hostel for the long-term care of people with mental health problems. The agency paid her wages and deducted tax and National Insurance. Eventually, after some trouble, the council asked the agency to withdraw Ms Dacas from the contract. She then made a complaint of unfair dismissal on the basis that she was either an employee of the agency or of the Council.

The first question to be decided was who, if anyone, was the employer of Ms Dacas. The Court of Appeal concluded that it could not be Brook Street Bureau because the agency was under no obligation to provide her with work and she was under no obligation to accept any work offered. There was thus no mutuality of obligation. On the other hand, the degree of control exercised by the Council, as well as a mutuality of obligation between the parties, suggested that she was actually an employee of the client.

Thus in cases involving a triangular relationship consisting of a worker, an employment agency and an end-user, tribunals should consider the possibility of an implied contract between the worker and the end-user.[56] According to the Court of Appeal, the relevant question is whether it is necessary to imply mutual contractual obligations between the end-user to provide work and the worker to perform it. Thus the implication of a contract of employment is not inevitable in a long-term agency situation.[57] It should also be remembered that it is impossible to imply into a contract a term that contradicts an express one.[58]

In October 2008 the European Parliament approved a Temporary Agency Work Directive which comes into force in December 2011. This will provide equal treatment from Day 1 in terms of basic working and employment conditions unless the social partners agree otherwise. In the UK, an agreement between the CBI and the TUC currently provides for equal treatment to be afforded after 12 weeks.

EMPLOYMENT AGENCIES

The implementation of the Employment Agencies Act 1973 was changed by the Conduct of Employment Agencies and Employment Businesses Regulations 2003,[59] which came into effect in April 2004. The government's stated objective in producing regulations has been to help promote a flexible labour market, which is underpinned by a set of regulations that ensure fairness and minimum standards in the industry.

In seeking the 'proper conduct' of agencies and employment businesses, the government aims to protect the interests of work-seekers and those of hirers. There is an attempt to ensure clarity of agreement between the work-seeker and the employment agency or business. Generally the Act and the Regulations regulate the relationship between the hirer and the agency or business and the relationship between the job-seeker and the agency or business. They set down the requirements for communicating of information between all the parties involved and the terms of the agreements between each of the parties. Anyone who contravenes the prohibition of charging fees to work-seekers, fails to comply with regulations to secure the proper conduct of the agency or business, falsifies records, or fails without reasonable excuse to comply with a prohibition order, will be guilty of an offence and subject to a fine.[60]

An employment tribunal may make an order prohibiting a person from operating an employment agency or business for up to 10 years on the grounds that the person is unsuitable because of misconduct or any other sufficient reason. In addition, terms of contracts with hirers or work-seekers that are invalid in terms of the Act or Regulations will be unenforceable.

SHOULD A PROBATIONARY PERIOD BE IMPOSED?

We shall see in Chapter 12 that (save in exceptional circumstances) only those who have been continuously employed for one year can claim that they have been unfairly dismissed. In a sense this requirement serves to impose a probationary period. However, some employers may regard one year as excessive for the purpose of establishing whether a person's appointment should be confirmed and frequently a shorter period will be deemed appropriate. Some employers prefer to make an assessment within four weeks in order to avoid having to give statutory notice to terminate the contract (see Chapter 11). The great advantage of operating a probationary period is that new recruits are made aware that they are on trial and must therefore establish their suitability.

REGULATORY CONSTRAINTS

At common law, employers have the right to decide what policies to adopt in relation to recruitment but this position has been altered by a series of statutory and non-statutory interventions designed to protect certain categories of job applicant. Such interventions mostly concern provisions designed to prevent discrimination in recruitment and employment on the grounds of gender, race, disability, sexual orientation, religion or belief, age and membership or non-membership of a trade union. Many of these issues are considered in later chapters.

REHABILITATION OF OFFENDERS ACT 1974

The law does not require applicants to disclose facts about themselves which could hinder them in getting jobs (unless their silence amounts to fraud). Thus if employers believe that certain information is important, they should seek it specifically before the job is offered.

Section 4 of this Act relieves certain rehabilitated persons from the obligation to disclose 'spent' convictions to a prospective employer and makes it unlawful for an employer to deny employment on the grounds that the applicant had a conviction which was 'spent'. It is the policy of the Act that applicants should not be questioned about spent convictions, although if this situation does arise, applicants are entitled to deny that they have ever been convicted. There are a number of exceptions to these rules. Protection under the Act is not given to certain occupations such as doctors, nurses, teachers, social workers and those working with children, including those applying to become registered day-care providers.

Sentences of over two-and-a-half years' imprisonment never become 'spent'; otherwise, convictions become 'spent' after periods which are related to the gravity of the sentence imposed. Thus for a sentence of imprisonment of between six months and two-and-a-half years the rehabilitation period is 10 years. Imprisonment for less than six months requires a seven-year rehabilitation period, and fines or community service orders take five years to become 'spent'. A probation order, conditional discharge or binding over need not be disclosed after a year or until the order expires (whichever is the longer), and absolute discharges can be concealed if six months have elapsed since sentence. Despite the existence of the Act, the courts cannot compel an employer to engage a rehabilitated offender: they can only declare the exclusion of the applicant to be unlawful.

MIGRANT WORKERS

A new method for migrant workers to enter the UK came into force in November 2008. Employers wanting to engage skilled persons from outside Europe and sponsor their entry to the UK must apply for a licence. Migrants have to pass a points-based assessment before they are given permission to enter or remain. The system consists of five tiers, each with different requirements. The number of points the migrant needs and the way the points are awarded depend on the tier they are applying under. Points are awarded to reflect the migrant's ability, experience, age and, when appropriate, the level of need within the sector the migrant will be working. Except for tier 1, migrants will have to be sponsored in order for their application to be successful. If an employer wishes to recruit a migrant under tiers 2, 4 or 5 they will have to apply for a licence. The tiers are: (1) highly skilled workers – for example, scientists and entrepreneurs; (2) skilled workers with a job offer – for example, teachers and nurses; (3) low-skilled workers filling specific temporary labour shortages – for example, construction workers for a particular project; (4) students; (5) youth mobility and temporary workers – for example, musicians coming to play in a concert.[61]

KEY LEARNING POINTS

- Organisations have to decide whether to use employees or independent contractors; there are differences in taxation and employment costs as well as vicarious liability.

- It is not always clear whether a worker is employed under a contract of employment or is working under a contract for services; the intention of the parties is important, but may not be the deciding factor.

- The factors leading to a decision on whether a contract of employment exists or not are likely to include a 'sufficient' level of control by the employer and an 'irreducible minimum' of mutuality of obligation between employer and worker.

- Outsourcing is an option for many employers, but it is important to be aware of the effect of the Transfer of Undertakings (Protection of Employment) Regulations 2006.

- Employers may be faced with decisions regarding whether to employ individuals on part-time, fixed-term or temporary contracts. Care will have to be taken with the regulatory constraints on the way an employer treats such employees/workers

- There are Regulations dealing with employment agencies which aim to clarify the rights of both hirers and work-seekers.

- Probationary periods may be useful in deciding whether to confirm an appointment; the law normally places a requirement for one year's continuous employment before there is a right to claim unfair dismissal.

- Rehabilitated offenders have the right, in certain circumstances, not to reveal information about spent convictions.

- Employers may have to apply for a licence in order to recruit certain types of migrant labour.

Reinforce your understanding of this chapter by visiting www.cipd.co.uk/sss for activities, questions, weblinks and additional case studies

REFERENCES

1 See *Gravil v Redruth R.F.C.* (2008) IRLR 829

2 (2001) IRLR 472

3 See *Heasmans v Clarity Cleaning* (1987) IRLR 286

4 See *Sime v Sutcliffe Catering (Scotland) Ltd* (1990) IRLR 228

5 (1994) IRLR 171

6 See *Lane v Shire Roofing* (1995) IRLR 493

7 See *Young & Woods v West* (1980) IRLR 201

8 See *McLeod v Hellyer Brothers Ltd* (1987) IRLR 232

9 *Carmichael v National Power plc* (2000) IRLR 43 HL

10 See *James v Redcats (Brands) Ltd* (2007) IRLR 296

11 (1999) IRLR 367

12 *MacFarlane v Glasgow City Council* (2001) IRLR 7

13 See *Clark v Oxfordshire Health Authority* (1998) IRLR 125

14 SI 2006/246

15 See *DJM International Ltd v Nicholas* (1996) IRLR 76

16 *Wren v Eastbourne B.C.* (1993) IRLR 425

17 *ECM (Vehicle Delivery Services) Ltd v Cox* (1999) IRLR 559

18 *Securicor Guarding Ltd v Fraser Security Services* (1996) IRLR 552

19 Council Directive 99/70/EC

20 SI 2002/2034

21 Regulations 3 and 4

22 Regulation 2

23 Case C-212/04 *Adeneler v Ellinikos Organismos Galaktos* (2006) IRLR 716

24 *Alonso v Osakidetza-Servicio* (2007) IRLR 911

25 (2005) IRLR 288

26 Regulation 7

27 SI 2000/1551; subsequently amended by the Part-time Workers (Prevention of Less Favourable Treatment) Regulations 2001 SI 2001/1107

28 Council Directive 97/81/EC OJ L14/9 20.1.98

29 Regulation 5(1) PTW Regulations

30 See *Sharma v Manchester City Council* (2008) IRLR 336 but compare *McMenemy v Capita Business Services LN* (2007) IRLR 400

31 Regulation 1(3) PTW Regulations

32 Regulation 2(4)(i) PTW Regulations; amended in 2002 (SI 2002/2035) so that there was no distinction between permanent and fixed-term contracts

33 Regulation 2(4)(ii) PTW Regulations

34 Regulation 2(5) PTW Regulations

35 (2006) ICR 365

36 Regulation 3 PTW Regulations

37 Regulation 4 PTW Regulations

38 Regulation 5(3) PTW Regulations

39 Regulation 2(2) PTW Regulations

40 Regulation 7(1) PTW Regulations

41 If the less favourable treatment is dismissal, the employee would be able to exercise his or her right to request written reasons for the dismissal under section 92 ERA 1996.

42 Regulation 6(3) PTW Regulations

43 There are special rules for members of the armed forces; see regulation 13 PTW Regulations

44 Regulation 8(1)–(3) PTW Regulations

45 Regulation 8(7) PTW Regulations

46 Regulation 8(11)–(12) PTW Regulations

47 Regulation 8(14) PTW Regulations

48 (1997) IRLR 353

49 (1984) ICR 365

50 See *O'Kelly v Trust House Forte* (1983) IRLR 286

51 (2001) IRLR 269

52 *Carmichael v National Power plc* (2000) IRLR 43

53 *Motorola Ltd v (1) Davidson and (2) Melville Craig Group Ltd* (2001) IRLR 4

54 This was a quotation from MacKenna, J. in *Ready Mixed Concrete (South East) Ltd v Minister of Pensions and National Insurance* (1968) 1 All ER 433

55 (2004) IRLR 358

56 See *Cable & Wireless v Muscat* (2006) IRLR 355

57 See *James v London Borough of Greenwich* (2008) IRLR 302

58 See *Consistent Group Ltd v Kalwak* (2008) IRLR 505 where it was alleged that some of the contractual obligations were a sham.

59 SI 2003/3319

60 See Sections 15 and 16 of EA 2008

61 see http://www.ukba.homeoffice.gov.uk/

CHAPTER 5

Pay Issues

OVERVIEW

This chapter is concerned with a number of issues related to pay, beginning with the duty to pay wages or salaries. There is then some detailed consideration of the National Minimum Wage Act 1998 and the complexities associated with trying to establish the actual rates paid in a variety of work circumstances. We then consider the employer's duty to provide pay statements and make guarantee payments when employees are not provided with work. Finally, we examine issues related to pay and sickness, including statutory sick pay and the right of employers to suspend employees on medical grounds.

THE DUTY TO PAY WAGES

This is a basic obligation of employers and is normally dealt with by an express term. There are a number of issues to be considered.

1 *An employer may be required to pay wages even if there is no work for the employee to do*
   The general rule is that wages must be paid if an employee is available for work,[1] but everything will depend on whether there is an express or implied term of fact in the contract which deals with the matter. Thus an express term to the effect that 'no payment shall be made during a period of lay-off' will eliminate the possibility of a contractual claim being brought in such a situation.

2 *Deductions from wages or payment by the employee are unlawful unless required or authorised by statute – for example, PAYE or social security contributions – or the worker has agreed to it*[2]
   Section 27(1) ERA 1996 defines 'wages' as 'any sum payable to the worker in connection with his employment'. This includes holiday pay and commission earnings which are payable after an employee has left. It also includes discretionary bonus payments where the employee has been told that he or she will receive the payments.[3] Before payment of such 'wages' the employer would

be entitled to deduct an amount to repay any advances that had been given to the employee.[4]

The worker must give oral or written consent to the deduction before it is made,[5] and where the agreement constitutes a term of the contract of employment, it must be in writing and drawn to the employee's attention (or its effect must have been notified to the worker in writing).[6] To satisfy the requirements of ERA 1996 there must be a document which clearly states that a deduction is to be made from the employee's wages and that the employee agrees to it.[7] Even if an employee has entered into a compromise agreement to settle an unfair dismissal complaint over non-payment of wages, he or she may still be able to make a claim for that underpayment.[8] If a tribunal is not persuaded on the evidence that a deduction was authorised by a provision of the employee's contract, the individual is entitled to be paid the money deducted. Thus, in *IPC Ltd v Balfour*,[9] the EAT held that a reduction in pay following the unilateral introduction of short-time working amounted to an unauthorised deduction. However, if the contract of employment allowed the employer to change the hours or shift-patterns of an employee, the employer would be entitled to adjust the pay levels to reflect those changes.[10]

For these purposes there is no valid distinction between a deduction and a reduction of wages. The issue is whether, for whatever reason, apart from an error of computation, the worker is paid less than the amount of wages properly payable.[11] However, employers who take a conscious decision not to make a payment because they believe that they are contractually entitled to take that course are not making an error of computation.[12] Although section 13(4) refers to an 'error of any description', it does not include an error of law.[13] Where there is a dispute over the justification for a deduction, it is the employment tribunal's task to resolve it.[14] However, tribunals do not have jurisdiction to determine whether a deduction by reason of industrial action was contractually authorised.[15]

Written agreements under which employers pay a proportion of wages to third parties are not affected by ERA 1996 and in retail employment deductions or payments made to an employer in relation to stock or cash shortages are subject to a limit of one-tenth of gross pay, except for the final payment of wages.[16]

3 *Payments in lieu are not wages within the meaning of ERA 1996 if they relate to a period after the termination of employment*

According to the House of Lords in *Delaney v Staples*,[17] ERA 1996 requires wages to be construed as payments in respect of the rendering of services during employment. Thus the only payments in lieu covered by the legislation are those in respect of 'garden leave' (see below), since these can be viewed as wages owed under a subsisting contract of employment. In the same case the Court of Appeal accepted that non-payment of wages constitutes a deduction for these purposes, as does the withholding of commission and holiday pay.[18] Indeed, the withholding of commission may amount to an unlawful deduction even where it is discretionary so long as commission was normally expected by the employee.[19]

4 *A complaint that there has been an unauthorised deduction must normally be lodged with an employment tribunal within three months of the deduction being made*[20]

If the complaint is well-founded, the tribunal must make a declaration to that effect and must order the reimbursement of the amount of the deduction or payment to the extent that it exceeded what should lawfully have been deducted or received by the employee. Employment tribunals can also provide compensation for workers who suffer financial losses as a result of unlawful deductions from wages.[21] The only method of contracting out of the requirements of ERA 1996 is if an agreement is reached following action taken by ACAS or there is a valid compromise agreement (see Chapter 15).

5 *Overpayments*

Employers may be entitled to restitution of overpayments made to an employee owing to a mistake of fact but *not* a mistake of law. For example, an overpayment that arose as the result of a misunderstanding of the National Minimum Wage Act would be irrecoverable.[22] Indeed, employees may commit theft if they fail to notify the employer of an accidental overpayment.[23] Section 16(1) ERA 1996 makes specific provision for the recovery of overpayments, and tribunals cannot inquire into the lawfulness of a deduction for this purpose.[24]

THE NATIONAL MINIMUM WAGE

The National Minimum Wage Act 1998 (NMWA 1998) provides for a minimum hourly wage for workers. 'Worker' is defined in section 54(3) as someone working under a contract of employment or any other contract under which an individual undertakes to do or perform in person any work or service for another. From October 2008, the standard rate was £5.73 per hour. There are also two development rates for younger workers: for those aged 18 years to 21 years inclusive it was set at £4.77 per hour and for 16- and 17-year-olds it was set at £3.53 per hour.[25] Any other allowances paid by the employer to workers in relation to their work cannot be used to offset the fact that an individual's basic hourly rate is less than the NMW. It is possible to reduce those other rates in order to increase the basic rate without contravening the requirements of the NMW Regulations 1999, although doing this might result in the employer being guilty of an unlawful deduction of wages in contravention of section 13(1) ERA 1996.[26]

Regulation 12 of the National Minimum Wage Regulations 1999[27] (NMW Regulations) describes those who do not qualify for the national minimum wage at all. These include:

- a worker who is employed under a contract of apprenticeship and is in the first 12 months of that contract, or who has not reached the age of 19

- a worker who is participating in a scheme designed to provide him or her with training, work, or temporary work, or which is designed to assist him or her to obtain work[28]

- a worker who is attending higher education up to first degree level or a teacher-training course, and who, before the course ends, is required as part of the course to attend a period of work experience not exceeding one year

- a homeless person who is provided with shelter and other benefits in return for performing work.

WHEN IS A WORKER 'WORKING'?

Workers who work and live in the employer's household and who are treated as members of the family are also excluded.[29] However, workers who, by arrangement, sleep on the employer's premises may be entitled to payment for all the hours that are required to be spent at those premises. In *Scottbridge Ltd v Wright*[30] a night-watchman was required to be on the premises between 5 pm and 7 am each night. Apart from some minor duties he was mainly required to be present in case of intruders. He was provided with sleeping facilities and allowed to sleep during the course of the night. The Court of Session upheld the EAT decision that he was entitled to be paid at least the national minimum wage rate for the specific hours that he was required to be at work. It was up to the employer to provide him with work and the fact that he was not required to do any did not nullify his entitlement to be paid.

CASE STUDY

British Nursing Association v Inland Revenue[31]

The employers were a national organisation providing emergency 'bank' nurses for nursing in homes and other institutions. Part of the work involved a 24-hours-per-day telephone booking service. This service was carried on at night by employees working from home. The 'duty' nurse would take the diverted call and contact the appropriate person to do the work requested. The duty nurse was paid an amount per shift.

The issue was whether this person was 'working' within the meaning of the NMW Regulations when they were not actually receiving or making phone calls – even when watching television while waiting for calls. The Court of Appeal endorsed the EAT's view that in deciding when a worker is working for the purposes of the NMW Regulations, an employment tribunal should look at the type of work involved and its different elements to see if altogether it could be properly described as work. Aspects to be examined include:

- the nature of the work
- the extent to which the worker's activities are restricted when not performing the particular task
- the mutual obligations of employer and worker, although the way in which remuneration is calculated is not conclusive
- the extent to which the period during which work is being performed is readily ascertainable.

Thus the duty nurses were held to be working throughout their shift and entitled to payment for it.

CALCULATING REMUNERATION

The hourly rate is calculated by adding up the total remuneration, less reductions, and dividing by the total number of hours worked[32] during a pay reference period.[33] Total remuneration[34] in a pay reference period is calculated by adding together:

- all money paid by the employer to the worker during the reference period
- any money paid by the employer to the worker in the following reference period which is in respect of work done in the current reference period
- any money paid by the employer to the worker later than the end of the following pay reference period in respect of work done in the current reference period and for which the worker is under an obligation to complete a record and has not done so
- the cost of accommodation, calculated by an approved formula.[35]

Deductions that can be made from this total remuneration figure are set out in Regulation 31 and include:[36]

- any payments made by the employer to the worker in respect of a previous pay reference period
- in the case of non-salaried work, any money paid to the worker in respect of periods when the worker was absent from work or engaged in taking industrial action
- in the case of time-work, the difference between the lowest rate of pay and any higher rates of pay paid during the reference period
- any amounts paid by the employer to the worker that represent amounts paid by customers in the form of service charge, tips, gratuities or cover charge – that is, not paid through the payroll[37]
- the payment of expenses.

CALCULATING HOURS

The calculation of the hours worked can be complex. There are four different types of hours of work. These are:

1 *salaried hours work*[38]
   This is where the worker is paid for a number of ascertainable hours in a year (the basic hours) and where the payment, which normally consists of an annual salary and perhaps an annual bonus, is paid in equal instalments, weekly or monthly.

2 *time-work*[39]
   This is work that is paid for under a worker's contract by reference to the time worked, and is not salaried hours work.

3 *output work*[40]
   This is work that is paid for by reference to the number of pieces made or processed, or by some other measure of output such as the value of sales made

or transactions completed. The rated output hours, in a reference period, will be the total number of hours spent by the worker in doing output work. The employer has to arrive at a 'fair' piece rate by reference to the the time taken by the average employee doing the same job.

4 *unmeasured work*[41]

This is any work that is not salaried hours work, time-work or output work, especially work where there are no specified hours and the worker is required to work when needed or whenever work is available. The unmeasured work hours will be the total hours, in a pay reference period, spent by the worker in carrying out his or her contractual duties.[42] Regulation 28 allows for a 'daily average' agreement to be reached between the employer and the worker.[43]

UNDERPAYMENT OF THE NMW

Section 9 NMWA 1998[44] allows the Secretary of State to require employers to keep and preserve records for at least three years. Workers have the right to inspect these records if they believe, on reasonable grounds, that they are being paid at a rate less than the national minimum wage.[45] When inspecting these records a worker may be accompanied by another person of his or her choice.[46] That choice must be stated in the 'production notice' that the worker gives to the employer requesting the production of the records.[47] The employer must produce these records within 14 days following receipt of the notice and must make them available at the worker's place of work or some other reasonable place.[48] Failure to produce the records or to allow the workers to exercise their rights can lead to a complaint at an employment tribunal.[49] In these circumstances the tribunal can make an award of up to 80 times the national minimum wage. If a worker has been remunerated, during the reference period, at a rate less than the national minimum wage, there is a contractual entitlement to be paid the amount underpaid. There is a reversal of the normal burden of proof and a presumption that the worker qualifies for the national minimum wage and that he or she is underpaid.[50]

Sections 5–8 of the NMWA 1998 established the Low Pay Commission and gave the Secretary of State discretion to refer matters to it. The HM Customs and Revenue has the task of ensuring that workers are remunerated at a rate that is at least equivalent to the NMW. It has wide powers to inspect records and enforce the Act's requirements.[51] If it is discovered that workers are not being paid the national minimum wage, the Revenue can issue notices of underpayment requiring payment of the national minimum wage together with arrears and a financial penalty.[52] Section 14 allows HMRC officers to take information away from the employer's premises in order to copy it and section 31 enables serious offences to be tried in the Crown Court.

Workers have a right not to suffer detriment[53] if they assert in good faith their right to the national minimum wage, to inspect records or to recover underpayment.

PAY STATEMENTS

Under section 8 ERA 1996 employers must give their employees an itemised pay statement. The statement must contain the following particulars:

- the gross amount of wages or salary
- the amount of any variable or fixed deductions and the purposes for which they are made (on the legality of such deductions see above)
- the net wages or salary payable and, where the net amount is paid in different ways, the amount and method of payment of each part.

Such a statement need not contain separate particulars of a fixed deduction – for example, of union dues – if it specifies the total amount of fixed deductions and each year the employer provides a standing statement of fixed deductions which describes the amount of each deduction, its purpose and the intervals at which it is made. If no pay statement is issued, an employee may refer the matter to an employment tribunal to determine what particulars ought to have been included. Where a tribunal finds that an employer failed to provide such a statement or the statement does not contain the required particulars, the tribunal must make a declaration to that effect. Additionally, where it finds that any unnotified deductions have been made during the 13 weeks preceding the application, it may order the employer to pay compensation to the employee. This refund cannot exceed the total amount of unnotified deductions.[54] Thus there is here a penal aspect to the discretion that tribunals have to exercise.

GUARANTEE PAYMENTS

Employees with one month's continuous service qualify for a guarantee payment if they are not provided with work throughout a day in which they would normally be required to work in accordance with their contract of employment because of:

- a diminution in the requirements of the employer's business for work of the kind which the employee is employed to do, or
- any other occurrence that affects the normal working of the employer's business in relation to work of that kind.[55]

The words 'normally required to work' are significant for two reasons. First, an employee who is not obliged to work when requested may be regarded as not being subject to a contract of employment.[56] Second, if contracts of employment are varied to provide for a reduced number of working days – for example, four instead of five – employees will be unable to claim a payment for the fifth day because they are no longer 'required to work' on that day. 'Any other occurrence …' would seem to comprehend something like a power failure or natural disaster rather than works holidays.

No guarantee payment is available if the workless day is a consequence of a strike, lock-out or other industrial action involving any employee of the employer or any associated employer.[57] The entitlement to a guarantee payment may be lost in two other circumstances:

- where the employer has offered to provide alternative work which is suitable in the circumstances (irrespective of whether it falls inside or outside the scope of the employee's contract) but this has been unreasonably refused;[58] and

- where the employee does not comply with reasonable requirements imposed by the employer with a view to ensuring that his or her services are available.[59] This is to enable the employer to keep the workforce together, perhaps in the hope that the supplies which have been lacking will be delivered.

CALCULATING GUARANTEE PAYMENTS

A guarantee payment is calculated by multiplying the number of normal working hours on the day of lay-off by the guaranteed hourly rate. Accordingly, where there are no normal working hours on the day in question, no guarantee payment can be claimed.[60] The guaranteed hourly rate is one week's pay divided by the number of normal hours in a week and, where the number of normal hours varies, the average number of such hours over a 12-week period will be used.[61] Payment cannot be claimed for more than five days in any period of three months.[62] There is a maximum daily sum payable of £21.50 in 2009 but this increases or decreases each year in line with the retail price index.[63] It should be noted that contractual payments in respect of workless days not only discharge an employer's liability to make guarantee payments for those days[64] but are also to be taken into account when calculating the maximum number of days for which employees are entitled to statutory payments.[65] Where guaranteed weekly remuneration has been agreed, this sum is to be 'apportioned rateably between the workless days'.[66] If an employer fails to pay the whole or part of a guarantee payment, an employee can complain to an employment tribunal within three months of the last workless day. Where a tribunal finds a complaint to be well-founded, it must order the employer to pay the amount which it finds owing to the employee.[67]

If guaranteed remuneration is the subject of a collective agreement currently in force, all the parties may choose to apply for an exemption order. So long as the Secretary of State is satisfied that the statutory provisions should not apply, the relevant employees will be excluded from the operation of section 28 ERA 1996. However, the Secretary of State cannot make an order unless a collective agreement permits employees to take a dispute about guaranteed remuneration to arbitration, an independent adjudicating body or an employment tribunal.[68]

PAY AND SICKNESS

THE RIGHT TO SICK PAY AT COMMON LAW

In the absence of an express term in the contract of employment, the correct approach to determining whether there is an obligation upon the employer to pay wages to an employee absent through sickness is to look at all the facts and circumstances to see whether such a term can be implied. Such a term may derive from the custom or practice in the industry or from the knowledge of the parties at the time the contract was made. The nature of the contract will have to be taken into account and, on occasions, it will be permissible to look at what the parties did during the period of the contract. Only if all the factors and circumstances do not indicate what the contractual term is will it be assumed that wages should be paid during sickness. If such a term is implied, it is likely to provide for the deduction of sums received under social security legislation.[69] In *Howman & Sons v Blyth*[70] it was held that the reasonable term to be implied in respect of duration in an industry where the normal practice is to give sick pay for a limited period only is the term normally applicable in the industry. The EAT did not accept that where there is an obligation to make payments during sickness, in the absence of an express term to the contrary, sick pay is owed so long as the employment continues.

ENTITLEMENT TO BENEFITS AND THE INDIVIDUAL'S CONTRACT OF EMPLOYMENT

The courts have intervened to ensure that employees' entitlements to disability benefits under health insurance schemes have not been frustrated by a strict interpretation of the contract of employment. In *Adin v Sedco Forex International*[71] an employee's contract of employment included provisions for short-term and long-term disability benefits. It also contained a clause which allowed the employers, at their sole discretion, to terminate the contract for any reason whatsoever. The Court of Session concluded that because the right to these benefits was established in the contract of employment, the employer could not take them away by dismissing the employee. The courts have also been willing to imply terms into contracts which will give effect to agreed health insurance schemes. In *Aspden v Webbs Poultry Group*,[72] a manager had a contract of employment which did not mention the generous health insurance scheme which, the High Court held, had been mutually agreed by the employers and the senior management. The employee was dismissed while on sick leave as a result of angina. It was claimed that there was an implied term that the employee would not be dismissed while incapacitated because this would frustrate the permanent health insurance scheme. The court accepted this argument, even though there was an express term in the contract that allowed the employer to dismiss employees for reasons of prolonged incapacity. It should also be noted that an employee can rely on contractual terms to pay long-term benefits, even if the employer has stopped paying the premiums on his or her health insurance policy.[73]

CASE STUDY

Hill v General Accident[74]

Mr H started employment with the company in 1988. In March 1994 he became ill and remained absent from work for medical reasons until his employer terminated his employment on the grounds of redundancy in November 1995.

During his absence he had received sick pay in accordance with the contractual scheme. Under that scheme employees could receive full pay for 104 weeks. After this period employment was to be terminated and the employee would receive either an ill-health retirement pension or sickness and accident benefit. When Mr H was made redundant he was still four months away from qualifying for his long-term sickness provision. He claimed that there was an implied term in his contract of employment that he would not be made redundant where this would frustrate his entitlement to long-term benefit.

The contract contained an express provision for the retention of sick employees for a period of two years' absence before they were able to qualify for the ill-health retirement scheme. The Court held that this did not exclude the possibility of the employee being dismissed for redundancy, despite the unfortunate consequence. To allow this exclusion would put sick employees at an advantage compared to those who were well and attending work when it came to selecting those who would be dismissed.

STATUTORY SICK PAY

The Social Security Contributions and Benefits Act 1992 (SSCBA 1992) and the Statutory Sick Pay Act 1994 make employers responsible for paying statutory sick pay (SSP) to such of their employees as work within the EU. SSP will be paid for up to 28 weeks of absence due to sickness or injury in any single 'period of entitlement' (see below).[75] As well as those who pay full Class 1 National Insurance contributions, married women and widows paying reduced contributions are eligible for SSP. Part-timers who earn more than the lower earnings limit (£95 per week in 2009) are to be treated in the same way as full-time employees, and there is no minimum service qualification. Indeed, an employee may be entitled to SSP under more than one contract or with more than one employer if the relevant conditions are satisfied.

The rate of SSP in 2009 is £79.15 per week, and the daily rate will be the appropriate weekly rate divided by the number of 'qualifying days' in the week (starting with Sunday).[76] Employers must pay the stipulated amount of SSP for each day that an employee is eligible, but any other sums paid in respect of the same day can count towards the SSP entitlement – eg normal wages.[77] Any agreement which purports to exclude, limit or modify an employee's right to SSP or which requires an employee to contribute (directly or indirectly) towards any cost incurred by the employer will be void.[78] For many employees SSP will be worth less than state incapacity benefit because the former is subject to tax and National Insurance contributions and will be paid at a flat rate without additions for dependants. It is therefore hardly surprising that trade unions endeavour to negotiate sick pay schemes which ensure that their members do not suffer any detriment as a result of this legislation.

Normally employers cannot recover the sums they pay out by way of SSP. However, if in any tax month the amount of SSP exceeds 13 per cent of National Insurance contributions' liability for that month, the employer can recoup the excess from the contributions due.[79]

Section 14(3) of the Social Security Administration Act 1992 gives employees the right to ask their employer for a written statement, in relation to a period before the request is made, of one or more of the following matters:

- the days for which the employer regards himself or herself as liable to pay SSP
- the reasons the employer considers himself or herself not liable to pay for other days
- the amount of SSP to which the employer believes the employee to be entitled.

And, to the extent to which the request is reasonable, the employer must comply with it within a reasonable time.

THE DUTY TO KEEP RECORDS

Employers are obliged to keep records showing:

- the amount of SSP paid to each employee on each pay day
- the amount of SSP paid to each employee during each tax year
- the total amount of SSP paid to all employees during the tax year.

Additionally, Regulation 13 of the SSP Regulations 1982 (as amended) stipulates that for three years after the end of each tax year employers must in relation to each employee keep a record of the following matters:

a) any day in that tax year which was one of four or more consecutive days of incapacity for work, whether or not the employee would normally have been expected to work on that day

b) any day recorded under (a) for which the employer paid SSP.

PENALTIES

An employer who knowingly produces false information in order to recover a sum allegedly paid out as SSP commits an offence.

SUSPENSION ON MEDICAL GROUNDS

Employees with at least one month's continuous service who are suspended from work in consequence of a requirement imposed by specified health and safety provisions or a recommendation contained in a code of practice issued or approved under section 16 HASAWA 1974 are entitled to a week's pay (see Chapter 16) for each week of suspension up to a maximum of 26 weeks.[80] The relevant health and safety provisions are listed in section 64(3) ERA 1996 and cover hazardous substances and processes – for example, lead and ionising radiation. It should be observed that this statutory right can be invoked only where the specified safety legislation has affected the employer's undertaking and not the employee's health. Employees are therefore not entitled to remuneration under this provision for any period during which they are incapable of work by reason of illness or injury. Additionally, if employees unreasonably refuse to perform suitable alternative work (whether or not it is within the scope of their contract), or they do not comply with reasonable requirements imposed by their employer with a view to ensuring that their services are available, no payment is owed.[81]

It is important to note that these sections do not grant employers the right to suspend: they merely give rights to employees who are lawfully suspended. If there is no contractual right to suspend, employees will be entitled to sue for their full wages anyway, although any amounts already paid in respect of this period can be set off.[82] Where the employer fails to pay remuneration which is owed to the employee by virtue of the statute, the employee can apply to an employment tribunal normally within three months. Section 70(3) ERA 1996 provides that if the tribunal finds a complaint to be well-founded, the employer must be ordered to pay the amount due to the employee. As long as any replacement for a suspended employee is informed in writing by the employer that the employment will be terminated at the end of the suspension, dismissal of the replacement in order to allow the original employee to resume work will be deemed to have been for a 'substantial reason of a kind such as to justify the dismissal of an employee holding the position which that employee held'.[83] However, an employment tribunal must still be satisfied that it was reasonable in all the circumstances to dismiss (see Chapter 13).

KEY LEARNING POINTS

- Subject to express or implied contractual terms, an employer is normally obliged to pay wages if there is no work.

- Deductions from wages are unlawful unless approved by statute or by agreement with the employee.

- The standard rate for the national minimum wage is set at £5.73 per hour from October 2008.

- The types of hours worked, for the purposes of the NMWA 1998, are salaried hours work, time-work, output work and unmeasured work.

- Employers are obliged to give their employees itemised pay statements.

- Statutory sick pay is payable for up to 28 weeks of absence due to sickness or injury in any single period of entitlement.

- Employees suspended from work as a result of a requirement imposed by any provisions or code of practice under the HASAWA 1974 are entitled to a week's pay for each week of suspension up to a maximum of 26 weeks.

Reinforce your understanding of this chapter by visiting www.cipd.co.uk/sss for activities, questions, weblinks and additional case studies

REFERENCES

1 See *R v Liverpool City Corporation* (1985) IRLR 501

2 See sections 13(1) and 15(1) ERA 1996; wages are defined in section 27 and a worker is defined in section 230(3) ERA 1996.

3 *Farrell, Matthews & Weir v Hansen* (2005) IRLR 160

4 See *Robertson v Blackstone Franks Investment Management Ltd* (1998) IRLR 376

5 See *Discount Tobacco v Williams* (1993) IRLR 327

6 Section 13(2) ERA 1996; see *Kerr v The Sweater Shop* (1996) IRLR 424

7 See *Peninsula Business Services Ltd v Sweeney* (2004) IRLR 49

8 See *Dattani v Trio Supermarkets Ltd* (1998) IRLR 240

9 (2003) IRLR 11

10 *Hussman Manufacturing Ltd v Weir* (1998) IRLR 288

11 See sections 13(3) ERA 1996 and *New Century Cleaning v Church* (2000) IRLR 27. On the distinction between a deduction in respect of wages and a deduction in respect of expenses, see *London Borough of Southwark v O'Brien* (1996) IRLR 240.

12 See *Yemm v British Steel* (1994) IRLR 117

13 See *Morgan v West Glamorgan County Council* (1995) IRLR 68

14 See *Fairfield Ltd v Skinner* (1993) IRLR 3

15 See section 14(5) ERA 1996 and *Sunderland Polytechnic v Evans* (1993) ICR 196

16 See section 13 ERA 1996

17 (1992) IRLR 191

18 *Delaney v Staples t/a De Montfort Recruitment* (1991) IRLR 112

19 See *Kent Management Services v Butterfield* (1992) IRLR 394 and compare *Coors Ltd v Adcock* (2007) IRLR 440

20 'Or, within such further period as the tribunal considers reasonable in a case where it is satisfied that it was not reasonably practicable for the complainant to be presented within three months': sections 23(2)–(4) ERA 1996. This 'escape clause' applies to other statutory provisions and throughout the rest of the book will be referred to as the 'time-limit escape clause'; see *List Design Ltd v Douglas & Catley* (2003) IRLR 14.

21 See section 24 ERA 1996

22 See *Avon C.C. v Howlett* (1993) 1 All ER 1073

23 See Attorney General's reference (No 1 of 1983) 1 All ER 369

24 See *SIP Ltd v Swinn* (1994) IRLR 323

25 The development rate can also apply to workers aged 22 years and above during their first six months of employment in a new job with a new employer and who are receiving accredited training.

26 This was the case in *Laird v A K Stoddart Ltd* (2001) IRLR 591

27 SI 1999/584 (as amended)

28 See National Minimum Wage Regulations 1999 (Amendment) Regulations 2001 SI 2001/1108, which ensure that all trainees on government training schemes are excluded from entitlement to the NMW during the first 12 months of their engagement or if they are under 19 years of age.

29 Regulation 2 NMW Regulations 1999

30 (2003) IRLR 21

31 (2002) IRLR 480

32 Regulation 14 NMW Regulations 1999

33 Regulation 10 NMW Regulations 1999; a pay reference period is one month or a shorter period if a worker is usually paid at more frequent intervals.

34 Regulation 30 NMW Regulations 1999

35 Regulation 36 NMW Regulations 1999

36 On deductions for gas and electricity in tied accommodation see *HM Revenue and Customs v Leisure Management Ltd* (2007) IRLR 450

37 See *Revenue and Customs Commissioners v Annabel's Ltd* (2008) ICR 1076

38 Regulation 16 NMW Regulations 1999

39 Regulation 15 NMW Regulations 1999

40 Regulation 17 NMW Regulations 1999

41 Regulation 18 NMW Regulations 1999

42 Regulation 27 NMW Regulations 1999

43 See *Walton v Independent Living Organisation* (2003) IRLR 469

44 See also regulation 38 NMW Regulations 1999

45 Sections 10(1) and 10(2) NMWA 1998

46 Section 10(4)(b) NMWA 1998

47 Sections 10(5) and 10(6) NMWA 1998

48 Sections 10(8) and 10(9) NMWA 1998

49 Section 11 NMWA 1998; section 11(3) requires that the complaint should normally be made within three months of the end of the 14-day notice period.

50 Section 28 NMWA 1998

51 Sections 13–17 NMWA 1998

52 See the National Minimum Wage (Enforcement Notices) Act 2003 and Sections 19–19H NMWA 1998

53 Section 23 NMWA 1998

54 Section 12(4) ERA 1996

55 Section 28(1) ERA 1996

56 See *Mailway (Southern) Ltd v Willsher* (1978) IRLR 322

57 Section 29(3) ERA 1996; 'associated employer' is defined by section 231 ERA 1996.

58 Section 29(4) ERA 1996

59 Section 29(5) ERA 1996

60 Section 30(1) ERA 1996

61 Section 30(2)–(4) ERA 1996

62 Section 31(1)–(3) ERA 1996

63 Section 34 ERel Act 1999

64 Section 32(2) ERA 1996

65 See *Cartwright v Clancey Ltd* (1983) IRLR 355

66 Section 32(3) ERA 1996

67 Section 34(3) ERA 1996

68 Section 35 ERA 1996

69 See *Mears v Safecar Security* (1982) IRLR 501

70　(1983) IRLR 139

71　(1997) IRLR 280

72　(1996) IRLR 521

73　See *Bainbridge v Circuit Foil UK Ltd* (1997) IRLR 305

74　(1998) IRLR 641

75　Section 155 SSCBA 1992 sets the entitlement limit at '28 times the appropriate weekly rate'.

76　See section 157 SSCBA 1992

77　See Schedule 12 paragraph 2 SSCBA 1992

78　Section 151(2) SSCBA 1992

79　SSP Percentage Threshold Order 1995 SI 1995/512

80　Section 64(1) ERA 1996

81　Section 65 ERA 1996

82　See section 69(3) ERA 1996

83　See section 106(3) ERA 1996

CHAPTER 6

Discrimination Against Employees on the Grounds of Sex, Sexual Orientation, Race, Religion or Belief

OVERVIEW

Here we consider five important pieces of anti-discrimination legislation: the Equal Pay Act 1970, the Sex Discrimination Act 1975, the Race Relations Act 1976, the Employment Equality (Sexual Orientation) Regulations 2003 and the Employment Equality (Religion or Belief) Regulations 2003. Included in this is the important role played by the EU and decisions of the European Court of Justice. We begin with an explanation of the differences between direct and indirect discrimination and then look at those occasions when discrimination is lawful – eg when there is a genuine occupational qualification or requirement. There is an examination of issues raised by the Equal Pay Act and we look at the meaning of such terms as 'like work', 'work rated as equivalent' and 'work of equal value'.

THE EQUALITY BILL 2009

The Government has introduced an Equality Bill with a number of objectives.[1] The Bill aims to replace nine major pieces of legislation by a single Act, in order to provide a clearer legal framework on equality matters. It will eventually, therefore, replace such legislation as the Sex Discrimination Act 1975 and the Race Relations Act 1976. In addition to this the Bill aims to

(i) ban age discrimination in the provision of goods, facilities and services. This is already the case for all the other unlawful grounds of discrimination, but, prior to the Bill, age discrimination regulation was confined to tackling age discrimination in employment

(ii) increase transparency, particularly to tackle the gender pay gap which persists. One way of helping this is to ban secrecy clauses in agreements which stop individuals discussing their own pay

(iii) extend the Equality Duty, which public bodies currently have for gender, race and disability, to include sexual orientation, religion or belief and age. This ensures that public bodies tackle discrimination and encourage equality of opportunity. The Bill will also ensure that public bodies report on equality issues

(iv) encourage the public sector to influence equality issues in the private sector through the use of its purchasing power

(v) extend the scope for positive action so giving employers an opportunity to ensure diversity in their workforces. They will be able to select on this ground if two candidates are of equal merit

(vi) strengthen enforcement by enabling tribunals, in discrimination cases, to make wider recommendations on improvements to employers

(vii) simplify the law on disability discrimination so that people are clearer about when they are protected.

It is likely that the implementation of the Bill will be carried out by a number of new Regulations. To keep up to date with this, please visit the website associated with this book – www.cipd.co.uk/sss .

THE SEX DISCRIMINATION ACT 1975, THE RACE RELATIONS ACT 1976, THE SEXUAL ORIENTATION REGULATIONS 2003 AND THE RELIGION OR BELIEF REGULATIONS 2003

It is important to note that the titles of these measures do not fully reflect the matters that are covered. The Sex Discrimination Act 1975 (SDA 1975) outlaws, for example, discrimination and harassment against civil partners and married (but not single) persons. A civil partnership is a relationship between two people of the same sex which is formed when they register.[2] 'Sexual orientation' means an orientation towards persons of the same sex, the opposite sex or both sexes. It does not include sexual practices or preferences.[3] The Race Relations Act 1976 (RRA 1976) defines 'racial grounds' as meaning colour, race, nationality, national or ethnic origins.[4] A racial group that is defined by colour may include people of more than one ethnic origin.[5] In *Mandla v Lee*[6] the House of Lords held that 'ethnic origins' described the background of a group which was a segment of the population distinguished from others by a sufficient combination of shared customs, beliefs, traditions and characteristics derived from a common or presumed common past. This was so even if not drawn from what in biological terms was a common racial stock, in that it was that combination which gave them a historically determined social identity in their own eyes and in the eyes of those outside the group. In relation to 'national origins', it has been held that this concept is not limited to 'nationality' and thus to citizenship acquired at birth. A person can become a member of a racial group defined by reference to origins through adherence – for example, by marriage.[7] Although a racial group cannot be defined by language or religion alone,[8] it has been accepted that Sikhs, Jews and Gypsies all fall within the scope of the Race Relations Act 1976. In contrast, in *Dawkins v Department of the Environment*[9] it was accepted that Rastafarians are a separate group with identifiable characteristics, but the Court of Appeal concluded that they have not established a separate identity by reference to their ethnic origins and are therefore not protected by the 1976 Act. This group should now get the benefit of the RB Regulations 2003, which define 'religion' as meaning any religion and 'belief' as meaning 'any religious or philosophical belief'.[10]

It is unlawful for a public authority to discriminate or commit acts of harassment on the grounds of sex when performing its functions.[11] In addition, specified public authorities are required to carry out their functions having due regard to the need to:

- eliminate unlawful sex and race discrimination and sexual harassment; and

- promote equality of opportunity and good relations between men and women and persons of different racial groups.[12]

The Equal Opportunities Commission and the Commission for Racial Equality (both now replaced by the Commission for Equality and Human Rights) have issued Codes of Practice for the purpose of eliminating discrimination in employment.[13] A failure to observe any of the provisions of these codes does not render a person liable to legal proceedings but the Commissions' recommendations are admissible in evidence before employment tribunals.[14]

Anti-discrimination legislation recognises that discrimination can be either direct or indirect.

DIRECT DISCRIMINATION

Direct discrimination occurs where on the grounds of sex, sexual orientation, civil partnership, marital status, race, religion or belief a person is treated less favourably than a person of the opposite sex, a single person or a person not of the same racial group, etc, would be treated.[15] This would cover situations where there has been a generalised assumption that people in a particular group possess or lack certain characteristics.[16]

In Azmi v Kirklees B.C.,[17] Mrs Azmi worked at a junior school. She was a devout Muslim who usually wore a veil which covered all her head and face apart from her eyes. She asked if she could wear it when teaching in the presence of male teachers. The EAT observed that the question was whether the wearing of the veil was because of a genuinely held belief or whether it was a manifestation of that belief. In terms of direct discrimination the comparator had to be a woman, whether Muslim or not, who wore a face covering for a reason other than religious belief – the less favourable treatment was the instruction not to wear the veil.

Section 1(1)(a) RRA 1976, the RB and the EESO Regs 2003 cover all cases of discrimination on the grounds of race, religion or belief or sexual orientation grounds whether the characteristics in question are those of the person treated less favourably or some other person. Thus in Weathersfield Ltd v Sargent[18] it was held that a white European woman was unlawfully discriminated against on grounds of race when she resigned as a result of being given an unlawful instruction to discriminate on racial grounds against black and Asian people. However, the expression 'on racial grounds' does not cover every situation in which the discriminator's less favourable treatment was significantly influenced by racial considerations. For example, an employee who is sacked for racially abusing fellow employees is dismissed for misconduct.[19]

Section 1(1)(a) of the SDA covers discrimination on the 'grounds of her sex' only, which implies that it is more specific than the other legislation, only applying to the individual discriminated against. This limitation has been placed in question by a disability discrimination case (see Chapter 7), *Coleman v Attridge Law*,[20] which interpreted European Community law as extending protection from discrimination to those associated with an individual, rather than to just the individual alone.

Section 1(2) RRA 1976 states that segregation on racial grounds amounts to less favourable treatment, although it has been decided that allowing members of a racial group to congregate voluntarily – eg in a particular department – will not render an employer liable.[21]

Section 3A SDA 1975 deals with discrimination on the grounds of pregnancy where, during the protected maternity period, a woman is treated less favourably than she would have been treated if she had not become pregnant or not exercised (or sought to exercise) a statutory right to maternity leave.

It appears that the phrase 'on the grounds of' does not refer to the alleged discriminator's reason or motive but to the intention to provide less favourable treatment. According to the House of Lords, the relevant question is: 'Would the complainant have received the same treatment but for his or her sex, race, etc?'[22] Words or acts of discouragement can amount to less favourable treatment.[23]

Sextion 2A SDA makes discrimination for a reason related to gender reassignment unlawful. Although the Court of Appeal has ruled that a male-to-female transsexual had to be treated as female,[24] problems still remain in relation to the rights of pre-operative transsexuals – for example, in granting access to toilet facilities.[25] Once recognition of the new gender has been acquired, however, there can be no exception for a genuine occupational requirement resulting from that gender acquisition. The Gender Recognition Act 2004 contains the procedure for acquiring this recognition.

HARASSMENT

The anti-discrimination provisions discussed in this chapter all describe harassment as 'unwanted conduct which has the purpose or effect of violating that other person's dignity, or creating an intimidating, hostile, degrading, humiliating or offensive environment'. In addition, section 4A SDA 1975 outlaws harassment in the form of unwanted verbal, non-verbal or physical conduct of a sexual nature. However, conduct will only be regarded as having this effect if 'having regard to all the circumstances, including in particular the perception of that other person, it should reasonably be considered as having that effect'.[26] In *Reed and Bull Information Systems v Stedman*[27] the EAT said that it is for the recipient themselves to decide what is acceptable and what is unwelcome or offensive. Provided that any reasonable person would understand him or her to be rejecting the conduct of which he or she is complaining, then a continuation of that conduct would generally be regarded as harassment. Tribunals should not make judgments as to the significance, if any, of individual incidents but should assess the impact of the totality of events.[28] In *Jones v Tower Boot Co. Ltd*[29] an employee whose mother was white and father black was held to have been racially harassed as a result of a number of incidents at work which included being called offensive names and having an arm burned with a hot screwdriver. The employer was held to be vicariously liable for the harassment because the acts were carried out 'during the course of employment'.[30] This expression has been given a broad interpretation. It includes, for example, actions that take place during a social event held immediately after work and during a leaving party for a colleague.[31]

In *English v Thomas Sanderson Blinds Ltd*,[32] an individual had suffered long-term harassment by work colleagues who voiced homophobic abuse towards him, even though they knew that he was not homosexual. The EAT held that the EESO Regulations inadequately implemented the Equal Framework Directive by referring to harassment 'on the grounds of sexual orientation'. The individual here could not show this, even though the harassment was related to homosexuality. The Directive was concerned with harassment related to sexual orientation and this was not reflected in the terminology of the Regulations. Subsequently, however, the Court of Appeal took a purposive approach to the implementation of the Directive and held that the Regulations could be interpreted as protecting this individual from the homophobic abuse.[33]

It is worth noting that both employment tribunals and the EAT are allowed to make a 'restricted reporting order' in cases where allegations of sexual misconduct are made. Whether such an order is made is up to the discretion of the tribunal, and its effect will be to prohibit the publication or broadcasting of anything likely to lead the public to identify either the person making the allegation or any person affected by it. This relates only to individuals, so tribunals do not have the ability to make a restricted reporting order protecting a corporate body.[34] Unless revoked earlier, an order will lapse when the tribunal makes its decision.[35]

Section 1(1) of the Protection from Harassment Act 1997 declares that a person must not pursue a course of conduct which amounts to the harassment of another or which he or she knows, or ought to know, amounts to harassment of another. Section 2 makes such action a criminal offence, and section 3 provides for a civil remedy against the offender.[36] It is also worth noting that it is also a criminal offence intentionally to cause another person harassment, alarm or distress. This applies not only to sexual and racial harassment but also to other grounds – for example, sexual orientation or disability.[37]

INDIRECT DISCRIMINATION

As regards colour and nationality discrimination, an individual can complain where an employer applies a requirement or condition which would apply equally to a person not of the same racial group but which is such that the proportion of the applicant's racial group who can comply with it is considerably smaller than the proportion of persons not of the same racial group. The applicant must also show that he or she suffered a detriment as a result of being unable to comply with the requirement or condition. Employers can avoid liability by demonstrating that the requirement or condition is 'justifiable' irrespective of the colour or nationality of the person to whom it is applied.[38] In relation to race, religion or belief, ethnic or national origins, sex and sexual orientation, indirect discrimination occurs where a provision, criterion or practice applies or would apply to persons not of the same race, religion or belief, ethnic or national origins, sex or sexual orientation but such people would be put at a particular disadvantage and this cannot be shown to be a proportionate means of achieving a legitimate aim.[39] The legislation stipulates that when drawing comparisons the relevant circumstances must be the same or not materially different.[40]

PROVISION, CRITERION OR PRACTICE (REQUIREMENT OR CONDITION)

The term 'provision, criterion or practice' is not defined other than stating that it includes a 'requirement or condition'. However, it is likely to cover informal work practices. The words 'requirement or condition' are capable of including any obligation of service – for example, an obligation to work full-time,[41] have a permanent contract,[42] or be mobile.[43] Indeed, the mere fact that the employer requires workers to perform the jobs they were employed to do may be regarded as 'applying a requirement'.[44] Similarly, the inclusion of a contractual term can amount to an application of a requirement or condition even though that term has not been invoked.[45] A requirement or condition can be discriminatory even if it is only expressed as being desirable, rather than essential. In *Falkirk Council v Whyte*[46] some prison officers failed to gain promotion because management training and supervisory experience were desirable before a promotion could be agreed. In practice this requirement turned out to be essential, and because most of the people in the basic grade posts were women, it was held to be discriminatory.

'CAN COMPLY'

The courts have interpreted the words 'can comply' to mean 'can in practice comply' rather than physically or theoretically comply.[47] Thus it has been held that an age-limit of 28 for recruitment could amount to indirect discrimination against women since they are less likely than men to be available for work below that age owing to child-bearing and -rearing.[48] However, the expression 'can comply' cannot be equated with 'may wish to comply'; ultimately it is a question of reasonableness, taking into account all the surrounding circumstances. In *Clarke and Powell v Eley (IMI) Kynoch Ltd*[49] the issue arose whether the words 'can comply' and 'cannot comply' include past opportunities to comply. The EAT decided that the date on which the detriment must be demonstrated was the date the discriminatory conduct operated so as to create the alleged detriment.

PROPORTION

As regards the relative proportion of persons who can comply, much will depend on the tribunal's own knowledge and experience and its selection of the appropriate section of the population for comparison. In *Jones v University of Manchester*,[50] for example, the Court of Appeal ruled that in finding that the requirement for a career adviser to be a graduate aged between 27 and 35 years had a disproportionate impact on women, the employment tribunal had erred in restricting the pool for comparison to mature students. According to the Court of Appeal, the appropriate pool was all men and women with the required qualifications not including the requirement complained of, in this case graduates with the necessary experience. The decision on what is a considerably smaller (or larger) proportion is a question of fact for the employment tribunal.[51]

DETRIMENT

The words 'subjecting ... to any other detriment' are to be given their broad ordinary meaning, so it is clear that almost any discriminatory conduct by an employer is potentially unlawful.[52] Thus in *Garry v London Borough of Ealing*[53] the Court of Appeal accepted that the applicant had suffered a detriment when, for reasons connected with her ethnic origin, an investigation into her activities was continued longer than an ordinary investigation would have been, even though she was unaware that the investigation was continuing. For a detriment to occur, it must be shown that a reasonable worker would or might take the view that he or she had been disadvantaged in the circumstances that she or he had to work.[54] However, it is not necessary to demonstrate some physical or economic consequence.[55] Finally, it should be noted that rules concerning appearance will not be discriminatory because their content is different for men and women so long as they enforce a common principle of smartness or conventionality and, taken as a whole, neither sex is treated less favourably in enforcing that principle.[56]

JUSTIFICATION

Where a *prima facie* case of indirect discrimination has been established, the employer will have to satisfy the tribunal that the discriminatory requirement or condition (provision, criterion or practice) was justifiable. Clearly, a connection must be established between the function of the employer and the imposition of the requirement or condition (provision, criterion or practice). In addition, a tribunal must assess both the quantitative and the qualitative effects of the requirement or condition (provision, criterion or practice) on those affected by it.[57] In order to justify a requirement or condition (provision, criterion or practice) which has a disproportionate impact the employer must demonstrate that the requirement or condition (provision, criterion or practice) is designed to meet a legitimate objective and that the means chosen are appropriate and necessary (proportionate) to achieving that objective.[58] *Allen v GMB*[59] concerned a collective agreement between a local authority and a trade union. This agreement discriminated against female employees by agreeing to a lower pay increase than they were entitled to if there had been a complete implementation of a proper equal pay policy. This was done to protect the pay of other members, recognising that the local authority had limited resources. The Court held that the aim was legitimate, but the means were not proportionate to achieving this aim. These 'means' included the manipulation of female members of the union and the provision, criterion or practice could not therefore be justified.

Finally, it should be noted that neither sex nor race discrimination can be justified on the basis of customer or union preferences.[60]

RECRUITMENT AND SELECTION

It is unlawful to discriminate on the prohibited grounds in the arrangements made for the purpose of determining who should be offered employment, in the terms on which employment is offered, or by 'refusing or deliberately omitting' to offer employment.[61] These arrangements can include the interviewing and assessing of candidates for a post. If racial grounds, for example, are the reason for the less favourable treatment resulting from the arrangements made, then direct discrimination is established. The reason for the discrimination is not relevant.[62] Harassment of an applicant for employment on the grounds of race, religion or belief, ethnic or national origins, sex or sexual orientation is specifically covered by the legislation.[63]

'Employment' covers engagement under a contract of service or a contract personally to execute any work or labour.[64] According to the Court of Appeal, the legislation contemplates a contract of which the dominant purpose is that the party contracting to provide services under it personally performs the work or labour which constitutes the subject matter of the contract.[65] The legislation aims to prevent the emergence or continuation of discriminatory practices – ie conduct which does not, in itself, amount to unlawful discrimination but which in fact results in discriminatory treatment.[66] If it becomes common knowledge that an employer will not employ people of a certain ethnic origin, then there will be a presumption of discriminatory practices, as happened in *Frima Feryn* where the employer publicly stated that this was its position.[67]

Advertisements must not indicate, or reasonably be understood as indicating, an intention to discriminate unlawfully; nor should they adopt a job title with a sexual connotation – eg waiter or stewardess – because this will be taken to indicate a discriminatory intent unless there is an indication to the contrary.[68] The word 'advertisement' is defined to include 'every form of advertisement, whether to the public or not'.[69]

It would seem to follow that human resource managers should ensure that application forms and interviewers ask only questions and insist on minimum qualifications that are relevant to the requirements of the job.[70] Thus a height requirement and certain conditions relating to past experience – eg having served an apprenticeship – might be difficult to justify under either Act. Clearly, word-of-mouth recruitment is suspect, and refusing to employ those who live in a particular geographical area could amount to indirect discrimination if there was a racial imbalance in the population residing there.[71]

LAWFUL DISCRIMINATION

Despite what has been stated above, discrimination may be lawful in certain circumstances:

1 *Genuine occupational qualifications or requirements*

The major exception, which is common to both statutes and both sets of regulations, is where sex, sexual orientation, race, religion or belief is a genuine occupational qualification (GOQ) or requirement. In the case of sex, this occurs where:[72]

- the essential nature of the job demands a particular physiology (excluding physical strength) or authenticity in entertainment
- the job needs to be held by a particular sex to preserve decency or privacy either because it is likely to involve physical contact in circumstances where members of the opposite sex might reasonably object to its being carried out (eg searching, for security purposes) or because people are in a state of undress or are using sanitary facilities. In *Sisley v Britannia Security*[73] it was held that this exclusion covers all matters reasonably incidental to an employee's work and is not confined to cases where the job itself requires the holder to be in a state of undress
- the nature or location of the employer's establishment makes it impracticable for the job-holder to live anywhere other than on the employer's premises and the premises are not equipped with separate sleeping accommodation and sanitary facilities for more than one sex and it is unreasonable to expect the employer to equip those premises with separate facilities or to provide separate premises (eg where the employment is on a remote site). The words 'to live in' involve the concept of residence (either permanent or temporary) and do not cover the situation where the employee is obliged to remain on the premises for a limited period eating or resting[74]
- the nature of the establishment demands a person of a particular sex because it is an establishment for persons requiring special care or attention and those persons are all of a particular sex and it is reasonable, 'having regard to the essential character of the establishment', that the job should not be held by a person of the opposite sex[75]
- the job-holder provides personal services which can most effectively be provided by a person of a particular sex (eg in a team of social workers)
- the job is one of two to be held by a married couple
- the job is likely to involve the holder's working or living in a private home and the job has to be done by a member of one sex because objection might reasonably be taken to allowing someone of the other sex the degree of physical or social contact with a person living in the home or the knowledge of such a person's private affairs which the job is likely to entail

– the job is likely to involve the performance of duties outside the UK in a country of which the laws or customs are such that the duties could not effectively be performed by a woman.

The only GOQs allowed for under the 1976 Act depend on authenticity in the provision of food and drink, in entertainment and modelling, and where the job-holder provides personal welfare services which can most effectively be provided by a person of a particular racial group. In relation to personal welfare services the Court of Appeal has ruled that the word 'personal' indicates that the identity of the giver and the recipient of the services is important and appears to contemplate direct contact between the giver and the recipient.[76]

The concept of a genuine occupational requirement was introduced in the 2003 Regulations. It applies where 'having regard to the nature of the employment or the context in which it is carried out' (being of a particular race, religion or belief, ethnic or national origin, sex or sexual orientation is a 'genuine and determining occupational requirement'.[77] It must also be proportionate to apply the requirement and either the person to whom it is applied does not meet it or 'the employer is not satisfied, and in all the circumstances it is not reasonable for him to be satisfied, that that person meets it'.[78] In *Glasgow C.C. v McNab*[79] a school teacher, who was an atheist and had been employed at a school for many years, applied for a post as acting principal of pastoral care. He was not successful in even getting an interview. If he had been a Roman Catholic he would have done so. One question was whether the education authority could qualify for the protection offered by Regulation 7(3) of the RB Regulations if only part of the organisation had an ethos based on religion or belief. The EAT held that if this had been intended it would have been expressly stated in the legislation. In any case it could not be said that an education authority as a whole had a religious ethos.

GOQs apply even though they relate to only some of the job duties, and unless a duty is so trivial that it ought to be disregarded altogether, it is not for tribunals to assess its importance.[80] However, a GOQ will not provide a defence if the employer already has sufficient employees capable of carrying out those duties and whom it would be reasonable to employ in that way.[81] Although the GOQ defence is unavailable where there is a discriminatory dismissal, a genuine occupational requirement can be pleaded in relation to dismissal or other detriments suffered.

2 Statutory provisions

It is lawful to discriminate if it is necessary to do so to comply with a requirement of an existing statutory provision of which the purpose is to protect women as regards pregnancy or maternity or other circumstances giving rise to risks specifically affecting women.[82]

It is also lawful to discriminate if it is necessary to do so to comply with a requirement of Part 1 HASAWA 1974 (see Chapter 9), or certain other health and safety legislation. For this exception to apply, the employer must demonstrate not only that the discriminatory act was necessary to comply with the statutory duty but also that it was done for the purpose of protecting the woman in relation to pregnancy, maternity or other circumstances giving rise to risks specifically affecting women. It should be noted that section 2(2) of SDA 1975 prevents men from complaining that special treatment has been afforded to women in connection with pregnancy or childbirth.

UNEQUAL TREATMENT IN EMPLOYMENT AND DISMISSALS

Turning our attention to unequal treatment in the course of employment and to discriminatory dismissals, it is unlawful for employers to discriminate:[83]

- in the terms of employment afforded[84]

- in the way they afford access to opportunities for promotion, transfer or training, or to any other benefits,[85] facilities or services, or by refusing or deliberately omitting to afford access to them

- by dismissing or subjecting the employee to any other detriment. In relation to dismissal the grounds of race, ethnic or national origins or sexual orientation, dismissal specifically includes the non-renewal of a limited term contract or a constructive dismissal.[86] Equally, where there has been a dismissal involving unlawful harassment or an act of discrimination on the grounds of race, ethnic or national origins, religion or belief, sex or sexual orientation, it is unlawful to inflict further harassment or discrimination on these grounds if it 'arises out of and is closely connected to' the employment relationship.[87] Additionally, the failure to provide a reference for an ex-employee might be construed as victimisation.[88] In *Coote v Granada Hospitality Ltd*[89] an ex-employee who had settled a complaint of sex discrimination was able to rely upon Article 6 of the Equal Treatment Directive[90] to show that the failure to provide the reference was victimisation

- by way of harassment on the grounds of race, religion or belief, ethnic or national origins, sex or sexual orientation.

The following points should be noted:

- Positive action may be permissible in certain circumstances. The European Court of Justice has held that rules which allow women to be preferred for promotion over male colleagues are acceptable provided that the male and female candidates in question are equally qualified and that the sector in question is one in which women are under-represented.[91] Special arrangements can be made to train persons of a particular sex or racial group if it can be shown that within the previous 12 months only a small minority of that sex or racial group was performing a particular type of work.[92] In relation to religion or belief and sexual orientation, positive action can be taken if it 'reasonably appears to the person doing the act that it prevents or compensates for disadvantages linked to sexual orientation (religion or belief) suffered by persons of that sexual orientation (religion or belief) doing that work or likely to take up that work'.[93] A refusal to investigate complaints of unfair treatment may amount to a refusal of access to 'any other benefits, facilities or services'.[94]

- Occupational pensions schemes must contain an equal treatment rule which ensures that men and women are offered the same rights to join a scheme as well as being entitled to the same benefits.[95] However, equal treatment is enforceable only in relation to pensionable service after 17 May 1990. Enforcement is via the Equal Pay Act 1970 (see below) and actions can be brought against scheme trustees or managers.[96]

- Good motive cannot excuse discriminatory behaviour. Thus, despite the Court of Appeal's decision in *Peake*'s case,[97] it is submitted that allowing one sex, racial group, etc, to arrive late or leave work early constitutes unlawful discrimination because those not specially favoured have been either denied access to a benefit or have suffered a detriment. The Court of Appeal has subsequently recognised that such arrangements cannot be condoned on the grounds of chivalry or administrative convenience and it is no trifling matter that an employer has introduced a discriminatory scheme when the same objective could be achieved in a non-discriminatory fashion.

- When considering termination, it is automatically unfair to dismiss a woman, irrespective of her hours of work or length of service, if the reason for dismissal is that she is pregnant or if the reason is in any way connected with her pregnancy (see Chapter 8). The critical question is whether, on an objective consideration of all the surrounding circumstances, the treatment complained of is on the ground of pregnancy or some other ground. This must be determined by an objective test of causal connection. The event or factor alleged to be causative of the matter complained of need not be the only or even the main cause of the result complained of. It is enough if it is an effective cause.[98] Thus in *Caruana v Manchester Airport plc*[99] it was held that there had been unlawful sex discrimination when the employee's fixed-term contract was not renewed because she would be unavailable for work at its commencement owing to pregnancy.

- Selection for redundancy on the prohibited grounds will also be unlawful. However, suppose a woman was selected for redundancy on the grounds that although she had a longer period of cumulative service, she had less continuous service than a man. It could be argued that because women are likely to have shorter periods of continuous service than men as a consequence of child-bearing and rearing, such a basis for selection constitutes indirect discrimination and would have to be shown to be a proportionate means of achieving a legitimate aim.[100] In *Clarke*'s case[101] the EAT decided that redundancy selection criteria which resulted in the selection of part-timers first was unlawful because they had a disproportionate impact on women and could not be justified on the particular facts of the case. Dismissal on the prohibited grounds cannot be excused simply because there was pressure from other employees.

- A term in a contract or collective agreement is void[102] where its inclusion renders the making of the contract unlawful by virtue of the SDA 1975 or it provides for the doing of an act which would be unlawful under this legislation. This section also applies to the rules of employers, employers' associations, professional or qualifying bodies and trade unions. Employees (or job-seekers) can complain to an employment tribunal that a term of a collective agreement or a works rule is void. However, to do so they must believe that the term or rule may have some effect on them in the future, or that the term provides for the doing of an unlawful discriminatory act which might be done to them, and the collective agreement was made by or on behalf of the employer or an employers' organisation to which the employer belongs. It is interesting to note that tribunals have no power to amend the term so as to make it non-discriminatory. Where the victim of the discrimination is a party to the contract, the term is unenforceable against that person.[103]

LIABILITY

If the provisions of the anti-discrimination legislation are not complied with, both the employing body and named individuals may be sued. Individuals may be liable for instructing or putting pressure on someone to perform an unlawful act and for knowingly aiding another person to do an unlawful act.[104] In relation to aiding, it does not matter whether or not the help is substantial and productive provided it is not so insignificant as to be negligible.[105] Employers are liable for the acts of employees in the course of employment, whether or not they were done with the employer's knowledge or approval, unless it can be proved that the employer 'took such steps as were reasonably practicable to prevent the employee from doing that act'.[106] According to the EAT, tribunals should first identify whether the employer took any steps to prevent the employee from doing the act or acts complained of. Secondly, they should consider whether there were any further acts that the employer could have taken which were reasonably practicable.[107] Hence it is not sufficient to adopt an equal opportunities policy: it is also necessary to check that such a policy has been communicated to all staff, and has been understood and implemented. Additionally, employers should ensure that informal practices do not develop which could lead to an act of unlawful discrimination.[108]

The legislation permits individuals to bring complaints before an employment tribunal within three months of an 'act complained of' occurring.[109] For these purposes an act which extends over a period is to be treated as done at the end of that period. In *Owusu v London Fire Authority*[110] the EAT ruled that an act extends over a period if it takes the form of some policy, rule or practice in accordance with which decisions are taken from time to time.[111] Over the years the courts have struggled to distinguish a continuing act from a one-off act with a continuing consequence. The following have been held to constitute continuing acts: the refusal of a mortgage subsidy;[112] the failure to re-grade and give an employee the opportunity to act up when opportunities arose;[113] an employer's failure to implement promised remedial measures;[114] and a requirement to work on less favourable pension terms.[115] Although in *Sougrin v Haringey Health Authority*[116] the Court of Appeal thought that the placing of a black nurse at a lower grade than a white colleague and the rejection of her appeal was not a continuing act, it is difficult to see why the appeal itself could not constitute a separate 'act complained of'. According to the EAT, in determining when the 'act complained of was done' the question is whether the cause of action had crystallised on the relevant date, not whether the complainant felt that he or she had suffered discrimination on that date.[117] Out-of-time claims can be heard if it is just and equitable to do so,[118] and in this respect the strength of the employee's complaint may be a factor.[119]

'EVASIVE' REPLIES FROM EMPLOYERS MAY IMPLY UNLAWFUL DISCRIMINATION

It is recognised that obtaining information can be particularly difficult where discrimination is alleged, and so there is provision in the legislation for aggrieved persons to obtain information. Although special forms are not necessary, an aggrieved person's questions and any reply by the employer are admissible in evidence. If there is a failure to reply within an eight weeks period, or an 'evasive or equivocal' response is received, the inference may be drawn that an unlawful act has been committed.[120] Thus, where an employer failed to answer all but one of nine questions asked by an unsuccessful job applicant, the reply was regarded as evasive and the inference drawn that the applicant had suffered unlawful discrimination in the selection arrangements.[121] Additionally, the House of Lords has ruled that the contents of documents must be revealed if such disclosure is necessary to dispose fairly of the proceedings.[122] In this context 'fair disposal' means a disposal of the proceedings which is fair to the applicant.[123] However, a tribunal is not empowered to order an employer to disclose information which is not available at the time.[124]

The EHRC is able to devote resources to assisting actual or prospective complainants, and if it thinks it desirable it can instigate formal investigations of anyone believed to be discriminating or harassing unlawfully.[125] However, the Commission cannot embark on a 'named person' investigation in the absence of any belief that the person named might have committed an unlawful act.[126] The Commission also has the power to require the production of documents, to make recommendations, and, if necessary, to issue non-discrimination notices.[127] As a last resort, it may seek a county court injunction to prohibit discriminatory acts.

DISCRIMINATION AND THE BURDEN OF PROOF

The burden of proof is formally reversed in anti-discrimination cases.[128] According to the Court of Appeal, this requires a two-stage process. First, the claimant has to prove facts from which the employment tribunal could conclude in the absence of an adequate explanation that the respondent committed, or is to be treated as having committed, an unlawful act of discrimination. Second, the respondent has to prove that it did not commit, or is not to be treated as having committed, the unlawful act against the claimant. If the explanation is inadequate, the employment tribunal must uphold the complaint.[129]

However, where the discrimination is on the grounds of colour or nationality the following principles set out by the Court of Appeal in *King v GB-China Centre*[130] will apply:

- It is unusual to find direct evidence of discrimination.

- The outcome of a case will therefore usually depend on what inferences it is proper to draw from the facts found by the tribunal.[131]

- A finding of discrimination and of a difference in race (or sex) will often point to the possibility of discrimination. In such circumstances it will be for the employer to explain. If no explanation is offered or the tribunal considers the explanation to be unsatisfactory, it will be legitimate to infer that the discrimination was on racial (or sexual) grounds.

- It is unnecessary and unhelpful to introduce the concept of a shifting evidential burden of proof. Tribunals should reach a conclusion on the balance of probabilities, bearing in mind the difficulties which face a person who complains of unlawful discrimination and the fact that it is for the complainant to prove his or her case.

Evidence of events subsequent to the alleged act of discrimination can be taken into account if it provides proof of a relevant fact.[132]

Compensation awards

If no settlement is reached,[133] and the complaint is held to be well-founded, three possible remedies are available:[134]

- The tribunal can make a declaration of the complainant's rights.

- It can require the respondent to pay unlimited compensation. In principle, successful complainants should be restored to the position they would have been in but for the unlawful conduct.[135] However, as regards unintentional indirect discrimination on the grounds of sex, sexual orientation, religion or belief, or marital status, the tribunal can only award compensation if it has already made a declaration or recommendation (see below) and considers it just and equitable.[136] The RRA 1976 provides that in cases of indirect discrimination no compensation can be awarded if the employer shows that there was no intention to discriminate.[137] For these purposes the requisite intention is established if, at the time the relevant act is done, the employer (i) wants to bring about the state of affairs which constitutes the unfavourable treatment; and (ii) knows that this prohibited result will follow from the act. Complainants are entitled to compensation if they can show a direct causal link between an act of unlawful discrimination and their loss.[138] A tribunal can award compensation for both physical and psychological injury,[139] and a claim for hurt feelings is almost inevitable in discrimination cases.[140]

- There may be a recommendation that the employer takes action within a specified period to reduce the effect of the discrimination which has taken place. Where a recommendation is not complied with, the tribunal can award compensation or increase it.[141]

If the relevant statutory procedure was not completed before the proceedings were commenced, and this was wholly or mainly attributable to a failure by the employer, the tribunal is required to increase the level of any award. Similarly, if the non-completion of the procedure was wholly or mainly caused by the employee's failure to comply with its requirements, or exercise a right of appeal under it, the tribunal must reduce the award.[142]

Finally, the anti-discrimination legislation outlaws the victimisation of people simply because they have given evidence in connection with proceedings, have brought proceedings or intend to do so against someone (eg some other employer) under the Equal Pay Act 1970, the SDA 1975, the RRA 1976, the RB or EESO Regulations 2003.[143] According to the House of Lords, in order to determine whether a person has suffered less favourable treatment there should be a simple comparison between the treatment afforded the complainant who has done a protected act and the treatment that was or would be afforded other employees who have not done the protected act.[144] Thus in *Commissioners of Inland Revenue v Morgan*,[145] the EAT held that a memorandum about Ms Morgan's case circulated by her head of department amounted to unlawful victimisation in that it had an adverse effect on the attitude of her colleagues.

CASE STUDY

Lakhbir Rihal is a Sikh who worked as a senior surveyor in his employer's central technical team. When the acting head of the planned maintenance subdivision retired in 1996, Mr Rihal was not promoted but a white employee more junior to Mr Rihal was raised to his level to share the duties. Subsequently, the head of the team retired and was replaced by a white man. In 1998 Mr Rihal unsuccessfully applied for three managerial posts. One of those posts went to a white man on the basis that he had interviewed better. Mr Rihal brought a grievance under the organisation's procedure but this complaint was not dealt with for 14 months.

In upholding the findings of race discrimination, the Court of Appeal ruled that an employment tribunal is required to look at all the relevant evidence put before it. This might include evidence about the conduct of the alleged discriminator before or after the act about which the complaint is made. Moreover, the employment tribunal was entitled to take into account its finding that a 'glass ceiling' operated in the specific department in respect of non-white employees.[146]

THE EQUAL PAY ACT 1970

According to the Equal Pay Act 1970, an equality clause operates when a person is employed on 'like work', work rated as equivalent or work of equal value to that of a person of the opposite sex in the same employment.[147] For these purposes men and women are to be treated as in the same employment if they are employed at the same establishment or at establishments in Great Britain which observe common terms and conditions of employment.[148] For these purposes 'common terms and conditions' means terms and conditions which are substantially comparable on a broad basis rather than the same terms and conditions.[149]

It should be noted that the class of comparators defined in section 1(6) EPA 1970 is more restricted than applies under Article 141 EC (formerly Article 119 EC). Because Article 141 EC takes precedence, the crucial question is whether the applicant and the comparators are employed 'in the same establishment or service'. Thus the EAT has allowed a teacher employed by a Scottish local education authority to bring an equal pay claim comparing herself with a teacher employed by a different education authority in Scotland.[150] However, according to the European Court of Justice, a situation where the differences in pay of employees performing work of equal value cannot be attributed to a single source does not come within Article 141. This is because there is no body which is responsible for the inequality and which could restore equal treatment.[151]

The effect of the equality clause is that any term in a person's contract (whether concerned with pay or not) which is less favourable than in the contract of a person of the opposite sex is modified so as to be not less favourable. In *Evesham v North Hertfordshire Health Authority*[152] the EAT held that this meant being placed at the same point on an incremental scale as the comparator, not being placed on that scale at a level that was commensurate with her experience. It should also be noted that paragraph 2 of Article 141 EC states that 'pay' means 'the ordinary basic minimum wage or salary and any other consideration, whether in cash or in kind, which the worker receives, directly or indirectly, in respect of his employment from his employer'.[153] According to the European Court of Justice, a benefit is pay if the worker is entitled to receive it from his or her employer by reason of the existence of the employment relationship. Thus Article 141 EC covers not only occupational retirement and survivors' pensions,[154] travel concessions on retirement, end-of-year bonuses and statutory and contractual severance payments, but also paid leave or overtime for participation in training courses given by an employer under a statutory scheme.[155] Attention focuses on each aspect of remuneration rather than any general overall assessment of all the consideration paid to the workers.[156] However, for the purposes of comparison, the Court of Appeal has accepted that attention should focus on all the monetary payments that an employee receives for performing the contract during normal working hours.[157] Section 6 of the EPA 1970 provides that an equality clause does not operate where there are terms affording special treatment to women in connection with pregnancy or childbirth.[158]

WHAT IS 'LIKE WORK'?

The concept of 'like work' focuses on the job rather than the person performing it. Once a person has shown that his or her work is of the same or broadly similar nature as that of a person of the opposite sex, unless the employer can prove that any differences are of practical importance in relation to terms and conditions of employment, that person is to be regarded as employed on 'like work'.[159] In comparing work, a broad approach should be taken and attention must be paid to the frequency with which any differences occur in practice as well as their nature and extent. Trivial differences or 'differences not likely in the real world to be reflected in terms and conditions of employment' are not to be taken into account.[160] Similarly, tribunals are required to investigate the actual work done rather than rely on theoretical contractual obligations. The performance of supervisory duties may constitute 'things done' of practical importance[161] but the time at which the work is done would seem to be irrelevant. In *Dugdale v Kraft Foods*[162] the men and women were employed on broadly similar work but only men worked the night shift. It was held that the hours at which the work was performed did not prevent equal basic rates being afforded because the men could be compensated for the night shift by an additional payment. Thus an equality clause will not result in equal pay if persons of one sex are remunerated for something which persons of the other sex do not do.[163] It is not permissible, however, to ignore part of the work which a person actually performs on the grounds that his or her pay includes an additional element in respect of that work,[164] although there might be an exception where part of the work is, in effect, a separate and distinct job. Finally, in determining whether differences are of practical importance a useful guide is whether the differences are such as to put the two employments in different categories or grades in an evaluation study.[165]

WHAT IS 'WORK RATED AS EQUIVALENT'?

According to section 1(5) EPA 1970, a person's work will only be regarded as rated as equivalent to that of a person of the opposite sex if it has been given equal value under a properly conducted job evaluation scheme, including the allocation to a grade or scale at the end of the evaluation process. Thus in *Springboard Trust v Robson*[166] it was accepted that the applicant was employed on work rated as equivalent, notwithstanding that the comparator's job scored different points, where the result of converting the points to grades provided for under the evaluation scheme was that the jobs were to be treated as in the same grade.

A valid job evaluation exercise will evaluate the job and not the person performing it, and if evaluation studies are to be relied on they must be analytical in the sense of dividing a physical or abstract whole into its constituent parts. It is clearly insufficient if benchmark jobs have been evaluated using a system of job evaluation whereas the jobs of the applicant and comparators have not.[167] Employers are not prevented from using physical effort as a criterion if the tasks involved objectively require a certain level of physical strength, so long as the evaluation system as a whole precludes all sex discrimination by taking into account other criteria.[168] If the work has been rated as equivalent, a complainant does not have to show that the employees concerned have actually been paid in accordance with the evaluation scheme.[169]

According to the Court of Appeal, where there is one group which contains a significant number, though not a clear majority, of females whose work is evaluated as equal to that of another group who are predominantly male and receive more pay, the presence of a significant number of men in the disadvantaged group should not preclude an employment tribunal from holding that the disparity requires justification.[170]

Equal value claims

The House of Lords has ruled that an equal value claim can be pursued so long as the applicant's comparator is not engaged on like work or work rated as equivalent.[171]

Where, for example, a woman can show that she is employed on like work, or work rated as equivalent, an employer can still defeat a claim for equal pay by proving on the balance of probabilities that the variation is 'genuinely due to a material difference (other than the difference of sex) between her case and his'.[172] If there is an equal value claim, the employer need only show that a variation between a woman's and a man's contract is genuinely due to a factor which is (a) material and (b) not the difference of sex. In this context 'material' means significant and relevant. The requirement for 'genuineness' is satisfied if the tribunal concludes that the reasons put forward were not a sham or pretence. An employer seeking to establish a material factor has to prove: that there were objective reasons for the difference unrelated to sex; that they corresponded to a real need on the part of the undertaking, were appropriate to achieve the objective pursued and were necessary to that end; that the difference conformed to the principle of proportionality; and that that was the case throughout the period during which the differential existed.[173] One of the important messages to be sent out to pay negotiators by the Equal Pay Act is that they need to be aware that any agreed differences in pay may indirectly discriminate against employees of one gender.[174] According to the ECJ, the employer cannot rely on the fact that rates of pay have been set by collective bargaining even if the bargaining process is untainted by sex discrimination. In the same case the ECJ acknowledged that market forces cannot constitute a complete defence where they account only for part of the difference in pay.[175]

The objectively justified grounds need not be solely economic and could include administrative efficiency in appropriate cases.[176] It is worth noting that the following have been regarded as genuine material differences: the method of entering employment;[177] working in a different part of the country;[178] responsibility allowances;[179] financial constraints;[180] longer service;[181] physical effort and unpleasantness;[182] better academic qualifications; and higher productivity.

In the *Danfoss* case[183] the Equal Pay Directive 75/117 was interpreted as meaning that where employees do not understand how the criteria for pay increments are applied, if a woman establishes that the average pay of females is lower than that of men, the burden of proof is on the employer to show that the pay system is not discriminatory. Thus where vocational training or flexibility operates to the disadvantage of women, the employer will have to justify their application. According to the European Court of Justice, vocational training can be justified as a criterion if the employer shows that such training is important for the performance of specific work tasks. Similarly, insofar as flexibility refers to adaptability to variable work schedules rather than to the quality of the work, it can be justified by demonstrating that such adaptability is of importance for the performance of specific job duties.

PIECEWORK

In relation to piecework, the ECJ has ruled that where individual pay includes a variable element depending on each worker's output and it is impossible to identify the factors which determined how the variable element in pay was calculated, the burden of proving that the differences found are not the result of sex discrimination may shift to the employer. For these purposes any comparisons must cover a relatively large number of employees in order to ensure that the differences found are not purely fortuitous or differences in individual output.[184]

RED-CIRCLING

The practice of drawing a circle around the names of those within a protected group – for example, employees demoted through no fault of their own as the result of reorganisation – is one device that has to be scrutinised as a result of the EPA 1970. Such action may be perfectly lawful – eg where employees accept lower-paid work in a redundancy situation – but if the underlying reason for different treatment is sex-based it cannot be accepted as a defence.[185] Employers have to justify the inclusion of every employee in a red-circled group and must prove that at the time of admission to the circle the more favourable terms were related to a consideration other than sex.[186] Again, if a person's wages are protected on a transfer, perhaps because of age or illness, tribunals must be satisfied that this was not merely because of sex or that the new job was not one which was open only to one sex. The prolonged maintenance of a red circle may not only be contrary to good industrial relations practice but may in all the circumstances give rise to a doubt as to whether the employers have discharged the statutory burden of proof imposed on them by section 1(3) EPA 1970. Thus in *Home Office v Bailey*,[187] the EAT ruled that arrangements that were objectively justified in 1987 provided an unsatisfactory explanation 12 years later. In their Code of Practice on Equal Pay, the EOC recommends an internal pay review as the most appropriate method of ensuring that a pay system delivers equal pay free from sex bias. It also provides a model equal pay policy.[188]

ENFORCEMENT

Where there is a dispute as to the effect of an equality clause, both the employee and the employer can apply to an employment tribunal.[189] Equal pay claims must be lodged on or before a qualifying date. Normally, this will be six months after the last day on which the claimant was employed.[190] Similarly, where the proceedings relate to a period during which a stable employment relationship subsists, the qualifying date is six months after the day on which that stable employment relationship ended.[191] Arrears can be awarded back to the 'arrears date' in respect of any time when there was unequal pay. Normally the arrears date will be six years before the date on which the claim is made.[192] Complainants must identify a comparable person of the opposite sex and cannot launch an application without some sort of *prima facie* case.[193] Although a comparison cannot be made with a hypothetical person, the ECJ has decided that Article 141 EC allows a complainant to compare himself or herself with a previous job incumbent.[194]

In relation to the burden of proof, once a claimant demonstrates that his or her job is either like work or work of equal value to that of the chosen comparator, there is a presumption of discrimination on the grounds of sex which the employer has to rebut. However, according to the EAT, there is no requirement for objective justification of differences in pay where the employer has satisfactorily rebutted direct sex discrimination and there is no independent evidence to show that sex has had any influence on the difference in pay.[195]

Under section 7B(2) EPA 1970 the Secretary of State has prescribed forms by which an employee can question the employer on any matter that may be relevant to an equal pay claim. Similarly, forms have been published by which the employer can reply.[196] If an employee asks the questions before a complaint is made or within 21 days of presentation, the questions and replies may be used in evidence at a tribunal hearing, whether or not they were asked or answered in the prescribed form. If the employer, deliberately or without reasonable excuse, fails to answer the questions within eight weeks, or answers them evasively or equivocally, a tribunal may draw any inference it considers just and equitable, including an inference that the employer has contravened the provisions of the equality clause.[197]

KEY LEARNING POINTS

- A new Equality Bill is due to be adopted and will come into effect over a number of years. It will replace all the current discrimination statutes. The Sex and Race Discrimination Acts cover more than their names suggest; the SDA 1975, for example, covers discrimination and harassment against married persons and civil partners, while the RRA 1976 defines racial grounds as referring to colour, race, nationality, and national or ethnic origins.

- Direct discrimination occurs when on the grounds of sex, marital status or race a person is treated less favourably than a person of the opposite sex, a single person or a person not of the same racial group.

- Indirect discrimination on the grounds of colour or nationality occurs where an employer applies a requirement or condition which would apply equally to a person not of the same racial group but which is such that the proportion of the applicant's racial group who can comply with it is considerably smaller than the proportion of persons not of the same racial group.

- Indirect discrimination on the grounds of race, religion or belief, ethnic or national origins, sex or sexual orientation occurs where a provision, criterion or practice applies or would apply to persons not of the same race, ethnic or national origins, or sexual orientation but such people would be put at a particular disadvantage and this cannot be shown to be a proportionate means of achieving a legitimate aim.

- There are occasions when it is lawful to discriminate; these include when there is a statutory requirement of which the purpose is to protect women in relation to pregnancy or maternity provisions and when there is a genuine occupational qualification or requirement.

- The EPA 1970 inserts an equality clause into all contracts of employment when a person is employed on like work or work rated as equivalent or work of equal value to that of a person of the opposite sex in the same employment.

- An employer will have to be able to show that any differences in pay between any two employees are the result of a genuine material difference not related to the sex of either employee.

Reinforce your understanding of this chapter by visiting www.cipd.co.uk/sss for activities, questions, weblinks and additional case studies

REFERENCES

1   As of 1 April 2009 we were still waiting for the promised piece of legislation.

2   Section 1 Civil Partnership Act 2004

3   Regulation 2 EESO Regs 2003

4   Section 3(1) RRA 1976

5   See section 2(2) RRA 1976 and *London Borough of Lambeth v CRE* (1990) IRLR 231

6   (1983) IRLR 209

7   See *BBC v Souster* (2001) IRLR 150

8   See *Gwynedd C.C. v Jones* (1986) ICR 833; *Nyazi v Rymans Ltd* (1988) IRLIB 367

9   (1993) IRLR 284

10 Reg. 2(1)RB Regulations 2003 also makes it clear that 'lack of religion' and 'lack of belief' are both covered.

11 Section 21A SDA

12 See Section 76A SDA 1975, section 71(1) RRA, and *The General Duty to Promote Racial Equality*, CRE (2001)

13 EOC Code of Practice on sex discrimination 2006; CRE Code of Practice on racial equality in employment 2005. See also CIPD Equal Opportunities Code

14 Section 56A(10) SDA 1975 and section 47(10) RRA 1976. The CEHR has the power to produce Codes of Practice under sections 14–15 Equality Act 2006

15 On the use of actual and hypothetical comparators see *Balamoody v UKCC* (2002) IRLR 288

16 See *Moyhing v Barts NHS Trust* (2006) IRLR 860

17 *Azmi v Kirklees B.C.* (2007) IRLR 484

18 (1999) IRLR 94

19 See *Redfearn v Serco Ltd* (2006) IRLR 623

20 *Coleman v Attridge Law* (2008) IRLR 722

21 See *FTAT v Modgill* (1980) IRLR 142

22 See *James v Eastleigh B.C.* (1990) IRLR 288

23 See *Tower Hamlets v Rabin* (1989) ICR 693

24 See *A v Chief Constable of West Yorkshire Police* (2004) IRLR 754

25 See *Croft v Consignia plc* (2003) IRLR 592

26 Section 4A SDA 1975, section 3A RRA 1976 and Regulation 5 of RB and EESO Regulations 2003. On good practice see CRE Code

27 (1999) IRLR 299

28 *Driskell v Peninsula Business Services* (2000) IRLR 151

29 (1997) IRLR 168

30 Section 32 RRA 1976 and section 41 SDA 1975

31 *Chief Constable of Lincolnshire Police v Stubbs* (1999) IRLR 81

32 *English v Thomas Sanderson Blinds Ltd* (2008) IRLR 342

33 (2009) IRLR 206

34 See *Leicester University v A* (1999) IRLR 352

35 Sections 11 and 13 ETA 1996; see also *Chief Constable of West Yorkshire v A* (2000) IRLR 465

36 See *Majrowski v Guys NHS Trust* (2005) IRLR 340

37 Section 4A Public Order Act 1986

38 Section 1(2) and 3(1) SDA 1975 and section 1(1) RRA 1976

39 Section 1(2)(b) SDA 1975, section 1A RRA 1976 and Reg 3(1)(b) of RB and EESO Regs 2003. See *R v Elias* (2006) IRLR 934

40 Section 5(3) SDA 1975, section 3(4) RRA 1976, Regulation 3(2) EESO Regulations 2003 and Regulation 3(3) RB Regulations; see *Shamoon v RUC* (2001) IRLR 520 and *Wakeman v Quick Corporation* (1998) IRLR 424

41 See *Hardys and Hansons v Lax Plc* (2005) IRLR 726

42 *Whiffen v Milham Ford Girls School* (2001) IRLR 468

43 *Meade-Hill v British Council* (1995) IRLR 478

44 See *Briggs v North Eastern Education and Library Board* (1990) IRLR 181

45 See *Meade-Hill v British Council* (note 41)

46 (1997) IRLR 560

47 See *Coker v Lord Chancellor* (2002) IRLR 80

48 *Price v Civil Service Commission* (1978) IRLR 3

49 (1982) IRLR 482

50 (1993) IRLR 218

51 *London Underground v Edwards* (1998) IRLR 364

52 See *Barclays Bank v Kapur* (1991) IRLR 136

53 (2001) IRLR 681

54 See *Moonsar v Fiveways Express Transport* (2005) IRLR 9

55 *Shamoon v RUC* (2003) IRLR 285

56 See *Department of Work and Pensions v Thompson* (2004) IRLR 338 and CRE Code page 55. On possible human rights issues relating to appearance see Chapter 18

57 See *Jones v University of Manchester* (1993) IRLR 218

58 See *British Airways v Starmer* (2005) IRLR 862. On justifying statutory provisions see *Secretary of State v Rutherford (No. 2)* (2006) IRLR 551

59 *Allen v GMB* (2008) IRLR 690

60 Section 40 SDA 1975 and section 31 RRA 1976 deal with inducement or attempted inducement to perform an unlawful act.

61 Section 6(1) SDA 1975 and section 4(1) RRA 1976. For good practice in recruitment see the EOC Code and CRE Code

62 See *Nagarajan v London Regional Transport* (1999) IRLR 572

63 See section 6(2A) SDA, section 4(2A) RRA 1976 and Regulation 6(3) of both RB and EESO Regulations 2003

64 See section 82(1) SDA 1975 and section 78(1) RRA 1976. On employment wholly outside Great Britain see section 10 SDA 1975 and section 8 RRA 1976

65 See *Mirror Group Ltd v Gunning* (1986) IRLR 27 and *Percy v Church of Scotland* (2006) IRLR 195. Section 9 SDA 1975 and section 7 RRA 1976 outlaw discrimination against contract workers: see *Allonby v Accrington and Rossendale College* (2004) IRLR 224.

66 Section 37 SDA 1975 and section 28 RRA 1976

67 *Centrum voor Gelijkheid van Kansen en voor Racismebestrijding v Frima Feryn* (2008) IRLR 732

68   Section 38 SDA 1975 and section 29 RRA 1976

69   Section 82(1) SDA 1975 and section 78(1) RRA 1976

70   See EOC Code, CRE Code and CIPD Recruitment Code; see also *Martins v Marks & Spencer* (1998) IRLR 326

71   See EOC Code, CRE Code and CIPD Recruitment Code

72   Section 7 SDA 1975

73   (1983) IRLR 404

74   *Sisley v Britannia Security* (1983) IRLR 404

75   See *Lasertop Ltd v Webster* (1997) IRLR 498

76   See *London Borough of Lambeth v CRE* (note 5)

77   According to Reg. 7(3) RB Regs, where the employer has an 'ethos based on religion or belief' the genuine occupational requirement does not have to be 'determining'.

78   Section 4A(2) RRA 1976 and Regulation 7(2) of both RB and EESO Regulations 2003. On sexual orientation and employment for the purposes of organised religion see also Regulation 7(3) EESO Regulations 2003

79   *Glasgow C.C. v McNab* (2007) IRLR 476

80   See *Tottenham Green Under-Fives v Marshall (No.2)* (1991) IRLR 161 and EOC Code paragraphs 14–17, Appendix 1 of CRE Code

81   See *Etam plc v Rowan* (1989) IRLR 150

82   Section 51(1)(2) SDA 1975; compare section 41 RRA 1976 and *Hampson v DES* (1990) 3 WLR 42

83   Section 6(2) SDA 1975; section 4(2)(2A) RRA 1976; Regulation 6 EESO Regulations 2003; EOC Code paras 25, 28, 32 and CRE Code pages 56–71. On employment for the purposes of a private household see Section 4(3) RRA 1976

84   Section 4(2)a RRA 1976; in relation to sex, the EPA 1970 deals with discrimination in contractual matter.

85   Regulation 25 EESO Regulations 2003 provides an exception for benefits dependent on marital status.

86   See section 4(4A) RRA 1976 and Regulation 6(5) of both RB and EESO Regulations 2003

87   See section 27A RRA 1976, Regulation 21 of both RB and EESO Regulations 2003 and section 20A SDA 1975. Also *Rhys-Harper v Relaxion* (2003) IRLR 484

88   Section 4 SDA 1975

89   (1999) IRLR 452

90   Directive 76/207

91   *Marschall v Land Nordrhein-Westfalen* (1998) IRLR 39; *EFTA Surveillance Authority v Norway* (2003) IRLR 318

92   Section 47 SDA 1975 and section 37 RRA 1976

93   Regulation 26 EESO Regulations and Regulation 25 RB Regs 2003

94   *Peake v Automotive Products* (1977) IRLR 365

95   See *Eke v Commissioners of Customs and Excise* (1981) IRLR 384; EOC Code para 31

96   See sections 62–66 Pensions Act 1995. Section 64 deals with exclusions – for example, in relation to bridging pensions and actuarial factors.

97   See Occupational Pension Schemes (Equal Treatment) Regulations 1995 SI 1995/3183;

on the possible impact of Article 141 on access to a statutory scheme see *Allonby v Accrington and Rossendale College* (see note 65)

98 See *O'Neill v Governors of St Thomas More School* (1996) IRLR 372

99 (1996) IRLR 378; see also *Tele-Danmark* case [*Tele Danmark A/S v Handels- og Kontorfunktionaerernesforbund i Danmark*] (2001) IRLR 853

100 See *Whiffen v Milham Ford Girls School* (2001) IRLR 468 and *Allonby v Accrington and Rossendale College* (2001) IRLR 364

101 (1982) IRLR 482

102 Section 77 SDA 1975. On colour and nationality see section 72 RRA 1976; and on race, ethnic or national origins see Section 72A RRA 1976

103 See *Meade-Hill v British Council* (note 43)

104 Sections 30–40, 42 SDA 1975; sections 30–31, 33 RRA 1976; Regulations 22–3 of both RB and EESO Regulations 2003. See *Yeboah v Croftan* (2002) IRLR 634

105 See *Gilbank v Miles* (2006) IRLR 538

106 Section 41 SDA 1975 and section 32 RRA 1976

107 *Canniffe v East Riding Council* (2000) IRLR 555

108 See EOC Code paras 33–40

109 Employees wishing to complain under this legislation must first submit a statement of grievance to their employer: see paragraphs 6 and 9 Schedule 2 EA 2002.

110 (1995) IRLR 574; see also *Tyagi v BBC World Service* (2001) IRLR 465

111 See *Hendricks v Commissioner of Police for the Metropolis* (2003) IRLR 96

112 *Calder v Finlay* (1989) IRLR 55

113 *Owusu v London Fire Authority* (1995) IRLR 574

114 *Littlewoods v Traynor* (1993) IRLR 54

115 *Barclays Bank v Kapur* (1991) IRLR 136

116 (1992) IRLR 416

117 See *Clarke v Hampshire Electro-Plating* (1991) IRLR 491

118 Section 76 SDA 1975 and section 68 RRA 1976; see *Robertson v Bexley Community Centre* (2003) IRLR 434

119 See *Foster v South Glamorgan H.A.* (1988) IRLR 277

120 Section 74 SDA 1975 and section 65 RRA 1976

121 See *Virdee v ECC Quarries* (1978) IRLR 295

122 See *Nasse v Science Research Council* (1979) IRLR 465

123 See *British Library v Palyza* (1984) IRLR 307

124 See *Carrington v Helix Ltd* (1990) IRLR 6

125 Sections 57–8 SDA 1975 and sections 48–9 RRA 1976

126 See *Re Prestige Group plc* (1984) IRLR 166

127 Sections 59–60, 67 SDA 1975 and sections 50–51, 58 RRA 1976; see *R v CRE ex parte Westminster C.C.* (1985) IRLR 426

128 Section 63A(2) SDA 1975, section 54A RRA 1976 and Regulation 29 of both RB and EESO Regulations 2003

129 *Igen Ltd v Wong* (2005) IRLR 258. See also *Network Rail v Griffiths-Henry* (2006) IRLR 865, and *Laing v Manchester City Council* (2006) IRLR 748; also see *London Borough of Islington v Ladele* (2009) IRLR 154 where the EAT held that there are times when it is not neccessary to go through the two-stage process.

130 (1991) IRLR 513

131 See *Law Society v Bahl* (2003) IRLR 640

132 See *Eke*'s case (note 95) and *Chattopadhyay v Headmaster of Holloway School* (1981) IRLR 487

133 On conciliation see *Clarke v Redcar Borough Council* (2006) IRLR 324

134 Section 65 SDA 1975 and section 56 RRA 1976

135 See *Ministry of Defence v Cannock* (1994) IRLR 509

136 Section 65(1B) SDA 1975 and Regulation 30(2) of both RB and EESO Regulations 2003

137 Section 57(3) RRA 1976

138 See *Essa v Laing Ltd* (2004) IRLR 313

139 See *Sheriff v Klyne Tugs* (1999) IRLR 481

140 See *Orlando v Didcot Social Club* (1996) IRLR 262

141 Section 65(3) SDA, section 56(4) RRA, Regulation 30(3) of both RB and EESO Regulations 2003

142 Section 31 and Schedule 3 EA 2002

143 Section 4 SDA 1975, section 2 RRA 1976 and Regulation 4 of both RB and EESO Regs 2003. See *National Probation Service v Kirby* (2006) IRLR 508

144 *Chief Constable of West Yorkshire v Khan* (2001) IRLR 830

145 (2002) IRLR 776

146 *Rihal v London Borough of Ealing* (2004) IRLR 649

147 Section 1(2) EPA 1970; on work of greater value see *Murphy v Bord Telecom Eireann* (1988) IRLR 267

148 See section 1(6)(6A) EPA 1970

149 *British Coal v Smith* (1996) IRLR 404

150 *South Ayrshire Council v Morton* (2002) IRLR 256; see also *South Ayrshire Council v Milligan* (2003) IRLR 153

151 See *Allonby v Accrington and Rossendale College* (2004) IRLR 224 and *Armstrong v Newcastle NHS Trust* (2006) IRLR 124

152 (1999) IRLR 155

153 Section 1(2)(d) –(f) EPA 1970 covers increases to maternity-related pay

154 See *ten Oever*'s case [*ten Oever v Stichting Bedrijfspensioenfonds voor het Glazenwassers- en Schoonmaakbedrijf*] (1993) IRLR 601

155 See *Botel*'s case [*Arbeiterwolfahrt der Stadt Berlin eV v Botel*] (1992) IRLR 423

156 See *Brunnhofer v Bank der Österreichischen Postsparkasse AG* (2001) IRLR 571

157 *Degnan v Redcar B.C.* (2005) IRLR 615

158 See *Abdoulaye v Renault* (1999) IRLR 811 on lump sum maternity payments

159 Section 1(4) EPA 1970

160 See *Capper Pass Ltd v Lowton* (1976) IRLR 366

161 See *Eaton v Nuttall* (1977) IRLR 71

162 (1976) IRLR 368

163 See *Thomas v NCB* (1987) IRLR 451 and *Calder v Rowntree Mackintosh* (1993) IRLR 212

164 See *Maidment v Cooper & Co.* (1978) IRLR 462

165 See *British Leyland v Powell* (1978) IRLR 57

166 (1992) IRLR 261

167 See *Bromley v Quick Ltd* (1988) IRLR 249

168 See *Rummler v Dato-Druck GmbH* (1987) IRLR 32

169 See *O'Brien v Sim-Chem Ltd* (1980) IRLR 373

170 *Bailey v Home Office* (2005) IRLR 369

171 See *Pickstone v Freemans plc* (1988) IRLR 357

172 See *Financial Times v Byrne (No.2)* (1992) IRLR 163

173 See *Barton v Investec Ltd* (2003) IRLR 332

174 *British Airways plc v Grundy (No.2)* (2008) IRLR 815

175 *Enderby v Frenchay Health Authority* (1993) IRLR 591

176 See *Rainey v Greater Glasgow H.B.* (1987) IRLR 26

177 *Rainey v Greater Glasgow H.B.* (note 176)

178 *NAAFI v Varley* (1976) IRLR 408

179 *Avon and Somerset Police Authority v Emery* (1981) ICR 229

180 *Beneviste v University of Southampton* (1989) IRLR 122

181 On the relationship between experience and the better performance of duties see *Cadman v Health and Safety Executive* (2006) IRLR 969

182 *Christie v Haith Ltd* (2003) IRLR 670

183 (1989) IRLR 532

184 See the *Dansk Industri* case [*Specialarbejderforbundet i Danmark v Danmark Industri*] (1995) IRLR 648

185 See *Snoxell v Vauxhall Motors* (1997) IRLR 123

186 See *Methuen v Cow Industrial Polymers* (1980) IRLR 289

187 (2005) IRLR 757

188 EOC 2003

189 An employee wishing to complain under the legislation must first submit a statement of grievance to his or her employer: see paragraphs 6 and 9 Schedule 2 EA 2002.

190 See section 2(4) EPA 1970 and *Powerhouse Retail v Burroughs* (2006) IRLR 381

191 Section 2ZA EPA 1970. See *Jeffery v Secretary of State for Education* (2006) IRLR 1062

192 Section 2ZD EPA 1970

193 See *Clwyd C.C. v Leverton* (1985) IRLR 197

194 See *Kells v Pilkington plc* (2002) IRLR 693 and *Alabaster v Barclays Bank (No.2)* (2005) IRLR 576

195 *Villalba v Merrill Lynch & Co.* (2006) IRLR 437

196 See Equal Pay (Questions and Replies) Order 2003 SI No.722 and the EOC Code of Practice Section One.

197 Section 7B(4)(6)

CHAPTER 7

Age Discrimination and Disability Discrimination

OVERVIEW

The Employment Equality (Age) Regulations 2006[1] came into effect on 1 October 2006. They implement the age aspects of the EU Framework Directive on Equal Treatment in employment and occupation.[2] As a result of the Regulations it is unlawful to directly or indirectly discriminate on the grounds of age, unless objectively justified; subject someone to harassment on the grounds of his or her age or perceived age; victimise someone because he or she has made a complaint or an allegation or has given or plans to give evidence concerning a complaint of age discrimination; discriminate against someone, in certain circumstances, after the working relationship has ended.

This chapter also deals with discrimination by employers on the grounds of disability. The Disability Discrimination Act 1995 makes it unlawful to discriminate against current or prospective employees for a reason relating to their disability. We examine how the Act defines disability and the duties of the employer to take such steps as are reasonable in the circumstances to stop any physical or other arrangements that place a disabled person at a disadvantage.

AGE DISCRIMINATION

THE FRAMEWORK DIRECTIVE

The purpose of the Directive is set out in article 1 as being to lay down a general framework for combating discrimination and putting into effect the principle of equal treatment. The Directive is intended to introduce a minimum level of protection and the principle of equal treatment here means, according to article 2, that there should be no direct or indirect discrimination on the grounds of age. Thus article 2.2(a) states that direct discrimination shall be taken to occur where one person is treated less favourably than another in a comparable situation.

Article 2.2(b) states that indirect discrimination is

> taken to occur where an apparently neutral provision, criterion or practice would put persons having a particular age at a particular disadvantage with other persons, unless

(i) that provision, criterion or practice is objectively justified by a legitimate aim and the means of achieving that aim are appropriate and necessary.

JUSTIFICATION

Article 2.2(b)(i) provides a defence of justification. This can be where the provision, criterion or practice is 'objectively justified by a legitimate aim and the means of achieving that aim are appropriate and necessary'. Thus there can be objective justification for a difference in treatment between groups if:

- the difference in treatment deserves protection
- the difference in treatment is sufficiently substantial for it to take precedence over the principle of equal treatment
- the means for achieving this difference in treatment are both appropriate and necessary.

It is for the employer to justify the difference in treatment, if necessary, in accordance with article 9 of the Directive on the Burden of Proof.[3]

CASE STUDY

Mangold v Helm Case C-144/04 (2006) IRLR 143

In the case of Werner Mangold[4] the European Court of Justice considered a situation where German law allowed for the employer to conclude, without restriction, fixed-term contracts of employment with employees over the age of 52 years.

There were issues connected to the Fixed-term Workers Directive, but also with regard to the age aspects of the Framework Directive on Equal Treatment. The purpose of the German legislation, according to the national government, was to encourage the vocational integration of unemployed workers. The Court agreed that such a purpose could be 'objectively and reasonably' justified. The question then was whether this legitimate aim was 'appropriate and necessary'. The problem was that the national legislation applied to all people over the age of 52 years and not just to those who were unemployed. The Court concluded:

In so far as such legislation takes the age of the worker concerned as the only criterion for the application of a fixed-term contract of employment, it has not shown that fixing an age threshold, as such, regardless of any other consideration linked to the structure of the labour market in question or the personal situation of the person concerned, is objectively necessary to the attainment of the objective pursued. Observance of the principle of proportionality requires every derogation from an individual right to reconcile, so far as is possible, the requirements of the principle of equal treatment with those of the aim pursued.

Thus the Court held the measure to be not in accord with Community law. Taking away the employment protection rights from employed older workers was not appropriate and necessary when introducing a measure to help unemployed older workers.

HARASSMENT

Article 2.3 declares that harassment is another form of discrimination. It occurs when there is unwanted conduct which takes place for the purpose or effect of violating a person's dignity or of creating an intimidating, hostile, degrading, humiliating or offensive environment.

INSTRUCTION TO DISCRIMINATE

An instruction to discriminate against persons on the grounds of age will be deemed to be a form of direct or indirect discrimination. This is intended to stop discrimination by third parties on behalf of the employer. One example might be with employment agencies used by employers to supply permanent and/or temporary staff. An express or implied instruction to supply only candidates within a particular age range will effectively discriminate against others on the grounds of age. Presumably also instructing an advertising agency only to place recruitment advertising in certain journals which appeal to a particular age group might also be seen as an instruction to discriminate.

FURTHER EXCEPTIONS

Article 2.5 states that the Directive is without prejudice to 'measures laid down by law which, in a democratic society, are necessary for'

- public security
- the maintenance of public order
- the prevention of criminal offences
- the protection of health
- the protection of the rights and freedoms of others.

SCOPE

The Directive applies to both the public and the private sector and has a wide scope, albeit limited to the areas of employment and vocational guidance and training. In particular it applies to:

- conditions for access to employment, self-employment or to occupation – this includes selection criteria and recruitment conditions
- all types of activity and at all levels of the professional hierarchy, including promotion
- access to all types and all levels of vocational guidance and vocational training, including practical work experience
- employment and working conditions
- pay
- dismissals

- membership of, or involvement in, workers' and employers' organisations, including any benefits provided
- any organisation of which the members carry on a profession, including any benefits provided.

The Directive also specifically excludes:

- payments of any kind made by state schemes, including social security or social protection schemes
- the armed forces, at the Member State's discretion.

Thus the scope is wide, but it is limited to the fields of employment and vocational training, although the new Equality Bill will extend it to include discrimination in the provision of goods and services.

OCCUPATIONAL REQUIREMENTS AND JUSTIFICATION OF DIFFERENCES OF TREATMENT ON GROUNDS OF AGE

Articles 4 and 6 of the Framework Directive provide for the exceptions to the principle of equal treatment as they apply to age. Article 4.1 specifies that Member States may determine that a difference of treatment which is based on a characteristic related to age shall not constitute discrimination where such a characteristic 'constitutes a genuine and determining occupational requirement, provided that the objective is legitimate and the requirement is proportionate'.

Article 6 then takes this further. It actually provides for specific exceptions to the principle of equal treatment. They must be

objectively and reasonably justified by a legitimate aim, including legitimate employment policy, labour market and vocational training objectives.

In addition, the means of achieving the aim must be 'appropriate and necessary'. It is not clear what 'legitimate employment policy' means. Article 6 then continues to give some specific examples of differences in treatment which could be justified. The list is:

(i)   the setting of special conditions on access to employment and vocational training, employment and occupation (including dismissal and remuneration conditions) for young people, older workers and persons with caring responsibilities in order to promote their vocational integration or ensure their protection

(ii) the fixing of minimum conditions of age, professional experience or seniority of service for access to employment or to certain advantages linked to employment

(iii) the fixing of a minimum age for recruitment which takes into account the training period and the need for a reasonable period of work before the individual retires.

This difference of treatment assumes a retirement age which will limit a person's working life and therefore limit the return that an employer might receive in return.

POSITIVE ACTION

The Directive (Article 7.1) provides that the principle of equal treatment will not stop Member States from maintaining or adopting specific measures 'to prevent or compensate for disadvantages' linked to age.

Positive action is a term that includes measures designed both to counter the effects of past discriminatory practices and to assist members of the protected group to compete on an equal basis with those not in the protected group. This may include, for example, the encouragement of applications from the disadvantaged group, through extra advertising; or the provision of special training opportunities for employees in the disadvantaged group.

INFORMATION AND DIALOGUE

Member States are required to ensure that the provisions of the national rules 'are brought to the attention of the persons concerned by all appropriate means, for example at the workplace'. There is therefore a need to publicise and disseminate information about the Age Regulations.

THE AGE REGULATIONS

DIRECT DISCRIMINATION

Regulation 3(1)(a) states that a person A discriminates against a person B if, on the grounds of B's age, A treats B less favourably than he or she treats or would treat others.

The obvious example of direct discrimination with regard to age is the placing of age limits in job advertisements. Stipulating that a person must be of a certain age or within a certain age range is likely to be direct discrimination against those of other ages, except for those nearing retirement age (see below). Less obvious examples of discrimination in recruitment might be the stipulation of a certain length of experience or of the requirement for certain qualifications if such requirements cannot be justified. The use of advertising media which only appeals, or is accessed by, a certain age group might also infer discrimination. Of course direct discrimination is unlikely to be as obvious as this, and the problem to be tackled might be an unwritten policy within an organisation not to recruit outside a certain age range.

A major issue here is that it is possible to objectively justify direct age discrimination. There is a proviso in Regulation 3(1) which allows A to show that the less favourable treatment is a 'proportionate means of achieving a legitimate aim'. The meaning of this is discussed below, but discrimination on the grounds of age is the only ground for which it is possible to justify direct discrimination apart from the limited possibility of a genuine occupational requirement.

Regulation 4(b) provides that a reference to B's age includes B's apparent age. This is an important inclusion because it applies to all those who appear to be older (or younger) than they actually are. It is also important because, in a way, it is a step towards stopping discrimination because of a person's appearance.

INDIRECT DISCRIMINATION

Section 3(1)(b) declares that discrimination takes place when A applies to B a provision, criterion or practice which he or she applies or would apply equally to persons not of the same age group as B, but which puts or would put persons of the same age group as B at a disadvantage when compared with other persons and which also puts B at that disadvantage.

This, of course, is now a standard definition of indirect discrimination. One example might be that of a business which requires applicants for a driving job to have held a driving licence for ten years. The requirement does not mention age, but it is likely that a higher proportion of workers over the age of, say, 40 years will meet the requirement than those aged, say, 25 years.

OBJECTIVE JUSTIFICATION

One of the areas that weakens the impact of the Age Regulations is the wide scope for justifying exceptions to the principle of equal treatment. The tests for objective justification are, firstly, that the discrimination has a legitimate aim, and, secondly, that it is an appropriate and proportionate means of achieving that aim. The Directive uses the words 'appropriate and necessary', rather than the word 'proportionate'. The Courts in the UK have held that held that this means that the test is 'appropriate and *reasonably* necessary'.[5]

In the 2005 draft Regulations some specific examples of treatment which 'depending upon the circumstances' may be a legitimate and proportionate aim and being justified exceptions to the rule on direct discrimination were included. In the event these examples were left out of the final Regulations, but it is likely that any Court might first turn to Article 6 of the Framework Directive, which permits exceptions in a way that it does not to other forms of discrimination. Two examples of legitimate aims are 'business needs' and 'considerations of efficiency'. In themselves, of course, these are meaningless phrases but the scope that they imply is potentially wide.

DISCRIMINATION BY WAY OF VICTIMISATION

Regulation 4(1) provides that victimisation is less favourable treatment by A on the grounds that B had done something in relation to the Age Regulations, such as bringing proceedings or giving evidence or information. This protection is subject to something done being done or said in good faith[6] and is identical in wording to the provisions in other measures on discrimination.

INSTRUCTIONS TO DISCRIMINATE

If A instructs B to carry out an act which is unlawful under the Age Regulations and B does not carry out the instruction, or complains to A or another about the instruction, then any less favourable treatment of B by A would amount to discrimination on the grounds of age.

HARASSMENT ON GROUNDS OF AGE

Throughout the Age Regulations there are statements that it is unlawful to subject a person to harassment.[7] Harassment is then defined in Regulation 6(1). There now seems to be a standard definition of harassment in all the anti-discrimination measures. The Age Regulations adopt this standard approach. Thus harassment on the grounds of age takes place when A engages in unwanted conduct which has the effect of violating B's dignity, or creating an intimidating, hostile, degrading, humiliating or offensive environment for B. There is also a reasonableness test, including taking into account B's perception, in Regulation 6(2). Harassment is always unlawful and there is no possibility of justification.

DISCRIMINATION IN EMPLOYMENT AND VOCATIONAL TRAINING

APPLICANTS AND EMPLOYEES

Regulations 7(1) and 7(2) set out what an employer may or may not do in relation to age discrimination in employment. Two limitations are that it is (i) only the employer's actions in relation to employment that count, and (ii) only employment at an establishment in Great Britain.

Insofar as applicants are concerned, it is unlawful for an employer to discriminate in the arrangements made for the purpose of deciding to whom employment should be offered, in the terms on which the person's employment is offered or by not offering employment.[8] As far as those who are employed at an establishment in Great Britain, an employer may not discriminate in the terms of employment offered; in offering promotion, transfers or training; or in receiving any other benefits or refusing or deliberately stopping such opportunities; or by dismissing[9] or subjecting to any other detriment.[10]

Regulation 7(4), however, does allow discrimination on the basis of age for those applicants who would be employees if recruited and who are older than the employer's normal retirement age or 65 years of age if the employer does not have such an age. This exception also applies to applicants who would reach such an age within a period of six months from the date of the application. In such cases it will be permissible for employers to discriminate in the recruitment process on the basis of age. An employer may decide not to offer employment or may decide to offer less favourable terms than to other employees.

The provision in Regulation 7(4) is closely connected to the age limit on retirement. It would not be logical to have a default retirement age of 65 and then not allow employers to discriminate so that they did not recruit a replacement who was the same age or older. If an employee was forcibly retired at the age of 65 and the employer advertised the post, receiving an application from someone aged 66, it would be absurd if the employer was not allowed to discriminate against that person. The problem really starts with having a default retirement age in the first place. It this were removed, there would not be a logic in having this age limit on recruitment.

The 2005 consultation document did state that recruitment, selection and promotion decisions should be made on the skills required, rather than age, but there are situations where direct or indirect discrimination can be justified.

Age issues

Examples of where there might be issues are:[11]

● birth dates on job application forms might help an employer to make decisions based upon age

● requiring a certain length of experience for recruitment or promotion might have to be objectively justified because it is likely to discriminate against young people

● requiring a certain qualification might put people at a disadvantage. The example given is of an older person who may never have had the opportunity to take media studies

● graduate recruitment schemes might have to be open to students of all ages or open to other sources of recruitment

● vocational training – any age limits concerning access will have to be objectively justified

● employment agencies will have to be able to justify any age limits or specialisms related to age.

Regulation 7(3) makes harassment in relation to those employees or those who are applicants unlawful. Regulation 7(6) states that benefits provided by the employer for the public, or for part of the public, from which the employee benefits as a member of the public or of that part are not covered by the Regulations. This is unless there are differences in the benefits given to the employees and the public, or unless the benefits are regulated by the contract of employment or are concerned with training.

EXCEPTIONS FOR GENUINE OCCUPATION REQUIREMENT, ETC

This Regulation is identical to the equivalent provisions contained in the Sexual Orientation and the Religion or Belief Regulations. It declares that all the provisions, except those relating to terms of employment, in Regulation 7(1) and 7(2) concerning applicants and those in employment do not apply where 'possessing a characteristic related to age is a genuine and determining occupational requirement'.[12]

The example given in the 2005 consultation is that of an actor who might be required to be of a certain age, but even that would need objective justification to show that it was 'proportionate to apply that requirement in the particular case'.[13] The same consultation pointed out that it is unlikely to be a great issue for age discrimination. This Regulation is used in the other statutes and regulations concerning discrimination because it is an exception to the rule that there can be no justification of direct discrimination. As we have seen above, somewhat depressingly, this rule does not apply in the case of age discrimination, where it is permissible to justify such discrimination generally.

CONTRACT WORKERS

This Regulation provides for contract[14] workers to be given similar rights in relation to Regulations 7 and 8, where relevant, to those workers in employment. Thus Regulation 9(1) makes discrimination against a contract worker by a principal unlawful in respect of the terms on which he allows him or her to do the work, by not allowing him or her to do it or continue to do it, in granting access to benefits or refusing the same, or by subjecting the contract worker to any detriment.[15] A principal is defined as 'a person who makes work available for doing by individuals who are employed by another person who supplies them under a contract made with the principal'; contract work is the work which is made available; and a contract worker is an individual supplied to the principal to do the work.[16]

Regulations 9(2) to 9(4) provide the same protection as before concerning harassment, genuine occupational requirement and benefits supplied to workers and the public, as in Regulation 7(6).

THE PROVISION OF VOCATIONAL TRAINING

It is unlawful for a training provider to discriminate against a person seeking or undergoing training in the arrangements made for the purpose of selecting who should be offered training; in the terms on which the training provider affords access to any training; refusing access; terminating the training; or subjecting the applicant or person to be trained to any other detriment during the training.[17] Regulation 20(2) also makes harassment of an applicant or a person undergoing training unlawful.

'Training' here means

- all types of instruction that help fit a person for any employment
- vocational guidance
- facilities for training
- practical work experience
- assessment related to the award of a professional or trade qualification.

There is one exception in the Regulations. This is that it will not be unlawful to discriminate if the training is for employment which the trainee or potential trainee would not get because the employer could lawfully refuse to offer employment on the grounds of Regulation 8 (genuine occupational requirement).[18]

EMPLOYMENT AGENCIES, CAREER GUIDANCE, ETC

This Regulation applies to employment agencies, including agencies that provide guidance on careers or any other service related to employment.[19] It is unlawful for an employment agency to discriminate in the terms on which it offers its services, or by refusing to provide its services, or in the way it provides its services, or for it to subject a person to harassment.[20]

There is also an exception in Regulation 21(3) which states that it is not discrimination if it concerns employment for which the employer will claim a genuine occupational requirement. An employment agency will not be liable for a claim of discrimination if it can show that it relied upon a statement by the employer that the genuine occupational requirement exception applied, and that it was reasonable for the agency to rely on the statement. The agency will, therefore, still have to exercise its own judgement, although it is difficult to see how it could avoid relying on an employer's statement. There is provision, though, in Regulation 21(5) for a person who knowingly or recklessly makes such a statement to be liable to a fine.

RELATIONSHIPS WHICH HAVE COME TO AN END

If, during a 'relationship', an act of discrimination has taken place against B, then it is unlawful for A to discriminate against B, by subjecting him or her to detriment, or to subject B to harassment, after their relationship has ended, if this discrimination 'arises out of or is closely connected to the relationship'.[21] This is true even if the relationship came to an end before the Age Regulations came into force in October 2006, provided that the original act of discrimination would have been unlawful if it had taken place after the commencement date of the Age Regulations.

This same provision applies to the Sexual Orientation and Religion or Belief Regulations and is designed to stop continuing discrimination or harassment, such as inhibiting a person's attempts to get another job.

OTHER UNLAWFUL ACTS

LIABILITY OF EMPLOYERS AND PRINCIPALS

Anything done by a person in the course of his or her employment is to be regarded as having been done by the employer as well as him or her. It is not relevant whether the employer had knowledge of the things done or approved them. Similarly, anything done by an agent for another person with the authority[22] will be treated as having been done by the original person as well as the agent. There is a defence in Regulation 25(3) where a person such as an employer can prove that he or she took steps 'as were reasonably practicable to prevent the employee from doing that act or acts in the course of employment'.

AIDING UNLAWFUL ACTS

If a person knowingly aids another person to commit an act that is made unlawful by the Age Regulations, then that person is to be treated as having done an unlawful act of 'the like description'. A person may have a defence to the provisions of this Regulation if he or she relies upon a statement by the other person that the act done would not be unlawful by virtue of some aspect of the Age Regulations and that it is reasonable for him or her to rely on the statement. Again, if a person knowingly or recklessly makes such a statement which 'in a material respect is false or misleading', then that person will be liable to a fine on conviction.

GENERAL EXCEPTIONS

The Age Regulations 2006 contain eight general exceptions.[23] These are exceptions for:

- statutory authority
- national security
- positive action
- retirement
- national minimum wage
- the provision of benefits based on length of service
- the provision of enhanced redundancy payments
- the provision of life assurance cover for retired workers.

EXCEPTIONS FOR STATUTORY AUTHORITY AND NATIONAL SECURITY

These provide that nothing in Parts 2 or 3 shall make unlawful any act done in order to comply with a statutory provision or for the purpose of safeguarding national security. An obvious statutory example quoted in the 2005 consultation document is the Licensing Act 1964, which prohibited the employment of persons under the age of 18 years in a bar when it is open for the sale of alcohol.

EXCEPTIONS FOR POSITIVE ACTION

Because of the availability of the test of objective justification in direct and indirect discrimination, the need for something more is seen only narrowly by the Regulations and the 2005 consultation. There are only two areas described in the Regulations as fulfilling a less demanding test for positive discrimination. These are, firstly, allowing persons of a particular age or age group to have access to facilities for training which will help them find particular work, and, secondly, encouraging persons of a particular age or age group to take advantage of opportunities for doing particular work.

EXCEPTION FOR RETIREMENT AND THE DUTY TO CONSIDER WORKING BEYOND RETIREMENT

Regulation 30(1) is concerned with the exception for retirement and states that

> Nothing in Part 2 or 3 shall render unlawful the dismissal of an employee at or over the age of 65 years where the reason for the dismissal is retirement.[24]

This also applies to those in Crown employment and relevant members of the House of Commons and the House of Lords staff.[25]

What this means, of course, is that provided the employer follows the rules (see below), the employee may be dismissed for reasons of retirement at any age on or after the age of 65 years. Section 98(2) of the Employment Rights Act 1996 had a new subsection (ba) inserted wherein the retirement of the employee was made an additional 'fair' reason for dismissal.[26]

Whether the Directive permits the introduction of this retirement age has been challenged by Age Concern at the European Court of Justice. In the meantime, all challenges at employment tribunals claiming that compulsory retirement amounted to age discrimination, have been stayed pending the outcome of that case.[27] If the operative date of termination for such an employee is before the employee's 65th birthday, retirement shall not be taken as the reason for the dismissal (unless there is an objectively justified earlier retirement age).[28] If the operative date of termination falls on or after the employee's 65th birthday and the employer has followed the correct notification procedure (see below), retirement is the only reason that can be taken for dismissal, provided that the employment does terminate on the intended date of retirement.[29] If, despite following the duty to notify procedure, the contract is terminated before the intended date, retirement cannot be the reason for dismissal.

There are particular matters to be considered with regard to the fairness of the reasons for dismissal.[30] These are:

- whether or not the employer has notified the employee in accordance with paragraph 4 of Schedule 6.[31] This paragraph is concerned with an employer's continuing duty to notify the employee of the intended retirement date and the employee's right to make a request (see below)

- if the employer has notified the employee, in accordance with paragraph 4, how long before the notified retirement date the notification was given

- whether or not the employer has followed, or tried to follow, the procedures in paragraph 7 of Schedule 6. Paragraph 7 is concerned with arranging and holding a meeting to consider the employee's request.

It is clear that employers' procedures will have to be robust in order to ensure that events take place at the correct time and that all the procedures are correctly followed. A retirement dismissal will be unfair if the employer fails to comply with obligations under paragraph 4 (notification of retirement if not already given under paragraph 2), paragraphs 6 and 7 (duty to consider employee's request not to be retired) and paragraph 8 (duty to consider the appeal) of Schedule 6.[32] The one-year qualifying employment period for protection against unfair dismissal does not apply in these cases, and, of course, the upper age limit on being able to make a claim for unfair dismissal was removed.[33]

SCHEDULE 6

Schedule 6 of the Age Regulations is about the duty to consider working beyond retirement.

The Schedule imposes two duties upon an employer.

(i)   Firstly, there is the duty to inform the employee of his or her intended retirement date and of his or her right to make a request. This information must be given not more than one year and not less than six months before the dismissal. This is a continuing duty of the employer and such an obligation exists until the fourteenth day before dismissal.[34] The employee may make a request to the employer not to retire on the intended retirement date. The employee must propose that, following the intended date of retirement, his or her employment should continue indefinitely, for a stated period or until a stated date. This request must be in writing and can only be made once under this paragraph.[35] In a case where the employer has complied with its duty to notify, the employee's request must be made more than three months but not more than six months before the intended retirement date; in a case where the employer has not complied with the duty, then within the six months before the intended date.[36]

(ii) Secondly, there is the duty to consider the request.[37]

According to paragraph 6, considering a request means:

- holding a meeting with the employee to discuss the request
- the employer and employee taking all reasonable steps to attend the meeting.

The meeting is to be held within 'a reasonable period' after the request has been received. In the draft Regulations there was a time limit of 14 days for the employer to notify the employee of the decision. In the final Regulations this changed to 'as soon as reasonably practicable'. The decision, which must be in writing, is either to grant the request, stating whether the employee's employment will continue indefinitely or whether it will continue for a specified period, or to refuse it and to confirm the date of dismissal as well as informing the employee of his or her right to appeal.[38]

It is possible for the decision to be given in writing without a meeting taking place, if it has not proved reasonably practicable to hold one within a period that is reasonable (again there was a time limit of two months in the draft).[39] The appeals procedure, contained in paragraph 7, follows a similar procedure and, again, time-limits for decision-making were removed. Employees have a right to be accompanied to the first meeting and any subsequent appeal meeting.[40] The accompanying person must be a fellow-employee, which excludes trade union representatives who are not employees. The accompanying employee may address the meeting and confer with the employee, but not answer questions on behalf of the employee.

If the employer dismisses the employee after the request has been made but before a decision has been reached, the contract of employment will continue in force for all purposes including the purpose of determining the period for which the employee has continuity of employment until the day after the date of the employer's notice of the decision made.[41] Where an employer fails to inform the employee of the retirement date or of his or her right to make a request, an employment tribunal may award compensation of a maximum 8 weeks' pay from the employer to the employee.[42]

It was proposed in an earlier consultation by the government that the duty to consider procedure would be modelled on the right of parents with young children to request flexible working.[43] In the Age Regulations, however, there is no list of possible reasons for turning down a request not to retire, nor is there any obligation upon the employer to give any reasons for turning down the request. The only obligation is to notify the employees of the decision and their right of appeal.

EXCEPTION FOR THE NATIONAL MINIMUM WAGE

This allows for differential rates of pay related to age. Such pay is in relation to the hourly rate set by the Secretary of State[44] or in relation to differential pay for contracts of apprenticeship.[45]

There are, of course, two lower bands for young people: one for those aged 16 and 17 years; the other for those aged between 18 and 21 inclusive. This measure only applies to the age bands and pay levels established by the statutory measures on the national minimum wage. Objective justification would be needed to pay a 16-year-old at a different rate from a 17-year-old. Similarly, if an employer were paying rates which were above the levels of the national minimum wage, he or she would have to justify this, even if the same age bands were used.

The objective in having a lower rate for young people is, according to the government, to make young people more attractive to employers but, at the same time, not set the rates at a level that would act as an incentive for young people to give up education and go into work. If the government was ever challenged on these lower rates (which do discriminate against younger workers), then it would have to show that these were legitimate aims and that the means for achieving these aims – namely the national minimum wage – are proportionate, or appropriate and necessary.

EXCEPTION FOR PROVISION OF CERTAIN BENEFITS BASED ON LENGTH OF SERVICE

Regulation 32 is concerned with the issue of benefits related to length of service and seniority. It is not uncommon for employees to be given extra benefits related to length of service with an organisation. Holiday entitlement is one example of a benefit that might be linked to length of service. Without further provisions such benefits might constitute unlawful age discrimination, because it will tend to mean that older (and longer-serving) employees receive greater benefits than less experienced (and often younger) employees.

It will not be unlawful for A to award a benefit to employee B less than that awarded to employee C, when the reason for the difference is the relative length of service.[46] There is a further proviso relating to service that is longer than five years. In this case it must reasonably appear to A that the way in which the criterion of length of service is used 'fulfils a business need of his undertaking (for example, by encouraging the loyalty or motivation, or rewarding the experience, of some or all of his workers)'.[47] It is difficult to see why the government bothered with this proviso for service over five years when it has such a broad justification that will be almost impossible to disprove.

Obvious benefits that are linked to service include pay scales, and entry into health and employee discount schemes. It is for the employer to decide which formula to use to calculate length of service. It may be either the length of time a worker has been working at or above a particular level or it can be the length of time the worker has been working for the employer in total.

This distinction is important because it means that the five-year rule can be used again and again. Thus if a worker is employed as a shopfloor operative for a few years, doing work of a like nature, and is then promoted to being supervisor, then the five-year period can start all over again while he or she does work of a like nature which is different from that done previously.

EXCEPTION FOR PROVISION OF ENHANCED REDUNDANCY PAYMENTS

The payments were calculated using a combination of the length of service and age. The older the redundant employee, the higher the rate of payment, at least until the age of 64 years when there was a severe tapering off of benefit. This exception based on age is permitted by the Regulations and employers are to be allowed to pay more so long as they follow the same formula. The age restrictions at both ends were also removed.

There have been a number of cases concerning redundancy schemes which were all much more generous than the state scheme but which were claimed to discriminate against individuals in particular circumstances. The essential point in all the cases is whether redundancy schemes which are related to length of service can be objectively justified in having legitimate aims with the means of achieving those aims being proportional.

Rolls-Royce plc v Unite the Union[48] concerned two collective agreements which had an agreed matrix to be used to choose who should be selected for redundancy. There were five criteria against which an individual could score between 4 and 24 points. In addition there was a length-of-service criterion which awarded 1 point for each year of continuous service. Thus older employees would have an important advantage over younger ones. *MacCulloch v ICI plc*[49] concerned a redundancy scheme which had been in existence since 1971. The amount of payment was linked to service up to a maximum of 10 years, and the size of the redundancy payment increased with age. The claimant was 37 years old and received 55% of her salary as a payment and she claimed that someone aged between 50 and 57 years would have received 175% of salary under the scheme. *Loxley v BAE Systems*[50] had a contractual redundancy scheme in which each employee received two weeks' pay for the first five years of employment, three weeks' for each of the next five years, and four weeks' pay for each year after 10 years. There was also a further age-related payment of two weeks' pay for each year after the age of 40 years. All this was subject to a maximum of two years' pay. Essentially, the claimant, who was 61 years of age, was not entitled to any enhanced payments for voluntary redundancy because he had an entitlement to a pension.

In *Rolls-Royce* the employers argued that even if it were true that length of service recognised and rewarded loyalty, it was not related to the purpose of the exercise which was to fulfil a business need. Length of service was reflected in the other measured criteria, such as that of experience and skill. Indeed, according to them, a long-serving employee could be disloyal throughout his or her employment! The employers were arguing that the length of service provisions were discriminatory.

The Union argued, and the EAT agreed, that Regulation 32 provides for three stages:

- whether inclusion of a length of service criterion in redundancy selection is a benefit – in this case long-service points are an advantage because they protect workers from redundancy
- if so, whether it is reasonable for Rolls-Royce to consider that the inclusion of the criterion fulfils a business need of the undertaking
- whether the benefit is one awarded to a worker by virtue of his ceasing to work – the answer here is yes, because it is awarded in the context of a scheme to determine who retains employment.

ENFORCEMENT

The Commission for Equality and Human Rights includes age diversity and age discrimination within its scope. It has similar roles in relation to advice and guidance on age as with regard to other grounds of discrimination, as well as powers to investigate and challenge discrimination itself and through the support of others.

BURDEN OF PROOF

The complainant must prove facts from which the court could infer discrimination in the absence of an adequate explanation. It is for the respondent to prove facts showing that age discrimination was not the reason or part of the reason for the action. Alternatively, the respondent may show objective justification for the difference in treatment in the case of direct and indirect discrimination. There is no justification defence for victimisation or harassment.

REMEDIES ON COMPLAINTS TO EMPLOYMENT TRIBUNALS

An employment tribunal may make an order declaring the rights of the complainant, award damages,[51] and make a recommendation to the respondent to take action within a specified period obviating or reducing the adverse effect complained of.

HELP FOR PERSONS IN OBTAINING INFORMATION

Like the other anti-discrimination Regulations there is a procedure for sending a questionnaire to respondents or prospective[52] respondents. The questionnaire is contained in Schedule 3 and there is provision within Regulation 41(1) for the questions to be varied 'as the circumstances require'. The form is simple and invites the questioner to give a factual description of the circumstances and the treatment received and why such treatment was unlawful. It then asks the respondent whether he or she agrees with the facts and whether he or she agrees that this amounts to unlawful discrimination or harassment. If the respondent disagrees, he or she is invited to say why, what the reason was for the treatment and how far considerations of age affected the treatment of the questioner. Question 4 is then simply a statement of any other questions to be asked. Schedule 4 merely asks the respondent to reply to these questions or, if he or she refuses to do so, to give reasons for not answering.

There are time-limits for serving such questionnaires[53] and rules about how they may be served.[54] The questions and answers, subject to the time-limits, are admissible as evidence in the proceedings and the court will take them into account, and may draw inferences, if it appears that the respondent deliberately failed to reply (without a reasonable excuse) within eight weeks of the questions being served or if it appears that the replies are evasive or equivocal.[55]

PERIOD WITHIN WHICH PROCEEDINGS ARE TO BE BROUGHT

There are the normal periods for submission: three months for an employment tribunal and six months for a county or sheriff court beginning when the act[56] complained of was done, with discretion to extend these periods if it is just and equitable to do so.

DISABILITY DISCRIMINATION

DISABILITY

The Disability Discrimination Act 1995 (DDA 1995) makes it unlawful for employers to discriminate against existing or prospective staff for a reason relating to their disability.[57] People are also protected if they have recovered from a disability that is covered by this Act.[58] The Act also is to be interpreted as applying to other persons who are discriminated against by virtue of associating with a disabled person. In *Coleman v Attridge Law*,[59] a person, who was a legal secretary, suffered poor treatment because of the need to take time off work to look after her disabled child. The employers denied that she was covered by the DDA because she was not herself disabled. The European Court of Justice held that such an interpretation would undermine the objectives of the Equal Treatment Directive (see above) and held that she was protected.

The DDA 1995 covers employees and contract workers, apprentices and those working under a contract to do any work. The Act was amended by the Disability Discrimination Act 2005 which, amongst other matters, introduced a general duty for employers to take into account the need to eliminate unlawful discrimination and harassment in carrying out its functions.

The forms of discrimination made unlawful by the DDA are:

- direct discrimination
- failure to comply with a duty to make reasonable adjustments
- disability related discrimination
- victimisation.[60]

DIRECT DISCRIMINATION AND HARASSMENT

A person discriminates against a disabled person if he or she, for a reason related to the disabled person's disability,

- treats the disabled person less favourably than he or she would treat others to whom that reason does not apply
- cannot show that the treatment in question is justified.[61]

Thus direct discrimination depends not only upon the treatment taking place because of a person's disability, but also in comparison with the treatment given to an appropriate comparator. This must be a person who does not have the disability in question. It can be a non-disabled person or another person with a different disability.

Less favourable treatment can only be justified if it meets two tests. The reasons for the treatment must be both material to the circumstances and must be substantial. If the treatment amounts to direct discrimination against the disabled person then it cannot be justified at all. Direct discrimination means treating the disabled person less favourably than a person who does not have the particular disability, but whose relevant circumstances (including his or her abilities) are the same as, or similar to, those of the disabled person.[62]

> ## 🍎 CASE STUDY
>
> A disabled person with arthritis who can type at 30 words per minute applies for a job which includes typing. The disabled person is rejected because the typing speed is too slow. The correct comparator in a claim of direct discrimination would be a person not having arthritis who also has a typing speed of 30 words per minute.[63]

The approach to be taken is similar to that taken in unfair dismissal cases when the 'range of reasonable responses' test is used with regard to the employer's actions (see Chapter 13). In disability discrimination cases the test is whether the reasons for the employer's response were both 'material and substantial'.[64]

DISABILITY-RELATED DISCRIMINATION

Sometimes discrimination takes place for a disability-related reason that cannot be shown to be direct discrimination. It is when the reason for the discrimination is not necessarily the disability itself, but that relates to the disability.[65] There has been a difficulty in deciding who is the correct comparator for disability-related discrimination. In *London Borough of Lewisham v Malcolm*,[66] the House of Lords decided, contrary to previous decisions of the Court of Appeal, that the correct comparator is a non-disabled person to whom the same reason applied. Thus, if a disabled person is dismissed because of an inability to do a job, then the correct comparator would be an able-bodied person also not able to do the job. This is a very narrow interpretation of the Act.

DEFINING DISABILITY

According to section 1(1) DDA 1995, a person has a disability 'if he has a physical or mental impairment which has a substantial and long-term adverse effect on his ability to carry out normal day-to-day activities'.

THE MEANING OF 'IMPAIRMENT'

Impairment[67] is generally determined by looking at the effect that an impairment has on the person's ability to carry out normal day-to-day activities. Some impairments are easy to identify, but some are not so obvious.

A disability can arise from a wide range of impairments which can be:

- sensory impairments, such as those affecting sight or hearing
- impairments with fluctuating or recurring effects, such as rheumatoid arthritis or myalgic encephalitis (ME) or chronic fatigue syndrome

- progressive, such as motor neurone disease or forms of dementia

- organ-specific, including respiratory conditions like asthma and cardiovascular diseases such as thrombosis, stroke and heart disease

- developmental, such as dyslexia

- learning difficulties

- mental health conditions and mental illnesses

- produced by injury to the body or brain.

The cause of the impairment is not relevant – eg liver disease caused by alcohol addiction, even though the latter does not count as an impairment. See the three example cases below.[68]

CASE STUDY

A woman has obesity which gives rise to impairments such as mobility restrictions and breathing difficulties. She is unable to walk more than 50 yards without having to rest.

A man has borderline-moderate learning difficulties which have an adverse impact on his short-term memory and his levels of literacy and numeracy – for example, he cannot write any original material, as opposed to slowly copying existing text, and he cannot write his address from memory.

It is the effects of those impairments that must be taken into account, rather than the conditions which cause the effects. This was the case in *Millar v Inland Revenue Commissioners*,[69] where doctors were unable to find an organic medical reason for physical ailments which included sensitivity to light, headaches and a drooping eyelid. The court stated that many physical impairments resulted from conditions which could not be described as illnesses. It is the fact of the claimant's condition that is important.

The 2005 Disability Discrimination Act removed the requirement that mental illness had to be 'clinically well recognised' for it to be regarded as a disability, although the illness must still meet the definition in Section 1.

PERSONS DEEMED TO BE DISABLED

Some people are automatically said to meet the definition of disability, so do not have to show that they have an impairment that has a substantial long-term effect on the ability to carry out normal day-to-day activities:

- a person who has cancer, HIV infection or multiple sclerosis

- a person who is certified blind or partially sighted.

Some conditions are not to be regarded in themselves as impairments:

- addiction to or dependency on alcohol, nicotine or any other substance
- seasonal allergic rhinitis (hay fever)
- a tendency to set fires
- a tendency to steal
- a tendency towards the physical or sexual abuse of other persons
- exhibitionism
- voyeurism
- disfigurements which consist of tattoos or non-medical body-piercing.

Think about each of the items on this list,[70] and consider whether you think it should be regarded as a disability or not.

Someone who met the requirements of the Act in the past – eg with a mental illness – is still covered by the Act.

The definition covers impairments affecting the senses such as hearing and sight, together with learning difficulties or a mental illness. However, addictions, tattoos and body-piercing are all excluded from the protection of the Act.[71]

Day-to-day activities are normal activities carried out on a regular basis and must involve one of the following:

- mobility
- manual dexterity (this covers the ability to use hands and fingers with precision)
- physical co-ordination
- continence
- the ability to lift, carry or move everyday objects
- speech, hearing or eyesight
- memory or ability to concentrate, learn or understand
- perception of the risk of physical danger.

However, severe disfigurements are treated as disabilities although they have no effect on a person's ability to carry out normal day-to-day activities.[72]

IMPAIRMENTS WITH A 'SUBSTANTIAL ADVERSE EFFECT'

'Substantial' can be defined by looking at:

- the length of time it takes to carry out an activity
- the way in which a day-to-day activity is carried out – eg someone with obsessive compulsive disorder may wash hands after handling any single element of a meal he or she is preparing
- the cumulative effect of impairments.

There is a need to take into account the effects of, firstly, behaviour by considering what is a reasonable expectation of the modification of behaviour – eg a person with a back problem might be expected to not go parachuting, but not give up lesser activities like gardening – and, secondly, the environment, because some aspects might exacerbate an impairment, like lighting, temperature, weather.

Medication, equipment or other control measures are not taken into account when assessing whether an impairment has a substantial effect. One exception to this is when people wear glasses or contact lenses.[73] Thus in *SCA Packaging Ltd v Boyle*,[74] a voice management scheme aimed at reducing stress on an individual's throat and voice was held to constitute a measure, but for which the person would have suffered from a long-term and substantial effect on her ability to carry out day-to-day activities.

WHO HAS A DISABILITY?

The proper approach to the question whether a person has a disability, within the meaning of the Act, was considered in *Goodwin v The Patent Office*.[75] The EAT concluded that a tribunal should look at the evidence by reference to four different conditions:

1 *The impairment condition*

   Does the applicant have an impairment which is either physical or mental? The term 'impairment' should carry its ordinary and natural meaning. It can be the result of an illness or be the illness itself. The onus is on the applicant to prove the impairment, on the balance of probabilities.[76] How the illness or impairment was caused is not relevant. Thus a person suffering liver damage as a result of alcohol abuse may come within the ambit of the DDA 1995, even though addiction to alcohol itself is expressly excluded from being treated as an impairment under the Act.[77]

   In *Chacón Navas*,[78] a Spanish case at the European Court of Justice, an employee was dismissed after being absent through sickness for eight months. She claimed that dismissal because of sickness amounted to disability discrimination. The Court of Justice disagreed and stated that disability referred to a limitation resulting from a physical, mental or psychological impairment which hindered participation in professional life. This is different from sickness and is likely to be much longer-lasting, so workers who are off work because of sickness are not necessarily protected by the prohibition of discrimination on the grounds of disability.

2 *The adverse effect condition*

   Does the impairment affect the applicant's ability to carry out normal day-to-day activities as set out in paragraph 4(1) of Schedule 1 to the Act (see below)? This condition is concerned with the ability to carry out normal day-to-day activities whether at work or at home[79] – eg a person may be able to cook, but only do so with the greatest difficulty. When an employment tribunal considers whether an impairment affects the ability to carry out these day-to-day activities, it should focus on the list in paragraph 4(1) and ask whether the ability to carry out any of these has been affected. If the answer is yes, then there is likely to have been an adverse effect on the person's abilities.[80] It is not necessarily appropriate to examine each individual's normal day-to-day activity. In *Abadeh v British Telecommunications plc*,[81] for example, the employment tribunal had found that travelling by Underground was not a normal day-to-day activity, because the applicant did not live or work in London. It also found that flying was not such an activity because the applicant's work did not involve plane travel. The EAT held that it was inappropriate to examine each form of transport, but to look at transport as a whole, when deciding whether a person's ability to carry out normal activities had been impaired.

3 The substantial condition

Is the adverse condition 'substantial'? The tribunal will need to look at how the person's abilities were affected at the material time while receiving treatment, and then try to deduce what he or she would have been like without this treatment. This treatment can include counselling for someone suffering from a form of depression.[82] The question is then whether the actual or deduced effects on the applicant's ability to carry out normal day-to-day activities are more than trivial. In *Leonard v Southern Derbyshire Chamber of Commerce*,[83] a management adviser was dismissed on the grounds of (in)capability after being away from work for some time with clinical depression. The EAT upheld her complaint of disability discrimination. It held that the employment tribunal should concentrate, in deciding whether the adverse effect was substantial, on what the individual could not do, rather than on what she was still able to do. In this case account had to be taken of the serious tiredness which affected the employee's ability to sustain an activity over a period of time.

Consideration of whether a condition is the result of an impairment should not be taken too narrowly. In *Kirton v Tetrosyl Ltd*[84] a person had an operation for prostate cancer which resulted in urinary incontinence. The Court of Appeal held that the urinary impairment should be taken as being as a result of the prostate cancer and not just of the surgical treatment, which was a common one for such complaints. As a result it was correct to conclude that the impairment resulted from the progressive condition.

4 The long-term condition

Is the adverse condition long-term? In *Cruickshank v Vaw Ltd*[85] the EAT held that the material time at which to assess a person's disability is at the time of the alleged discriminatory act. Schedule 1 paragraph 2 of the DDA states that a long-term effect is one

- which lasts at least 12 months, or

- which is likely to last 12 months.

THE DUTY TO MAKE ADJUSTMENTS

The DDAA Regulations 2003 make it very clear that a failure by an employer to comply with the duty to make reasonable adjustments in relation to the disabled person will amount to discrimination.[86]

The rule is that where an employer applies

- a provision, criterion or practice, or
- any physical feature of the employer's premises

which places the disabled person at a substantial disadvantage compared to someone who is not disabled, the employer has a duty to take such steps as are reasonable in order to prevent the provision, criterion, practice or physical feature having that effect.[87] The duty concerning provisions, criterion or practice applies to applicants as well as employees of the employer.

A tribunal, when considering whether there has been a failure in the duty to make reasonable adjustments, must identify a number of matters. Firstly, it must identify the provision, criterion or practice applied by, or on behalf of, an employer, or the physical feature of the premises occupied by the employer; next it must identify the non-disabled comparators (where appropriate); and then identify the nature and extent of the substantial damage suffered by the claimant.[88]

These rules will also apply to contract workers, where the duty to make adjustments rests with the principal who is providing work for the disabled contract worker, unless the disabled worker has an employer with whom the duty rests.

The following are examples of steps that an employer may have to take in order to comply with this obligation:

- making adjustments to premises
- allocating some of the disabled person's duties to another
- transferring the disabled person to fill an existing vacancy
- altering the disabled person's working hours
- assigning him or her to a different place of work
- allowing him or her to be absent during working hours for rehabilitation, assessment or treatment
- training or arranging for training to be given to him or her
- acquiring or modifying equipment
- modifying instructions or reference manuals
- modifying procedures for testing or assessment
- providing a reader or interpreter
- providing supervision.[89]

In deciding whether it is reasonable for an employer to take a particular step, regard will be had, in particular, to:

- the extent to which taking the step would prevent the particular effect in question

- the extent to which it is practicable for the employer to take the step

- the financial and other costs which would be incurred and the extent to which taking it would disrupt the employer's activities

- the extent of the employer's financial and other resources

- the availability to the employer of financial and other assistance in making the adjustment.

The DDAA Regulations 2003 also provide that the employer needs knowledge of the disability. If the employer did not know, or could not reasonably be expected to know, then the provisions relating to the duty to make adjustments do not arise.

According to the EAT the test under section 6 DDA is an objective one. The question to be asked is whether the employer has taken such steps as were reasonable in the circumstances to prevent the arrangements made by the employer from placing the disabled person at a substantial disadvantage in comparison with others who are not disabled. The test of whether it was reasonable for the employer to have to take a particular step does not relate to what the employer considered, but to what the employer did and did not do.[90] This includes making an assessment of what is required to eliminate a disabled person's disadvantage. It is clear that an employment tribunal cannot make a decision that less favourable treatment of a disabled person was justified unless it is satisfied that any reasonable adjustments that an employer had a duty to make had been carried out.[91]

In *Mid-Staffordshire General Hospitals NHS Trust v Cambridge*[92] an employer failed to do this assessment when an employee became ill and was absent from work for a long period of time. She was only able to work for short hours and was adversely affected by the office conditions in which she was required to work. She was eventually dismissed on the grounds of incapacity due to ill health. In this case the duty required by section 6(1) DDA to make adjustments also included a duty to make an assessment of her condition and prognosis, the effect of the disability on her and her ability to perform the duties of her post as well as what steps might be taken to remove or reduce the disadvantages to which she was subject. The EAT held that the making of this assessment could not be separated from the duty to actually make the adjustments and so a failure to make the assessment was a breach of section 6(1) DDA. In *Nottinghamshire County Council v Meikle*,[93] a schoolteacher eventually resigned after her employer had failed to make reasonable adjustments over a long period of time. The teacher had lost the sight in one eye and some sight in the other. She had made various suggestions about adjustments to help her, but few were actually taken up. The Court of Appeal held that the employer had been in fundamental breach of contract because of its continuing failure to deal with this issue, and that the employee was entitled to claim that she had been constructively dismissed.

There is a limit to the adjustments that an employer is required to make. They do not include the provision of personal carer services for a person who might need such help. They might, however, include the accommodation of such a carer if provided by others.[94]

CASE STUDY

Archibald v Fife Council (2004) IRLR 651

Susan Archibald was employed as a road sweeper. Her job involved refuse collection, cleaning of public toilets and road sweeping. She had a minor operation which led to severe complications, as a result of which she was unable to walk. Her employer tried to find her alternative work within the Authority. Over a period of months she unsuccessfully applied for over 100 different posts. Because almost every other post was of a higher grade than her previous position of road sweeper, she could only apply for these posts, according to the employer's rules, as part of a competition with other applicants. Eventually, the employer decided that all alternatives were exhausted, so it decided to dismiss her.

She complained of discrimination on the grounds of disability, stating that she should not have been made to compete for alternative employment and that the employer had failed to make a reasonable adjustment in her case.

The House of Lords held that the duty to make adjustments may require the employer to treat a disabled person more favourably in order to remove the disadvantage resulting from the disability. In this case the arrangements placed Susan Archibald at a substantial disadvantage, compared to those who were not disabled. They could have considered transferring her to another job without a competitive interview. Section 6(7) of the DDA not only permits an employer to treat a disabled employee more favourably than others, but it obliges them to do so.

UNLAWFUL DISCRIMINATION

It is unlawful for employers to discriminate against disabled people:

- in the arrangements made for determining who should be offered employment[95]
- in the terms on which employment is offered
- by refusing or deliberately not offering employment.

It is also unlawful to discriminate against disabled employees:

- in the terms of employment
- in the opportunities afforded for promotion, training, transfer or receiving any other benefit
- by refusing to afford or deliberately not affording any such opportunity
- by dismissing or subjecting the disabled person to any other detriment.[96]

With reference to the last point, in *British Sugar plc v Kirker*,[97] for example, an individual selected for redundancy claimed that he had been discriminated against because of a visual impairment suffered since birth. The employers had carried out an assessment exercise in order to select those to be dismissed. This had consisted of marking employees against a set of factors. The complainant claimed that the marks attributed to him were the result of a subjective view arising out of the disability. The employee had scored 0 for promotion potential and 0 out of 10 for performance and competence. The EAT observed that such marks would indicate that the employee did not always achieve the required standard of performance and required close supervision. Yet the employee had never been criticised for poor performance and was not subject to any supervision. There was no need to consider the scores of other employees because the DDA did not require comparisons. It was clear that this individual had been undermarked by reason of his disability. The fact that many of the relevant events took place before the coming into force of the DDA did not stop the employment tribunal from looking at them in order to help draw inferences about the employer's conduct.[98]

Section 68(1) DDA 1995 defines the term 'employment' as being employment under either a contract of service or a contract to personally do any work. The EAT has interpreted this to mean that the dominant purpose of the contract was the execution of personal work or labour. Thus, for example, a subpostmaster who, though answerable to the Post Office, was not obliged to carry out the work in person, was unable to claim discrimination on the grounds of a disability.[99]

RECRUITMENT ADVERTISEMENTS AND THE DISABLED

Recruitment advertisements which discriminate against applicants with a disability are unlawful.[100] Where an advertisement might reasonably be understood to have indicated that a person might not get the job because of a disability or that an employer is unwilling to make adjustments for disabled people, and a disabled person who was not offered the post complains, the employment tribunal must take the advertisement into account. Unless it can be proved otherwise, the tribunal will assume that the reason the complainant did not get the job related to his or her disability.[101] It should be noted that, apart from section 6, employers are not obliged to treat disabled persons more favourably than others, although such discrimination in itself will not necessarily be unlawful.[102] Equally, there is nothing in this statute which prevents positive discrimination.

DISCRIMINATION AGAINST CONTRACT WORKERS

Similar provisions apply to contract workers.[103] It is unlawful for a 'principal', in relation to contract work, to discriminate against a disabled person. In *Abbey Life Assurance Co Ltd v Tansell*[104] the principal was described as the 'end-user' in a situation where a contract computer person was employed by his own limited liability company which had a contract with a consultancy who supplied services to the end-user. Taking a purposive approach to the statute, the Court of Appeal concluded that it was the end-user who should be the target for the complaint since the agency would simply justify their actions by reference to their instructions.

LODGING A COMPLAINT UNDER THE DDA

Claims that the DDA 1995 has been infringed must normally be lodged with an employment tribunal within three months of the act complained of. As with other tribunal proceedings, ACAS conciliation officers will make their services available in order to assist the parties to reach a settlement. There is an obligation upon the tribunal to enquire about what steps the employer has taken and whether they were reasonable.[105] If, however, a tribunal finds that a complaint is well-founded, it may provide any of the following remedies it considers just and equitable:

- a declaration as to the rights of the parties
- an order for compensation to be paid to the complainant
- a recommendation that the employer takes action within a specified period for the purpose of obviating or reducing the adverse effect on the complainant of any matter to which the complaint relates.[106]

It is made clear that compensation is available for injury to feelings, and there is no limit on the amount of money that can be awarded.[107]

HARASSMENT

Harassment is defined in a similar way to the provisions contained in the Regulations concerning discrimination on the grounds of sexual orientation and religion or belief (see Chapter 6). Here harassment occurs when a person subjects a disabled person, for a reason related to the person's disability, to unwanted conduct whose purpose is to

- violate the disabled person's dignity, or
- create an intimidating, hostile, degrading, humiliating or offensive environment for the disabled person.[108]

CASE STUDY

A man with a learning disability is often called 'stupid' and 'slow' by a colleague at work. This is harassment, whether or not the disabled man was present when the comments were made. They were said with the intention of humiliating him.[109]

VICTIMISATION

Section 55 makes it unlawful for a person to victimise another for:

- bringing proceedings under the DDA
- giving evidence or information in connection with such proceedings

- doing anything under the DDA

- alleging that another person contravened the DDA 1995 (unless the allegation was false and not made in good faith).

The rules regarding discrimination also apply to those whose relationship has come to an end. Thus it will be unlawful to discriminate against, or subject to harassment, any ex-employee where the discrimination or harassment arises out of, or is closely connected to, the previous employment relationship.

EMPLOYER LIABILITY UNDER THE DDA

As with sex and race discrimination, anything done by a person in the course of employment is treated as also done by the employer, whether or not it was done with the employer's approval. However, employers will not be liable if they can show that they took such steps as were reasonably practicable to prevent the employee's action.[110] Similarly, section 57 provides that anyone who knowingly aids another to perform an unlawful act is to be treated as having committed the same unlawful act.

The Disability Rights Commission[111] advises the government on ways to eliminate and reduce discrimination and on the operation of the Act generally. The Commission produces Codes of Practice and carries out formal investigations in particular sectors or where it is concerned that the law is not being followed. The Secretary of State can also produce Codes of Practice and has the power to appoint people to advise him or her on matters relating to the employment of disabled persons.[112]

PUBLIC AUTHORITIES

Section 49A of the DDA requires that public authorities will, in carrying out their functions, have due regard to:

- the need to eliminate unlawful discrimination

- the need to eliminate any harassment of disabled persons

- the need to take steps to take account of disabled persons' disabilities, even where this means treating the disabled persons more favourably than others

- the need to promote positive attitudes towards disabled persons and to encourage their participation in public life.

There is a duty to promote equality of opportunity between disabled persons and other persons. These obligations are further developed in Regulations[113] which require public authorities to prepare and publish a Disability Equality Scheme. This Scheme will show how the authority will fulfil its duty under Section 49A DDA.

KEY LEARNING POINTS

- Although the Age Regulations 2006 are similar to those measures taken on other grounds of discrimination, there are important differences, such as: direct discrimination can be justified if it is a proportionate means of achieving a legitimate aim.

- There is an entire part of the Regulations (Part 4) which lists general exemptions comprising some eight separate clauses, in comparison to the Regulations on Religion or Belief and also those concerned with Sexual Orientation, which have three such clauses. These exemptions reflect the complexity of regulation in this area, but include discrimination against the young, in terms of the lower rate of national minimum wage, and the provision of benefits for long service.

- A default retirement age is retained. It is difficult to see this as anything but a national retirement age which must be open to challenge as an inadequate implementation of the Framework Directive. The position of those workers aged 65 and over continues to be weak. They are to negotiate continuation of their working lives from a position of considerable weakness and the provisions removing the upper limit on unfair dismissal claims could turn out to have little meaning.

- A disability, within the meaning of the Act, is a physical or mental impairment which has a substantial and long-term adverse effect on the ability to carry out normal day-to-day activities.

- A tribunal must approach the question whether a person has a disability by reference to the impairment condition, the adverse effect condition, the substantial condition and the long-term condition.

- An employer has a duty to take steps and make adjustments in order not to place a disabled person at a substantial disadvantage.

- Public authorities have a duty to promote equality of opportunity between disabled persons and others.

Reinforce your understanding of this chapter by visiting www.cipd.co.uk/sss for activities, questions, weblinks and additional case studies

REFERENCES

1   SI 2006/1031

2   Directive 2000/78/EC

3   Directive 1997/80/EC

4   Case C-144/04 (2006) IRLR 143

5   *Hampton v Lord Chancellor* (2008) IRLR 258

6   Regulation 4(2)

7   Regulations 7(3) in relation to employees and Regulation 9(2) in relation to contract workers

8   Regulation 7(1)(a)–(c)

9   Regulation 7(7) ensures that those on fixed-term contracts and those who effect a constructive dismissal are included in the definition of dismissal from employment

10 Regulation 7(2)(a)–(d)

11 These are taken from the 2005 consultation.

12   Regulations 8(1) and 8(2)(a)

13   Regulation 8(2)(b)

14   For further definition of contract work see note on Regulation 10 below

15   Detriment does not include harassment, Regulation 2(2).

16   Regulation 9(5)

17   Regulation 20(1)

18   Regulation 20(3)

19   Regulation 21(6)(b)

20   Regulation 21(1)–(2)

21   Regulation 24(1)–(2)

22   Regulation 25(2) whether express or implied and whether precedent or subsequent

23   Regulations 27–34; this is an improvement on the draft Regulations 2005 which contained eleven such exceptions.

24   According to Regulation 30(1) 'employee' has the same meaning as in Section 230(1) Employment Rights Act 1996.

25   Regulation 30(1)

26   See Schedule 6 Amendments to unfair dismissal legislation

27   See *Johns v Solent SD Ltd* (2008) IRLR 820

28   Section 98ZA Employment Rights Act 1996

29   Section 98ZB(1) Employment Rights Act 1996

30   Section 98ZF Employment Rights Act 1996

31   Schedule 6 is concerned with the duty to consider working beyond retirement.

32   Section 98ZG Employment Rights Act 1996

33   Schedule 5 paragraphs 24–25 Age Regulations 2006

34   Paragraphs 2 and 4 Schedule 6

35   Paragraph 5 Schedule 6

36   Paragraph 5(5) Schedule 6

37   Paragraph 6 Schedule 6

38   Paragraph 7(3) Schedule 6

39   Paragraph 7(4) and 7(5) Schedule 6

40   Paragraph 9 Schedule 6

41   Paragraph 10 Schedule 6; the continuation of employment contained here does not count for the purposes of Sections 98ZA to 98ZH Employment Rights Act 1996.

42   Paragraph 11 Schedule 6; the rule on calculating a week's pay contained in Part XIV Employment Rights Act 1996 and the limit in Section 227(1) apply here; see paragraphs 11(3)–(5) Schedule 6

43   See Part VIIIA Employment Rights Act 1996

44   Section 1(3) National Minimum Wage Act 1998

45   Regulation 12(3) National Minimum Wage Regulations 1999

46   Regulation 32(1) Age Regulations

47   Regulation 32(2) Age Regulations

48   *Rolls-Royce plc v Unite the Union* (2009) IRLR 49

49   *MacCulloch v ICI plc* (2008) IRLR 846

50   *Loxley v BAE Systems Land Systems (Munitions and Ordnance) Ltd* (2008) IRLR 853

51   As with other areas of discrimination there are no statutory ceilings to the amount that can be awarded.

52   Regulation 41 Age Regulations 2006

53   See Regulations 41(3)–(4)

54   Regulation 41(5) Age Regulations 2006

55   Regulation 41(2) Age Regulations 2006

56   Including omission to act

57   Regulation 7 DDAA Regulations 2003: a small-firm exemption of firms with 15 or fewer employees is removed by 1 October 2004.

58   See section 2 and Schedule 1 paragraph 2(2)

59   (2008) IRLR 722

60   See the Code of Practice 2004 issued by the Disability Rights Commission

61   Section 3A(1) DDA as amended

62   Section 3A(4) and (5) DDA as amended

63   Taken from the DRC Code of Practice; see above (note 60)

64   *Jones v Post Office* (2001) IRLR 384

65   Taken from the DRC Code of Practice; see above (note 60)

66   (2008) IRLR 700

67   See *Guidance to be taken into account in determining questions relating to the definition of disability*, DTI, May 2006

68   Taken from the DTI Guidance; see above (note 67)

69   (2006) IRLR 112

70   Taken from the DTI Guidance; see above (note 67)

71   See the Disability Discrimination (Meaning of Disability) Regulations 1996, SI 1996/1455

72   Schedule 1 paragraphs 3 and 4 DDA 1995

73   Schedule 1 paragraph 6 DDA 1995

74   (2009) IRLR 54

75   (1999) IRLR 4

76   See *McNicol v Balfour Beatty Rail Maintenance Ltd* (2002) IRLR 711

77   See *Power v Panasonic UK Ltd* (2002) IRLR 153

78   *Chacón Navas v Eurest Colectividades SA* Case C-13/05 (2006) IRLR 706

79   See *Cruickshank v VAW Motorcast Ltd* (2002) IRLR 24

80   See *Ekpe v Commissioner of Metropolitan Police* (2001) IRLR 605

81   (2001) IRLR 23

82   See *Kapadia v London Borough of Lambeth* (2000) IRLR 699

83   (2001) IRLR 19

84   (2003) IRLR 353

85   (2002) IRLR 24

86   Regulation 3A(2) DDAA Regulations 2003

87   Section 4A DDA 1995 inserted by Regulation 5 DDAA Regulations 2003, with effect from 1 October 2004

88   *Environment Agency v Rowan* (2008) IRLR 20

89   See Code of Practice for the elimination of disability discrimination in employment 1996

90   See *British Gas Services Ltd v McCaull* (2001) IRLR 60

91   See *Rothwell v Pelikan Hardcopy Scotland Ltd* (2006) IRLR 24

92   (2003) IRLR 566

93   (2004) IRLR 703

94   See *Kenny v Hampshire Constabulary* (1999) IRLR 76

95   The Code of Practice makes helpful suggestions about job specifications and interviews.

96   Section 4 DDA 1995

97   (1998) IRLR 624

98   See also *Kent County Council v Mingo* (2000) IRLR 90 where a redeployment policy that gave preference to redundant or potentially redundant employees in preference to those with a disability amounted to discrimination in accordance with sections 5(1) and 5(2) DDA 1995.

99   *Sheehan v Post Office Counters Ltd* (1999) ICR 734

100 Section 10 DDA 2005

101 Section 11 DDA 1995

102 *Clark v Novacold Ltd* (1999) IRLR 318. Section 6(7) DDA 1995 states that 'Nothing in this part is to be taken to require an employer to treat a disabled person more favourably than he treats or would treat others.'

103 Section 12 DDA 1995

104 (2000) IRLR 387

105 See *Morse v Wiltshire County Council* (1998) IRLR 352

106 The Employment Tribunals (Constitution and Rules of Procedure) (Amendment) Regulations 1998 SI 1996/1757 oblige tribunals to give extended reasons for their decisions and enable them to make restricted reporting orders in DDA 1995 cases.

107 Section 8 and Schedule 3 DDA 1995

108 Section 4 DDA as amended

109 Taken from the DRC Code of Practice; see above (note 60)

110 Section 58 DDA 1995

111 Disability Rights Commission Act 1999

112 See sections 53 and 60 DDA 1995

113 The Disability Discrimination (Public Authorities) (Statutory Duties) Regulations 2005, SI 2005/2996

CHAPTER 8

Parental Rights

OVERVIEW

This chapter discusses the rights of parents in certain circumstances – in particular, the rights of pregnant women and those who have recently given birth together with the right to ordinary, compulsory and additional maternity leave. Other rights examined here are the rules associated with parental leave, adoption leave and paternity leave. We then consider the right to time off to deal with emergencies and the right to ask for more flexible working arrangements for the care of children and adults.

TIME OFF FOR ANTENATAL CARE

Irrespective of the length of service or the number of hours she works, a pregnant woman who, on the advice of a registered medical practitioner, midwife or health visitor, has made an appointment to receive antenatal care has the right not to be unreasonably refused time off during working hours to enable her to keep the appointment. Apart from the first appointment, the woman may be required to produce a certificate and some documentary evidence of the appointment for the employer's inspection. A woman who is permitted such time off is entitled to be paid for her absence at the appropriate hourly rate.[1]

If time off is refused or the employer has failed to pay the whole or part of any amount to which she feels she is entitled, a woman can complain to an employment tribunal. Unless the 'time-limit escape clause' applies, her claim must be presented within three months of the date of the appointment concerned.[2] Where a tribunal finds that the complaint is well-founded, it must make a declaration to that effect, and if time off has been unreasonably refused, the employer will be ordered to pay a sum equal to that which she would have been entitled to had the time off not been refused. If the complaint is that the employer failed to pay the amount to which she was entitled, the employer must pay the amount that the tribunal finds due to her. Any contractual remuneration paid to a woman in respect of a period of time off under this section, however, goes towards discharging any statutory liability to pay that arises. Conversely, any payment made as a result of this section goes towards discharging any contractual liability to pay for the period of time off.[3]

MATERNITY LEAVE

European Community law, in particular the Pregnant Workers Directive,[4] and the European Court of Justice have played an important part in developing rules that protect women during their pregnancy and maternity leave period. The ECJ has regarded discrimination against pregnant women as acts of sex discrimination which are in breach of Article 141, the Equal Treatment Directive[5] and the Equal Pay Directive.[6]

In *Pedersen*,[7] for example, the ECJ held that a policy which stated that workers who are unfit for work because of illness would receive full pay, but that pregnant women off sick from work for an illness related to the pregnancy would not, was in breach of Article 141 EC and the Equal Pay Directive, although there was no Community rule that pregnant women off sick were entitled to full pay as long as the rules applied equally to women and men who were absent through sickness.[8] This developed further the view of the ECJ as expressed in *Brown v Rentokil*,[9] in which the Court of Justice held that the dismissal of a woman at any time during her pregnancy for absences caused by illness resulting from that pregnancy is direct discrimination on the grounds of sex contrary to the EC Equal Treatment Directive.[10] Thus, in *Patefield v Belfast City Council*,[11] the replacement of a pregnant temporary agency worker with a permanent employee while the temporary worker was on maternity leave amounted to discrimination on the grounds of sex. The employer could have lawfully replaced her with a

CASE STUDY

Herrero v Instituto Madrileno Case C-294/04 (2006) IRLR 296

Carmen Herrero was a temporary worker for the Spanish National Institute for Health. She successfully applied for a permanent post, but was unable to take up the position on the required date because she was about to give birth. The employer extended the period for starting, but refused to give her seniority from the date of her appointment, saying that they would give it from the day she actually started work.

Mrs Herrero claimed that she had been discriminated against as a result of taking maternity leave.

The European Court of Justice agreed with her. It said that the Equal Treatment Directive was aimed at substantive equality, not just formal equality. The Directive had to be interpreted as forbidding any unfavourable treatment of a female worker because of her maternity leave. So when an employee is on maternity leave at the time of her appointment, deferring the start of her career, for the purposes of calculating seniority, to the date when she actually started in the post amounted to discrimination on the grounds of sex.

permanent replacement at any time before she went on leave. Replacing her while she was unavailable for work because of her pregnancy was to treat her less favourably than a man (who would not have become unavailable for work because of pregnancy) would have been treated. Similarly, in *GUS Home Shopping Ltd v Green and McLaughlin*,[12] not paying employees a loyalty bonus because they were absent from work owing to pregnancy was also held to amount to unlawful sex discrimination.

Part VIII of the ERA 1996 contains provisions for maternity rights and is more generous than the minimum requirements in the EU Directive. The provisions are further detailed in the Maternity and Parental Leave Regulations 1999[13] (MPL Regulations), as amended.

ORDINARY MATERNITY LEAVE AND THE ADDITIONAL MATERNITY LEAVE

Changes have resulted in the extension of the right to additional maternity leave for all those who are entitled to ordinary maternity leave, and the differences in treatment of those on ordinary and those on additional maternity leave have been limited. All qualifying employees are entitled to a maximum of 52 weeks' ordinary and additional maternity leave.

The dates of maternity leave are calculated as being periods before or after the 'expected week of childbirth'. This is defined as the week, beginning with midnight between Saturday and Sunday, in which it is expected that childbirth will occur.[14]

Regulation 2 of the MPL Regulations defines childbirth as 'the birth of a living child or the birth of a child whether living or dead after 24 weeks of pregnancy'. This means that a woman who gives birth to a stillborn child after 24 weeks of pregnancy will be entitled to the same leave as a person who gave birth to a live child.

The MPL Regulations state that an employee is entitled to ordinary and additional maternity leave if she satisfies certain conditions. These are:[15]

- that no later than the 15th week before her expected week of childbirth she notifies her employer of her pregnancy and the date on which she intends to start her ordinary maternity leave. If it is not reasonably practicable to inform the employer by this time, then the requirement is that notice must be provided as soon as is reasonably practicable. The employee may subsequently vary the date, provided that she does so at least 28 days before the date to be varied or the new date, whichever is earlier

- that the employee must give these notices in writing if the employer so requests

- that the employer is able to request, for inspection, a certificate from a registered medical practitioner or a registered midwife stating the expected week of childbirth. Failure to provide such a certificate, if requested, will remove the employee's entitlement to ordinary maternity leave.

Regulation 6 MPL Regulations 1999 provides that if the ordinary maternity leave has not commenced

- by the first day after the beginning of the fourth week before the expected week of childbirth on which the employee is absent from work wholly or partly because of pregnancy, or

- by the day on which childbirth occurs,

- then the ordinary maternity leave will be deemed to have commenced on that day, provided that the employee notifies her employer, in writing if requested, as soon as reasonably practicable.

Ordinary maternity leave continues for a period of 26 weeks from its commencement, or until the end of the compulsory maternity leave period, whichever is later.[16] This period can be extended if there is a statutory provision that prohibits the employee from working after the end of the ordinary maternity leave period, for a reason related to the fact that she had recently given birth. An employee who is entitled to ordinary maternity leave is also entitled to additional maternity leave. This additional maternity leave period commences on the day after the last day of the ordinary maternity leave period and continues for 26 weeks from the day on which it commenced.[17]

THE COMPULSORY MATERNITY LEAVE PERIOD

An employer may not permit an employee to work during her compulsory maternity leave period. An employer who allows an employee to work during this period will be subject to a fine.[18] This compulsory period will not be less than two weeks in length, commencing with the day on which childbirth occurs, and it is included in the ordinary leave period (see above).[19]

THE DATE OF THE RETURN TO WORK

To avoid confusion, an employer who has been notified under Regulation 4 about when an employee's ordinary maternity leave will commence, or has commenced, has an obligation to notify the employee of the date on which the additional maternity leave will end. This must be done within 28 days of the date on which the employer received notification of the commencement.[20]

If the employee wishes to return early and not take her full entitlement of maternity leave, then she must give 8 weeks' notice, in writing, of her intended return date. If she does not give the required notice, the employer may delay her return for up to 8 weeks.[21]

Employers and employees are encouraged to stay in contact with each other. Regulation 12A provides that employers are entitled to maintain 'reasonable' contact with the employee during maternity leave and enables the employee to do up to 10 days' work for her employer without prejudicing her maternity leave. Work done on any day constitutes a day's work. This is to be done by agreement between the employer and employee. The employer cannot demand that this work be done, nor can the employee demand the work.

Where the employer has engaged a replacement for the absent woman, provided that person has been informed in writing that his or her employment will be terminated on the woman's return to work, the dismissal of the replacement will be regarded as having been for a substantial reason (see Chapter 13). This does not mean that such a dismissal will always be fair, because a tribunal will have to be satisfied that it was reasonable to dismiss in the circumstances. For instance, it might be unfair to dismiss if the employer had a vacancy that the replacement could have filled.

If during ordinary or additional maternity leave it becomes clear that the employer cannot continue to employ the employee under her existing contract of employment by reason of redundancy, the employee is entitled to be offered any other suitable employment which may be available. The work to be done must be both suitable and appropriate in the circumstances, and its provisions as to the capacity and place of work and other terms and conditions to be not substantially less favourable than if she had continued to be employed under the previous contract.[22]

STATUTORY MATERNITY PAY

Employees who meet the qualifying conditions are entitled to receive statutory maternity pay (SMP) for the first 39 weeks of maternity leave (it is the government's intention to eventually extend this to 52 weeks).[23] Those who do not qualify may be entitled to Maternity Allowance. In order to qualify for SMP an employee must have been employed by the same employer for at least 26 weeks preceding the 14th week before the week in which the baby is due, and must have been earning at least at or above the lower earnings limit for the payment of National Insurance contributions (£95 per week for 2009/10) for at least 8 weeks.

SMP may start as early as the 11th week before the week in which the baby is due, but no later than the day following the baby's birth. If the pregnant woman is off sick from work for a pregnancy-related reason at the start of, or during, the four weeks before the week in which the baby is due, then SMP will start on the first day of absence.

During the first six weeks the employee will receive a sum equivalent to 90 per cent of her average weekly earnings (usually calculated as the 8-week period up to and including the 15th week before childbirth), with no upper limit. During the remaining weeks she will receive a flat-rate sum (£123.06 in 2009) or 90 per cent of average earnings if this is less than the £123.06 figure for 2009. The employer must deduct tax and National Insurance contributions from these sums.

The Maternity Allowance (MA) is managed by Jobcentre Plus. In order to qualify for MA a pregnant woman must

- not qualify for SMP

- have been employed or self-employed for at least 26 weeks in the 66-week period before the week in which the baby is due

- have earned at least £30 per week in any 13-week period during this time.

The earliest time at which MA can start is the 11th week before the week in which the baby is due. The amount paid (in 2009) is a flat rate of £123.06 per week or 90 per cent of the employee's average earnings if less than this amount.

PARENTAL LEAVE

An employee who has been continuously employed for a period of not less than one year and who has, or expects to have, responsibility for a child[24] is entitled to be absent from work on parental leave for the purposes of caring for that child.[25]

The entitlement to parental leave is in respect of a child who is less than five years old. When the child reaches his or her fifth birthday, the entitlement ceases. There are three exceptions to this:

- when a child is adopted or placed for adoption with an employee – In such cases the entitlement ceases on the fifth anniversary of the date on which the placement began and the upper age limit, therefore, cannot apply. The Regulations place an absolute upper age limit of the date of the child's eighteenth birthday.

- when a child is in receipt of, or entitled to, a disability living allowance – In this case the upper age limit of 18 years applies.

- when the employer exercises his or her right to delay parental leave (see below) and this results in the child's passing the fifth birthday – The entitlement can still be taken at the end of the period for which leave has been postponed, even though the child will now be over five years old.

CASE STUDY

Rodway v South Central Trains (2005) IRLR 583

Mr Christopher Rodway was employed as a train conductor and had a son, aged 2 years, who lived with his former partner. His former partner informed him that he would have to look after his son on Saturday 26 July. He applied for annual leave for that day but was told that this could not be guaranteed. Because of this uncertainty he applied for parental leave for that day, but this was refused on the grounds that his job could not be covered. He took the day off and was subsequently disciplined for it.

He brought a complaint stating that he had suffered a detriment because he had sought to take parental leave.

The Court of Appeal held that the default regulations in Schedule 2 of the MPL Regulations 1999 state that an employee 'may not take parental leave in a period other than the period which constitutes a week's leave'. In other words such leave, except where it is in respect of a child entitled to a disability living allowance, must be taken in blocks of one week, not in single days. Such an approach, according to the Court, made practical sense as employers might well prefer to be able to make arrangements for temporary employees to cover for a week during an employee's absence, rather than to face the problems arising from an employee wishing to be away for a single day or two odd days.

An employee is entitled to 13 weeks' leave in respect of any individual child.[26] The leave entitlement is for 'any individual child', so that an employee/parent of multiple-birth children will be entitled to 13 weeks' leave in respect of each child. This figure is increased to 18 weeks for those with responsibility for a child who is entitled to a disability living allowance.[27]

NOTICE PROVISIONS

Before employees can exercise their rights to parental leave, they must, unless otherwise stipulated by collective or workforce agreements (see Chapter 2):

- comply with any request from the employer to produce for inspection evidence of the employee's responsibility or expected responsibility for the child as well as evidence of the child's age

- give the employer notice of the period of leave that is proposed. This notice must specify the dates on which the leave is to begin and end and be given at least 21 days before the date upon which the leave is to start. Where the leave to be taken is in respect of a child to be adopted and the leave is to begin on the date of the placement, then the notice must specify the week in which the placement is expected to occur and the period of leave. The notice is to be given to the employer at least 21 days before the beginning of that week, or if that is not reasonably practicable, as soon as it is so. These rules also apply to a situation where the employee is the father of the child and the leave is to be taken when the child is born (but see below on paternity leave)

- ensure that the employer has not postponed the leave in accordance with the MPL Regulations (see below).

POSTPONING PARENTAL LEAVE[28]

An employer may postpone a period of parental leave, subject to any collective or workforce agreements, where:

- the employee has applied and given the necessary notice, and

- the operation of the employer's business would be unduly disrupted if the employee took leave during the period identified in the notice, and

- the employer permits the employee to take a period of leave of the same length that had been requested within six months of the date on which it was due to begin, and

- the employer gives notice in writing of the postponement, stating the reasons for it and specifying the dates on which the employee may take parental leave. This notice must be given to the employee not later than seven days after the employee's notice was given to the employer.

An employee may complain to an employment tribunal if the employer has unreasonably postponed a period of parental leave or attempted to prevent the employee from taking it.[29] The tribunal may award such compensation that it considers 'just and equitable'.

TERMS AND CONDITIONS DURING PERIODS OF MATERNITY LEAVE AND PARENTAL LEAVE

Sections 71(4) ERA and 73(4) 1996 state that an employee on ordinary or additional maternity leave is:

- entitled to the benefit of the terms and conditions of employment which would have applied had she not been absent. This does not include terms and conditions relating to remuneration[30]

- bound by obligations arising under those terms and conditions

- entitled to return to a job of a prescribed kind (see below).

Sections 77(1) to (4) ERA 1996 make the same provisions for those on parental leave. In addition, Regulation 17 MPL Regulations 1999 states that employees on parental leave are:

- entitled to the benefit of the employer's implied obligation of trust and confidence (see Chapter 3) and any terms of employment relating to

  - notice of the termination of the employment contract by the employer

  - compensation in the event of redundancy

  - disciplinary and grievance procedures

- bound by an implied obligation of good faith to the employer and any terms and conditions of employment relating to

  - notice of the termination of the employment contract by the employee

  - the disclosure of confidential information

  - the acceptance of gifts or other benefits, or

  - the employee's participation in any other business.

THE RIGHT TO RETURN TO WORK AFTER MATERNITY LEAVE OR PARENTAL LEAVE

The Regulations distinguish between those employees who take shorter periods of leave from those who take longer periods. Thus, if an employee is returning to work after a period of ordinary maternity leave or of parental leave of less than four weeks' duration, that employee will be entitled to return to the job in which she was employed before her absence. This is provided that the period of leave was an isolated one or that it was the last of two consecutive periods of statutory leave which did not include any periods of additional maternity or adoptive leave, or parental leave of more than four weeks.[31]

Unless subject to dismissal through redundancy, an employee who takes additional maternity leave or parental leave of more than four weeks is entitled to return from that leave to the job in which he or she was employed prior to the absence. If this is not reasonably practicable, the employer must permit the employee to return to another job which is both suitable and appropriate in the circumstances.[32] This right to return to work is a right to return with seniority, pension rights and similar rights preserved as they would have been if she had not been absent.[33]

PATERNITY LEAVE

The provisions relating to paternity leave, introduced by the Employment Act 2002[34] and the Paternity and Adoption Leave Regulations 2002 (the PAL Regulations)[35] were amended by the Maternity and Parental Leave etc and the Paternity and Adoption Leave (Amendment) Regulations 2006, which came into effect on 1 October 2006.[36] In addition, the Work and Families Act 2006 provides for Regulations to introduce additional paternity leave under certain circumstances. Entitlement to paternity leave is, according to Regulation 4(1), for the purpose of caring for a child or supporting the child's mother. In order to qualify for paternity leave an individual must meet certain conditions and comply with the notice requirements.[37] The conditions are:

- that the employee has been continuously employed for a period of at least 26 weeks ending with the week immediately preceding the 14th week before the expected week of childbirth
- that the employee is the father of the child or, if not the father, then married to, or partner of, the child's mother
- that if he is the father, he has, or expects to have, responsibility for bringing up the child; if he is not the father but the partner of the mother, that he has, or expects to have, the main responsibility (apart from any responsibility of the mother) for bringing up the child.

There are a number of complications to this simple formula, which are dealt with by the Regulations. These are, firstly, that if the child is born earlier than expected, then the original date is still used in order to calculate whether the employee has 26 weeks' service before the 14th week preceding the expected week of childbirth. Secondly, if the child's mother dies, her husband or partner would still be assumed to be married to or the partner of the mother. Thirdly, an employee will be assumed to have responsibility for bringing up the child even if the child is stillborn after 24 weeks of pregnancy or dies. All these measures are aimed at ensuring that the employee is still entitled to paternity leave when these issues arise.

The notice and evidence requirements are:[38]

- An employee must give his employer notice of his intention to take paternity leave, specifying the expected week of childbirth, the length of the period of leave (see below) and the date on which the employee has chosen that his period of leave will begin.
- This notice must be given to the employer in or before the 15th week before the expected week of childbirth, or if it was not reasonably practicable to do so, then as soon as it is so.
- If the employer requests it, the employee must give a signed declaration stating

that the purpose of the leave is either for caring for the child or supporting the child's mother and that he satisfies the conditions of entitlement listed above.

Unlike parental leave, multiple births from the same pregnancy do not have any effect on the amount of paternity leave the father is entitled to.[39] An employee may take one or two weeks' leave in respect of the child (or children). This leave must be taken between the date of the birth and a date 56 days after that. It is for the employee to choose whether he takes the leave commencing with the date of the birth or at some time after that, within the 56-day period.[40] Partly because dates of birth are not entirely predictable, there are opportunities for the employee to vary the start date for the leave, provided that the employee gives the employer 28 days' notice or, if this is not reasonably practicable, then gives such notice as soon as it is reasonably practicable.

Employees who are married to, or the partner of, an adopter have the same entitlement to paternity leave. They must meet similar conditions and abide by similar notice rules. The important date is that on which the child is placed with the adopter, as this is the date from which the critical 56-day period commences.[41] Regulations resulting from the Work and Pensions Act 2006 will provide for the extension of paternity leave up to a maximum of 26 weeks.

Other rules relating to paternity leave are identical to those connected with maternity leave. There is the same right to return to the job in which employed before the absence, in a case where the paternity leave is an isolated period of leave or the last of two consecutive periods of statutory leave not including additional maternity leave or a period of parental leave of more than four weeks. Where other combinations of leave occur, there is the right to return to the same job or, if that is not reasonably practicable, to one that is similar and appropriate in the circumstances. The employee will return with his seniority, pension and other rights as if he had not been absent.[42]

ADOPTION LEAVE

The right to adoption leave was introduced by the Employment Act 2002 and the PAL Regulations 2002.[43] Some amendments were made by the 2006 Regulations, which apply to an employee whose child is expected to be placed with him or her for adoption on or after 1 April 2007. In addition, the Work and Families Act 2006 provides for Regulations to introduce additional adoption leave under certain circumstances. An employee who meets the necessary conditions and complies with the notice and evidential requirements is entitled to adoption leave. As with maternity leave this is divided into ordinary and additional adoption leave, although there is no equivalent of compulsory maternity leave.

An employee is entitled to adoption leave if the employee[44]

- is the child's adopter
- has been continuously employed for a period of not less than 26 weeks ending

with the week in which the employee was notified of being matched with the child, and

- has notified the agency that he agrees that the child should be placed with him on the date of placement.

An employee's entitlement to adoption leave is not affected by the placement for adoption of more than one child as part of the same arrangement.

ORDINARY ADOPTION LEAVE

An employee may choose between two options when deciding when ordinary adoption leave starts. The choices are between the date on which the child is placed for adoption, and some other predetermined date which is no more than 14 days before the date on which the child is expected to be placed, and no later than this date. Thus the notice and evidential requirements are[45]

- An employee must give the employer notice of intention to take ordinary adoption leave, specifying the date on which the child is expected to be placed for adoption and the date on which the employee has chosen when the period of leave should begin.

- The notice must be given to the employer no more than seven days after the date on which the employee has been notified of having been matched with a child or, if this was not reasonably practicable, then as soon as it is so.

- Where the employer requests it, the employee must provide evidence, in the form of documents issued by the adoption agency, of the name and address of the agency, the name and birth date of the child, the date on which the employee was notified of the match and the date on which the agency expects to place the child with the employee.

Within 28 days of the receipt of the employee's notification, the employer must give the employee notice of when the period of additional adoption leave, if there is an entitlement, will end. There are also provisions for the employee to vary the start date, subject to notice to the employer.

ADDITIONAL ADOPTION LEAVE

An employee is entitled to additional adoption leave if
- the child was placed with the employee for adoption
- the employee took ordinary adoption leave
- the ordinary adoption leave did not end prematurely (see below).

The leave begins on the day after the last day of ordinary adoption leave.[46]

PREMATURE ENDING

Ordinary adoption leave and additional adoption leave will normally last for 26 weeks each. It may be less, of course, if the employee were dismissed before the end of this period.[47] It may also end early if the placement is disrupted.[48] The circumstances where this applies are:

- where the adoption leave commences prior to the placement and the employee is subsequently notified that the placement will not take place
- if the child dies
- if the child is returned to the adoption agency under section 30(3) of the Adoption Act 1976.

Unless the employee has less than eight weeks to go before his or her leave comes to an end, the adoption leave, in these circumstances, will end after a period of eight weeks after the week in which the employee was informed that the placement is not to be made, or the child dies, or the child is returned.

OTHER ISSUES

The other matters concerning adoption leave are identical to those concerning maternity leave, as outlined earlier in this chapter. These matters concern the right to return to work,[49] notice periods for early return,[50] matters concerning terms and conditions during adoption leave, and contact between the employer and employee during adoption leave, including the right to carry out up to 10 days' work with the employer without bringing the statutory adoption leave period to an end.[51]

TIME OFF FOR DEPENDANTS

Section 57A ERA 1996 states that an employee is entitled to be permitted by the employer to take a reasonable amount of time off during the employee's working hours in order to take action necessary

- to provide assistance on an occasion when a dependant falls ill, gives birth or is injured or assaulted
- to make arrangements for the provision of care for a dependant who is ill or injured
- in consequence of the death of a dependant
- because of the unexpected disruption or termination of arrangements for the care of a dependant, or
- to deal with an incident which involves a child of the employee and which occurs unexpectedly in a period during which an educational establishment which the child attends is responsible for him or her.

The use of the words 'unexpected disruption' is not necessarily intended to mean a 'sudden' and unexpeced disruption. Thus a mother who knew that she had a problem with her child care arrangements in two weeks' time, but failed to solve the problem in the interim, is still entitled to time off at the end of the two weeks. Although the tribunal is entitled to take into account the time gap between the problem arising and the taking of time off, it is not necessarily conclusive.[52]

There is an obligation on the employee to inform the employer of the reason for absence and of its duration as soon as reasonably practicable. The time off is limited to incidents involving a dependant, who is defined as:[53]

- a spouse
- a child
- a parent
- a person who lives in the same household as the employee but who is not an employee, tenant, lodger or boarder
- any person who reasonably relies on the employee for assistance if he or she is ill or assaulted[54]
- any person who reasonably relies on the employee to make arrangements for the provision of care in the event of illness or injury.[55] The references to illness or injury include mental illness or injury.[56]

Section 57B ERA 1996 asserts that an employee may apply to an employment tribunal to complain about a failure to be allowed time off. A tribunal may make a declaration and award compensation which the tribunal considers 'just and equitable in the circumstances'.

In *Qua v John Ford Morrison Solicitors*[57] the EAT considered a situation where a single mother with a child who had medical problems was dismissed after taking time off on 17 different days. The EAT held that the right to time off did not enable employees to take time off for themselves to look after a sick child, except for enabling the parent to deal with an immediate crisis. Such longer-term care would be covered by the employee's parental leave entitlement. The right to time off is the right to a 'reasonable' amount of time in order to take action that is 'necessary'. The decision as to whether it was necessary depended upon a number of factors, including, for example:

- the nature of the incident that has occurred
- the closeness of the relationship between the employee and the dependant, and
- the extent to which anyone else was available to help out.

All of this would depend upon the individual circumstances. An employee is not, however, entitled to unlimited amounts of time off, and the employer may take into account the number and length of previous absences, as well as the dates on which they occurred, when deciding whether the time off sought for a subsequent occasion is reasonable. The time off is to deal with unforeseen circumstances. Thus if a child were known to suffer regular relapses needing attention, then time off for dealing with these illnesses would not come within the terms of section 57A ERA 1996.

In determining the reasonableness of the amount of time taken off, the disruption to an employer's business by the employee's absence cannot be taken into account. This, unfortunately perhaps for an employer, is not a relevant factor.

FLEXIBLE WORKING

Section 47 of the Employment Act 2002 inserted sections 80F to 80I into the ERA 1996, concerned with flexible working. There are also two sets of Regulations spelling out the details of employee rights. These are the Flexible Working (Eligibility, Complaints and Remedies) Regulations 2002[58] and the Flexible Working (Procedural Requirements) Regulations 2002.[59] Section 12(10) of the Work and Families Act 2006 changed the definition of a child to include all persons up to the age of 18 years and introduced in section 12(2)(b) the right to include adults who needed care.

A qualifying employee may make an application to the employer to vary his or her contractual terms in relation to hours of work, times when required to work or place of work. The purpose of the application is to enable the employee to care for a child or an adult with whom the care has a relationship prescribed by the Secretary of State.

A qualifying employee is an individual who

- has been continually employed for a period of not less than 26 weeks, and
- is the mother, father, adopter, guardian or foster parent of the child, or is married to, or partner of, the child's mother, father, adopter, guardian or foster parent, and
- has, or expects to have, responsibility for the upbringing of the child.

The application must be made by 14 days before the child reaches the age of 6 or, if disabled, 18 years. The application must be in writing.

The employer must hold a meeting with the employee within 28 days from the date when the application is made, unless the contract variation is agreed to and the employee is notified accordingly.

Where the meeting is held, the employer must give notice, in writing, of the decision within 14 days of the meeting. The notice must consist of

- *either* the employer's agreement, and the date on which the change becomes effective
- *or* notice of the employer's decision to refuse the application, together with the reasons and details of an appeals procedure.

An employee is entitled to appeal, in writing, against the employer's decision within a further 14 days. The appeal meeting itself must take place within 14 days of the date of the appeal notice and the employer then has a further 14 days in which to give written notice of the decision. This can be either agreement and the date on which the change will come into effect, or refusal with reasons.

All these periods of time can be extended by agreement between the employer and the employee.

The times and dates of the meetings must be convenient for both parties and the employee has the right to be accompanied by a single companion. The employee may complain to an employment tribunal and obtain an award of up to two weeks' pay if the employer fails to allow and make provision for the employee to be accompanied.

The employer may only refuse the application for one of these reasons:

- burden of additional costs
- detrimental effect on the ability to meet customer demand
- inability to reorganise work amongst existing staff
- inability to recruit additional staff
- detrimental impact on quality
- detrimental impact on performance
- insufficiency of work during the periods the employee proposes to work
- planned structural changes
- such other grounds as the Secretary of State may specify.

An employee may complain to an employment tribunal that his or her employer has failed to comply with the duty under section 80G, or that a decision to reject the application was based upon incorrect facts. Failure to comply with the duty includes a failure to hold the required meeting, or a failure to notify a decision. The maximum amount of compensation that can be awarded is 8 weeks' pay.

CASE STUDY

Commotion Ltd v Rutty (2006) IRLR 171

Mrs Rutty was an employee of a mail order company when she became legally responsible for the care of her grandchild. She had problems coping with her full-time job as a warehouse assistant and informally asked her employer if she could change to a three-day week. After being turned down, she put in a formal application under section 80F ERA 1996. Her employer refused the application giving as the reason that it would have a detrimental effect on their ability to meet customer demand and a detrimental effect on performance.

Mrs Rutty resigned and claimed, amongst other matters, a breach of her right to request flexible working.

The EAT held that the employer had failed to establish that they had refused her request on one of the grounds set out in section 80G ERA 1996. In order to establish whether or not the employer's decision to reject the request was based on incorrect facts, the tribunal is entitled to enquire what would be the effect of granting the application – eg could it have been coped with without disruption? What did other staff feel about it? Could they have made up the time? In this case the tribunal was entitled to find that the evidence did not support the employer's statements about the effects of agreeing to the request.

PROTECTION FROM DETRIMENT[60]

An employee is entitled not to be subjected to any detriment by any act, or failure to act, on the part of the employer for one of the following reasons:

- that she is pregnant or has given birth to a child

- that the employee is subject to a relevant requirement or a relevant recommendation as defined by section 66(2) ERA 1996

- that she took paternity leave, ordinary or additional maternity or adoption leave or availed herself of the benefits of her terms and conditions of employment during such leave

- that the employee took time off under section 57A ERA 1996

- that the employee declined to sign a workforce agreement for the purposes of the MPL Regulations 1999

- that the employee was a representative of the workforce, a candidate for election as a representative or performed any activities or functions related to being a representative or a candidate.

UNFAIR DISMISSAL[61]

It is automatically unfair to dismiss an employee, irrespective of the length of service, if:

- the reason or principal reason for dismissal is that she is pregnant or is in any way connected with her pregnancy

- she is dismissed during her maternity leave period and the reason or principal reason for dismissal is that she has given birth or is connected with her having given birth[62]

- she is dismissed after the end of her maternity leave period and the reason or principal reason for dismissal is that she took, or availed herself of the benefits of, maternity leave, adoptive leave or paternity leave

- the reason or principal reason for dismissal is a requirement or recommendation referred to in section 66 ERA 1996 (suspension on maternity grounds)

- she is dismissed during the maternity or adoption leave period and the principal reason for dismissal is that she is redundant and the employer has not offered her any suitable alternative vacancy

- the employee failed to return to work after additional maternity or adoption leave and the employer had failed to notify the employee of the date on which the period would end and the employee reasonably believed that the period had not ended; or the employer had given the employee less than 28 days' notice of the date on which the period would end, and it was not reasonably practicable for the employee to return on that date[63]

- the employee took time off for maternity leave, adoption leave, parental leave or time off for dependants in accordance with section 57A of the ERA 1996

- the employee refused to sign a workforce agreement for the purposes of the MPL Regulations 1999

- the reason is that, for the purposes of the MPL Regulations, the employee was a representative of the workforce, stood for election as a representative or performed any of the functions or activities of such a representative or a candidate for such representation.

Where an employee is dismissed while she is pregnant or during her maternity leave period, she is entitled to written reasons for her dismissal. This right does not depend on any qualifying period of service and the woman does not need formally to request the reasons.[64]

There are exceptions to the application of these automatically unfair dismissal rules. They do not apply if it is not reasonably practicable for an employer to offer a suitable position, but an associated employer does offer such a job and the employee accepts or unreasonably refuses that offer.

The onus for showing that these provisions are satisfied rests on the employer.

RISK ASSESSMENT

Where an employee is pregnant, has given birth within the past six months or is breast-feeding, the employer must assess the special risks which the woman faces in the workplace and take measures to avoid them.[65] If preventive action is impossible or would be inadequate to avoid the risk, the employee's working conditions or hours of work must be altered. If that would be unreasonable or would not avoid the risk, the employer must offer suitable alternative work, or where none is available, suspend her from work on full pay.[66] Alternative work will be suitable if it is both suitable in relation to the employee and appropriate for her to do in the circumstances. The terms and conditions applicable must not be substantially less favourable than those which apply to her normal work. An employment tribunal may award compensation to a woman if her employer fails to offer suitable alternative employment.[67] An example of this can be seen in *British Airways v Moore and Botterill*.[68] The case concerned two cabin crew employees who became grounded, by agreement, after their 16th week of pregnancy. They were given alternative duties and continued to receive their normal levels of pay less the allowances that they had previously received while flying. Despite the fact that these arrangements were in accord with a collective agreement, the EAT held that the reduction in pay was enough to show that the employees concerned had not been offered suitable alternative employment.

A woman who is suspended on maternity grounds is entitled to be paid by her employer during the suspension. However, this right is lost if she unreasonably refuses an offer of suitable alternative work. The remuneration payable is a week's wage for each week of suspension and pro rata for any part of a week of entitlement. Any contractual remuneration paid goes towards discharging the employer's liability. Conversely, any suspension payment goes towards discharging any contractual obligation the employer may have. Where an employer fails to pay all or any of the amount due, an employment tribunal will order the employer to pay the remuneration owed.[69]

KEY LEARNING POINTS

- A pregnant woman is entitled to paid time off for antenatal care.

- The maternity leave period is divided into ordinary, compulsory and additional leave periods; adoptive leave is divided into ordinary and additional leave periods.

- An employee has the right to return to his or her job under the original contract of employment and on terms and conditions not less favourable than those which would have applied if the employee had not taken maternity, adoption, parental or paternity leave; if this is not practicable, the right is to be offered a suitable and appropriate alternative position.

- Where an employee is pregnant, has given birth within the last six months, or is breast-feeding, the employer must assess the special risks faced by the woman in the workplace and take measures to avoid those risks.

- It is automatically unfair, regardless of length of service, to dismiss an employee for reasons connected with pregnancy or the taking of maternity, adoption, parental or paternity leave.

- Parents with child responsibilities are entitled to time off for parental leave for a maximum of 13 weeks or 18 weeks for a child in receipt of invalidity benefit.

- Employees are entitled to time off to provide assistance for dependants in certain circumstances.

- A qualifying employee may make an application to the employer to vary his or her contractual terms in relation to hours of work, times when required to work or place of work. The purpose of the application is to enable the employee to care for a child.

Reinforce your understanding of this chapter by visiting www.cipd.co.uk/sss for activities, questions, weblinks and additional case studies

REFERENCES

1 See section 56(1) ERA 1996

2 Section 57 ERA 1996

3 Section 56(6) ERA 1996

4 Directive 92/85/EEC of 19 October 1992

5 Directive 76/207/EEC, amended by Directive 2002/37/EC and, from August 2009, consolidated into Directive 2006/54/EC

6 Directive 75/117/EEC, also to be consolidated into Directive 2006/54/EC from August 2009

7 *Handels- og Kontorfunktionærernes Forbund i Danmark acting on behalf of Pedersen v Fællesforeningen for Danmarks Brugsforeningen acting on behalf of Kvickly Skive* Case C-66/96 (1999) IRLR 55, ECJ

8 *North Western Health Board v McKenna* Case C-191/03 (2005) IRLR 895

9   Case 394/96 (1998) IRLR 445

10 See also *Caledonia Bureau Investment & Property v Caffrey* (1998) IRLR 110

11 (2000) IRLR 664

12 (2001) IRLR 75

13 SI 1999/3312

14 Regulation 2(1) MPL Regulations 1999

15 Regulation 4 MPL Regulations 1999

16 Regulation 7 MPL Regulations 1999

17 Regulation 7(4) MPL Regulations 1999

18 Section 72(5) ERA 1996

19 Section 72(3) ERA 1996 and Regulation 8 MPL Regulations 1999

20 Regulation 7(6) MPL Regulations 1999

21 Regulation 11 MPL Regulations 1999

22 Regulation 10 MPL Regulations 1999

23 Section 171ZN(2) Social Security Contributions and Benefits Act 1992

24 Responsibility for a child means having parental responsibility or being registered
    as the child's father in accordance with the provisions of the Births and Deaths
    Registration Act 1953 or the Registration of Births, Deaths and Marriages (Scotland) Act
    1965 – Regulation 13(2) MPL Regulations 1999.

25 Regulation 13(1) MPL 1999

26 Regulation 14 MPL Regulations 1999

27 Regulation 14(1)(A) MPL Regulations 1999

28 Schedule 2 section 6 MPL Regulations 1999

29 Section 80 ERA 1996

30 Section 73(5) ERA 1996

31 Regulation 18(1) MPL Regulations 1999

32 Regulation 18 MPL Regulations 1999

33 Regulation 18A(1) MPL Regulations 1999

34 Now contained in sections 80A–80D ERA 1996 and sections 171ZA–171ZK Social Security
    Contributions and Benefits Act 1992

35 SI 2002/2788

36 SI 2006/2014

37 Regulation 4(1) PAL Regulations 2002

38 Regulation 6 PAL Regulations 2002

39 Regulation 4(6) PAL Regulations 2002

40 Regulation 5 PAL Regulations 2002

41 See Regulations 8–11 PAL Regulations 2002

42 See Regulations 12–14 PAL Regulations 2002

43 Now contained in sections 75A–75D ERA 1996 and sections 171ZL–171ZT Social Security
    Contributions and Benefits Act 1992

44 Regulation 15 PAL Regulations 2002

45 Regulation 17 PAL Regulations 2002

46 Regulation 20 PAL Regulations 2002

47 Regulation 24 PAL Regulations 2002

48 Regulation 22 PAL Regulations 2002

49 Regulation 26 PAL Regulations 2002

50 Regulation 25 PAL Regulations 2002; changed to 8 weeks from 28 days for those whose adoption placements start after 1 April 2007

51 Regulation 21 PAL Regulations 2002 and Regulation 21A for those whose adoption placements start after 1 April 2007

52 *Royal Bank of Scotland v Harrison* (2009) IRLR 28

53 Section 57A(3) ERA 1996

54 Section 57A(4)(a) ERA 1996

55 Section 57A(4)(b) ERA 1996

56 Section 57B ERA 1996

57 (2003) IRLR 184

58 SI 2002/3236

59 SI 2002/3207

60 Regulation 19 MPL Regulations 1999 and section 47C ERA 1996

61 See Regulation 20 MPL Regulations 1999

62 In *Rees v Apollo Watch Repairs* (1996) ICR 467 it was held that a woman was unfairly dismissed during her maternity leave after the employers hired a replacement whom they found to be more efficient.

63 Regulation 4 MPL Regulations 1999 and Regulation 29 PAL Regulations 2002

64 Section 92(4) ERA 1996

65 See the revised ACOP issued with the 1999 Health and Safety (Miscellaneous Modifications) Regulations; the revised ACOP refers employers to HSE guidance entitled *New and Expectant Mothers at Work: A guide for employers.*

66 Regulation 16 of the Management of Health and Safety at Work Regulations 1999, SI 1999/3242

67 Sections 66–67 ERA 1996

68 *British Airways (European Operations at Gatwick) Ltd v Moore and Botterill* (2000) IRLR 296

69 Sections 68–70 ERA 1996

CHAPTER 9

Health and Safety at Work

This chapter is a slightly amended version of one originally written by Professor
Brenda Barrett of Middlesex University

OVERVIEW

In this chapter we examine some aspects of health and safety law. Having distinguished
between injury prevention and injury compensation law, consideration is given to the Health
and Safety at Work Act 1974, noting the roles of the Health and Safety Commission and
Executive, and the duties of employers to ensure the health, safety and welfare of their
employees and others. There is then an examination of the Management of Health and
Safety at Work Regulations 1999 and a brief description of other Regulations, including the
COSHH Regulations 2002. Finally, we consider the Access to Medical Reports Act and issues
concerning an employer's wish to consult an employee's medical records.

INJURY PREVENTION AND INJURY COMPENSATION

The primary purpose of the law should be to make work safe so that it does not
cause personal injury – but provision also has to be made for the compensation
of people who nevertheless suffer injury. 'Injury' covers both physical and mental
impairment caused by accident or illness. In the UK legislation with criminal
sanctions imposes duties on employers and others for the purpose of injury
prevention. The victims of work-related injury may sue in the civil courts for
damages, claiming that the defendant has caused the injury either by negligent
conduct or by breaking a statutory duty. This chapter focuses on the principal
preventative legislation but makes some reference to compensation case law.

SCOPE OF THE CURRENT INJURY PREVENTION LEGISLATION

The principal Act is the Health and Safety at Work Act 1974 (HASAWA 1974).
It is a framework Act enabling the making of regulations and it is the vehicle
through which EC directives are normally implemented. An important feature
of the Act and the Management of Health and Safety at Work Regulations 1999
(MHSW Regulations),[1] the most important and comprehensive set of regulations,
is that they apply to people rather than premises and, with certain exceptions,

all persons are covered. The Act sets out general duties which employers have towards their employees, other workers and members of the public. It also imposes duties on employees to protect themselves and others.

The MHSW Regulations generally make more explicit what employers are required to do to manage health and safety under the Act. Like the Act these Regulations apply to every work activity. They also seek to protect persons other than those at work against risks to their health and safety arising out of, or in connection with, work activities. While a breach of HASAWA 1974 or Regulations issued under it amounts to a criminal offence, civil liability arises only if there is a failure to comply with Regulations.[2]

The Act is administered by the Health and Safety Commission (HSC) and the Health and Safety Executive (HSE).[3] HSC is responsible for keeping the law under review and for initiating research. HSE has to make arrangements for enforcing the law, either through its own or local authority inspectors. Where the Health and Safety Commission (HSC) considers the law is not functioning well, it has three main options. It can issue:

1   *Guidance*, which has three purposes. Firstly, to help people understand the law by interpreting it; secondly, to help people comply with the law; and thirdly, to provide technical advice. Guidance has no standing in a prosecution.

2   *Approved codes of practice* (ACOP), which offer practical guidance about how to comply with the law. A failure to observe any provision of an approved code of practice does not of itself render a person liable to any civil or criminal proceedings. However, such a code is admissible in evidence in a criminal court, and proof of a failure to meet its requirements will be sufficient to establish a contravention of a statutory provision, unless a court is satisfied that the provision was complied with in some other way.[4] The HSC considers that a duty-holder who has complied with an ACOP will have done enough to satisfy the law on the specific issues addressed by the code.

3   *Regulations*, which are made under the HASAWA 1974. Regulations are proposed by HSC and approved by Parliament. They identify specific risks and set out particular actions that must be taken.[5] In practice most Regulations are made to comply with EC Directives.

THE HEALTH AND SAFETY AT WORK ACT 1974

Section 2(1) provides that 'It shall be the duty of every employer to ensure, so far as is reasonably practicable, the health, safety and welfare at work of all his employees.' The inclusion of the words 'so far as reasonably practicable' was unsuccessfully challenged[6] by the European Commission as an incorrect implementation of Directive 89/391 which introduced measures to encourage improvements in health and safety. The European Court of Justice held that the Commission were arguing that the legislation should impose a no-fault liability on employers for all accidents in the workplace – a proposition which the Court did not accept.

The matters to which this duty extends include:[7]

- the provision and maintenance of plant[8] and systems of work that are, so far as is reasonably practicable, safe and without risks to health

- arrangements for ensuring, so far as is reasonably practicable, safety and absence of risks to health in connection with the use, handling, storage and transport of articles and substances[9]

- the provision of such information, instruction, training and supervision as is necessary to ensure, so far as is reasonably practicable, the health and safety at work of employees

- so far as is reasonably practicable as regards any place of work under the employer's control, the maintenance of it in a condition which is safe and without risks to health and the provision and maintenance of means of access to and egress from it which are safe and without such risks

- the provision and maintenance of a working environment for his employees that is, so far as is reasonably practicable, safe, without risks to health, and adequate as regards facilities and arrangements for their welfare at work.[10] (On working time see Chapter 11.)

HASAWA 1974 requires the duty-holder (usually an employer) to ensure that systems set down on paper are actually observed. In *R* v *Gateway Foodmarkets Ltd*,[11] the employer set down procedures for the maintenance of lifts in all its stores. However, when failings at store management level led to the death of an employee, the company was held to be in breach of its duties under section 2(1) HASAWA 1974.

It could be argued that these statutory duties merely enact the employer's common-law obligations developed in compensation cases. Although this is largely true, compensation law requires the defendant merely to take reasonable care whereas the statutory duties are usually either actually or virtually absolute, for even where the standard is qualified the burden lies on the accused to escape liability by proving that it was not 'reasonably practicable' to do more than was in fact done to achieve a safe situation.[12] This defence is rarely invoked. It does not mean that the defendant must do everything that is physically possible to achieve safety, only that the risks be weighed against the trouble and expense of eliminating or reducing them.[13] Defendants are to be judged according to the knowledge they had or ought to have had at the time. In compensation cases it has been held that the existence of a universal practice is evidence which goes to the question whether any other method was reasonably practicable but it does not necessarily discharge the onus on the employer.[14]

EMPLOYEE INVOLVEMENT

From the outset it was intended that employees should be well informed and consulted about developing and maintaining measures to ensure the health and safety of employees. Section 2(4–7) HASWA 1974 enabled regulations to be made for safety representatives. The Safety Representatives and Safety Committees

Regulations 1977[15] enabled recognised trade unions to appoint representatives and required employers to set up a safety committee if the appointed representative(s) so required. The Health and Safety (Consultation with Employees) Regulations 1996[16] gave similar rights to be consulted to employees without union representation. For further consideration of employee consultation see Chapter 17.

SAFETY POLICIES

Except where fewer than five employees are employed at any one time in an undertaking,[17] every employer must:

> prepare and, as often as may be appropriate, revise a written statement of his general policy with respect to the health and safety at work of his employees, and the organisation and arrangements for the time being in force for carrying out that policy, and bring the statement and any revision of it to the notice of all of his employees.[18]

The Act does not give any further indication of what the statement should contain, but advice and guidance notes, which are not legally enforceable, are available from the HSE. Clearly, it is intended that employers will seek solutions to their own particular safety problems and it will not be sufficient simply to adopt a model scheme drawn up by some other body. As an absolute minimum the safety policy should deal with the various responsibilities of all employees, from the board of directors down to the shop floor. Indeed, the statement may be used as evidence if a prosecution is launched under section 37 HASAWA 1974 (see below). It should also deal with general safety precautions, mechanisms for dealing with special hazards, routine inspections, emergency procedures, training and arrangements for consulting the workforce.

In industrial relations terms, it is obviously desirable to reach agreement with employee representatives on the contents of the written statement. However, this is not a legal requirement. No guidance is given as to how the statement should be brought to the notice of employees, although ideally a copy should be supplied to each person. Special precautions may have to be taken in relation to those who have language difficulties.

PERSONS OTHER THAN EMPLOYEES

Section 3 HASAWA 1974 imposes a duty on employers and self-employed persons to conduct their undertakings in such a way as to ensure, so far as is reasonably practicable, that persons not in their employment who may be affected thereby are not exposed to risks to their health and safety. More specifically, Regulation 12 of the MHSW Regulations 1999 obliges employers and self-employed people to supply any person working in their undertaking who is not their employee with comprehensible information and instruction on any risks which arise out of the conduct of the undertaking.[19] It is clear that the word 'risk' should be given its ordinary meaning of denoting the possibility of danger rather than actual danger.[20] This may apply to subcontractors working on the employer's premises. The duty of the employer towards visiting workers is not very different from that owed to its own employees under section 2 HASAWA 1974, since it may need to instruct the visitors (see *R v Swan Hunter Shipbuilders Ltd and Telemeter Installations Ltd*[21]).

The question of employer control

An employer cannot delegate its duty under section 3 HASAWA 1974 and criminal liability is not limited to the acts of the 'directing mind' or senior management of a company.[22] In *R v Associated Octel*[23] the House of Lords held that cleaning, repair and maintenance was necessary for the carrying out of the employer's business and part of the conduct of the undertaking and fell within the scope of section 3 when carried out by contractors.[24] It is unnecessary to show that the employer has some actual control over how the work is done. Nevertheless, as far as operations carried out by independent contractors are concerned, the question of control may be relevant. In most cases, the employer has no control over how a competent contractor does the work and it may not be reasonably practicable to do other than rely on the contractor. Thus it is important to clarify when making the contract the way the work should be done and, if it is clear that the contractor is not honouring the agreed system, the employer should order it offsite.

SAFE PREMISES

Section 4 HASAWA 1974 provides that a person who has control of non-domestic premises used as a place of work must take such measures as are reasonably practicable to ensure that the means of access and egress and any plant or substance in the premises is safe and without risks to health. According to the House of Lords, once it is proved that:

- the premises made available for use by others are unsafe and constitute a risk to health

- the employer had a degree of control over those premises, and

- having regard to the employer's degree of control and knowledge of the likely use, it would have been reasonable to take measures to ensure that the premises were safe,

the employer must demonstrate that, weighing the risk to health against the means (including cost) of eliminating it, it was not reasonably practicable to take those measures. However, if the premises are not a reasonably foreseeable cause of danger to people using them in the circumstances that might reasonably be expected to occur, it is not reasonable to require further measures to be taken. Unlike section 3 this section provides for shared responsibility where there is more than one occupier of the premises. This possibly explains why the employer was not liable under section 4 in a case[25] where the facts were very similar to those in the *Octel* case.

EMPLOYEE DUTIES

Section 7 of HASAWA 1974 imposes two general duties on employees while they are at work:[26]

- to take reasonable care of the health and safety of themselves and of others who may be affected by their acts or omissions

- as regards any duty imposed on their employers or any other person by any of the relevant statutory provisions, to co-operate with them so far as is necessary to enable that duty to be performed.

REGULATIONS

It is not possible to review all the sets of Regulations made under HASAWA 1974. The following paragraphs outline the Regulations made to implement the EC Framework Directive, the five sets of Regulations immediately subsidiary to this, and the Control of Substances Hazardous to Health Regulations.

THE MHSW REGULATIONS

These Regulations are intended to implement the EC Framework Directive[27] and Regulation 4 requires an employer to implement preventative and protective measures on the basis of certain general principles of prevention set out in this Directive. These general principles are:

- avoiding risks

- evaluating the risks which cannot be avoided

- combating the risks at source

- adapting the work to the individual, especially as regards the design of workplaces and the choice of work equipment and the choice of working and production methods with a view in particular to alleviating monotonous work and work at a predetermined work rate and to reducing their effect on health

- adapting to technical progress

- replacing the dangerous by the non-dangerous or less dangerous

- developing a coherent overall prevention policy which covers technology, organisation of work, working conditions, social relationships and the influence of factors related to the work environment

- giving collective protective measures priority over individual protective measures

- giving appropriate instructions to employees.

RISK ASSESSMENT

The MHSW Regulations impose a duty on all employers and the self-employed to conduct a risk assessment. This assessment must be both suitable and sufficient and must consider the risk to the health and safety of all employees and other persons arising from the conduct of the undertaking.[28] The purpose of the assessment is to identify the measures that have to be taken to ensure compliance with the relevant statutory provisions. These provisions are specified in the Approved Code of Practice and include the duties under HASAWA 1974. The risk assessment must be reviewed if there is reason to suspect that it is no longer valid or there has been a significant change in the matters to which it relates. An employer is specifically forbidden from employing a young person (someone under the age of 18 years[29]) unless a review has occurred which takes particular account of certain special characteristics such as the inexperience, lack of awareness of risks and the immaturity of young persons.[30] Regulation 19 provides employers with a particular duty to ensure that young employees are protected from risks to their health and safety arising out of their inexperience. If there are any women of child-bearing age working in an undertaking, there is a special obligation, in Regulation 16, to assess any potential risk that might affect the health and safety of a new or expectant mother.

Regulation 5 requires employers to give effect to appropriate arrangements for the effective planning, organisation, control, monitoring and review of the measures they need to take as a result of the risk assessment. Again, such arrangements must be recorded if the employer has five or more employees. Regulation 6 obliges employers to provide appropriate health surveillance for their employees.

Relating risk assessment to compensation cases

While the risk assessment requirements are clearly part of the preventative legislation, compensation cases can give insights into factors that the employer may have to consider when carrying out a risk assessment. For example, the employer may need to have regard to any particular issues relating to individual employees. Thus in *Tasci v Pekalp of London Ltd*[31] a Kurdish refugee, who spoke little English, was employed as a wood machinist. The Court of Appeal (Civil Division) held that, given the claimant's background, the system of work operated by the employer fell short of that which was required by the relevant safety regulations and the employer's common-law duty of care.

It may be possible to identify a wide range of compensation cases which, like the one above, are indicative of the requirements of a comprehensive risk assessment, but of general importance is the developing awareness of the incidence of stress at the workplace. The HSE website states that

- About 1 in 5 people says that he or she finds work either very or extremely stressful.
- Over half a million people report experiencing work-related stress at a level they believe has actually made them ill.

- Each case of stress-related ill health leads to an average of 29 working days lost.

- A total of 13.4 million working days were lost to stress, depression and anxiety in 2001.

- Work-related stress costs society between £3.7 billion and £3.8 billion a year (1995/6 values).

Recent compensation litigation has established that the employer must compensate an employee who suffers stress-related injury as a result of the employer's negligence, whether the injury is physical or psychological.[32] Yet health and safety legislation makes no express reference to the employer's having any duty to protect employees from stress-related ill health. However, HSE considers that section 2 of the Act implicitly requires employers to take steps to make sure employees do not suffer stress-related illness as a result of their work. It similarly believes that employers must take account of the risk of stress-related ill health when carrying out risk assessments as required by Regulation 3.[33] The implication is therefore that employers can be criminally liable for operating stressful workplaces that put their employees at risk of ill health. For criminal liability to occur it is not necessary that any employee becomes ill; it is sufficient that employees are at risk of becoming ill.

Defining and appointing 'competent persons'

Under Regulation 7 employers must appoint one or more 'competent persons' to assist them in implementing the measures they need in order to comply with the relevant statutory provisions. The number of people appointed, the time available for them to fulfil their functions, and the means at their disposal must be adequate, having regard to the size of the undertaking and the risks to which employees are exposed. A 'competent person' is defined as someone who has sufficient training and experience or knowledge to enable him or her to assist properly in the undertaking.[34] However, there is a requirement for the employer to give preference to the appointment of a 'competent person' in his employment over one from outside.[35]

Regulation 8 obliges an employer to establish appropriate procedures to be followed in the event of 'serious and imminent danger to persons at work in his undertaking'. Employers must nominate a sufficient number of competent persons to implement these procedures and to be sure that employees are unable to enter dangerous areas without having received adequate health and safety instruction. It is made clear that this Regulation requires both the provision of information and procedures which enable employees to leave their work immediately in the event of 'serious and imminent danger'.[36]

THE SUBSIDIARY DIRECTIVES

At about the time of the adoption of the Framework Directive, the EC adopted five subsidiary Directives. The following sets of Regulations were made in Britain to implement these Directives and many of them have been more tested in the civil than in the criminal courts.

THE MANUAL HANDLING OPERATIONS REGULATIONS

These Regulations[37] require an employer to:

- avoid hazardous manual handling where reasonably practicable
- assess unavoidable hazardous manual handling operations
- reduce the risk of injury as far as possible.

Manual handling is a major cause of workplace injuries and there have been many compensation claims. HSE has published guidance.[38]

THE WORKPLACE (HEALTH, SAFETY AND WELFARE) REGULATIONS 1992

These Regulations[39] provide standards for matters such as temperature, lighting, space, passageways, floors, doors, toilets, washing, eating and changing facilities, drinking water, and for maintenance of the workplace, equipment and facilities.

THE PERSONAL PROTECTIVE EQUIPMENT AT WORK REGULATIONS 1992

These Regulations[40] set out principles for selecting, providing, maintaining and using PPE. They do not apply where there are specific regulations relating to PPE.

THE HEALTH AND SAFETY (DISPLAY SCREEN EQUIPMENT) REGULATIONS 1992

These Regulations[41] apply where there is a 'user'.[42] Employers have to:

- assess DSE workstations and reduce risks discovered by the assessment
- make sure that workstations satisfy minimum regulatory standards
- plan DSE work so that there are breaks or changes of activity
- provide information and training for users.

THE PROVISION AND USE OF WORK EQUIPMENT REGULATIONS 1998

These revised Regulations[43] were originally made in 1992. Work equipment is broadly defined to include everything from a hand tool to a complete plant. 'Use' includes starting, stopping, repairing, modifying, installing, dismantling, programming, setting, transporting, maintaining, servicing and cleaning. Minimum requirements are set down for work equipment to deal with selected hazards. HSE has published an Approved Code of Practice and several sets of guidance.

THE CONTROL OF SUBSTANCES HAZARDOUS TO HEALTH (COSHH) REGULATIONS 2002

Each year, approximately 16,000 to 25,000 people become ill as a result of exposure to substances hazardous to health at work – eg respiratory disease, dermatitis, etc. This includes an estimated 3,000 to 12,000 cancer deaths mostly related to chemicals, including asbestos.[44] The Control of Substances Hazardous to Health (COSHH) Regulations originally came into force in October 1989 but have been amended and replaced several times. The most recent version came into effect in November 2002.[45]

According to the Health and Safety Executive hazardous substances are anything that can harm your health when you work with them if they are not properly controlled – eg by using adequate ventilation. They can include:

- substances used directly in work activities – eg glues, paints, cleaning agents
- substances generated during work activities – eg fumes from soldering and welding
- naturally occurring substances – eg grain dust, blood, bacteria.

For the vast majority of commercial chemicals, the presence (or not) of a warning label will indicate whether COSHH is relevant. For example, household washing-up liquid doesn't have a warning label but bleach does – so COSHH applies to bleach but not washing-up liquid when used at work.[46]

COSHH provides employers with a general duty to prevent or adequately control the exposure of their employees and others who may be affected to hazardous substances. In addition there are a number of specific duties:

1 *Risk assessment*

An employer must not carry out work which is liable to expose any employees to any substance hazardous to health unless the employer has carried out an assessment of the risk to the health of employees and the steps that need to be taken to meet the requirements of the Regulations.[47] The risk assessment is to be reviewed regularly and appropriate changes made as a result of these reviews. All but the smallest of employers (those employing fewer than five employees) must record the 'significant' findings of the risk assessment and the steps that have been taken as a result.

2 *Prevention or control of exposure*

Every employer must ensure that the exposure of his employees to substances hazardous to health is either prevented or, where this is not reasonably practicable, adequately controlled.[48] Substitution of the hazardous substance is preferred. However, if this is not reasonably practicable, the employer must comply with this duty by applying protection measures such as adequate ventilation, using appropriate work processes, and the provision of suitable protective equipment.

3 *Maintenance, examination and testing*

All employers who provide control measures must ensure, where relevant, that they are maintained in an efficient state, in efficient working order, in good repair and in a clean condition.[49] A suitable record of the examinations and tests plus any subsequent repairs carried out must be kept and made available for at least five years after it was done.

Where employees are, or are liable to be, exposed to a hazardous substance, they must be kept under suitable health surveillance. The employer should ensure that a health record is kept in respect of each of these employees and must make sure that it is kept and available for 40 years from the date it was made. Employees, and the Health and Safety Executive, have a right of access to their own records.[50] The employer also has a duty to ensure that all employees who may be exposed to hazardous substances are provided with suitable information, instruction and training. This will include details about the substances, maximum exposure limits, findings of the risk assessment and the precautions and actions that must be taken by the employee to safeguard himself or herself and others at the workplace.[51] The Regulations are supported by an Approved Code of Practice which gives detailed practical advice on compliance. The ACOP includes appendices dealing with carcinogens, biological agents and substances that cause occupational asthma.

Dugmore v Swansea NHS Trust[52] concerned a nurse who developed an allergy to latex protein as a result of using powdered latex gloves in the course of her work. She was given vinyl gloves to use instead but still came into contact with the latex ones and suffered an illness which stopped her returning to work as a nurse. She claimed damages from her employers, alleging, amongst other matters, a breach of Regulation 7(1) of the COSHH Regulations (see point **2** above). The Court of Appeal held that the purpose of the COSHH Regulations was protective and preventative. Lady Justice Hale stated that they did not simply rely on criminal sanctions or civil liability to induce good practice. They involved positive obligations to seek out the risks and take precautions. In this case the employer had a duty to ensure that exposure was adequately controlled. The Court suggested that it would have been a simple matter to change the latex gloves to vinyl ones and the onus was on the employer to show that they were unable to do this. They failed to do so and the Court allowed Ms Dugmore's claim.

REGULATIONS ON REPORTING INJURIES

The Reporting of Injuries, Diseases and Dangerous Occurrences Regulations 1995[53] (RIDDOR 1995) apply to events which arise 'out of or in connection with work'[54] activities covered by HASAWA 1974. Whenever any of the following arises it must be reported to the enforcing authority in writing and a record kept.[55] If any of (a)–(d) happens, the enforcing authority must first be notified by the quickest practicable means:

(a) the death of any person as a result of an accident, whether or not he or she is at work

(b) someone at work suffers a major injury as the result of an accident[56]

(c) someone who is not at work suffers an injury as the result of an accident and is taken to a hospital for treatment

(d) one of a list of specified dangerous occurrences takes place[57]

(e) someone is unable to do his or her normal work for more than three days as the result of an injury caused by an accident at work

(f) the death of an employee, if it occurs after a reportable injury which led to the employee's death, but not more than one year afterwards

(g) a person at work suffers a specified disease, provided that a doctor diagnoses the disease and the person's job involves a specified work activity.[58]

The duty to report the events listed above is imposed on the 'responsible person'.[59] Regulation 13 gives the HSE a limited power to grant exemptions from the requirements imposed by RIDDOR 1995.

OFFENCES

Apart from the Crown, any person or body corporate can be prosecuted for an offence under HASAWA 1974. However, if an offence is proved to have been committed with the consent or connivance of, or to have been attributable to neglect on the part of, any director, manager, secretary or other similar officer, then that person as well as the body corporate may be found guilty of an offence.[60] Thus in *Armour* v *Skeen*[61] a local authority director of roads was prosecuted for failing to prepare and carry out a sound safety policy. His neglect led to breaches of safety provisions that resulted in the death of a Council employee.

Where the commission of an offence by any person is due to the act or default of some other person, that other person may be charged whether or not proceedings are taken against the first-mentioned person.[62] Crown servants may be prosecuted despite the immunity of the Crown itself. Proceedings under this Act can be brought only by an inspector or with the consent of the Director of Public Prosecutions.

The normal maximum penalty for a person found guilty of an offence on summary conviction (ie in a magistrate's court) is a fine not exceeding level 5 on the standard scale. However, where there is a breach of sections 2–6 of HASAWA 1974, or of an improvement or prohibition notice, a fine of up to £20,000 can be imposed. If there is a breach of a notice or a court order under section 42 HASAWA 1974 (see below), an offender may receive a sentence of up to six months' imprisonment. When proceedings are brought on indictment (in a Crown court) there is the possibility of an unlimited fine and, in specified circumstances, up to two years' imprisonment.[63]

In deciding on the level of the fine to be imposed, the court will take into account the ability of the defendant to pay. Generally, fines will not be so large as to endanger the earnings of employees or create a risk of bankruptcy, unless the offence is so serious that the firm should not be in business.[64] The questions to be asked, according to the Court of Appeal, which should guide courts in assessing fines were:

- What financial penalty does the offence merit?
- What financial penalty can a defendant reasonably be ordered to meet, and over what period? A longer period might be acceptable in the case of a company as opposed to an individual.[65]

In reaching a decision on the fine, the aggravating features to be taken into account will include:

- whether the defendant has failed to heed warnings
- whether the defendant deliberately profited financially from the failure to take the necessary health and safety measures.

Conversely, the features which might be taken in mitigation include:

- prompt admission of responsibility and a timely plea of guilty
- steps to remedy the deficiencies once they have been drawn to the defendant's attention
- a good safety record.

Where people are convicted of offences in respect of any matters that appear to the court to be within their power to remedy, the court may, in addition to or instead of imposing any punishment, order them to take such steps as may be specified to remedy those matters.[66]

CASE STUDY

Following a fatal accident at his plant hire business, Mr Davies was charged with an offence under section 3 HASAWA 1974. The judge ruled that section 40 HASAWA 1974, which states that 'it shall be for the accused to prove … that it was not reasonably practicable to do more than was in fact done' was compatible with Article 6(2) of the European Convention on Human Rights. This provides that 'Everyone charged with a criminal offence shall be presumed innocent until proved guilty according to law.'

In dismissing an appeal against conviction, the Court of Appeal held that the imposition of a reverse legal burden of proof was justified, necessary and proportionate in the circumstances. Before any question of reverse onus arises, the prosecution must prove that the defendant owed the duty and that the safety standard was breached. Additionally, the facts relied on by the defendant should not be difficult to establish because they will be within the defendant's knowledge. Finally, whether the defendant could have done more will be judged objectively.[67]

ENFORCING THE ACT

Except for the enforcement responsibilities of local authorities, HASAWA 1974 is enforced by the HSE, whose director is appointed by the HSC with the approval of the Secretary of State. Although the HSE is to give effect to any directions issued by the HSC, the former cannot be *directed* to enforce a statutory provision in a particular case.

HSE is empowered only to enforce HASAWA 1974 and 'relevant statutory provisions' (that is, in effect, regulations made under the Act). If a person has been killed and homicide proceedings appear appropriate, these can only be taken by the police, with the Crown Prosecution Service. In practice HSE and the police carry out a joint investigation. It is very difficult to convict a company of manslaughter and there is considerable public demand for reform, although in fact no greater penalty could be imposed on a company convicted of manslaughter than under HASAWA 1974. Indeed, in August 2006 Transco plc was fined £15 million under HASAWA 1974 at the High Court of Justiciary in Edinburgh following a massive pipeline explosion that destroyed a house and killed the occupants.

INSPECTORS' POWERS

The enforcing authorities appoint inspectors who may exercise the following powers:[68]

(a) at any reasonable time (or, if there is a dangerous situation, at any time) to enter premises

(b) to take with them a police officer, if they have reasonable cause to be apprehensive of any serious obstruction in the execution of their duty

(c) to take with them any other authorised person and any equipment or materials required

(d) to make such examination and investigation as may be necessary

(e) to direct that the premises be left undisturbed for so long as is reasonably necessary for the purpose of examination or investigation

(f) to take such measurements, photographs and readings as they consider necessary

(g) to take samples of any articles or substances found in any premises and of the atmosphere in, or in the vicinity of, any such premises[69]

(h) in the case of an article or substance which appears to have caused or to be likely to cause danger, to dismantle it or subject it to any process or test. The article or substance may be damaged or destroyed if it is thought necessary in the circumstances. However, if they are so requested by a person who is present and has responsibilities in relation to those premises, this power must be exercised in that person's presence unless the inspector considers that to do so would be prejudicial to the safety of the state

(i) in the case of an article or substance which appears to have caused or to be likely to cause danger, to take possession of it and detain it for so long as is necessary in order to examine it, to ensure that it is not tampered with before the examination is completed, and to ensure that it is available for use as evidence in any proceedings for an offence or any proceedings relating to a notice under section 21 or 22 HASAWA 1974 (see below). An inspector must leave a notice giving particulars of the article or substance stating that he or she has taken possession of it and, if it is practicable, he or she should give a sample of it to a responsible person at the premises[70]

(j) if carrying out examinations or investigations under (d), to require persons whom they have reasonable cause to believe to be able to give any information to answer such questions as the inspector thinks fit to ask and to sign a declaration of the truth of their answers

(k) to require the production of, inspect and take copies of an entry in, any books or documents which are required to be kept and any other books or documents which it is necessary for them to see for the purpose of any examination or investigation under (d) above

(l) to require any persons to afford them such facilities and assistance with respect to any matters within that person's control or responsibilities as are necessary for the inspectors to exercise their powers

(m) any other power which is necessary for the purpose of carrying into effect the statutory provisions.

IMPROVEMENT NOTICES

Where an inspector is of the opinion that a person is contravening or has contravened a relevant statutory provision in circumstances that make it likely that the contravention will continue or be repeated, he or she may serve an 'improvement notice' stating that opinion. The notice must specify the provision, give particulars of the reasons why he or she is of that opinion, and will require that person to remedy the contravention within such period as may be specified in the notice.[71] This period must not be less than the time allowed for appealing against the notice – ie 21 days [72]

PROHIBITION NOTICES

In respect of an activity covered by a relevant statutory provision, if any inspector believes that activities are being carried on or are about to be carried on which will involve a risk of serious personal injury, the inspector may serve a 'prohibition notice'. Such a notice will state the inspector's opinion, specify the matters which give rise to the risk, and direct that the activities to which the notice relates must not be carried on by or under the control of the person on whom the notice is served (unless the matters specified in the notice have been remedied). A prohibition notice will normally take effect immediately. Both types of notice may (but need not) include directions as to the measures to be taken to remedy the contravention or the matter to which the notice relates. Where a notice which is not to take immediate effect has been served, that notice may be withdrawn by the inspector within 21 days. Similarly, the period specified for rectification may be extended by an inspector at any time when an appeal against the notice is not pending.

A person on whom a notice is served may appeal to an employment tribunal, which has the power to cancel or affirm the notice or affirm it in a modified form.[73] For the purpose of hearing such appeals the tribunal may include specially appointed assessors. Bringing an appeal against an improvement notice has the effect of suspending the operation of that notice until the appeal is disposed of. Lodging an appeal against a prohibition notice suspends it only if the tribunal so directs and then only from the time when the direction is given.[74] Failure to comply with a notice is an offence.[75]

Because it is not possible to bring a prosecution against the Crown[76] it is equally impossible to enforce improvement and prohibition notices against Crown bodies. However, the HSE has been prepared to issue 'Crown notices' where, in its opinion, an improvement or prohibition notice would have been appropriate. Such notices have no legal effect but may be of some value insofar as they put moral pressure on the employing body. Of course, trade union representatives who receive copies of these notices may be in a position to apply industrial pressure.

ACCESS TO MEDICAL REPORTS ACT 1988

This Act provides a right of access to any medical report relating to an individual which is to be, or has been, supplied by a medical practitioner for employment or insurance purposes. The AMRA 1988 applies to 'medical reports' which are commissioned both before employment commences and during employment from 'a medical practitioner who is or has been responsible for the clinical care of the individual'.[77]

An employer who wishes to apply for a medical report covered by this legislation is required to notify the individual that he or she proposes to make an application, and must obtain that person's consent.[78] In addition, the employer must inform the individual in writing of the following rights created by the Act:

- the right to withhold consent to such an application[79]

- if the individual does consent, the right to state that he or she wants access to the report. Where the individual so states, the employer must notify the medical practitioner of this fact at the time the report is sought[80]

- the right of access is to the report before it is supplied to the employer[81] and to any medical report relating to him or her that the practitioner has supplied during the previous six months.[82] A person who wants access to the report before it is supplied to the employer has 21 days to contact the medical practitioner about arrangements for access. For these purposes, giving access to a report means supplying the individual with a copy of it or making the report (or a copy) available for inspection. A reasonable fee may be charged for the cost of supplying a report

- the right to request the amendment of, or record a difference of opinion over, any details contained in the report which the individual regards as misleading or incorrect. If the individual requests in writing that the medical practitioner should attach to the report a statement of that individual's views about any part of the report which the doctor refuses to amend, the doctor is obliged to do so[83]

- the right to refuse consent to the disclosure of the report to the employer.[84]

Doctors' duty of care is to the person for whom a report is made – not to the applicant.

An employer who applies for a medical report from a doctor must also inform that doctor of certain matters.[85] However, there is nothing to prevent employers from using standard forms for notifying either employees or doctors. The courts have held that medical practitioners who carry out pre-employment medical assessments and examinations do not owe a duty of care to the potential employee. The duty of care is owed to the person for whom the report is made and who is relying on it.

CASE STUDY

Kapfunde v Abbey National plc and another[86]

This case concerned a part-time employee who applied for a full-time position with the same employer. She was asked to complete a medical questionnaire and disclosed that she suffered from sickle-cell anaemia.

The questionnaire was referred to a general practitioner to whom the employer paid an annual retainer. The GP stated that the medical evidence showed a likelihood of higher-than-average levels of absenteeism and the employer declined to give the employee a full-time post.

The court held that the GP was under a contract of service with the employer when assessing medical questionnaires and that there was no special relationship from which a duty of care to the applicant could be shown. This approach was also followed in *London Borough of Hammersmith and Fulham v Farnsworth*,[87] where an occupational health physician was held to be an agent of the employer when preparing a report on a potential employee.

An individual can be denied access to the whole or part of a report if the medical practitioner thinks that its disclosure would be likely:

- to cause serious physical or mental harm to the individual involved, or
- to reveal information about another individual, or
- to reveal the intentions of the practitioner in relation to the individual, or
- to reveal the identity of another non-medical person who has supplied information to the medical practitioner.[88]

Where the medical practitioner decides that access to the report should be withheld (wholly or in part) because of one or more of the statutory exemptions, he or she must notify the individual of that fact. If a person is unhappy about the disclosure of information in these circumstances, he or she may choose to refuse consent to the report being supplied to the employer. Obviously, both job-seekers and job-holders will think hard about the conclusions that employers might draw from the withholding of consent to a medical report.

People who feel that their rights under this Act have been infringed can complain to the County Court.[89] If the court is satisfied that a person has failed (or is likely to fail) to comply with a requirement relating to the complainant, it may order compliance. Thus if a medical report has already been supplied without the individual's consent or access to it has been denied, all that can be enforced is the right of access to the report and to have a statement of views attached to it.

Reinforce your understanding of this chapter by visiting www.cipd.co.uk/sss for activities, questions, weblinks and additional case studies

REFERENCES

1 SI 1999/3242; see also Management of Health and Safety at Work Regulations 1999 Approved Code of Practice and Guidance, HSE 2000

2 Except insofar as the regulations provide otherwise. See section 47(2) HASAWA 1974

3 Section 10 HASAWA 1974

4 Section 17 HASAWA 1974

5 The website of the Health and Safety Executive contains a large amount of free information about various regulatory requirements.

6 *Commission v UK* (2007) IRLR 721

7 Section 2(2) HASAWA 1974. Note the illustrations provided by s.2(2) are not intended to be exhaustive.

8 Defined in section 53 HASAWA 1974 as including any machinery, equipment or appliance

9 Defined in section 54 HASAWA 1974 as 'any natural or artificial substance whether in solid or liquid form of a gas or vapour'

10 The legislation makes little explicit reference to welfare; but it may prove to be relevant to physical and psychiatric stress injury. See also the guide *Tackling Work-Related Stress* (HSG218) (2001).

11 (1997) IRLR 189

12 Section 40 HASAWA 1974

13 See *Edwards v National Coal Board* (1949) 1 KB 704, and under the 1974 Act, *West Bromwich Building Society v Townsend* (1983) IRLR 147

14 *Cavanagh v Ulster Weaving Co Ltd* (1959) 2 All ER 745

15 SI 1977/500

16 SI 1996/1513

17 An 'undertaking' is not statutorily defined for these purposes, but is likely to cover all enterprises or businesses.

18 Section 2(3) HASAWA 1974

19 There are special requirements in relation to visiting workers where there is asbestos in the premises. See The Control of Asbestos at Work Regulations 2002, SI 2002/2675

20 See *R v Trustees of the Science Museum* (1993) 3 All ER 853

21 (1981) IRLR 403

22 See *R v British Steel* (1995) IRLR 310. Regulation 21 of MHWR 1999 now provides that an employer cannot raise as a defence that a breach of the employer's duty was due to the fault of an employee; so the controversial case of *R v Nelson Group Services (Maintenance) Ltd* (1998) 4 All ER 331 is not likely to be followed.

23 (1997) IRLR 123

24 The site was classified as a hazardous installation and the employer did not ensure that the visitors followed the work permit system.

25 See *Inspector of Factories* v *Austin Rover* (1989) IRLR 404

26 On the meaning of 'at work' see section 52(1) HASAWA 1974

27 Directive 89/391/EEC

28 See HSE leaflet *A Guide to Risk Assessment Requirements*, HSE (2001)

29 Regulation 1(2) MHSW Regulations 1999

30 Regulation 3(5) MHSW Regulations 1999

31 (2001) ICR 633

32 See *Pickford v ICI* (1998) IRLR 435 on repetitive strain injury, and *Sutherland v Hatton* (2002) IRLR 263 on psychological injury

33 *Tackling Work-Related Stress: A manager's guide to improving and maintaining employee health and well-being* (2001) HSG218 at paras 12 and 13

34 See Regulation 6(5)

35 Regulation 6(8) 1999 Regulations

36 See Regulation 7(2)

37 SI 1992/2793, implementing 90/269/EEC

38 *Simple Guide to Lifting Operations and Lifting Equipment Regulations 1998*

39 SI 1992/3004, implementing 89/6544/EEC

40 SI 1992/2966, implementing 89/656/EEC

41 SI 1992/2792 implementing 90/270/EEC

42 An employee who habitually uses DSE as a significant part of normal work

43   SI 1998/2306, revised to implement 95/63/EEC

44   Information from the Health and Safety Executive website

45   The Control of Substances Hazardous to Health Regulations 2002, SI 2002/2677

46   See HSE website

47   Regulation 6 COSHH Regulations 2002

48   Regulation 7 COSHH Regulations 2002

49   Regulation 9 COSHH Regulations 2002

50   Regulation 11 COSHH Regulations 2002

51   Regulation 12 COSHH Regulations 2002

52   (2003) IRLR 164

53   SI 1995/3163

54   Defined by Regulation 2(2)c RIDDOR 1995

55   Regulation 7 RIDDOR 1995

56   Major injuries are listed in Schedule 1 RIDDOR 1995

57   Dangerous occurrences are listed in Schedule 2 RIDDOR 1995

58   The specified diseases and corresponding work activities are listed in Schedule 3
     RIDDOR 1995

59   Defined in Regulation 2

60   Section 37 HASAWA 1974. Directors who are convicted of an offence can be disqualified
     from office under the Directors Disqualification Act 1986.

61   (1977) IRLR 310. See also *R v Boal* (1992) IRLR 420

62   Section 36 HASAWA 1974

63   Section 33(2)(5) HASAWA 1974 (as amended)

64   See *R* v *F Howe & Son* (1999) IRLR 434

65   See *R* v *Rollco Screw Co Ltd* (1999) IRLR 439

66   Section 42(1) HASAWA 1974

67   *Davies v HSE* (2003) IRLR 170

68   Section 20 HASAW 1974

69   See *Laws* v *Keane* (1982) IRLR 500

70   See also section 25 HASAWA 1974 on the power to deal with an imminent cause of
     danger

71   See *West Bromwich Building Society* v *Townsend* (note 13)

72   Rule 2 Schedule 4 Employment Tribunal (Constitution and Rules of Procedure)
     Regulations 1993, SI 1993/2687

73   Section 24(2) HASAWA 1974. Section 82(1)(c) defines 'modifications' as including
     additions, omissions and amendments. See *British Airways* v *Henderson* (1979) ICR 77

74   Section 24(3) HASAWA 1974

75   See section 33(1)(g) HASAWA 1974 and *Deary v Mansion Hide Upholstery Ltd* (1983)
     IRLR 195

76   Section 48 HASAWA 1974

77   Section 2(1) AMRA 1988

78   Section 3(1) AMRA 1988

79   Section 3(2) AMRA 1988

80   Section 4(1) AMRA 1988

81 Section 4(2) AMRA 1988
82 Section 6(2) AMRA 1988
83 Section 5(2) AMRA 1988
84 Section 5(1) AMRA 1988
85 Section 4(1) and (2) AMRA 1988
86 (1999) ICR 1
87 (2000) IRLR 691 CA
88 Section 7 AMRA 1988
89 Section 8 AMRA 1988

CHAPTER 10

The Regulation of Working Time

OVERVIEW

This chapter is concerned with the Working Time Regulations 1998 and those occasions when there is a statutory right to time off work. (Issues relating to parental rights, including maternity leave, parental leave and time off for dependants, are dealt with in Chapter 9.) There is an examination of the contents of the Regulations. This is followed by a consideration of the rights of trade unionists for time off to take part in trade union duties and activities. Finally we look at other rights to time off, including time off for carrying out public duties.

THE WORKING TIME REGULATIONS 1998

The Working Time Regulations[1] (WT Regulations) implement the Working Time Directive[2] and provisions of the Young Workers Directive.[3] The preamble to the Working Time Directive states that 'in order to ensure the safety and health of Community workers, the latter must be granted minimum daily, weekly and annual periods of rest and adequate breaks' and that 'it is necessary in this context to place a maximum limit on working time'. Thus the legal basis for the Directive was Article 118a EC (now Article 137 EC) relating to health and safety. This was the subject of an unsuccessful challenge by the United Kingdom,[4] which claimed that this was the wrong legal basis and that the regulation of working time was a matter for Member States and not a health and safety matter to be dealt with at Community level.

EXCLUSIONS FROM THE WT REGULATIONS

Certain activities and certain sectors were originally excluded from the scope of the WT Regulations, although these exclusions have been modified as a result of the Working Time (Amendment) Regulations 2003.[5] One of the problems with excluding whole sectors from the application of the Regulations is that all workers are affected. There may be special problems associated with limiting the number of hours of mobile workers, such as long-distance lorry drivers and those at sea, but a blanket exclusion includes non-mobile workers who perhaps should be included. This was the issue in *Bowden v Tuffnel Parcels Express Ltd*.[6] In this case three clerical workers employed in the road transport industry failed to receive paid holidays. The European Court of Justice held that the exclusion provisions of the Directive applied to all workers within an excluded sector. Thus the administrative workers were to be treated no differently from travelling workers in any such sector.

The effect of the 2003 Regulations was to distinguish between mobile workers and others.[7] A mobile worker is defined as 'any worker employed as a member of the travelling or flying personnel by an undertaking which operates transport services for passengers or goods by rail or air'.[8] Thus it is these mobile workers who are excluded from the WT Regulations and for whom special arrangements are made to cope with the special nature of the work. Specifically excluded groups include seafarers and those that work on board both seagoing ships and on ships or hovercraft operating on inland waterways; mobile road transport workers; mobile workers in aviation; and those in the armed or civil forces, such as the army or police, whose duties would inevitably conflict with the requirements of the WT Regulations. Also excluded are jobs in domestic service.[9] There are special transition arrangements for doctors in training,[10] whose maximum working hours have been progressively reduced and are set at 48 hours from 1 August 2009, although a 26-week reference period is used to calculate this.

Defining 'workers'

Regulation 2 defines a 'worker' as an individual who has entered into, or works under, a contract of employment or 'any other contract, whether express or implied and (if it is express) whether oral or in writing, whereby the individual undertakes to do or perform personally any work or services for another party to the contract whose status is not by virtue of the contract that of a client or customer of any professional or business undertaking carried out by the individual'. Thus there may be a distinction between a worker and a self-employed person. In *Bacica v Muir*[11] a self-employed painter and decorator who had worked for one employer for seven years was held not to be a worker but a self-employed person running his own business. He had claimed that he was entitled to be paid for his holidays under the Working Time Regulations because he met the definition of worker under those Regulations. The court, however, stated that there were enough indications to show that he was running his own business, such as being able to work for others, not being paid when not working and being paid an overheads allowance.

A young worker is defined as an individual who is at least 15 years of age, over the compulsory school-leaving age and who has not yet attained the age of 18 years. This does not include children who are covered by other legislation. Thus, in *Addison v Ashby*[12] a 15-year-old paperboy could not be classified as a worker, within the definition of the WT Regulations, because he was not over the compulsory school-leaving age. Regulation 36 deals with agency workers, who are not otherwise workers, by deeming the agency or principal to be the employer depending upon who is responsible for paying the worker. Labour-only subcontractors were held to be workers within the definition of worker in the WT Regulations.[13] This was despite the fact that their contracts allowed them to appoint substitutes in their place in certain circumstances. The subcontractors spent most of their time working personally and they were to be distinguished, according to the EAT, from others who might be seen as running a business undertaking, such as in *Commissioners of Inland Revenue v Post Office Ltd*,[14] where a number of sub-postmasters and postmistresses claimed that they were workers for the purposes of the WT Regulations. Their claim failed because, the EAT held, they were carrying on a business undertaking such that the Post Office was a client of their business. This was despite the fact that they gave undertakings to work personally for at least 18 hours per week in their sub-post office.

Working time, in relation to the worker, is defined[15] as:

- any period during which the worker is working, at the employer's disposal and carrying out the worker's activity or duties

- any period during which the worker is receiving relevant training

- any additional period which is to be treated as working time for the purpose of these Regulations under a relevant agreement (see below).

One issue concerning the WT Regulations has been the position of people who are on call, but not necessarily working all the time that they are required to be available. An example of this is a hospital doctor who is required to be on call and, inevitably, also be available in the hospital. The European Court of Justice[16] considered one case where a doctor spent three quarters of his working hours on call, sometimes for periods up to 25 hours. He was provided with a room where he could sleep when his services were not required. The Court decided that all his hours on call should be counted as working time. The crucial point was that he was required to be present at the place decided by the employer.

THE MAXIMUM WORKING WEEK

Regulation 4 provides that working time, including overtime, must not exceed 48 hours per week (seven days) averaged over a reference period of 17 weeks, unless the worker has first agreed in writing to perform such work. This must be agreed by the worker individually, 'expressly and freely', and it is not enough for the contract of employment just to refer to a collective agreement which allows an extension.[17]

The employer is unable to insist that the employee works longer hours. In *Barber v RJB Mining (UK) Ltd*[18] the employees were granted a declaration by the High Court that having worked in excess of the permitted hours during the reference period, they need not work again until such time as their average working time fell within the limits specified in Regulation 4(1).

> **Calculating average hours**
>
> The Regulations supply a formula for calculating the average hours over the reference period.[19] The formula is:
>
> $$\frac{A + B}{C}$$
>
> where A is the total number of hours comprised in the worker's working time during the reference period; B is the total number of hours comprised in the working time during the course of the period immediately after the end of the reference period and ending when the number of days in that subsequent period on which he or she has worked equals the number of excluded days during the reference period; and C is the number of weeks in the reference period. The excluded days in B are periods including annual leave, sick and maternity leave and periods in which an individual opting-out agreement is in effect. For new employees the reference period is the number of weeks actually worked.

Regulations 4 and 5 allow a worker to effectively opt out of the maximum working week provided that the agreement:

- is in writing
- relates either to a specified period or applies indefinitely
- may be terminable by the worker on seven days' notice, unless a different notice period is specified (subject to a maximum of three months), and
- requires the employer to keep up-to-date records of all the workers who have agreed to opt out.[20]

The Regulations set a maximum working time for young workers of eight hours per day or 40 hours per week.[21] There are wide some exceptions to this rule. These are where

- the young worker's employer requires him or her to undertake work necessary to maintain continuity of service or production, or to help cope with a surge in demand
- no adult worker is available to perform the work
- performing the work would not adversely affect the young worker's education or training.[22]

Night work

Regulation 2 defines 'night-time' as a period which is not less than seven hours in length and includes the hours of 12 midnight to 5 am. A 'night-worker' is a worker who, as a normal course, works at least three hours of working time during 'night-time'[23] or is a worker who is likely, during 'night-time', to work a certain proportion of his or her annual working time as defined by a collective or workforce agreement (see below). In *R v Attorney General for Northern Ireland*[24] the meaning of the term 'normal course' was considered. The employee in the case had been asked to change to a shift system which meant working a night shift, between 9 pm and 7 am, one week in three. The court held that the definition which requires an individual to work at least three hours during night-time as a 'normal course' meant no more than that this should be a regular feature of the individual's work. It would be wrong to confine the protection only to those who work night shifts exclusively or predominantly.

Regulation 6 states that a night-worker's normal hours of work must not exceed, in a reference period, an average of eight in any 24-hour period.

Night-worker's average hours

A night-worker's average normal hours of work for each 24 hours during a reference period are calculated by the formula:

$$\frac{A}{B-C}$$

where A is the number of hours during the reference period which are the normal working hours for that worker; B is the number of days during the reference period; and C is the total number of hours during the reference period spent in rest periods (see below) divided by 24.

There is an obligation upon the employer to ensure that no night-worker whose work involves special hazards or heavy physical or mental strain works for more than 8 hours in any 24-hour period during which night work is performed.[25] Such hazards or strain can be identified in a collective or workforce agreement or as a result of a risk assessment carried out in accordance with Regulation 3 of the Management of Health and Safety at Work Regulations 1999 (see Chapter 9). Night-workers are also entitled to a free health assessment prior to taking up night work and at regular intervals thereafter.[26]

Regulation 7(6) also stipulates that where a medical practitioner informs the employer that a worker is suffering from health problems connected with working night work, the employer should, if it is possible, transfer the worker to more suitable work or work which is not night work. The employer also has an obligation to provide adequate rest breaks where the pattern of work is likely to cause health problems, such as where there is monotonous work or a predetermined work-rate.[27] Regulation 9 also ensures that employers keep adequate records for a period of at least two years.

A restricted period for working is also introduced. This period is between 10 pm and 6 am, or if a worker's contract provides for him or her to work after 10 pm, then the restricted period is between 11 pm and 7 am. The significance of this restricted period is that employers must ensure that no young worker works during these hours.[28] This effective ban on night work for young workers is also qualified. The rule does not apply to work in hospitals or similar establishments and does not apply in connection with cultural, artistic, sporting or advertising activities. The restricted period is reduced to the hours between midnight and 4 am for young workers in a number of businesses such as agriculture, retail trading, postal or newspaper deliveries, catering, hotels and bakeries.[29]

Rest periods and rest breaks

According to Regulation 10, adult workers are entitled to a rest period of at least 11 consecutive hours in each 24-hour period. For young workers this period constitutes at least 12 consecutive hours. The rest period can be interrupted in the case of activities which involve periods of work that are split up over the day or are of short duration. In addition,[30] adult workers are entitled to an uninterrupted weekly rest period of at least 24 hours in each seven-day period. The employer may change this to two uninterrupted rest periods of 24 hours in each 14 days or one uninterrupted rest period of 48 hours every 14 days. Young workers are entitled to an uninterrupted 48-hour rest period every seven days, although this may be interrupted in cases of activities which involve periods of work that are split up over the day or are of short duration, or where there are technical or organisational reasons for reducing it.[31]

Regulation 12 provides that where an adult worker's daily working time is more than six hours, the worker is entitled to a rest break. The details of this rest break can be in accordance with a workforce or collective agreement, provided that it is for at least 20 minutes and the worker is entitled to spend it away from the workstation. Young workers are entitled to a break where their working time is more than four and a half hours. Their break is to be for at least 30 minutes and can be spent away from the workstation. There is an additional complication for employers in Regulation 12(5), which states that where a young worker is employed by more than one employer, the daily working time is the total number of hours that the young worker has worked.

CASE STUDY

MacCartney v Oversley House Management (2006) IRLR 514

Elizabeth MacCartney was employed as the resident manager of a development of privately owned homes for the over-sixties. She had a variety of duties, including being on call for emergencies. She was required to work for four days per week 'of 24 hours on site cover'. This meant that she had to stay on site, in her employer-provided accommodation, during the whole of this period. She could not go out, but could receive visitors, during the on-call period. On average she would have to deal with three to four emergency calls and ten or eleven non-emergency calls per month.

She made a claim that she was being denied the daily rest priods and rest breaks to which she was entitled under the WT Regulations 1999.

The EAT held that the whole period when she was on call could be classified as working time. It did not matter how many times she was actually called out or whether she was sleeping or resting during some of the period. Nor was it relevant that she was in accommodation intended to be her home. Workers who are on call at a place where they are required by their employer to remain can be said to be 'working' during the whole period. Elizabeth MacCartney was therefore entitled to the daily rest periods in accordance with Regulation 10(1). Following the decision in *Gallagher v Alpha Catering Services Ltd*[32] the EAT held that she was also entitled to her 20-minute rest breaks in accordance with Regulation 12.

ANNUAL LEAVE

In any leave year a worker is entitled to four weeks' paid leave.[33] Originally these four weeks included public and other state holidays, which meant that many workers only received 12 days' annual paid leave plus the eight statutory bank and public holidays. The government took the power to make Regulations amending this situation in Section 13 of the Work and Families Act 2006 with the intention of ensuring that workers receive four weeks' annual holiday in addition to the bank and public holidays. As a result, all full-time workers have been entitled to 28 days' paid leave since April 2009.

Unless there is a relevant agreement for another date, the worker's leave year begins on the date employment commenced and every anniversary thereafter. If the worker commences employment on a date that is different from the date agreed for the commencement of a leave year, he or she is entitled to a proportion for that first year. The leave may be taken during the year, but there is only an entitlement to the amount that has accrued so far. This is calculated on the basis of one-twelfth of the four-week entitlement for each month of service.[34] A worker is deemed to have been continuously employed if his or her relations with the employer have been governed by a contract during the whole or part of each of those weeks. The leave may only be taken in the leave year in respect of which it was due and cannot be replaced by a payment in lieu, unless the employment is terminated.[35] If leave is carried over to the next holiday year, it must not be replaced with a payment in lieu. The ECJ has stated[36] that the Directive includes the rule that a worker must be entitled to the actual rest. To pay money in lieu would create an incentive not to take leave and this would be incompatible with the health and safety objectives of the Working Time Directive.

The correct approach to calculating the appropriate daily rate when working out what is owed to an employee is to divide the annual salary by the number of working days in the year, rather than the number of calendar days.[37] If an employee's employment is terminated and he or she has taken in excess of the entitlement calculated on a pro rata basis, there is no opportunity for the employer to claw back any of the overpayment unless there is in existence a relevant agreement, such as a collective or workforce agreement, allowing it to be done.[38]

A worker may give the employer notice of when he or she wishes to take the leave.[39] This notice must be given by a date which is equivalent to twice the amount of leave the worker is proposing to take. An employer can, however, stipulate when holidays can be taken by giving the worker concerned notice using the same formula. In *Sumsion v BBC*[40] a worker objected to the employer's stipulating that some Saturdays should be taken as part of his statutory entitlement. He, and others, claimed that this practice was in breach of the WT Regulations. The EAT held that this was not so. Mr Sumsion had a contract which stated that his services would be required for up to six days per week. His holiday entitlement could be taken on one of these stipulated days when not required; sometimes this was a Saturday. The EAT held that this was not in breach of the Regulations. Many people worked on Saturdays and it could not be held that there was a norm of a working week when holiday entitlement could be taken. Regulation 16 provides that in respect of annual leave workers are entitled to be paid a sum equivalent to a week's pay for each week of leave.[41]

The entitlement to paid annual leave arises if an individual has been a worker during all or part of a leave year. There is no rule which states that the individual will actually have to be at work or do work. Thus the right to holiday pay continues to accrue during sick leave and, on termination of employment, a worker who has been on sick leave and unable to take paid annual leave is entitled to a payment in lieu.[42]

For a time there were contradictory approaches in the courts as to whether holiday pay could be 'rolled' over the year, so workers did not receive extra pay when they took their holidays. In effect the employer claimed that part of the worker's remuneration was holiday pay and that this was paid throughout the year, so that there was no obligation to pay the worker when he or she took the holiday, because it had already been included in the pay rate. The ECJ held[43] that the Working Time Directive precluded part of the remuneration payable to a worker, for work done, from being attributed to payment for annual leave without the worker receiving, in that respect, a payment additional to that for work done. The term 'paid annual leave' meant that a worker should be paid his or her normal remuneration for the duration of the annual leave, although the employer will be able to deduct any payments already made provided that these deductions were made in a transparent and comprehensible way.[44] According to the Court, the Working Time Directive treats entitlement to annual leave and to a payment on that account as 'being two aspects of a single right'. Its purpose is to put workers in the position that when they are on leave they are in a comparable position, with regard to remuneration, as when they are working.

RECORDS

There is an obligation, in Regulation 9, for employers to keep records in respect of the maximum weekly working time (in respect of those workers who have agreed to opt out of the 48-hour limit), night work and health assessment checks for night-workers. These records must be adequate to show that the relevant time limits are being complied with in the case of each worker employed. Such records must be retained for a period of two years.

THE RIGHT NOT TO SUFFER DETRIMENT

Workers have the right not to be subjected to any detriment by any act, or failure to act, on the part of the employer on the grounds that the worker

- refused, or proposed to refuse, to comply with any requirement in contravention of the WT Regulations
- refused, or proposed to refuse, to give up a right conferred by the WT Regulations

- failed to sign a workforce agreement (see below) or vary any other agreement with the employer which is provided for by the WT Regulations
- was a workforce representative or a candidate in an election for such representatives
- alleged that the employer had infringed the worker's rights under the WT Regulations
- was bringing proceedings to enforce rights under the WT Regulations.

The worker will be entitled to such compensation as the tribunal considers is just and equitable in all the circumstances, taking into account the default of the employer and the loss suffered by the worker.[45] If the detriment amounts to a dismissal for one of the above reasons, an employee may bring a complaint of unfair dismissal in accordance with Part X ERA 1996.[46] Any compensation awarded to a worker who is not an employee will be limited to that which an employee could claim under the unfair dismissal provisions.[47]

Derogation by agreement

Apart from the individual's ability to opt out of the maximum working week (see above), the WT Regulations allow derogations, in some instances, by agreement between the employer and representatives of the employees. The types of agreement are:

1 *collective agreements*

   which, according to Regulation 2, are defined in section 178 TULRCA. They are agreements between employers and independent trade unions recognised for collective bargaining purposes, which allow agreement to be reached on

   - extension of the reference period for averaging the 48-hour week from 17 weeks up to a maximum of 52 weeks[48]
   - modifying or excluding the application of the regulations concerning the length of night work, health assessments, daily and weekly rest periods and daily rest breaks[49]

2 *workforce agreements*

   which, according to schedule 1 to the Regulations, are valid if the following conditions are met:

   - the agreement is in writing
   - it has effect for a specified period not exceeding five years
   - it applies to all the relevant members of the workforce or to a particular group within the relevant workforce
   - the agreement is signed by representatives of the workforce or group
   - before the agreement is signed, the employer provides all the workers concerned with a copy plus any necessary guidance.

If the employer has fewer than 20 workers, a workforce agreement can be reached either by representatives of that workforce or by obtaining the support of the majority of the workforce. Representatives of the workforce are the elected representatives of the workforce concerned. A workforce agreement will allow the same derogations as those for collective agreement.

Regulation 2 also contains a definition of a relevant agreement. It is an agreement which can be a provision of a collective agreement which forms part of a contract between the worker and the employer, or a workforce agreement, or any other agreement in writing that is legally enforceable as between employer and worker.

TIME OFF FOR TRADE UNION DUTIES AND ACTIVITIES

No minimum period of service is required before trade unionists can claim time off.

TRADE UNION DUTIES

According to section 168 TULRCA 1992, employers must permit employees who are officials of independent trade unions recognised by them to take reasonable time off with pay during working hours to enable them to:

- carry out their duties which are concerned with negotiations with the employer that are related to or connected with any of the matters specified in section 178(2) TULRCA and in relation to which the employer recognises the union

- carry out any other duties which are concerned with the performance of any functions that are related to or connected with any matters listed in section 178(2) TULRCA 1992 and that the employer has agreed may be performed by the union – this includes accompanying workers, at their request, to disciplinary and grievance hearings[50]

- receive information from the employer and be consulted under section 188 TULRCA 1992 or the Transfer Regulations 1981

- undergo training in aspects of industrial relations which is both relevant to the carrying out of any of the duties mentioned in the first bullet point above and approved by their trade union or the TUC.

An official is defined as someone who is an officer of the union or branch of it, or someone who is elected or appointed in accordance with the rules to be a representative of its members or some of them[51] (see Chapter 18 on the meaning of 'independence' and recognition).

The amount of time off allowed, together with the purpose for which, the occasions on which, and any conditions subject to which, time off may be taken, depends on what is reasonable in all the circumstances having regard to any relevant provisions in the ACAS Code of Practice.[52] The Code does not lay down any fixed amount of time that employers should permit officials to take off. Its main theme is that employers and trade unions should reach agreements on arrangements for handling time off in ways appropriate to their situations.

PAY FOR PERMITTED TIME OFF

Officials who are permitted time off should receive normal remuneration as if they had worked. Where the remuneration varies with the work done, average hourly earnings should be paid.[53] No claim can be made for overtime which would normally have been worked unless that overtime was contractually required, and there is no entitlement to be paid for time spent on trade union duties outside working hours.[54] It follows that an employee on the night shift who attends a works committee meeting during the day will not be entitled to a payment, whereas a day shift worker would. Nevertheless, employees may reasonably require paid time off during working hours to enable them to undertake the relevant duties or training – for example, to travel to or return from a training course.[55] Two further points should be noted. First, the 'set-off formula' applies here.[56] Second, employers who give their part-time employees paid time off only up to the limit of their normal working hours may be discriminating contrary to Article 141 EC. In *Davies v Neath Port Talbot Borough Council*[57] the employee concerned worked a 22-hour week. The individual was a health and safety representative and was given time off to attend two five-day courses run by the union. The employer agreed to pay for the usual working hours, not the actual time spent on the courses. The employee made an equal pay claim under Article 119 (now Article 141) of the EC Treaty. The EAT agreed that part-time workers had a right to be paid on the same basis as full-timers when attending such courses and that to do otherwise would amount to indirect sex discrimination.

LEGITIMATE REASONS FOR TIME OFF

The Code of Practice recommends that officials of recognised trade unions should be allowed reasonable time off for duties concerned with negotiations related to or connected with:[58]

- terms and conditions of employment, or the conditions in which employees are required to work – eg pay, hours of work, holiday pay and entitlement, sick pay arrangements, pensions, learning and training needs, equal opportunities, notice periods, the working environment and the operation of digital equipment and other machinery

- engagement or non-engagement, or termination or suspension of employment or the duties of employment, of one or more workers – eg recruitment and selection policies, human resource planning, redundancy and dismissal arrangements

- allocation of work, or the duties of employment as between workers or groups of workers – eg job grading, job evaluation, job descriptions, flexible working practices and family-friendly policies

- matters of discipline – eg disciplinary procedures, arrangements for representing trade union members at internal interviews, arrangements for appearing on behalf of trade union members, or as witnesses before agreed outside appeal bodies or employment tribunals

- trade union membership or non-membership – eg representational agreements, any union involvement in the induction of new workers

- facilities for officials of trade unions – eg accommodation, equipment, names of new workers to the union

- machinery for negotiation and consultation and other procedures – eg arrangements for collective bargaining, grievance procedures, joint consultation, communicating with members, communicating with other union officials also concerned with collective bargaining with the employer.

The Code states that where an official is not taking part in industrial action but represents members who are, normal arrangements for time off with pay should apply.[59] Additionally, the code suggests that management should make available the facilities necessary for officials to perform their duties efficiently and to communicate effectively with members. The items mentioned are accommodation for meetings, access to a telephone, notice-boards and the use of office facilities.[60]

What has to be demonstrated is that there is a sufficient connection between the collective bargaining and the duty for which leave is sought.[61] Employment tribunals will have to decide whether the preparatory work is directly relevant to one of the matters specified in section 178(2), and if the employer does not negotiate on the issue, the employer's agreement to the performance of the duty will have to be demonstrated.[62] It also seems that the recognised union must, expressly or impliedly, require the performance of the duty; otherwise, it would be impossible to hold that the individual was 'carrying out those duties … as such an official'.[63] If no agreement on time off is reached in advance of a meeting, a sensible approach might be to determine claims for payment on the basis of what the minutes disclosed. Where only a proportion of the time was spent on section 168 TULRCA 1992 matters, a tribunal will probably find that only a proportion of the time should reasonably be paid for.

As regards industrial relations training, again no fixed amount of time is specified but the code recommends that officials should be permitted paid time off for initial basic training as soon as possible after their election or appointment. Time off should be allowed for further training, for example, where the official has special responsibilities or where it is necessary to meet changed industrial relations circumstances.[64] In determining whether a course meets the requirement of relevance to the specified duties, the description of people attending the course by those responsible for it will be pertinent.[65] Indeed, as a general principle it would seem wise for employers to insist on being shown a copy of course prospectuses.

TRADE UNION ACTIVITIES

An employer must also permit a member of a recognised independent trade union to take reasonable time off during working hours for trade union activities and to represent the union. However, in the absence of any contractual term to the contrary, an employer does not have to pay for such time off. Trade union activities are not statutorily defined, although the code gives the following examples of the activities of a member

- attending workplace meetings to discuss and vote on the outcome of negotiations with the employer

- meeting full-time officials to discuss issues relevant to the workplace

- voting in properly conducted ballots on industrial action

- voting in union elections.[66]

Paragraph 31 of the Code gives examples of activities where the member is acting as a representative of a union:

- branch, area or regional meetings of the union where the business of the union is under discussion

- meetings of official policy-making bodies such as the executive committee or annual conference

- meetings with full-time officials to discuss issues relevant to the workplace.

Not surprisingly section 170(2) TULRCA expressly excludes activities which consist of industrial action. Finally, in *Wignall v British Gas*[67] the EAT rejected the argument that the statute requires each proposed activity on the part of the employee in the service of his or her union to be weighed and tested on its own merits without regard to any other activities or duties on the union's behalf for which the employee might be taking time off. Thus every application for time off under section 170 should be looked at on its merits in the particular circumstances.

Employees wishing to complain of failure to permit time off or to pay the amount required by section 169 TULRCA 1992 must apply to an employment tribunal within three months of the date when the failure occurred.[68] According to the EAT, a complainant must establish on the balance of probabilities that a request for time off was made, that it came to the notice of the employer's appropriate representative, and that he or she refused it, ignored it or failed to respond to it.[69] If the tribunal finds that the claim is well-founded, it must make a declaration to that effect. It may also make an award of compensation, which can include reparation to the official for the wrong done to him or her,[70] of such amount as it considers 'just and equitable in all the circumstances having regard to the employer's default ... and to any loss sustained by the employee which is attributable to the matters complained of'.[71]

TIME OFF FOR PUBLIC DUTIES

Section 50 ERA 1996 permits employees who are, for example:

- members of a local authority[72]

- members of any statutory tribunal

- members of a health authority, NHS trust or a Health Board

- members of a relevant education body[73]
- members of a police authority[74]
- part of the Service Authority of the National Crime Squad or the National Criminal Intelligence Service
- members of a board of prison visitors or a prison visiting committee[75]
- members of the Environment Agency or the Scottish Environment Protection Agency
- members of Scottish Water Customer Consultation Panel

to take time off during working hours for the purpose of performing any of the duties of their office or as members. Employees are eligible for time off irrespective of their length of service, but are not entitled to a payment from their employer by virtue of this section.

The duties referred to are attendance at meetings of the body (or its committees or sub-committees) and 'the doing of any other thing approved by the body' for the purpose of discharging its functions. The amount of time off which is to be allowed and the occasions on which and conditions subject to which it may be taken are those that are reasonable in the circumstances. No code of practice exists for these purposes but what must be taken into consideration is:[76]

- how much time off is required for the performance of the public duty as a whole and how much is required for the particular duty
- how much time off has already been permitted for trade union duties and activities (see above)
- the circumstances of the employer's business and the effect of the employee's absence on the running of it.

The EAT has commented that an employee who undertakes a variety of public and other duties may have some responsibility to plan the absences from work, and to scale down the level of commitment which such public duties involve, so as to produce a pattern which can be regarded as reasonable in the circumstances.[77] A complaint that an employer has failed to permit time off in accordance with the above provisions must be lodged in the same way as a claim that the employer has not complied with sections 168 or 170 TULRCA 1992, and the remedies available are identical. However, two observations may be helpful at this stage. First, rearranging employees' hours of work but requiring them to perform the same duties does not constitute giving time off. Second, it is not the function of employment tribunals to stipulate what amounts of, or conditions for, time off would be appropriate in the future.[78]

TIME OFF FOR EMPLOYEE REPRESENTATIVES[79] AND EMPLOYEE TRUSTEES OF PENSION FUNDS

A person who is an employee representative for the purposes of consultation over redundancies or the transfer of undertakings (see Chapter 13), or a candidate in an election to be such a representative, is entitled to reasonable time off during working hours to perform the functions of such a representative or candidate.[80] Employees who are permitted time off are entitled to be paid at the appropriate rate.[81] Those who feel that their rights have been infringed can use the enforcement mechanisms available in relation to time off for antenatal care.[82]

Section 58(1) ERA 1996 allows employee trustees of a pension fund reasonable time off during working hours for the purpose of performing any of their duties as a trustee or undergoing training relevant to those duties. In ascertaining what is reasonable in all the circumstances, account must be taken of:

- how much time off is required for the performance of the trustee's duties and undergoing relevant training, and how much time off is needed for undertaking the particular duty or training, and

- the circumstances of the employer's business and the effect of the employee's absence on the running of it.[83]

Employees who feel that this right has been infringed must normally complain to an employment tribunal within three months. The remedies available are identical to those that apply to time off for trade union duties (see above).[84]

It should also be noted that employee representatives (or candidates in an election) and trustees of pension funds have the right not to be subjected to any detriment on the ground that they performed (or proposed to perform) their functions or activities.[85] Claims must be lodged within three months of the act (or failure to act) complained of, and the remedies available are the same as for the right not to be subject to detriment on trade union grounds (see above).[86]

TIME OFF FOR STUDY OR TRAINING

Section 63A of the ERA 1996 permits certain young employees to have time off for study or training. The employees concerned are those who:

- are aged 16 or 17 years, and

- are not receiving full-time or further education, and

- have not attained such standard of achievement as is prescribed by regulations made by the Secretary of State.[87]

These standards of achievement are set out in the Right to Time Off for Study or Training Regulations 2001[88] (RTOST Regulations). Examples of the standards of achievement are grades A–C in five subjects at GCSE or one intermediate level GNVQ or one GSVQ at level 2.[89]

In addition young employees who:

- are aged 18 years
- are undertaking training or study leading to a relevant qualification
- began that study before reaching the age of 18 years

are also entitled to time off during working hours.

The amount of time off permitted must be reasonable, taking into account the requirements of the employee's study or training and the circumstances of the employer's business and the effect of the time taken off on that business.[90] An employee who has the right to take time off for study and training also has the right to be paid remuneration by the employer at the normal hourly rate.[91] If an employee has been unreasonably refused permission for time off or has not been paid correctly for that time off, he or she may make a complaint to an employment tribunal.[92] The complaint must be made within three months, unless not reasonably practicable, beginning with the day that the time off was taken or should have been taken. If the complaint is well-founded, the tribunal may make a declaration to that effect or order the employer to pay compensation equal to the amount of remuneration to which the employee would have been entitled.

TIME OFF TO LOOK FOR WORK

A person who has been continuously employed for two years or more and is under notice of dismissal by reason of redundancy is entitled to reasonable time off during working hours to look for new employment or make arrangements for training for future employment.[93] Such an employee should be paid at the appropriate hourly rate for the period of absence. This is one week's pay divided by the number of normal weekly hours, or, where the number of working hours varies, the average of such hours.[94]

A complaint that an employer has unreasonably refused time off or has failed to pay the whole or any part of any amount to which the employee is entitled must be presented to an employment tribunal, if reasonably practicable, within three months of the day on which it is alleged that the time off should have been allowed or paid for.[95] If the complaint is well-founded, the tribunal must make a declaration to that effect and order the employer to pay the amount which it finds due to the employee. Curiously, although the employee is entitled to be paid 'an amount equal to the remuneration to which he would have been entitled if he had been allowed the time off', the maximum that a tribunal can award is two-fifths of a week's pay. In *Dutton v Hawker Siddeley Aviation Ltd*[96] the EAT rejected the argument that employees had to give details of any appointments or interviews for which they wished to take time off.

- The WT Regulations implement the WT Directive and parts of the Young Workers Directive.

- The Regulations provide for a maximum 48-hour week during a 17-week reference period and provide rules on night work, rest periods and annual leave.

- The individual is able to agree to opt out of the 48-hour week and there are provisions for determining the rules by collective and workforce agreements.

- No minimum period of service is required before trade unionists can claim time off.

- Employers must permit employees who are officials of independent trade unions recognised by them to take reasonable time off with pay.

- Members of a recognised independent trade union are entitled to reasonable time off during working hours for trade union activities and to represent the union.

- Employees are to be permitted time off, without pay, for a variety of public duties such as being a justice of the peace or a member of a local authority.

- Young employees who are not receiving full-time education are entitled to time off to study and train for certain qualifications.

- A person who has been continuously employed for two years or more and is under notice of dismissal for redundancy is entitled to reasonable time off, during working hours, to look for new work.

Reinforce your understanding of this chapter by visiting www.cipd.co.uk/sss for activities, questions, weblinks and additional case studies

REFERENCES

1   SI 1998/1833

2   Directive 93/104 concerning certain aspects of the organisation of working time

3   Directive 94/33 on the protection of young people at work

4   *UK v Council of the European Union* (1997) ICR 443

5   SI 2003/1684; see also the Road Transport (Working Time) Regulations 2005 SI 2005/639

6   (2001) IRLR 838

7   See amended Regulation 18 WT Regulations 1998

8   Amended Regulation 2 WT Regulations 1998

9   Regulation 20 WT Regulations 2003

10 Regulation 25A WT Regulations 2003

11 *Bacica v Muir* (2006) IRLR 35

12 (2003) IRLR 211

13 *Byrne Brothers (Formwork) Ltd v Baird* (2002) IRLR 96

14 (2003) IRLR 199

15 See Regulation 2 WT Regulations 1998

16 *Landeshauptstadt Kiel v Jaeger* (2003) IRLR 804

17 *Pfeiffer and others v Deutsches Rotes Kreuz, Kreisverband Waldshut eV* Case C-397/01 (2005) IRLR 137

18 (1999) IRLR 308

19 Regulation 4(6) WT Regulations 1998

20 This requirement was introduced by the Working Time Regulations 1999, SI 1999/3372. It had the effect of simplifying the records that had to be kept, thus making it easier for such opt-out agreements to be reached.

21 Regulation 5A WT Regulations 1998

22 Regulation 27A WT Regulations 1998

23 See *R v Attorney General for Northern Ireland* (1999) IRLR 315

24 (1999) IRLR 315

25 Regulation 6(7) WT Regulations 1998

26 Regulation 7 WT Regulations 1998

27 Regulation 8 WT Regulations 1998

28 Regulation 6A WT Regulations 1998

29 Regulation 27A(3) WT Regulations 1998

30 Regulation 11 WT Regulations 1998; Regulation 11(7) states that the weekly rest period may not be in addition to the daily rest period 'where this is justified by objective or technical reasons or reasons concerning the organisation of work'.

31 Regulation 11(8) WT Regulations 1998; the rest period may not be less than 36 consecutive hours

32 *Gallagher v Alpha Catering Services Ltd* (2005) IRLR 102; see also *Corps of Commissionaires Ltd v Hughes* (2009) IRLR 122

33 Regulation 13 WT Regulations 1998; see also *Gibson v East Riding of Yorkshire* (2000) IRLR 598, where a local authority employee tried unsuccessfully to rely on the Working Time Directive's being directly effective to claim four weeks' holiday.

34 Regulation 15A, inserted by the Working Time (Amendment) Regulations 2001, SI 2001/3256.

35 In which case the worker is entitled to a proportionate payment in lieu; see Regulation 14

36 *Federatie Nederlandse Vakbeweging v Staat der Nederlanden* Case C-124/05 (2006) IRLR 561

37 *Leisure Leagues UK Ltd v Maconnachie* (2002) IRLR 600

38 *Hill v Chapell* (2002) IRLR 19

39 Regulation 15 WT Regulations 1998

40 *Sumsion v BBC* (2007) IRLR 678

41 A week's pay is defined in sections 221–224 ERA 1996. See *Davies v MJ Wyatt (Decorators) Ltd* (2000) IRLR 759, where the EAT held that an employer could not unilaterally reduce an employee's contractual pay in order to provide for holiday pay.

42 *Stringer v HM Revenue & Customs* (2009) IRLR 214

43 *Robinson-Steele v RD Retail Services Ltd* Case C-131/04 (2006) IRLR 386

44 *Lyddon v Englefield Brickwork Ltd* (2008) IRLR 198

45 Regulation 30 WT Regulations 1998

46 Section 101A ERA 1996

47 Section 49(5A) ERA 1996

48 Regulation 23(b) WT Regulations 1998

49 Regulation 23(a) WT Regulations 1998, although Regulation 24 allows for compensatory rest periods and rest breaks

50 Section 10(7) ERel Act 1999

51 Section 119 TULRCA 1992

52 ACAS Code of Practice on time off for trade union duties and activities 2004

53 Section 169(3) TULRCA 1992

54 Working hours are defined in the same way as section 146(2) TULRCA 1992

55 See *Hairsine v Hull City Council* (1992) IRLR 211

56 Section 169(4) TULRCA 1992

57 (1999) IRLR 769

58 Paragraph 11

59 Paragraph 49

60 See paragraph 38

61 See *London Ambulance Service v Charlton* (1992) IRLR 510

62 See *British Bakeries v Adlington* (1989) IRLR 218

63 See *Ashley v Ministry of Defence* (1984) IRLR 57

64 Paragraph 21

65 See *Ministry of Defence v Crook* (1982) IRLR 488

66 Paragraph 30

67 (1984) IRLR 493

68 Unless the 'time-lapse escape clause' applies; section 171 TULRCA 1992

69 *Ryford Ltd v Drinkwater* (1995) IRLR 16

70 *Skiggs v South West Trains Ltd* (2005) IRLR 459

71 Section 172 TULRCA 1992

72 Defined in section 50(5) ERA 1996

73 Defined in section 50(9) ERA 1996

74 Defined in section 50(6) ERA 1996

75 Defined in section 50(7) ERA 1996

76 Section 50(4) ERA 1996

77 *Borders Regional Council v Maule* (1993) IRLR 199

78 See *Corner v Buckinghamshire Council* (1978) IRLR 320

79 Workers must be permitted to take time off during working hours for the purpose of accompanying another worker at a disciplinary or grievance hearing: section 10 ERel Act 1999.

80 Section 168(1) TULRCA 1992 and section 61(1) ERA 1996

81 See section 62 ERA 1996

82 Section 63 ERA 1996

83 See section 58(2) ERA 1996

84 Section 60(3)(4) ERA 1996

85 See sections 47 and 46 ERA 1996 respectively. Dismissal on these grounds is unfair (see Chapter 14)

86 Sections 48–49 ERA 1996

87 Section 63A(1)(a)–(c) ERA 1996

88 SI 2001/2801

89 Regulation 3 RTOST Regulations 2001; the awarding bodies that are recognised for these purposes are listed in the schedule to the Regulations.

90 Section 63A(5) ERA 1996

91 See section 63B(1) ERA 1996

92 Section 63C ERA 1996

93 Section 52 ERA 1996

94 Section 53 ERA 1996

95 Section 54 ERA 1996

96 (1978) IRLR 390

CHAPTER 11

Variation, Breach and Termination of the Contract of Employment at Common Law

OVERVIEW

This chapter deals with various issues raised by the common-law approach to the variation and ending of contracts of employment. To begin with we look at the consequences of unilateral variation of the contract by the employer. We then examine the options open when a breach of contract takes place by studying, firstly, the innocent party's choice in accepting the breach or not, and secondly, the principal remedies for a breach. Issues arising from frustration of the contract and summary dismissal are considered and, finally, we look at the consequences of termination without notice and the remedies for wrongful dismissal.

VARIATION

Theoretically, neither employer nor employee can unilaterally alter the terms and conditions of employment because these can only be varied by mutual agreement.[1] It follows that an employer cannot lawfully vary a contract simply by giving 'notice to vary'. Such a notice will have legal effect only if it terminates the existing contract and offers a new contract on revised terms.[2] Consent to change may be obtained through individual or collective negotiation or may be implied from the conduct of the parties. Thus if employees remain at work for a considerable period of time after revised terms have been imposed, they may be deemed to have accepted the changes.[3] However, where the employer purports to change terms unilaterally which do not immediately impact on the employee, the fact that the latter continues to work knowing that the former is asserting that a change has been effected, does not mean that the employee can be taken to have accepted the variation.[4] Where the individual continues in employment but works 'under protest', it is a question of fact whether or not the variation has been accepted. In *WPM Retail v Lang*[5] it was held that the employer's obligation to pay a bonus in accordance with the terms when the employee was promoted remained in force until the employment was terminated three years later, notwithstanding that the bonus had been paid only in the first month after promotion and the employee had carried on working thereafter. As a general rule, courts and tribunals will be reluctant to find that there has been a consensual variation 'where the employee has been faced with the alternative of dismissal and where the variation has been adverse to his interest'.[6]

A unilateral variation which is not accepted will constitute a breach and could amount to a repudiation of the contract. However, there is no law that any breach which an employee is entitled to treat as repudiatory brings the contract to an end automatically.[7] Where there is repudiatory conduct by the employer, the employee has the choice of affirming the contract (by continuing in employment) or accepting the repudiation as bringing the contract to an end. If the latter option is exercised and the employee resigns within a short period, there will be a constructive dismissal for statutory purposes (see Chapter 12). In practice, developments in the law of unfair dismissal make it very difficult for an employee to resist a unilateral variation. Suffice to say at this stage that employers can offer, as a fair reason for dismissal, the fact that there was a sound business reason for insisting on changes being put into effect. So long as a minimum amount of consultation has taken place, it is relatively easy to satisfy a tribunal, particularly where the majority of employees has been prepared to go along with the employer's proposals, that an employer has acted reasonably in treating a refusal to accept a variation as a sufficient reason for dismissing.[8]

BREACH OF CONTRACT

EMPLOYERS' OPTIONS: DISCIPLINARY AND LEGAL

The options open to an innocent party will depend on whether the breach is of a minor or serious nature. An innocent party may choose to continue with the contract as if nothing had happened (ie waive the breach), may sue for damages, or, in the case of a serious or fundamental breach, may regard the contract as at an end (ie accept the other party's repudiation of it).[9] Although the employer could sue or possibly dismiss for breach of contract, there are a number of reasons why disciplinary rather than legal action is preferred. First, the potential defendant may be unable to pay any damages awarded. Second, the amount likely to be obtained may not be worth the time and effort involved. Third, taking legal rather than disciplinary action against individual employees is not conducive to harmonious industrial relations.

What options are open to employers when employees refuse to carry out all or part of their contractual obligations? Apart from the measures outlined in the previous paragraph, the employer may withhold pay on the grounds that employees who are not ready and willing to render the services required by their contracts are not entitled to remuneration.[10] In *Wiluszynski v London Borough of Tower Hamlets*[11] the employee refused to perform the full range of his duties and had been told by the employer that until he did he would not be required for work or be paid. Although he went to work and performed a substantial part of his duties, the Court of Appeal held that the local authority was entitled to withhold the whole of his remuneration. Clearly, employees are not entitled to pick and choose what work they will do under their contracts. Yet if employers are prepared to accept part-performance, they will be required to pay for such work as is agreed.[12]

The principal remedies for breach of contract are an injunction (an order restraining a particular type of action), a declaration of the rights of the parties, and damages. An account of profits may be ordered in exceptional circumstances.[13] Traditionally, great emphasis was placed on the personal nature of the contract of employment and courts were extremely reluctant to order a party to continue to perform the contract. However, in recent years the courts have been more willing to grant injunctions against employers who act in breach of contract.[14] Nevertheless, they need to be satisfied not only that it would be just to make such an order but also that it would be workable.[15] The mere fact that the employer and employee are in dispute does not mean that mutual confidence has evaporated.[16] Although an employee cannot be compelled to return to work,[17] a tribunal has the power to order the re-employment of someone who has been unfairly dismissed and seeks this remedy (see Chapter 15). Those who seek damages can be compensated for the direct and likely consequences of the breach, although nothing can be recovered for the manner of the breach or for the mental stress, frustration or annoyance caused.[18] However, in *Gogay v Hertfordshire County Council*[19] the Court of Appeal confirmed that damages could be awarded for a psychological disorder brought on by an unlawful suspension. Compensation will not be recoverable for damage to an existing reputation unless pecuniary loss was sustained as a foreseeable consequence of the breach.[20]

CASE STUDY

Thomas Judge was one of three special operations managers. When another manager was appointed at a considerably higher salary than others were receiving, they were told that it was the employer's intention to bring the remuneration of all special operations managers roughly into line. After two years Mr Judge resigned because he was still earning substantially less than the new manager. He argued that the employer had failed to fulfil a contractually binding commitment to raise his pay. According to the claimant, during a conversation at the company's Christmas party, the special operations director had expressly promised to put Mr Judge on the same scale as the new manager within two years.

The Court of Appeal upheld the employment tribunal's decision that the statements made at the party did not amount to a contractual promise. For there to be a legally binding and enforceable contractual obligation there must be certainty as to the contractual commitment entered into, or alternatively facts from which certainty can be established. Although a promise to achieve parity within two years might be sufficiently certain, a promise of parity eventually or in due course was too vague.[21]

The jurisdiction of employment tribunals extends to breach of contract claims which have arisen or are outstanding at the end of employment.[22] Under section 3(2) ETA 1996 the claim must be for:

- damages for breach of a contract of employment or any other contract connected with the employment. However, this does not include the loss of an opportunity to claim unfair dismissal through being sacked prior to satisfying the requirement of having one year's service.[23]

- a sum owed under such a contract

- the recovery of a sum in pursuance of any enactment relating to the terms or performance of such a contract.

Certain claims are excluded – for example, personal injury, breach of confidence and restrictive covenant cases. Employers can bring proceedings (counterclaims) only if an employee has made a claim first, but the employer's claim can then continue even if the employee is unable to continue with the complaint.[24]

An employee's claim must normally be brought within three months of the effective date of termination[25] and an employer's counterclaim must be presented within six weeks of receiving a copy of the originating application. A case is heard by a chairperson sitting alone unless it is decided that a full tribunal should hear it. Although ACAS's services are available, the parties can reach their own agreement without any need for a conciliated settlement or compromise agreement.

AUTOMATIC TERMINATION: FRUSTRATION

A contract is said to have been frustrated where events make it physically impossible or unlawful for the contract to be performed, or where there has been a change such as to radically alter the purpose of the contract.[26] Once a contract has come to an end by reason of frustration, it cannot be treated by the parties as still subsisting. If the parties come to an arrangement to continue the employment relationship, then this may constitute a new contract or some other arrangement. It will not be a continuation of the original contract which has been frustrated.[27] A contract that is still capable of being performed but becomes subject to an unforeseen risk is not frustrated.[28] As long as the frustrating event is not self-induced, there is an automatic termination of the contract – ie there is no dismissal.[29] This being so, it was not uncommon for an employer to resist a claim for unfair dismissal by alleging that the contract had been frustrated – for example, on grounds of sickness. Although the EAT thought that the concept of frustration should normally come into play only where the contract is for a long term and cannot be determined by notice, the Court of Appeal has allowed this doctrine to be applied to contracts of employment that can be terminated by short periods of notice.[30]

FRUSTRATION OF THE CONTRACT THROUGH ILLNESS

The following principles are relevant to the application of the doctrine of frustration in the event of illness.[31] First, the courts must guard against too easy an application of the doctrine. Second, an attempt to decide the date that frustration occurred may help to decide whether it is a true frustration situation. Third, the factors below may help to decide the issue:

- length of previous employment

- how long the employment was expected to continue

- the nature of the job

- the nature, length and effect of the illness or disabling event[32]

- the employer's need for the work to be done and the need for a replacement employee

- whether wages have continued to be paid

- the acts and statements of the employer in relation to the employment. In *Hart v Marshall & Sons*[33] the EAT held that the employer's acceptance of sick notes did not prevent a tribunal from finding that the contract had been frustrated

- whether in all the circumstances a reasonable employer could have been expected to wait any longer

- the terms of the contract as to sick pay, if any

- a consideration of the prospects of recovery.

A prison sentence is a potentially frustrating event. However, the circumstances of each case have to be examined to discover whether such a sentence has in fact operated to frustrate the contract or whether its termination resulted from some other cause.[34]

TERMINATION WITHOUT NOTICE: SUMMARY DISMISSAL

A summary dismissal occurs where the employer terminates the contract of employment without notice. It must be distinguished from an instant dismissal which has no legal meaning but normally refers to a dismissal without investigation or inquiry. Whereas an instant dismissal is likely to be procedurally defective in unfair dismissal terms (see Chapter 13), a summary dismissal may be lawful under both common law and statute.

In order to justify summary dismissal the employee must be in breach of an important express or implied term of the contract – ie be guilty of gross misconduct. Although certain terms are always regarded as important – for example, the duty not to steal or damage the employer's property, the duty to obey lawful orders and not to engage in industrial action – the significance of other terms will depend on the nature of the employer's business and the employee's position in it. If an employer feels that a particular act or omission would warrant summary dismissal, this fact should be communicated clearly to all employees.[35]

One consequence of the contractual approach is that everything hinges upon the facts in the particular case and previous decisions usually have little bearing. Nevertheless, a number of general principles can be discerned:

- single acts of misconduct are less likely to give rise to a right of summary dismissal than a persistent pattern

- it is the nature of the act rather than its consequences that is relevant

- an employer is more likely to be entitled to dismiss summarily for misconduct within the workplace than outside it

- a refusal to obey instructions can still amount to repudiation even though the employee has mistakenly proceeded in the *bona fide* belief that the work which he or she had been instructed to do fell outside the scope of the contract.[36]

If employers do not invoke the right to end the contract within a reasonable period, they will be taken to have waived their rights and can only seek damages. What is a reasonable period will depend on the facts of the particular case. In *Allders International v Parkins*[37] it was held that nine days was too long a period to elapse in relation to an allegation of stealing before deciding what to do about the alleged repudiatory conduct. In *Gunton v London Borough of Richmond*[38] the Court of Appeal decided that the general doctrine that repudiation by one party does not terminate a contract applies to employment law. Thus an unlawful summary dismissal does not terminate a contract of employment until the employee has accepted the employer's repudiation and certain contractual rights and obligations will survive until that time, for example, in relation to a disciplinary procedure (see Chapter 12 on the effective date of termination for statutory purposes). Nevertheless, in the absence of special circumstances, a court will easily infer that the repudiation has been accepted.[39] Finally, at common law an employer is not required to supply a reason for dismissal, although this is now qualified by statute[40] (see Chapter 13).

TERMINATION WITH NOTICE

Usually, either party is entitled to terminate a contract of employment by giving notice,[41] and once notice has been given it cannot be unilaterally withdrawn.[42] (It almost goes without saying that an employer who makes a mistake could offer to re-employ.) The courts have consistently ruled that for notice to be effective it must be possible to ascertain the date of termination and, not infrequently, employees have confused an advanced warning of closure with notice of dismissal.[43] The length of the notice will be determined by the express or implied terms of the contract and, if no term can be identified, both parties are required to give a reasonable period of notice. What is reasonable will depend on the circumstances of the relationship – for example, the employee's position and length of service. Thus in *Hill v C. A. Parsons & Co. Ltd*[44] a 63-year-old engineer with 35 years' service was held to be entitled to at least six months' notice.

Apart from the situation where individuals are disentitled to notice by reason of their conduct,[45] section 86(1) ERA 1996 provides that certain minimum periods of notice must be given. After a month's service an employee is entitled to a week's notice and this applies until the employment has lasted for two years. At this point two weeks' notice is owed and from then on the employee must receive an extra week's notice for each year of service up to a maximum of 12 weeks. According to section 86(2) ERA 1996, an employee with a month's service or more need give only one week's notice to terminate but there is nothing to prevent the parties from agreeing that both should receive more than the statutory minimum.

Although the ERA 1996 does not prevent an employee from accepting a payment in lieu of notice, strictly speaking an employer must have contractual authority for insisting on such a payment. Without such authority a payment in lieu of notice will be construed as damages for the failure to provide proper notice.[46] Thus a payment in lieu can properly terminate a contract of employment if the contract provides for such a payment or the parties agree that the employee will accept a payment in lieu, provided the payment relates to a period no shorter than that of the notice to which the employee would be entitled either under the contract of employment or section 86(1) ERA 1996.[47] The date of termination at common law is the day notice expires or the day wages in lieu are accepted. Except where the notice to be given by the employer is at least one week more than the statutory minimum, an employee is entitled to be paid during the period of notice even if:

- no work is provided by the employer

- the employee is incapable of work because of sickness or injury

- the employee is absent from work wholly or partly because of pregnancy or childbirth or an adoption, parental or maternity leave

- the employee is absent in accordance with the terms of his or her employment relating to holidays.[48]

Any payments by the employer by way of sick pay, maternity pay, paternity pay, adoption pay, holiday pay or otherwise go towards meeting this liability.[49] If employees take part in a strike after they have been given notice, payment is due for the period when they were not on strike. However, where employees give notice and then go on strike, they do not qualify for any payment under section 88 or 89 ERA 1996.[50]

REMEDIES FOR WRONGFUL DISMISSAL

Basically, a wrongful dismissal is a dismissal without notice or with inadequate notice in circumstances where proper notice should have been given. The expression also covers dismissals which are in breach of agreed procedures. Thus where there is a contractual disciplinary procedure, an employee may be able to obtain an injunction or declaration from the courts so as to prevent a dismissal or declare a dismissal void if the procedure has not been followed.[51] However, an injunction will only be granted if the court is convinced that the employer's repudiation has not been accepted, that the employer has sufficient trust and confidence in the employee, and that damages would not be an adequate remedy.[52]

Judicial review is available where an issue of public law is involved, although employment by a public authority does not by itself inject any element of public law.[53] Indeed, where an alternative remedy is available, judicial review will only be exercised in exceptional circumstances. Factors to be taken into account in considering whether the circumstances are exceptional include the speed of the alternative procedure, whether it was as convenient and whether the matter depended on some particular knowledge available to the appellate body.[54]

For the reason mentioned earlier, the courts are reluctant to enforce a contract of employment, so in the vast majority of cases the employee's remedy will lie in damages for breach of contract. A person who suffers a wrongful dismissal is entitled to be compensated for such loss as arises naturally from the breach and for any loss which was reasonably foreseeable by the parties as being likely to arise from it. Hence an employee will normally recover only the amount of wages lost between the date of the wrongful dismissal and the date when the contract could lawfully have been terminated.[55] The following are examples of situations where damages have been awarded:

- an employee was allowed to keep share options, even though the terms of the share option scheme provided that the option to purchase lapsed on termination as a result of disciplinary action[56]

- a senior employee with a contract that allowed for a 10 per cent per annum salary increase and substantial annual bonuses during a three-year notice period was entitled to the benefit of those payments even though they were at the discretion of the board; for the board to exercise its discretion to reduce these payments to nil would have been capricious and a breach of contract[57]

- an employee was entitled to damages in respect of enhanced pension rights which he lost when his employment was terminated without proper notice 12 days before his 55th birthday. For these purposes there is no difference in principle between lost pension rights and lost pay.[58]

Damages are not available for hurt feelings or the manner in which the dismissal took place, even though the manner might have made it more difficult to obtain other employment.[59]

Except where employees have a contractual right to a payment in lieu of notice,[60] or are entitled to their full payments during a contractual notice period,[61] they have a duty to mitigate their loss. In effect, this means that they are obliged to look for another job. Where there is a failure to mitigate, the court will deduct a sum it feels the employee might reasonably have been expected to earn. As regards state benefits, it would appear that any benefit received by the dismissed employee should be deducted only where not to do so would result in a net gain to the employee.[62] Finally, the first £30,000 of damages is to be awarded net of tax but any amount above this figure will be awarded gross because it is taxable in the hands of the recipient.

Reinforce your understanding of this chapter by visiting www.cipd.co.uk/sss for activities, questions, weblinks and additional case studies

REFERENCES

1 See *Security & Facilities Division v Hayes* (2001) IRLR 81

2 *Alexander v STC Ltd* (1991) IRLR 119

3 *Aparau v Iceland Frozen Foods* (1996) IRLR 119

4 See *Harlow v Artemis Ltd* (2008) IRLR 629

5 (1978) IRLR 343

6 See *Sheet Metal Components Ltd v Plumridge* (1979) IRLR 86

7 See *Boyo v Lambeth Borough Council* (1995) IRLR 50

8 See *Hollister v National Farmers Union* (1979) IRLR 238

9 See *Macari v Celtic F.C.* (1999) IRLR 787

10 See *Ticehurst v British Telecom* (1992) IRLR 219; section 14(5) ERA 1996 allows deductions to be made in respect of participation in industrial action.

11 (1989) IRLR 279

12 See *Spackman v London Metropolitan University* (2007) IRLR 744

13 See *Attorney-General v Blake* (2001) IRLR 37

14 See *Gryf-Lowczowski v Hinchingbrooke Healthcare NHS Trust* (2006) IRLR 100

15 See *Robb v London Borough of Hammersmith* (1991) IRLR 72

16 See *Hughes v London Borough of Southwark* (1988) IRLR 55

17 Section 236 TULRCA 1992

18 See *Bliss v South East Thames Regional Health Authority* (1988) IRLR 308

19 (2000) IRLR 703

20 See *Malik v Bank of Credit and Commerce* (1997) IRLR 462 and *BCCI v Ali (No.3)* (1999) IRLR 508

21 *Judge v Crown Leisure Ltd* (2005) IRLR 823

22 See *Fraser v HLMAD Ltd* (2006) IRLR 687 on the problems caused by the financial limit of £25,000.

23 See *Harper v Virgin Net Ltd* (2004) IRLR 390

24 See *Patel v RCMS Ltd* (1999) IRLR 161

25 See *Capek v Lincolnshire County Council* (2000) IRLR 590

26 See *Rose v Dodd* (2005) IRLR 977

27 See *G F Sharp & Co. Ltd v McMillan* (1998) IRLR 632

28 See *Converform Ltd v Bell* (1981) IRLR 195

29 Where an employer dies or the business is destroyed, a dismissal is deemed to occur for the purpose of safeguarding an employee's right to a redundancy payment; section 174 ERA 1996.

30 See *Nottcutt v Universal Equipment Ltd* (1986) I WLR 641

31 See *Williams v Watsons Ltd* (1990) IRLR 164

32 Employers must be aware of the possible implications of the DDA 1995; see Chapter 7.

33 (1977) IRLR 61

34 See *F C Shepherd v Jerrom* (1986) IRLR 358

35 See ACAS Code of Practice on Disciplinary and Grievance Procedures 2009 paragraph 23

36 See *Blyth v Scottish Liberal Club* (1983) IRLR 245

37 (1981) IRLR 68

38 (1980) IRLR 321

39 See *Boyo v Lambeth Borough Council* (note 7)

40 Section 92 ERA 1996

41 A contract of apprenticeship is for a fixed term and the ordinary law relating to dismissal does not apply; see *Flett v Matteson* (2006) IRLR 277.

42 See *Harris & Russell Ltd v Slingsby* (1973) IRLR 221

43 See *ICL v Kennedy* (1981) IRLR 28

44 (1971) 3 WLR 995

45 See section 86(6) ERA 1996

46 See *Cerberus Ltd v Rowley* (2001) IRLR 160

47 See *Ginsberg Ltd v Parker* (1988) IRLR 483

48 Section 88(1) ERA 1996

49 Section 88(2) ERA 1996

50 Section 91(2) ERA 1996

51 See *Jones v Gwent County Council* (1992) IRLR 521

52 See *Dietman v London Borough of Brent* (1988) IRLR 299 and *Wall v STC* (1990) IRLR 55

53 See *R v East Berkshire Health Authority ex parte Walsh* (1984) IRLR 278 and *McLaren v Home Office* (1990) IRLR 338

54 See *R v Chief Constable of Merseyside Police ex parte Calveley* (1986) 2 WLR 144 and *R v Broxtowe Borough Council ex parte Bradford* (2000) IRLR 329

55 See *Marsh v National Autistic Society* (1993) ICR 453

56 See *Lovett v Biotrace International Ltd* (1999) IRLR 375

57 *Clark v BET plc* (1997) IRLR 348; see also *Clark v Nomura plc* (2000) IRLR 766

58 See *Silvey v Pendragon plc* (2001) IRLR 685

59 See *Johnson v Unisys Ltd* (2001) IRLR 716

60 See *Abrahams v Performing Rights Society* (1995) IRLR 486

61 See *Gregory v Wallace* (1998) IRLR 387

62 See *Westwood v Secretary of State* (1984) IRLR 209

CHAPTER 12

Unfair Dismissal (1): Exclusions and the meaning of dismissal

OVERVIEW

Here we are concerned with the meaning of dismissal for statutory purposes and with the various requirements that must be satisfied before an employee is entitled to protection against unfair dismissal. We start by looking at the hurdles to be overcome, such as the need to have one year's continuous service in order to claim. The ways in which a contract of employment can be ended are considered, such as termination with or without notice, by mutual agreement or by constructive dismissal. We then look at the importance of identifying the effective date of termination.

EXCLUSIONS AND QUALIFICATIONS

Every employee has the right not to be unfairly dismissed but this generally applies only to those working in Great Britain at the time of dismissal.[1] There are other general exclusions and qualifications – for example, the need to have one year's service.[2] Although there is no age limit for claiming unfair dismissal, retirement may be a potentially fair reason for dismissal. (The relevant statutory provisions on age discrimination are discussed in Chapter 7.)

CONTINUOUS SERVICE

In order to complain of unfair dismissal, one year's continuous service is required. This qualification does not apply if the reason or principal reason for dismissal was 'inadmissible' (see Chapter 13). Continuity is to be calculated up to the effective date of termination in accordance with sections 210–219 ERA 1996 (see Chapter 16). Employees who are wrongfully deprived of their statutory minimum entitlement to notice or receive a payment in lieu can add on that period of notice in ascertaining their length of service.[3] Longer contractual notice cannot be added and it should be remembered that employees who are guilty of gross misconduct forfeit their entitlement to notice.[4] Two other exceptions should be noted. First, if an employee is dismissed rather than suspended on medical grounds, only one month's service is required.[5] Second, where unlawful discrimination is being alleged, no minimum period of service is needed because the case will be brought under the relevant anti-discrimination legislation rather than ERA 1996.

CONTRACTING OUT

It is possible to contract out of the unfair dismissal and redundancy payment provisions in the following ways:

- An employee will be excluded if a dismissal procedures agreement has been designated by the Secretary of State as exempting those covered by it. An application must be made jointly by all the parties to the agreement and the Secretary of State must be satisfied about the matters listed in section 110(3) ERA 1996.

- An agreement to refrain from presenting a complaint will be binding if it has been reached after the involvement of a conciliation officer or satisfies the conditions regulating 'compromise agreements' (see Chapter 15).[6]

THE MEANING OF DISMISSAL

Apart from the lay-off and short-time provisions, an employee is to be treated as dismissed if:[7]

- the contract under which he or she is employed is terminated by the employer with or without notice, or

- a limited-term contract terminates by virtue of the limiting event without being renewed under the same contract, or

- the employee terminates the contract with or without notice in circumstances such that he or she is entitled to terminate it without notice by reason of the employer's conduct.

For redundancy purposes section 174 ERA 1996 provides that a contract is terminated by the employer's death unless the business is carried on by the personal representatives of the deceased. Similarly, if the employee dies after being given notice of dismissal, he or she is to be treated as dismissed.[8] Finally, a court order for the compulsory winding up of a company, the appointment of a receiver by a court and a major split in a partnership can all constitute a termination by the employer.

TERMINATION BY THE EMPLOYER WITH OR WITHOUT NOTICE

It is vitally important not to confuse a warning of impending dismissal – for example, through the announcement of a plant closure – with an individual notice to terminate.[9] For the giving of notice to constitute a dismissal at law, the actual date of termination must be ascertainable. Where an employer has given notice to terminate, an employee who gives counter-notice indicating that he or she wishes to leave before the employer's notice has expired is still to be regarded as dismissed.[10] However, in the case of redundancy this counter-notice must be given within the 'obligatory period' of the employer's notice. This 'obligatory period' is the minimum period which the employer is required to give by virtue of section 86(1) ERA 1996 (see Chapter 11) or the contract of employment.[11] Before the counter-notice is due to expire, the employer can write to the employee and ask for it to be withdrawn, stating that unless this is done liability to make a redundancy payment will be contested.[12] If employees do not accede to such a request, a tribunal is empowered to determine whether they should receive the whole or part of the payment to which they would have been entitled. Tribunals decide what is just and equitable 'having regard to the reason for which the employee seeks to leave the employment and those for which the employer requires him to continue in it'.[13] Another possibility is that an employee leaves before the expiry of the employer's notice of termination for reasons of redundancy by mutual consent. This will not affect entitlement to a redundancy payment.[14]

MUTUALLY AGREED TERMINATION

A mutually agreed termination does not amount to a dismissal at law, although as a matter of policy tribunals will not find an agreement to terminate unless it is proved that the employee really did agree with full knowledge of the implications. Thus in *Hellyer Bros v Atkinson*[15] it was held that the employee was merely accepting the fact of his dismissal rather than agreeing to terminate his employment.

Whether a mutual agreement is void because of duress is a matter for the employment tribunal.[16] Moreover, where a provision for automatic termination is introduced by way of a variation to a subsisting contract, it may be declared void if its effect is to exclude or limit the operation of ERA 1996.[17] It is possible to have a mutual determination of a contract in a redundancy situation. Thus in *Birch and Humber v University of Liverpool*[18] the Court of Appeal held that there was no dismissal when the employer accepted the employees' applications for premature retirement. However, where an employer seeks volunteers for redundancy, those who are dismissed will be eligible for a payment despite their willingness to leave.[19]

If people resign of their own volition there is no dismissal at law, but if pressure has been applied the situation is different – for example, where the employee is given the choice of resigning or being dismissed. However, an invitation to resign must not be too imprecise. Hence in *Haseltine Lake & Co. v Dowler*[20] it was held that there was no dismissal when the employee was told that if he did not find a job elsewhere his employment would eventually be terminated. It would also appear that there is no dismissal when an employee resigns on terms offered by an employer's disciplinary subcommittee. In *Staffordshire C.C. v Donovan*[21] the EAT stated:

> It seems to us that it would be most unfortunate if, in a situation where the parties are seeking to negotiate in the course of disciplinary proceedings

and an agreed form of resignation is worked out by the parties, one of the parties should be able to say subsequently that the fact that the agreement was reached in the course of disciplinary proceedings entitles the employee thereafter to say that there was a dismissal.

THE IMPORTANCE OF THE ACTUAL WORDS USED IN RESIGNING OR DISMISSING

Problems can arise in determining whether the words used by an employee can properly be regarded as amounting to a resignation. Normally, where the words are unequivocal and are understood by the employer as a resignation, it cannot be said that there was no resignation because a reasonable employer would not have so understood the words. However, exceptions may be made in the case of immature employees, or of decisions taken in the heat of the moment or under pressure exerted by an employer.[22] An objective test of whether the employee intended to resign applies only where the language used is ambiguous or where it is not plain how the employer understood the words. In *Southern v Franks Charlesly*[23] the Court of Appeal decided that the words 'I am resigning' were unambiguous and indicated a present intention of resigning. Equally, doubts can arise in relation to expressions used by an employer. Thus in *Tanner v Kean*[24] it was decided that the words 'You're finished with me' were merely spoken in annoyance and amounted to a reprimand rather than a dismissal. The EAT has advised tribunals that in deciding whether the employer's words constituted a dismissal in law they should consider all the circumstances of the case to determine whether the words were intended to bring the contract to an end.

WHERE A LIMITED-TERM CONTRACT TERMINATES

According to section 235(2A), a limited term contract is one which terminates by virtue of a limiting event. There are three categories of limiting event: the expiry of a fixed term (see Chapter 4); the performance of a specific task; or the occurrence of an event or failure of an event to occur.[25]

CONSTRUCTIVE DISMISSAL

The situation in which an employee terminates the contract with or without notice in circumstances such that he or she is entitled to terminate it without notice by reason of the employer's conduct is commonly referred to as a 'constructive' dismissal. In these circumstances the employer's behaviour constitutes a repudiation of the contract and the employee accepts that repudiation by resigning. The case of *RDF Group plc v Clements*[26] involved an individual who was subjected to a campaign of vilification in the press while on garden leave. The High Court held that because Clements' own disloyalty amounted to a fundamental breach of contract, he was not entitled to accept the employer's repudiation.

Employees are entitled to treat themselves as constructively dismissed only if the employer is guilty of conduct which is a significant breach going to the root of the contract or which shows that the employer no longer intends to be bound by one or more of its essential terms.[27] Thus a finding that there has been conduct which amounts to a breach of the implied term of trust and confidence will mean that the employee is entitled to claim constructive dismissal.[28] Whether the repudiatory conduct of a supervisor binds the employer depends on whether the acts were done in the course of the supervisor's employment.[29]

If employees continue for any length of time without leaving, they will be regarded as having elected to affirm the contract and will lose the right to treat themselves as discharged.[30] However, provided that employees make clear their objection to what is being done, they are not to be taken to have affirmed the contract by continuing to work and draw pay for a limited period of time.[31] Where the employer has allowed the employee time to make up his or her mind there is no need expressly to reserve the right to accept repudiation.[32] Even though a repudiatory breach of an express term has been waived, it could still form part of a series of acts which cumulatively amounted to a breach of the employer's implied duty to show trust and confidence. If there is merely a threat to repudiate, the employee is not to be treated as constructively dismissed unless there has been unequivocal acceptance of the repudiation before the threat is withdrawn.[33]

CASE STUDY

Tolu Omilaju was employed by a local authority and issued five sets of proceedings alleging race discrimination and victimisation. These were heard in July and August 2001 but the employer refused to pay Mr Omilaju his full salary when he was absent without leave in order to attend the employment tribunal. It was the authority's rule that employees in his position were required to apply for special unpaid leave or annual leave. In September 2001 Mr Omilaju resigned and claimed unfair dismissal.

The Court of Appeal upheld the employment tribunal's decision that the refusal to pay for the time attending the tribunal could not be regarded as the 'final straw' in a series of actions which together amounted to a breach of trust and confidence. According to the Appeal Court, a 'final straw' does not have to be of the same character as earlier acts. However, it must contribute something to the breach of the implied term even if what it adds may be relatively trivial.[34]

In *Robins UK v Triggs*[35] the EAT held that the employer's failure to conduct a proper investigation into grievances contributed materially to earlier acts so as to cumulatively amount to a breach of the implied duty of trust and confidence.

BREACH OF CONTRACT IS A QUESTION OF FACT

It is not necessary to show that the employer intended to repudiate the contract. The tribunal's function is to look at the employer's conduct as a whole and determine whether its cumulative effect judged reasonably and sensibly is such that the employee cannot reasonably be expected to tolerate it.[36] The mere fact that a party to a contract takes a view of its construction that is ultimately shown to be wrong does not of itself constitute repudiatory conduct. It has to be shown that he or she did not intend to be bound by the contract as properly construed.[37] According to the Court of Appeal, whether or not there is a fundamental breach of contract is a question of fact, so the EAT cannot substitute its decision for that of an employment tribunal unless the latter misdirected itself in law or the decision was one which no reasonable tribunal could reach.[38]

DEMOTION AND CHANGE OF DUTIES

A physical assault, demotion, or significant change in job duties[39] or place of work[40] can amount to a constructive dismissal. In relation to the place of work, it is now established that even an express right to transfer may be subject to an implied right to reasonable notice, because employers must not exercise their discretion in such a way as to prevent employees from being able to carry out their part of the contract.[41] However, this does not mean that an employer repudiates a contract simply by introducing a general rule with which a particular employee is unable to comply.[42]

In *Millbrook Furnishing Ltd v McIntosh*[43] the EAT accepted that 'if an employer, under the stresses of the requirements of his business, directs an employee to transfer to other suitable work on a purely temporary basis and at no diminution in wages, that may, in the ordinary case, not constitute a breach of contract'. Nevertheless, the EAT has also held that for a breach to go to the root of the contract it need not involve a substantial alteration to terms and conditions on a permanent basis. A substantial alteration is sufficient by itself.[44] As regards demotion, even where this is provided for within a disciplinary procedure it may amount to repudiation if it can be said that the punishment was grossly out of proportion to the offence.[45] Similarly issuing a final written warning in respect of a relatively minor incident could amount to a constructive dismissal.[46]

ISSUES OF PAY

It is clear that an employer is not entitled to alter the formula whereby wages are calculated but whether a unilateral reduction in additional pay or fringe benefits is of sufficient materiality as to entitle the employee to resign is a matter of degree.[47] A failure to pay an employee's salary or wage is likely to constitute a fundamental breach if it is a deliberate act on the part of an employer rather than a mere breakdown in technology.[48] In *Gardner Ltd v Beresford*,[49] where the employee resigned because she had not received a pay increase for two years while others had, the EAT accepted that in most circumstances it would be reasonable to infer a term that the employer will not treat employees arbitrarily, capriciously or inequitably in the matter of remuneration. However, if a contract makes no reference at all to pay increases, it is impossible to say that there is an implied term that there will always be a pay rise.[50]

Many cases have been decided on the basis that the employer failed to display sufficient trust and confidence in the employee (see Chapter 3).[51] Thus unjustified accusations of theft, foul language or a refusal to act reasonably in dealing with grievances, matters of safety or incidents of harassment could all give rise to a claim of constructive dismissal. According to the EAT, whatever the respective actions of employer and employee at the time of termination, the relevant question is: who really terminated the contract? So when an employer falsely inveigled an employee to resign and take another job with the express purpose of avoiding liability for redundancy it was held that there was a dismissal at law.[52] Similarly, where an employer unilaterally imposes radically different terms of employment, these will be a dismissal under section 95(l)(a) or section 136(1) (a) ERA 1996 if, on an objective construction of the employer's conduct, there is a removal or withdrawal of the old contract. This was held to be the case in *Alcan Extrusions v Yates*,[53] where the employer imposed a continuous rolling shift system in place of the traditional shifts provided for in contracts of employment.

THE EFFECTIVE AND RELEVANT DATE OF TERMINATION

Whether a person is qualified to complain of unfair dismissal or has presented a claim within the prescribed time period (see Chapter 15) must be answered by reference to the effective date of termination. Similarly, entitlement to a redundancy payment and the computation of it, together with the time-limit for submitting a claim, all depend on ascertaining the 'relevant date' of dismissal. Thus, as a matter of policy, employers should ensure that there is no doubt as to what constitutes the effective or relevant date. Sections 97 and 145 ERA 1996 provide that:

- where the contract is terminated by notice, the effective or relevant date is the date on which the notice expires even though the employee does not work out that notice.[54] Where the employee gives counter-notice, the effective date is when the employee ceased working in accordance with that notice.[55] If the employee has given counter-notice in accordance with section 136(3) ERA 1996, the 'relevant date' is the date the counter-notice expires. However, once an employee has been given notice of redundancy to take effect on a specified date, there is nothing to prevent the employer and employee from altering that date by mutual agreement.[56] In *West v Kneels Ltd*[57] the EAT concluded that oral notice starts to run the day after it is given. Logically, the same should be true of notice in writing

- where the contract is determined without notice, the effective or relevant date is the date on which the termination takes effect.[58] The date of termination of people dismissed with payments in lieu of notice is the date on which they are told they are dismissed.[59] According to the Court of Appeal, where an employee is summarily dismissed during the course of a working day, and no question arises as to whether that dismissal constitutes a repudiation which the employee has not accepted, both the contract of employment and the status of employee cease at the moment when the dismissal is communicated to the employee.[60] Where employees are given notice of dismissal and told to work it, but the employer subsequently requires them to leave immediately, the effective or relevant date is the date when they stop working.[61]

- where a limited-term contract terminates by virtue of the limiting event without being renewed under the same contract, the effective or relevant date is the date on which the termination takes effect

- where under the redundancy provisions a statutory trial period has been served, for the purpose of submitting a claim in time the relevant date is the day that the new or renewed contract terminated. This is to be assessed in accordance with the three points above.

According to the Court of Appeal, the effective date of termination is to be objectively determined and cannot be fixed by agreeement between the employer and employee.[62] It is also worth noting that the form P45 has nothing to do with the date on which employment terminates.[63]

Whether in a particular case the words of dismissal evince an intention to terminate the contract at once or an intention to terminate it only at a future date depends on the construction of those words. Such construction should not be technical but reflect what an ordinary, reasonable employee would understand by the language used. Moreover, words should be construed in the light of the facts known to the employee at the time of notification.[64] If the language used is ambiguous, it is likely that tribunals will apply the principle that words should be interpreted most strongly against the person who uses them.[65] It should also be observed that where a dismissal has been communicated by letter, the contract of employment does not terminate until the employee has actually read the letter or had a reasonable opportunity of reading it.[66] What is the effective (or relevant) date where there is an appeal against dismissal? According to the House of Lords, unless there is a contractual provision to the contrary, the date of termination is to be ascertained in accordance with the above formula and is not the date on which the employee was informed that his or her appeal had failed.[67]

Reinforce your understanding of this chapter by visiting www.cipd.co.uk/sss for activities, questions, weblinks and additional case studies

REFERENCES

1 See Section 94 ERA 1996 and *Lawson v Serco Ltd* (2006) IRLR 289

2 On national security see sections 193 ERA 1996 and *B v BAA* (2005) IRLR 927

3 Sections 97(2) and 213(1) ERA 1996. See *Staffordshire C.C. v Secretary of State* (1989) IRLR 117

4 See *Lanton Leisure v White* (1987) IRLR 119

5 Section 108(2) ERA 1996

6 Section 203(2)(e) and (f) ERA 1996

7 Sections 95 and 136 ERA 1996

8 See section 176 ERA 1996

9 See *Doble v Firestone Tyre and Rubber Co. Ltd* (1981) IRLR 300

10 Section 95(2) ERA 1996 and *Ready Case Ltd v Jackson* (1981) IRLR 312

11 Section 136(4) ERA 1996

12 Section 142(2) ERA 1996

13 Section 142(3) ERA 1996

14 See *CPS Recruitment Ltd v Bowen* (1982) IRLR 54

15 (1994) IRLR 88

16 See *Logan Salton v Durham C.C.* (1989) IRLR 99

17 See *Igbo v Johnson Matthey* (1986) IRLR 215

18 (1985) IRLR 165; see also *Scott v Coalite* (1988) IRLR 131

19 *Lassman v De Vere University Arms Hotel* (2003) ICR 44

20 (1981) IRLR 25

21 (1981) IRLR 108; see also *Logan Salton v Durham C.C.* (note 16 above)

22 See *Kwik-Fit v Lincham* (1992) IRLR 156

23 (1981) IRLR 278

24 (1978) IRLR 110

25 Section 235 (2B) ERA 1996

26 (2008) IRLR 208

27 See *Kerry Foods Ltd v Lynch* (2005) IRLR 680

28 See *Morrow v Safeway Stores* (2002) IRLR 9

29 See *Hilton Hotels v Protopapa* (1990) IRLR 316

30 See *Wilton v Cornwall Health Authority* (1993) IRLR 482

31 See *Cantor Fitzgerald v Bird* (2002) IRLR 867

32 See *Bliss v South East Thames Regional Health Authority* (1985) IRLR 308

33 See *Harrison v Norwest Holst* (1985) IRLR 240

34 *London Borough of Waltham Forest v Omilaju* (2005) IRLR 35

35 *Robins UK v Triggs* (2007) IRLR 857

36 See *Claridge v Rowney Ltd* (2008) IRLR 672

37 See *Brown v JBD Engineering Ltd* (1993) IRLR 568

38 See *Martin v MBS Fastenings* (1983) IRLR 198

39 See *Land Securities v Thornley* (2005) IRLR 765

40 See *Aparau v Iceland Frozen Foods* (1996) IRLR 119

41 See *White v Reflecting Roadstuds* (1991) IRLR 332

42 See *Dryden v Greater Glasgow Health Board* (1992) IRLR 469

43 (1981) IRLR 309

44 See *McNeil v Crimin Ltd* (1984) IRLR 179

45 See *Cawley v South Wales Electricity Board* (1985) IRLR 89

46 *Cole Ltd v Sheridan* (2003) IRLR 52

47 See *Rigby v Ferodo Ltd* (1987) IRLR 516

48 See *Cantor Fitzgerald International v Callaghan* (1999) IRLR 234

49 (1978) IRLR 63

50 See *Murco Petroleum v Forge* (1987) IRLR 50

51 See *Morrow v Safeway Stores plc* (2002) IRLR 9

52 *Caledonian Mining Ltd v Bassett* (1987) IRLR 165; on possible fraudulent misrepresentation, see *Post Office v Sanhotra* (2000) IRLR 866

53 (1996) IRLR 327

54 See *TBA Industrial Products Ltd v Morland* (1982) IRLR 331

55 See *Thompson v GEC Avionics* (1991) IRLR 448

56 See *Mowlem Northern Ltd v Watson* (1990) IRLR 500

57 (1986) IRLR 430

58 This principle was applied to a constructive dismissal in *BMK Ltd v Logue* (1993) ICR 601.

59 See *R. Cort & Son Ltd v Charman* (1981) IRLR 437

60 See *Octavius Atkinson Ltd v Morris* (1989) IRLR 158

61 See *Stapp v Shaftesbury Society* (1982) IRLR 326

62 *Fitzgerald v University of Kent* (2004) IRLR 300

63 See *Leech v Preston B.C.* (1985) IRLR 337

64 See *London Borough of Newham v Ward* (1985) IRLR 509

65 See *Chapman v Letheby & Christopher Ltd* (1981) IRLR 440

66 See *McMaster v Manchester Airport plc* (1998) IRLR 112

67 *West Midlands Co-op Ltd v Tipton* (1986) IRLR 112; see also *Drage v Governors of Greenford High School* (2000) IRLR 314

CHAPTER 13

Unfair Dismissal (2): Potentially fair reasons and the concept of reasonableness

OVERVIEW

We continue our examination of the rules concerning unfair dismissal by looking at the procedures to be followed after an employee has established that he or she qualifies to make a claim. We begin by looking at the burden on employers to show the reason for dismissal and then consider those reasons that are automatically unfair. We study the potentially fair reasons of capability or qualifications, conduct, statutory ban and some other substantial reason. We consider the particular rules that apply to dismissals during industrial action and look at the ACAS Code of Practice on Disciplinary and Grievance Procedures.

GIVING A REASON FOR DISMISSAL

Once employees have proved that they were dismissed, the burden shifts to the employer to show the reason, or, if there was more than one, the principal reason, for the dismissal and that it falls within one of the following categories:[1]

- It relates to the capacity or qualifications of the employee for performing work of the kind which he or she was employed to do.

- It relates to the conduct of the employee.

- The retirement of the employee

- The employee was redundant.

- The employee could not continue to work in the position held without contravention, either on the employee's part or that of the employer, of a duty or restriction imposed by or under a statute.

- There was some other substantial reason of such a kind as to justify the dismissal of an employee holding the position which the employee held.

Several points need to be made at this stage:

- Where no reason is given by the employer, a dismissal will be unfair simply because the statutory burden has not been discharged. Equally, if a reason is engineered in order to effect dismissal because the real reason would not be acceptable, the employer will fail because the underlying principal reason is not within section 98(1) or (2) ERA 1996.[2]

- The fact that an employer has inaccurately described the reason for dismissal is not necessarily fatal, for it is the tribunal's task to discover what reason actually motivated the employer at the time of dismissal.[3] That the correct approach is the subjective one has been confirmed by the Court of Appeal: 'A reason for the dismissal of an employee is a set of facts known to the employer, or it may be of beliefs held by him, which causes him to dismiss the employee.'[4] Subsequently the Court of Appeal has been prepared to attribute a reason for dismissal even where the employers had argued throughout the case that they had not dismissed but the employee had resigned.[5]

- The reason for dismissal must have existed and been known to the employer at the time of dismissal, which makes it impossible, for example, to rely on subsequently discovered misconduct.[6] The reason itself may be an anticipated event. For example, if an employee is subject to a long period of notice, it is possible to give notice in anticipation of a decision, giving what the employer expects to happen as a reason for the dismissal.[7]

- Section 107 ERA 1996 provides that in determining the reason for dismissal, or whether it was sufficient to dismiss, a tribunal cannot take account of any pressure, in the form of industrial action or a threat of it, which was exercised on the employer to secure the employee's dismissal. It is not necessary that those exerting the pressure explicitly sought the dismissal of the employee: the test is whether it could be foreseen that the pressure would be likely to result in dismissal.[8]

EMPLOYERS' DUTY TO PROVIDE A STATEMENT OF REASONS FOR DISMISSAL

According to section 92 ERA 1996, a person who has been continuously employed for one year[9] and has been dismissed or is under notice of dismissal has the right to be supplied with a written statement giving particulars of the reasons for dismissal. The employer must provide the statement within 14 days of a specific request being made. In *Gilham v Kent County Council*[10] the Court of Appeal held that the Council had responded adequately by referring the employee's legal representative to two previous letters in which the reasons for dismissal were fully set out, enclosing copies of those letters and stating that their contents contained the reasons for dismissal. A claim may be presented to an employment tribunal on the grounds that the employer unreasonably failed to provide such a statement or that the particulars given were inadequate or untrue. However, section 92 merely obliges employers to indicate truthfully the reasons they were relying on when they dismissed. Only if an unfair dismissal claim is brought will a tribunal have to examine whether the reasons given justify dismissal.[11] The same time-limit applies as for unfair dismissal claims (see Chapter 15).

The test for determining the reasonableness of an employer's failure is objective. Thus, where the employer maintains that there was no dismissal in law but the tribunal finds that there was, it must then decide whether there was an unreasonable failure to supply a statement.[12] If the complaint is well-founded, a tribunal may make a declaration as to what it finds the employer's reasons were for dismissing and must order that the employee receive two weeks' pay.[13] Perhaps the most important aspect of this section is that such a statement is admissible in evidence in any proceedings. This means that an employee who detects any inconsistency between the particulars given and the reasons offered as a defence to an unfair dismissal claim can exploit the situation to the full.

AUTOMATICALLY UNFAIR DISMISSAL

In certain circumstances a dismissal will be unfair because the reason for it was 'inadmissible'. A dismissal is thus automatically unfair if the reason for it related to any of the following:

- the assertion of a statutory right (see below)

- trade union membership or activities, or non-union membership

- pregnancy or maternity (see Chapter 8)

- certain health and safety grounds (see below)

- certain shop workers and betting workers who refuse to work on a Sunday[14]

- workers dismissed for refusing to comply with a requirement which is in contravention of the WT Regulations 1998 (see Chapter 10)[15]

- the reason, or the principal reason, for the dismissal is that the employee made a protected disclosure (see Chapter 3)[16]

- the employee is dismissed for trying to enforce the national minimum wage[17]

- the proposed or actual performance of any of the functions of an employee trustee of a pension scheme[18]

- the proposed or actual performance of any functions or activities as an employee representative or candidate[19]

- the dismissal of a worker for exercising rights in relation to the statutory recognition of a trade union (see Chapter 18)

- the dismissal of a worker within eight weeks of taking part in protected industrial action (see below)

- the application of the Tax Credit Act 1999[20]

- the exercise of a right to request a contract variation (see Chapter 8 on flexible working)[21]

- the exercise of rights under the Part-Time Workers Regulations 2000 and Fixed-term Employees Regulations 2002.[22]

Additionally, if any of the above 'inadmissible' reasons was used to select a person for redundancy, dismissal will also be unfair (see below). Other unfair reasons for dismissal are those connected to transfers of undertakings (see Chapter

16); to the anti-discrimination provisions, which stipulate that it is unlawful to discriminate on the prohibited grounds by way of dismissal (see Chapters 6 and 7); and to the Rehabilitation of Offenders Act 1974, which states that 'a conviction which has become spent ... shall not be a proper ground for dismissing' (see Chapter 4).[23]

ASSERTING STATUTORY RIGHTS

Employees are protected if they have brought proceedings against the employer to enforce one of the following 'relevant' statutory rights:

- any right conferred by ERA 1996 which may be the subject of a complaint to an employment tribunal

- minimum notice rights under section 86 ERA 1996

- certain rights relating to the unlawful deduction of union contributions from pay,[24] action short of dismissal on union membership grounds, time off for union duties and activities and union learning representatives

- rights afforded by the WT Regulations 1998[25]

- rights afforded by the TULRCA 1992 in relation to statutory recognition of trade unions.

It should be noted that employees are protected irrespective of whether they qualify for the right that has been asserted or whether the right was actually infringed. All that has to be demonstrated is that the employee's claim was made in good faith.[26]

HEALTH AND SAFETY

In relation to health and safety, section 100 ERA 1996 provides that a dismissal is unfair if the reason for it was that the employee:

- carried out, or proposed to carry out, activities designated by the employer in connection with preventing or reducing risks to the health and safety of employees

- performed, or proposed to perform, any of his or her functions as a safety representative or a member of a safety committee

- took part or proposed to take part in consultation with the employer pursuant to the HSCE Regulations 1996 (see Chapter 9) or in an election of representatives of employee safety within the meaning of those Regulations

- where there was no safety representative or committee or it was not reasonably practicable to raise the matter in that way, brought to the employer's attention, by reasonable means, circumstances connected with his or her work which he or she reasonably believed were harmful or potentially harmful to health and safety[27]

- left or proposed to leave, or refused to return to (while the danger persisted), his or her place of work or any dangerous part of the workplace, in circumstances of danger which he or she reasonably believed to be serious and imminent and which he or she could not reasonably have been expected to avert

- took, or proposed to take, appropriate steps to protect himself or herself or other persons, in circumstances of danger which he or she reasonably believed to be serious and imminent. Whether those steps were 'appropriate' must be judged by reference to all the circumstances, including the employee's knowledge and the facilities and advice available at the time. A dismissal will not be regarded as unfair if the employer can show that it was, or would have been, so negligent for the employee to take the steps which he or she took, or proposed to take, that a reasonable employer might have dismissed on these grounds.

POTENTIALLY FAIR REASONS FOR DISMISSAL

CAPABILITY OR QUALIFICATIONS

According to section 98(3) ERA 1996, 'capability' is to be assessed by reference to 'skill, aptitude, health or any other physical or mental quality', and it has been held that an employee's inflexibility or lack of adaptability came within his or her aptitude and mental qualities.[28] 'Qualifications' means 'any degree, diploma, or other academic, technical or professional qualification relevant to the position which the employee held'. In *Blue Star Ltd v Williams*[29] it was held that a mere licence, permit or authorisation is not such a qualification unless it is substantially concerned with the aptitude or ability of the person to do the job.

Poor performance

Paragraph 1 of the ACAS Code of Practice on Disciplinary and Grievance Procedures observes that poor performance may be regarded as a disciplinary matter and comments that 'If employers have a separate capability procedure, they may prefer to address performance issues under this procedure.'

Dealing with absence

Appendix 4 of the draft ACAS Guide on Discipline and Grievances at Work discusses how to handle absence problems. It provides informaton under the following headings:

- How should frequent and persistent short-term absence be handled?
- How should longer-term absence through ill health be handled?
- Specific health problems
- Failure to return from extended leave on the agreed date.

Types of ill health

In cases of intermittent absences owing to ill health, there is no obligation on an employer to call medical evidence. According to the EAT, an employer has to have regard to the whole history of employment and to take into account a range of factors including: the nature of the illness and the likelihood of its recurrence; the lengths of absences compared with the intervals of good health; the employer's need for that particular employee; the impact of the absences on the rest of the workforce; and the extent to which the employee was made aware of his or her position. There is no principle that the mere fact that the employee is fit at the time of dismissal makes that dismissal unfair.[30]

Where there is long-term absence for ill health an employer is usually expected to take reasonable steps to consult the employee, to obtain appropriate medical evidence about the nature and prognosis of the condition and to consider alternative employment. If employers provide an enhanced pension on ill-health retirement, they will also be expected to take reasonable steps to ascertain whether the employee is entitled to benefit from the scheme.[31]

Four further points must be made:

- An employee's incapability need only 'relate to' the performance of contractual duties; there is no requirement to show that the performance of all those duties has been affected.[32]

- Although employees who are sick will hope to remain employed at least until their contractual sick pay entitlement (if any) is exhausted, this does not mean that a person cannot be dismissed before the period of sick pay has elapsed. Equally, it will be unfair to dismiss simply because the sick pay period has expired.

- The fact that the employer caused the employee's incapacity does not prevent a finding of fair dismissal.[33]

- An employee who has become incapable of work may have to be treated as a person with a disability within the meaning of section 1 of the Disability Discrimination Act 1995 (see Chapter 7).

CONDUCT

It is not the function of tribunals to decide whether misconduct is gross or criminal but whether the employer has, in the circumstances of the case, acted reasonably in dismissing. Thus in *John Lewis plc v Coyne*[34] it was held that the employer had acted unfairly in dismissing the employee for using the company telephone for making personal calls without investigating the seriousness of the offence. There is no necessary inference that because an employee is guilty of gross misconduct in relation to his or her actual employment, he or she must necessarily be considered unsuitable for any employment whatsoever.[35] Clearly, there will be cases where the misconduct is sufficiently serious that an employee can be dismissed without warning, and paragraph 23 of the ACAS Code of Practice on Disciplinary and Grievance Procedures advocates that employees should be given 'examples of acts which the employer regards as acts of gross misconduct'.

Employers must clarify what conduct leads to summary dismissal

According to the EAT, disciplinary rules which fail to follow the ACAS Code in specifying those offences that constitute gross misconduct and justify dismissal at the first breach will be defective. In *Lock v Cardiff Railway Co. Ltd*[36] a train conductor was dismissed for gross misconduct when he asked a 16-year-old to leave the train because he did not have a valid ticket or sufficient money to pay the excess fare. The employer's disciplinary code did not specify which offences would be regarded as gross misconduct that would result in dismissal for the first offence. As a result the EAT held that no reasonable tribunal properly directing itself could have concluded that the dismissal was fair.

Fighting is an example of an area where it is not necessary to state that such behaviour will be regarded very gravely, because the courts have decided that whether or not to dismiss for this reason is essentially a matter for the employer. The test is what would be the reaction of a reasonable employer in the circumstances. Thus, if without proper inquiry an employer implements a policy of dismissing any employee who struck another, there could be a finding of unfairness.[37] Similarly, false clocking or claims in respect of hours done are serious offences which can justify dismissal without a warning if the employer has had due regard to all the circumstances.[38]

Disobedience: when it is and is not 'reasonable'

As a general rule, if an order is lawful, a refusal to obey it will be a breach of contract and amount to misconduct even when similar refusals have been condoned in the past. Nevertheless, in disobedience cases the primary factor to be considered is whether the employee is acting reasonably in refusing to carry out an instruction.[39] Thus in *Robinson v Tescom Corporation*[40] the employee had agreed to work under the terms of a varied job description while negotiations were ongoing. His subsequent refusal to do so was held to amount to disobedience of a lawful order. Acknowledging that employers are obliged to issue instructions in order to ensure compliance with health and safety legislation, tribunals have readily accepted that non-compliance with safety rules or procedures constitutes sufficient grounds for dismissal.

Dismissal arising from issues of competition

The intention to set up in competition with the employer is not in itself a breach of the implied duty of loyalty. Unless the employer has reasonable grounds for believing that the employee has done or is about to do some wrongful act, dismissal will not be justified.[41] Thus in *Marshall v Industrial Systems Ltd*[42] the EAT held that it was reasonable to dismiss a managing director after discovering that (with another manager) he was planning to set up in competition and take away the business of their best client, and that he tried to induce another key employee to join them in that venture.

Suspicion of dishonesty

Theft of an employer's property will amount to a fair reason for dismissal; far more difficult to handle are cases of *suspected* dishonesty. According to the Court of Appeal, fairness demands that serious allegations of dishonesty be put with sufficient formality and at an early enough stage to provide a full opportunity for answer.[43] The same court has approved of the approach taken in *British Home Stores v Burchell*,[44] where it was stated that tribunals had to decide whether the employer entertained a reasonable suspicion amounting to a belief in the guilt of the employee at that time. There are three elements to this:

- the employer must establish the fact of that belief

- the employer must show that there were reasonable grounds upon which to sustain that belief

- at the stage at which the belief was formed the employer must have carried out as much investigation into the matter as was reasonable in the circumstances.

Thus the question to be determined is not whether, by an objective standard, the employer's belief that the employee was guilty of the misconduct was well-founded but whether the employer believed that the employee was guilty and was entitled so to believe having regard to the investigation conducted.[45] If these requirements are met, it is irrelevant that the employee is acquitted of criminal charges or that they are dropped.

Where there is a reasonable suspicion that one or more employees within a group have acted dishonestly, it is not necessary for the employer to identify which of them acted dishonestly.[46] Thus, provided certain conditions are satisfied, an employer who cannot identify which member of a group was responsible for an act can fairly dismiss the whole group, even where it is probable that not all were guilty of the act. These conditions are:

- the act must be such that if committed by an identified individual it would justify dismissal

- the employer had made a sufficiently thorough investigation with appropriate procedures

- as a result of that investigation the employer reasonably believed that more than one person could have committed the act

- the employer had acted reasonably in identifying the group of employees who could have committed the act and each member of the group was individually capable of doing so

- between the members of the group the employer could not reasonably identify the individual perpetrator.

The fact that one or more of the group is not dismissed does not necessarily render the dismissal of the remainder unfair, provided the employer is able to show solid and sensible grounds for differentiating between members of the group.[47]

In certain cases it will be reasonable to rely on the results of extensive police investigation rather than carry out independent inquiries.[48] Similarly, where an employee admits dishonesty there is little scope for the kind of investigation referred to in *Burchell*'s case. Where the probability of guilt is less apparent, the safer course may be to suspend until any criminal proceedings have been completed.[49] Whether a conviction forms an adequate basis for dismissal will depend to some extent on the nature of the crime. Clearly, there may be cases where the offence is trivial and dismissal would be unreasonable.[50]

Employers' contact with employees under criminal investigation

The fact that employees have been charged with a criminal offence does not prevent the employer from communicating with them or their representatives to discuss the matter. What must be discussed is not so much the alleged offence as the action the employer is proposing to take. If the employee chooses not to give a statement to the employer, the latter is entitled to consider whether the evidence available is strong enough to justify dismissal.[51] However, it will not always be wrong to dismiss before a belief in guilt has been established, because involvement in an alleged criminal offence often involves a serious breach of duty or discipline. Even when charged by the police with a criminal offence, failure to give employees an opportunity to explain themselves may render the dismissal unfair.[52]

Offences committed outside the workplace

In the context of unfair dismissal, conduct may mean actions of such a nature, whether done in the course of employment or outside, that reflect in some way on the employer–employee relationship.[53] Thus it may cover the wilful concealment of convictions which are not 'spent', criminal offences outside employment, such as stealing or gross indecency, or even 'moonlighting'. Finally, in an appropriate case it may be unfair to dismiss without first considering whether the employee could be offered some other job.[54]

RETIREMENT

Where the reason (or principal reason) for dismissal is retirement, the provisions of sections 98ZA–G ERA 1996 apply. These have been discussed in Chapter 7.

STATUTORY BAN

Section 98(2)(d) ERA 1996 states that if it would be unlawful to continue to work in the position which the employee held, there is a valid reason for dismissing. In *Bouchaala v Trust House Forte*[55] the EAT held that the absence of the words 'related to' in this section were significant and that a genuine but erroneous belief is insufficient for these purposes. Again, a tribunal must be satisfied that the requirements of section 98(4) ERA 1996 have been met. Thus the loss of a permit or licence may fall within section 98(2)(d) ERA 1996 but, in deciding what is reasonable, attention will focus on whether the legal ban is permanent or temporary. If the former, an employer might be expected to consider the feasibility of redeployment, and if the latter, short-term alternative work might be offered. Whether such measures should be taken will depend on the type of business and the employee's work record. Indeed, in some circumstances it may be possible for employees to continue in their normal job by making special arrangements. For example, a sales representative who has been disqualified from driving may be prepared to hire a driver at his or her own expense in order to remain in employment.

SOME OTHER SUBSTANTIAL REASON

Section 98(1)(b) ERA 1996 was included in the legislative scheme so as to give tribunals the discretion to accept as a fair reason for dismissal something that would not conveniently fit into any of the other categories. It covers such diverse matters as dismissal for having been sentenced to imprisonment,[56] the loss of confidence in a manager because of his manner and management style,[57] being dismissed as manager of a public house because a partner had resigned from jointly holding the position,[58] dismissal for refusing to sign an undertaking not to compete,[59] or dismissal because the employer's best customer was unwilling to accept the particular individual.[60] However, in *Wadley v Eager Electrical*[61] the EAT decided that an employee's dismissal on the grounds that there had been breaches of trust by his wife during her employment with the employer did not amount to a substantial reason.

According to the Court of Appeal, tribunals have to decide whether the reason established by the employer falls within the category of reasons which *could* justify the dismissal of an employee holding the position that the employee held.[62] Employers cannot claim that a reason for dismissal is substantial if it is whimsical or capricious. Nevertheless, if they can show that they genuinely believed a reason to be fair and that they had it in mind at the time of dismissal,[63] this would bring the case within section 98(1)(b) ERA 1996. It may be held that the reason was substantial even though more sophisticated opinion can be adduced to demonstrate that the belief had no scientific foundation.[64] The notion of genuine belief has also been invoked to assist employers who are unable to rely on any other reasons for dismissal owing to an error of fact. Thus this subsection was relied on where an employee was dismissed as a result of the employer's mistaken belief that a work permit was needed.[65]

Dismissal for refusing new terms arising from a business reorganisation

'Some other substantial reason' has frequently provided a convenient context in which employees have been dismissed as a result of a reorganisation of the business. The Court of Appeal has taken the view that it is not necessary for an employer to show that in the absence of a reorganisation there would be a total business disaster. It is sufficient if there is a sound business reason, which means only that there is a reason which management thinks on reasonable grounds is sound.[66] If the employer can satisfy a tribunal that a certain policy has evolved which was thought to have discernible advantages, then dismissal in accordance with that policy can be said to be for 'some other substantial reason'.

Where an employee refuses to agree changes consequent upon a reorganisation, the test to be applied by tribunals is not simply whether the terms offered were those which a reasonable employer could offer. Looking at the employer's offer alone would exclude from scrutiny everything that happened between the time the offer was made and the dismissal. For example, a potentially significant factor is whether other employees accepted the offer.[67] Equally, there is no principle of law that if new contractual terms are much less favourable to an employee than the previous ones, dismissal for refusing to accept them will be unfair unless the business reasons are so pressing that it is vital for the survival of the business that the revised terms are accepted. In *Farrant v The Woodroffe School*[68] an employee was dismissed for refusing to accept organisational changes. The employer mistakenly believed that the employee was obliged to accept a new job description and that the dismissal was therefore lawful. The EAT held that dismissal for refusing to obey an unlawful order was not necessarily unfair. Of importance was not the lawfulness or otherwise of the employer's instructions but the overall question of reasonableness. In this case it was not unreasonable for the employer to act on professional advice, even if that advice was wrong. Tribunals will examine an employer's motive for introducing changes in order to ensure that they are not being imposed arbitrarily.[69] The reasonable employer will explore all the alternatives to dismissal but, like consultation with trade unions and the individual concerned, such a consideration is only one of the factors that must be taken into account under section 98(4) ERA 1996 (see below).

INDUSTRIAL ACTION AND LACK OF JURISDICTION

PROTECTED INDUSTRIAL ACTION

Section 238A TULRCA states that a dismissal will be unfair if the reason is that the employee took part in protected industrial action[70] and one of three situations applies:

- the dismissal takes place within a period of twelve weeks from the day on which the employee first took part in the protected industrial action
- the dismissal takes place after that twelve-week period and the employee had ceased to take part in protected industrial action before the end of that period
- the dismissal takes place after the end of the period and the employee has not ceased to take part in the protected industrial action before the end of that period but the employer has not taken such procedural steps as would have been reasonable for the purpose of resolving the dispute to which the action relates.

In deciding whether an employer has taken those steps mentioned in the last point above, tribunals will look at whether the employer or union:[71]

- has followed procedures established by a collective agreement
- had offered or agreed to start or resume negotiations after the start of the protected industrial action

- unreasonably refused a request that conciliation services be used

- unreasonably refused a request that mediation services be used.

Where there was an agreement to use conciliation or mediation services, section 238B TULRCA 1992 provides that regard should be had to four matters:

- whether the parties were represented at the meeting by an appropriate person

- whether the parties co-operated in the making of arrangements for meetings to be held

- whether the parties fulfilled any commitment given to take particular action

- whether the parties answered any reasonable question put to them at meetings.

The fact that employees are in breach of their duty to attend work is relevant to the question of whether they are taking part in a strike but it is not an essential ingredient. Thus employees who are off sick or on holiday could be held to be taking part in a strike if they associated themselves with it – for example, by attending a picket line.[72] By way of contrast, if sick employees merely wish their colleagues well, this may be regarded as supportive but would not amount to taking part in industrial action.[73]

UNOFFICIAL ACTION

By virtue of section 237 TULRCA 1992 employees cannot complain of unfair dismissal if at the time of dismissal they were taking part in an unofficial strike or other unofficial industrial action. For these purposes, a strike or other industrial action will be treated as unofficial unless the employee:

- is a union member and the action is authorised or endorsed by that union, or

- is not a union member but there are amongst those taking part in the industrial action members of a union by which the action has been authorised or endorsed within the meaning of section 20(2) TULRCA 1992 (see Chapter 19).

A strike or other industrial action will not be regarded as unofficial if none of those taking part in it is a union member. However, employees who were union members when they began to take industrial action will continue to be treated as such even if they have subsequently ceased to be union members.[74]

Section 237(4) states that the issue of whether or not the action is unofficial is to be determined by reference to the facts at the time of the dismissal. Nevertheless, where the action is repudiated in accordance with section 21 TULRCA 1992 the industrial action is not to be treated as unofficial before the end of the next working day after the repudiation has taken place. According to the EAT, this means midnight on the following working day.[75] On the absence of statutory immunity for acts in support of those dismissed for taking unofficial action see Chapter 19.

REASONABLENESS IN THE CIRCUMSTANCES

Where the employer has given a valid reason for dismissal (other than retirement), the determination of the question whether the dismissal was fair or unfair:

- depends on whether in the circumstances (including the size and administrative resources of the employer's undertaking) the employer acted reasonably or unreasonably in treating it as a sufficient reason for dismissing the employee, and

- will be in accordance with equity and the substantial merits of the case.[76]

As a matter of law, a reason cannot be treated as sufficient where it has not been established as true or that there were reasonable grounds on which the employer could have concluded that it was true.[77] Under section 98(4) ERA 1996, tribunals must take account of the wider circumstances. In addition to the employer's business needs, attention must be paid to the personal attributes of the employee – for example, seniority and previous work record. Thus when all the relevant facts are considered, a dismissal may be deemed unfair notwithstanding the fact that the disciplinary rules specified that such behaviour would result in immediate dismissal.[78] Conversely, employers may act reasonably in dismissing even though they have breached an employee's contract.[79] In appropriate cases the test of fairness must be interpreted, so far as possible, compatibly with the European Convention on Human Rights.[80]

Employers will be expected to treat employees in similar circumstances in a similar way. The requirement that the employer must act consistently between all employees means that an employer should consider truly comparable cases which were known about or ought to have been known about. Nevertheless, the overriding principle seems to be that each case must be considered on its own facts and with the freedom to consider both aggravating factors and mitigating circumstances.[81] The words 'equity and the substantial merits' also allow tribunals to apply their knowledge of good industrial relations practice and to ensure that there has been procedural fairness (see below).[82]

According to the Court of Appeal, employment tribunals should not ask themselves whether they would have done what the employer did in the circumstances. Their function is merely to assess the employer's decision to dismiss and decide if it falls within a range of responses that a reasonable employer could have adopted.[83] Even so, the 'range of reasonable responses' test does not mean that such a high degree of unreasonableness must be shown so that nothing short of a perverse decision to dismiss can be held unfair.[84] Finally, it would seem that in determining the reasonableness of a dismissal tribunals are not barred from taking into account events which occurred between the giving of notice and its expiry – for example, if alternative work becomes available after redundancy notices have been issued.[85]

CASE STUDY

Willow Oak Ltd specialised in the supply of agency workers for health and associated services. After a number of attempts by competitors to poach staff and business from them, some of which had been successful, the company sought to impose new restrictive covenants on its employees. Without prior consultation, everyone was presented with a new contract which restricted their post-employment activities and were told to sign and return it within half an hour. When they refused to do so they were given notice of termination, although none of them had been warned that they would be dismissed if they did not accept the new terms.

An employment tribunal decided that the covenants were unreasonably wide and, as a consequence, the employers could not establish that the dismissals were for 'some other substantial reason' (see above). However, the Court of Appeal ruled that it was inappropriate for an ET to decide the validity of a proposed restrictive covenant. The reasonableness of the covenant should have been examined as part of all the circumstances of the case as provided for in section 98(4) ERA 1996. Nevertheless, the appeal was dismissed since the ET had been entitled to hold that the employers had failed to follow a fair procedure.[86]

THE CODE OF PRACTICE AND PROCEDURAL FAIRNESS

The ACAS Code of Practice on Disciplinary and Grievance Procedures 2009 does not have the force of law, so failure to comply with it does not make a dismissal automatically unfair. However, it will weigh heavily against the employer if not followed[87] and tribunals will be able to adjust any awards made in relevant cases by up to 25 per cent for unreasonable failure to comply with any provision of the Code.[88] In addition, ACAS has produced a draft guide to good practice which complements its Code.

SITUATIONS IN WHICH THE CODE MAY BE IGNORED

In certain circumstances there may be a good excuse for not following the Code. For example, if the inadequacy of the employee's performance is extreme or the actual or potential consequences of a mistake are grave, warnings may not be necessary.[89] Although it is management's responsibility to ensure that there are adequate disciplinary rules and procedures, the Code mentions the desirability of involving employees and their representatives in the development of rules and procedures.[90] Naturally, tribunals tend to pay greater attention to agreed rather than unilaterally imposed procedures. The rules required will again depend on the nature of the employment but they should be reasonable in themselves, consistently enforced, and reviewed in the light of legal developments and organisational needs. Employees should know and understand the rules and be made aware of the likely consequences of breaking them.

KEYS TO HANDLING DISCIPLINARY PROBLEMS IN THE WORKPLACE

The ACAS Code of Practice suggests the following steps:

- Establish the facts of each case (see paragraphs 5–8, draft guide paragraphs 35–38).

- Inform the employee of the problem (see paragraphs 9–10).

- Hold a meeting with the employee to discuss the problem (see paragraphs 11–12, draft guide paragraphs 40–51).

- Allow the employee to be accompanied at the meeting (see paragraphs 13–16, draft guide paragraphs 52–68 and *Employee representation* below).

- Decide on appropriate action (see paragraphs 17–24, draft guide paragraphs 69–95).

- Provide employees with an opportunity to appeal (see paragraphs 25–28, draft guide paragraphs 96–102).

Paragraphs 29–30 of the ACAS Code of Practice suggest that special consideration be given to the way in which disciplinary procedures operate in relation to trade union officials and those charged or conviction of a criminal offence. Paragraphs 103–114 of the draft ACAS guide provide further advice about dealing with special cases.

PROCEDURAL FAIRNESS AND NATURAL JUSTICE

According to paragraph 2 of the ACAS Code of Practice on Disciplinary and Grievance Procedures 2008, 'rules and procedures for handling disciplinary and grievance situations ... should be set down in writing, be specific and clear'. Paragraph 4 identifies the following aspects of fairness:[91]

- Employers and employees should raise and deal with issues promptly and should not unreasonably delay meetings, decisions or confirmation of those decisions.

- Employers and employees should act consistently.

- Employers should carry out any necessary investigations, to establish the facts of the case.

- Employers should inform employees of the basis of the problem and give them an opportunity to put their case in response before any decisions are made.

- Employers should allow employees to be accompanied at any formal disciplinary or grievance meeting.

- Employers should allow an employee to appeal against any formal decision made.

In addition, the Foreword to the ACAS Code of Practice emphasises the desirability of keeping written records.[92] It is clear from the above that natural justice is an important element in such procedures, although legal representation might be excluded.[93] According to the Court of Appeal, employees should only be found guilty of offences with which they have been charged. Such charges should be precisely formulated and evidence confined to the particulars of the charge.[94]

EMPLOYEE REPRESENTATION

Section 10 ERel Act 1999 gives workers the right to make a reasonable request to be accompanied during a disciplinary or grievance hearing. For these purposes a disciplinary hearing is one which could result in the administration of a formal warning, the taking of some other action or the confirmation of previous actions.[95] Whether there is a disciplinary hearing depends on the nature of the meeting itself and not on the description the parties attach to it or its possible consequences.[96] Thus there was no disciplinary hearing where the purpose of the meeting was simply to inform the employee about dismissal for redundancy.[97] According to the EAT, a disciplinary warning becomes a 'formal warning' if it becomes part of the employee's disciplinary record.[98] A grievance hearing is one which concerns the performance of an employer's duty in relation to a worker.[99]

A worker may be accompanied by a single companion who is:

- chosen by the worker
- to be permitted to address the hearing
- not to answer questions on behalf of the worker
- to be allowed to confer with the worker during the hearing.

Such a person can be an official of a trade union or another of the employer's workers.[100] A worker may propose an alternative time for the hearing if his or her chosen companion is unavailable at the time proposed by the employer. The employer must postpone the hearing to the time proposed by the worker, provided that the alternative time is reasonable and falls within a period of five working days beginning with the first working day after the day on which the worker was informed of the time by the employer. An employer must permit a worker to take time off during working hours in order to accompany another of the employer's workers. Section 11 ERel Act 1999 provides that an employer who infringes these rights is liable to pay up to two weeks' pay. In addition, section 12 ERel Act 1999 protects workers who are subjected to a detriment on the ground that they have exercised a right under section 10 ERel Act 1999 or sought to accompany another worker pursuant to a request under that section.

Protecting informants

If allegations are made by an informant, a careful balance must be maintained between the desirability of protecting informants who are genuinely in fear and providing a fair hearing of the issues for employees who are accused.[101]

'RECTIFIABLE' AND 'FINAL' WARNINGS

Warnings are particularly appropriate in cases of misconduct but may also be useful in dealing with other types of case. Basically, there are two types of warning that must be distinguished: a 'rectifiable' warning means that the employee will be dismissed unless an existing situation is resolved, whereas a 'final' warning indicates that the employee will be dismissed if further unacceptable behaviour occurs. Warnings are dealt with in paragraphs 18–20 of the ACAS Code of Practice, where it is recommended that written warnings should set out the nature of the offence and the likely consequences of its being repeated. Because an ambiguous warning will be construed strictly against the employer who drafted it, the date and time on which a warning is to commence and expire should be clearly specified.[102]

According to the Court of Appeal, provided a formal disciplinary warning has been given on adequate evidence, and not for an oblique or improper motive, it is a relevant consideration to which an employment tribunal should have regard in deciding whether the dismissal was unfair, even where the warning was under appeal and the appeal had not been determined at the time of the dismissal.[103] It follows that systematic records will have to be kept by employers, although it is suggested in paragraph 20 of the Code of Practice that the employee 'should be told how long the warning will remain current'. It should be noted that in *Airbus Ltd v Webb*[104] the Court of Appeal held that an expired warning does not make the earlier misconduct an irrelevant circumstance under section 98(4) ERA 1996.

THE IMPACT OF APPEAL PROCEDURES

In *Rowe v Radio Rentals*[105] the EAT decided that the employer's appeal procedure did not conflict with the rules of natural justice because the person hearing the appeal had been informed of the decision to dismiss before it took place and the person who took that decision was also present throughout the appeal hearing. It was recognised as inevitable that those involved in the original decision to dismiss will be in daily contact with their supervisors who will be responsible for deciding the appeal. However, if it is not necessary for the same person to act as both witness and judge in the procedure leading to dismissal, there may be a finding of unfairness.[106]

The House of Lords has confirmed that a dismissal is unfair if the employer unreasonably treats the reason for dismissal as a sufficient one, either when the original decision to dismiss is made or when that decision is maintained at the conclusion of an internal appeal.[107] Indeed, a dismissal may also be unfair if the employer refuses to comply with the full requirements of the appeal procedure.[108] Where two employees are dismissed for the same incident, and one is successful on appeal and the other is not, in determining the fairness of the latter's dismissal the question is whether the appeal panel's decision was so irrational that no employer could reasonably have accepted it.[109] Whether procedural defects can be rectified on appeal will depend on the degree of unfairness at the original hearing.[110]

- Once employees have proved that they were dismissed, the employer must show the reason for the dismissal.

- The employer must demonstrate that the reason for the dismissal relates to capability or qualifications, conduct, retirement, a statutory ban or some other substantial reason of a kind to justify the dismissal.

- There are certain reasons which are automatically unfair, such as those relating to trade union membership or activities or to pregnancy and maternity.

- Employees cannot claim unfair dismissal if they are dismissed while taking part in unofficial industrial action.

- Capability is assessed by reference to 'skill, aptitude, health or any other physical or mental ability'.

- Misconduct is a potentially fair reason for dismissal, but the employment tribunal will decide whether dismissal was a reasonable course of action, taking into account all the circumstances.

- 'Some other substantial reason' is a category which gives tribunals the discretion to accept as fair reasons that have not been defined by statute, such as those arising out of the reorganisation of a business.

- An employer must act reasonably in treating a reason as sufficient for dismissal. It should be guided by the ACAS Code of Practice and must follow contractual procedures.

Reinforce your understanding of this chapter by visiting www.cipd.co.uk/sss for activities, questions, weblinks and additional case studies

REFERENCES

1   Sections 98(1) and (2) ERA 1996

2   See *ASLEF v Brady* (2006) IRLR 76

3   See *Wilson v Post Office* (2000) IRLR 834

4   See *Abernethy v Mott, Hay and Anderson* (1974) IRLR 213

5   See *Ely v YKK Ltd* (1993) IRLR 500

6   See *Devis & Sons Ltd v Atkins* (1977) IRLR 314

7   See *Parkinson v March Consulting* (1997) IRLR 308

8   See *Ford Motor Co. v Hudson* (1978) IRLR 66

9   No service qualification applies if a dismissal is on the grounds of pregnancy, maternity or adoption; see Chapter 8.

10 (1985) IRLR 16

11 See *Harvard Securities v Younghusband* (1990) IRLR 17

12 See *Bromsgrove v Eagle Alexander* (1981) IRLR 127

13 Section 93(2) ERA 1996

14 Section 101 ERA 1996

15 Section 101A ERA 1996

16 Section 103A ERA 1996

17 Section 104A ERA 1996

18   Section 102 ERA 1996

19   Section 103 ERA 1996

20   Section 104B ERA 1996

21   Section 104C ERA 1996

22   Regulation 7 Part-time Workers Regulations 2000 and Regulation 6 Fixed-term Employees Regulations 2002 respectively

23   Section 4(3)b Rehabilitation of Offenders Act 1974; see *Wood v Coverage Care Ltd* (1996) IRLR 264

24   See *Elizabeth Claire Ltd v Francis* (2005) IRLR 858

25   See *McClean v Rainbow Homeloans Ltd* (2007) IRLR 15

26   Section 104 ERA 1996; see *Mennell v Newell & Wright Ltd* (1997) IRLR 519

27   See *Balfour Kilpatrick Ltd v Acheson* (2003) IRLR 683

28   See *Aberneathy v Mott, Hay and Anderson* (note 4)

29   (1979) IRLR 16

30   See *Cereal Packaging Ltd v Lyncock* (1998) IRLR 510

31   See *First West Yorkshire Ltd v Haigh* (2008) IRLR 182

32   See *Shook v London Borough of Ealing* (1986) IRLR 46

33   See *McAdie v Royal Bank of Scotland* (2007) IRLR 895

34   (2001) IRLR 139

35   See *Hamilton v Argyll and Clyde Health Authority* (1993) IRLR 99

36   (1998) IRLR 358

37   See *Taylor v Parsons Peebles Ltd* (1981) IRLR 199 where the employee concerned had a good conduct record extending over 20 years.

38   See also *United Distillers v Conlin* (1992) IRLR 503

39   See *UCATT v Brain* (1981) IRLR 224

40   (2008) IRLR 408

41   See *Laughton v Bapp Industrial Ltd* (1986) IRLR 245

42   (1992) IRLR 294; see also *Adamson v B&L Cleaning Ltd* (1995) IRLR 193

43   See *Panama v London Borough of Hackney* (2003) IRLR 278

44   (1978) IRLR 379

45   *Scottish Midland Co-op v Cullion* (1991) IRLR 261. See also *Sainsburys Ltd v Hitt* (2003) IRLR 23

46   See *Parr v Whitbread plc* (1990) IRLR 39

47   *Frames Snooker v Boyce* (1992) IRLR 472

48   See *Rhondda Cynon Taff Borough Council v Close* (2008) IRLR 868

49   On suspension see ACAS Code of Practice on Disciplinary and Grievance Procedures 2009 paragraph 8 and draft Guide paragraphs 37–8

50   See *Secretary of State v Campbell* (1992) IRLR 263

51   See *Harris v Courage Ltd* (1982) IRLR 509

52   *Lovie Ltd v Anderson* (1999) IRLR 164

53   See *Thomson v Alloa Motor Co.* (1983) IRLR 403 and ACAS draft guide on discipline and grievances paragraphs 106–111

54   See *P v Nottingham County Council* (1992) IRLR 362

55   (1980) IRLR 382

56   See *Kingston v British Rail* (1984) IRLR 146

57   *Perkin v St Georges NHS Trust* (2005) IRLR 934

58   *Alboni v Ind Coope Retail Ltd* (1998) IRLR 131

59   *Willow Oak Ltd v Silverwood* (2006) IRLR 607(see case study below).

60   See *Scottpacking Ltd v Paterson* (1978) IRLR 166

61   (1986) IRLR 93

62   See *Dobie v Burns International* (1984) IRLR 329

63   See *Ely v YKK Ltd* (note 5)

64   See *Saunders v National Scottish Camps Association* (1981) IRLR 277

65   See *Bouchaala v Trust House Forte* (1980) IRLR 382

66   See *Hollister v National Farmers Union* (1979) IRLR 238

67   See *St John of God Ltd v Brooks* (1992) IRLR 546

68   (1998) IRLR 176

69   See *Catamaran Cruisers v Williams* (1994) IRLR 386

70   'Protected industrial action' consists of acts that are not actionable in tort; see section 219 TULRCA 1992.

71   Section 238A(6) TULRCA 1992

72   See *Bolton Roadways Ltd v Edwards* (1987) IRLR 392

73   See *Rogers v Chloride Systems* (1992) ICR 198

74   Section 237(6) TULRCA 1992

75   *Balfour Kilpatrick Ltd v Acheson* (2003) IRLR 683

76   Section 98(4) ERA 1996

77   See *Smith v City of Glasgow D.C.* (1987) IRLR 326

78   See *Ladbroke Racing v Arnott* (1983) IRLR 154

79   See *Brandon v Murphy Bros* (1983) IRLR 54

80   See *X v Y* (2004) IRLR 625 on Article 8 and respect for private life

81   See *London Borough of Harrow v Cunningham* (1996) IRLR 256

82   See *Whitbread plc v Hall* (2001) IRLR 275

83   See *Anglian Homes Ltd v Kelly* (2004) IRLR 793

84   See *Rentokil Ltd v Mackin* (1989) IRLR 286

85   See *Stacey v Babcock Power Ltd* (1986) IRLR 3

86   *Willow Oak Ltd v Silverwood* (2006) IRLR 607

87   See *Lock v Cardiff Railway Co.* (1998) IRLR 358

88   Section 207A TULRCA 1992

89   See *Alidair Ltd v Taylor* (1978) IRLR 82

90   See ACAS Code of Practice on Disciplinary and Grievance Procedures paragraph 2

91   Paragraph 24 of the draft ACAS guide provides considerable detail about the contents of good disciplinary procedures.

92   See also draft ACAS guide paragraphs 31–2

93   See *Kulkarni v Milton Keynes Hospital NHS Trust* (2008) IRLR 949

94   *Strouthos v London Underground Ltd* (2004) IRLR 636

95   Section 13(4) ERel Act 1999

96   *Skiggs v South West Trains* (2005) IRLR 560

97   *Heathmill Ltd v Jones* (2003) IRLR 865

98   See *Harding v London Underground* (2003) IRLR 252

99   See Section 13(5) ERel Act 1999

100   Paragraphs 56–61 of the draft ACAS guide concern the companion

101   See *Ramsey v Walkers Snack Foods Ltd* (2004) IRLR 754

102   See *Bevan Ashford v Malin* (1995) IRLR 360

103   See *Tower Hamlets Health Authority v Anthony* (1989) IRLR 394

104   (2008) IRLR 309

105   (1982) IRLR 177

106   See *Byrne v BOC Ltd* (1992) IRLR 505

107   See *West Midlands Co-op Ltd v Tipton* (1986) IRLR 112

108   See *Tarbuck v Sainsburys Ltd* (2006) IRLR 664

109   See *Securicor Ltd v Smith* (1989) IRLR 356

110   See *Taylor v OCS Ltd* (2006) IRLR 613

CHAPTER 14

Redundancy

OVERVIEW

In this chapter we consider dismissals on the grounds of redundancy. We begin by looking at the statutory definition and then consider the rules concerning offers of alternative employment and the opportunity for the employee to make a decision about them. Finally, there is an examination of possible unfairness in the redundancy process.

QUALIFICATIONS AND EXCLUSIONS

In order to qualify for a redundancy payment an employee must have been continuously employed for two years at the relevant date.[1] Only employees have a right to redundancy payments and there are a number of situations in which they can lose their right:

- employees who are dismissed with or without notice for reasons connected to their conduct[2]

- employees who give notice to the employer terminating the employment with effect from a date prior to the date upon which the employer's notice of redundancy is due to expire. In such a case employees may lose their right to a redundancy payment, although if they leave early by mutual consent this payment will not be affected[3]

- an employee whose contract of employment is renewed, or who is re-engaged under a new contract of employment, provided that the renewal or re-engagement takes place within four weeks of the ending of the employment[4]

- an employee who takes part in strike action after receiving notice of termination. In such a case the employer is entitled to issue a notice of extension. This notice, which must be in writing and indicate the employer's reasons, may request the employee to extend their contract beyond the termination date by a period equivalent to the number of days lost through strike action. Failure by the employee to agree to this extension, unless he or she has good reasons such as sickness or injury, may enable the employer to challenge the right to a redundancy payment[5]

- certain specifically excluded categories of employee, such as public-office-holders and civil servants.[6]

The ending of a limited-term contract is a dismissal and may be for reasons of redundancy. Thus the college lecturers in *Pfaffinger v City of Liverpool Community College*,[7] who were employed during each academic year only, were dismissed for redundancy at the end of each academic term.

THE DEFINITION OF REDUNDANCY

According to 139(1) ERA 1996, employees[8] are to be regarded as being redundant if their dismissals are attributable wholly or mainly to:

- the fact that the employer has ceased, or intends to cease, to carry on the business[9] for the purposes the employees were employed, or

- the fact that the employer has ceased, or intends to cease, to carry on that business in the place where the employees were so employed, or

- the fact that the requirement of that business for employees to carry out work of a particular kind, or for employees to carry out work of a particular kind in the place where they were so employed, has ceased or diminished or is expected to cease or diminish.

In this context 'cease' or 'diminish' mean either permanently or temporarily and from whatever cause.[10] The House of Lords has held[11] that the definition of redundancy requires two questions of fact to be answered:

- Have the requirements of the employer's business for employees to carry out work of a particular kind ceased or diminished, or were they expected to cease or diminish?

- Was the dismissal of the employee attributable, wholly or mainly, to this state of affairs?

This means looking at the employer's overall requirements to decide whether there has been a diminution of the need for employees irrespective of the terms of the individual's contract or of the function that each performed. The House of Lords approved the approach of the EAT[12] in deciding that 'bumping' could give rise to a redundancy payment. 'Bumping' is where an individual's job may continue but there is a reduction in requirement for the same number of people to carry out the work and that individual is made redundant.

DETERMINING WHAT CONSTITUTES THE PLACE OF EMPLOYMENT

For these purposes, the place where an employee was employed does not extend to any place where he or she could contractually be required to work. The question of what is the place of employment concerns the extent or area of a single place, not the transfer from one place to another.[13] If there is no express term relating to mobility, a tribunal will have to examine all the evidence to see if a term should be inferred.[14] However, even though an employee may be contractually justified in declining to move, a request to do so may have to be considered as an offer of suitable alternative employment (see below).

DETERMINING WHAT CONSTITUTES 'WORK OF A PARTICULAR KIND'

One of the most onerous tasks of tribunals is to determine what constitutes 'work of a particular kind'. It is clear that a change in the time when the work is to be performed will not give rise to a redundancy payment,[15] nor will a reduction of overtime if the work to be done remains the same. Thus in *Lesney Products Ltd v Nolan*[16] the Court of Appeal held that the company's reorganisation, by which one long day shift plus overtime was changed into two day shifts, was done in the interests of efficiency and was not the result of any diminution in the employer's requirements for employees to carry out work of a particular kind.[17] However, both the work that the employee actually carried out and the work that the employee was contractually required to do will be considerations when an employment tribunal decides this issue.[18]

Three further points must be made:

- Employees will be entitled to a payment notwithstanding that it could be seen from the commencement of the contract that they would be dismissed for redundancy. The fact that the contract was temporary and short-term makes no difference in this respect.[19]

- The statutory definition of redundancy focuses on the employer's requirements rather than needs. Thus – even where there is still a need for the work to be done – if, owing to lack of funds, the requirement for the employee's service has ceased, the employee is redundant.[20]

- Section 163(2) ERA 1996 states that an employee who is dismissed is presumed to have been dismissed by reason of redundancy unless the contrary is proved.[21]

OFFERS OF ALTERNATIVE EMPLOYMENT

If, before the ending of a person's employment, the employer or an associated employer makes an offer, in writing or not, to renew the contract or to re-engage under a new contract which is to take effect either on the ending of the old one or within four weeks, then section 141 ERA 1996 has the following effect:

- if the provisions of the new or renewed contract as to the capacity and place in which the person would be employed, together with the other terms and conditions, do not differ from the corresponding terms of the previous contract, or

- the terms and conditions differ, wholly or in part, but the offer constitutes an offer of suitable employment, and

- in either case the employee unreasonably refuses that offer, then he or she will not be entitled to a redundancy payment.

The burden is on an employer to prove both the suitability of the offer and the unreasonableness of the employee's refusal.[22] Offers do not have to be formal, nor do they have to contain all the conditions which are ultimately agreed.[23] However, supplying details of vacancies is not the same as an offer of employment[24] and sufficient information must be provided to enable the employee to take a realistic decision.[25]

The suitability of the alternative work must be assessed objectively by comparing the terms on offer with those previously enjoyed. A convenient test has been whether the proposed employment will be 'substantially equivalent' to that which has ceased.[26] Merely offering the same salary will not be sufficient[27] but the fact that the employment will be at a different location does not necessarily mean that it will be regarded as unsuitable.

'REASONABLE' REFUSAL BY EMPLOYEES OF ALTERNATIVE EMPLOYMENT

By way of contrast, in adjudicating upon the reasonableness of an employee's refusal, subjective considerations can be taken into account, for example, domestic responsibilities. In *Spencer v Gloucestershire County Council*[28] the employees had refused offers of suitable employment on the grounds that they would not be able to do their work to a satisfactory standard in the reduced hours and with lower staffing levels. The Court of Appeal held that it was for employers to set the standard of work they wanted carried out but it was a different question whether it was reasonable for a particular employee, in all the circumstances, to refuse to work to the standard set. This is a question of fact for the tribunal. Similarly, it might be reasonable for an employee to refuse an offer of employment which, although suitable, involved loss of status.[29] In theory the questions of suitability and the reasonableness of refusal are distinct but they are often run together in practice.

TRIAL PERIODS FOR NEW OR RENEWED CONTRACTS

To allow an employee to make a rational decision about any alternative employment offered, section 138(3) ERA 1996 states that if the terms and conditions differ, wholly or in part, from those of the previous contract, a trial period may be invoked. Such a period commences when the employee starts work under the new or renewed contract and ends four calendar weeks later,[30] unless a longer period has been agreed for the purpose of retraining. Any such agreement must be made before the employee starts work under the new or renewed contract; it must be in writing, and specify the date the trial period ends, and the terms and conditions which will apply afterwards.[31] In order to have an agreement, an employee must do something to indicate acceptance. However, it is not necessary for the employer to provide all the information required by section 1 ERA 1996; the agreement need embody only important matters such as remuneration, status and job description.[32] If, during the trial period, the employee for any reason terminates or gives notice to terminate the contract, or the employer terminates or gives notice to terminate it for any reason connected with or arising out of the change, the employee is to be treated, for redundancy payment purposes, as having been dismissed on the date the previous contract ended. It should be noted that the employee's contract may be renewed again, or he or she may be re-engaged under a new contract in circumstances which give rise to another trial period.[33] Indeed, the termination of a trial period could lead to a finding of unfair dismissal.[34]

UNFAIR REDUNDANCY

It is possible for a dismissed employee to claim both a redundancy payment and unfair dismissal, although double compensation cannot be obtained.[35] For unfair dismissal purposes the statutory presumption of redundancy does not apply, so it is up to the employer to establish this as the reason, or principal reason, for dismissal. However, tribunals will not investigate the background which led to the redundancy or require the employer to justify redundancies in economic terms. According to the EAT, employers do not have to show that their requirements for employees to carry out work of a particular kind have diminished in relation to *any* work that the employees could have been asked to do under their contracts. Thus where an employee is hired to perform a particular trade, it is that basic obligation which has to be looked at when deciding whether the employer's requirements have ceased or diminished, rather than any work that the employee could be required to carry out in accordance with a contractual flexibility clause.[36]

A dismissal on grounds of redundancy will be unfair if it is shown that 'the circumstances constituting the redundancy applied equally to one or more other employees in the same undertaking who held positions similar' and either the reason, or principal reason, for which the employee was selected was inadmissible (see Chapter 13).[37] A situation where a number of employees at a similar level are made to apply for a reduced number of jobs at that level may still result in a dismissal on the grounds of redundancy which is fair, even though the work of that particular employee still continues to be done.[38]

THE INVOLVEMENT OF TRADE UNIONS

Because section 105 ERA 1996 is concerned purely with selection on grounds that are not permissible, a failure to comply with a procedural requirement to consult trade unions and to consider volunteers will not automatically be unfair.[39] Nevertheless, section 98(4) ERA 1996 can still have a considerable impact on dismissals for redundancy, a point which has been emphasised by the decision in *Williams v Compair Maxam*.[40] In this case it was held that it is not enough to show that it was reasonable to dismiss *an* employee, a tribunal must be satisfied that the employer acted reasonably in treating redundancy as 'sufficient reason for dismissing the employee'. According to the EAT, where employees are represented by a recognised independent trade union, reasonable employers will seek to act in accordance with the following principles:

- The employer will seek to give as much warning as possible of impending redundancies so as to enable the union and employees who may be affected to take early steps to inform themselves of the relevant facts, consider possible alternative solutions, and, if necessary, find alternative employment in the undertaking or elsewhere.

- The employer will consult the union as to the best means by which the desired management result can be achieved fairly and with as little hardship to the employees as possible.[41] In particular, the employer will seek to agree with the union the criteria to be applied in selecting the employees to be made redundant.[42] When a selection has been made, the employer will consider with the union whether the selection has been made in accordance with those criteria.[43]

- Whether or not an agreement as to the criteria to be adopted has been reached with the union, the employer will seek to establish criteria for selection which so far as possible do not depend solely upon the opinion of the person making the selection but can be checked objectively against such things as attendance record, efficiency at the job or length of service.

- The employer will seek to ensure that the selection is made fairly in accordance with these criteria and will consider any representations the union may make as to such selection.

- The employer will seek to see whether instead of dismissing, an employee could be offered alternative employment.

FAIR APPLICATION OF SELECTION CRITERIA

In selecting employees for redundancy a senior manager is entitled to rely on the assessments of employees made by those who have direct knowledge of their work. However, employers may need to show that their method of selection was fair and applied reasonably.[44] An absence of adequate consultation with the employees concerned or their representatives might affect their ability to do this[45] (consultation issues are considered below). It will not always be possible to call evidence subsequently to show that adequate consultation would not have made a difference to the decision on those selected for redundancy. If the flaws in the process were procedural, it might be possible to reconstruct what might have happened if the correct procedures had been followed. However, where the tribunal decides that the flaws were more substantive, such a reconstruction may not be possible.[46] In practice many employers have established redundancy appeal procedures to deal with complaints that selection criteria have been unfairly applied.

ALTERNATIVES TO COMPULSORY REDUNDANCY

It is now well established that employers have a duty to consider the alternatives to compulsory redundancy. According to ACAS, the measures for minimising or avoiding compulsory redundancies may include:

- natural wastage

- restrictions on recruitment

- reduction or elimination of overtime

- the introduction of short-time working or temporary lay-off (where this is provided for in the contract of employment or by an agreed variation of its terms)

- retraining and redeployment to other parts of the organisation

- termination of the employment of temporary or contract staff

- seeking applicants for early retirement or voluntary redundancy.[47]

'Last-in, first-out' is still used as a criterion for selection and it is assumed to be based on periods of continuous rather than cumulative service.[48] Arguably, this form of selection indirectly discriminates on the grounds of both sex and age and therefore needs to be objectively justified (see Chapters 6 and 7). Selecting employees on part-time and/or fixed-term contracts may also be potentially discriminatory. In *Whiffen v Milham Ford Girls School*[49] those employees not employed under a permanent contract of employment were the first to be selected in a redundancy exercise. This was held to be indirectly discriminatory because a smaller proportion of women than comparable men were able to satisfy this condition.

As regards alternative employment, 'the size and administrative resources' of the employer will be a relevant consideration here. However, if a vacancy exists, an employer would be advised to offer it rather than speculate about the likelihood of the employee accepting it. This is so even if the new job entails demotion or other radical changes in the terms and conditions of employment. Nevertheless, only in very rare cases will a tribunal accept that a reasonable employer would have created a job by dismissing someone else. Finally, employers should consider establishing both redundancy counselling services – which would provide information on alternative employment, training, occupational and state benefits – and hardship committees, which would seek to alleviate 'undue hardship'.[50]

CONSULTATION

An important requirement in redundancy situations is the need for consultation (see Chapter 17 for specific requirements in relation to collective redundancies). Consultation may be directly with the employees concerned or with their representatives. In *Mugford v Midland Bank plc*[51] the EAT held that a dismissal on the grounds of redundancy was not unfair because no consultation had taken place with the employee individually, only with the recognised trade union. The EAT described the position with regard to consultation as follows:

- Where no consultation about redundancy has taken place with either the trade union or the employee, the dismissal will normally be unfair, unless the reasonable employer would have concluded that the consultation would be an 'utterly futile' exercise.

- Consultation with the trade union over the selection criteria does not of itself release the employer from considering with the employee individually the fact that he or she has been identified for redundancy.

- It will be a question of fact and degree for the tribunal to consider whether the consultation with the individual and/or the trade union was so inadequate as to render the dismissal unfair.

For the tribunal to decide whether or not the employer acted reasonably, the overall picture must be viewed at the time of termination. The consultation must be fair and proper, which means that there must be:

- consultation when the proposals are still at a formative stage

- adequate information and adequate time to respond

- a conscientious consideration by the employer of the response to consultation.[52]

Although proper consultation may be regarded as a procedural matter, it might have a direct bearing on the substantive decision to select a particular employee, since a different employee might have been selected if, following proper consultation, different criteria had been adopted. It is not normally permissible for an employer to argue that a failure to consult or warn would have made no difference to the outcome in the particular case. It is what the employer did that is to be judged, not what might have been done. While the size of an undertaking might affect the nature or formality of the consultation, it cannot excuse lack of any consultation at all.[53] Finally, it should be noted that the EAT has taken the view that warning and consultation are part of the same single process of consultation, which should commence with a warning that the employee is at risk.[54]

CASE STUDY

Mr Elkouil was a credit controller at a night club. He was made redundant with immediate effect, although at no time was he warned that his job was at risk. The EAT held that the employment tribunal was wrong to limit the compensatory award to two weeks' pay on the basis that if the employer had consulted with him properly, he would have been employed for a further two weeks.

The EAT ruled that this was not an appropriate measure of the claimant's loss when the employer knew at least ten weeks before the dismissal that Mr Elkouil was going to be made redundant. The ET should have considered what would have been the likely outcome if the employer had done what it ought to have done. Here the consequence of the failure to consult was that the employee was disadvantaged in seeking another job, and ten weeks' pay was awarded.[55]

Reinforce your understanding of this chapter by visiting www.cipd.co.uk/sss for activities, questions, weblinks and additional case studies

REFERENCES

1 Section 155 ERA 1996

2 See Section 140 ERA 1996

3 See *CPS Recruitment Ltd v Bowen* (1982) IRLR 54

4 Section 138(1) ERA 1996

5 Sections 143–4 ERA 1996

6 See sections 159 and 191 ERA 1996

7 (1996) IRLR 508

8 It is for the tribunal to decide if a person is an employee by considering the facts and concluding that there is a genuine contract of employment; see *Secretary of State v Bottrill* (1999) IRLR 326.

9 'Business' is defined in section 235(1) ERA 1996

10 Section 139(6) ERA 1996

11 See *Murray v Foyle Meats Ltd* (1999) IRLR 562

12 *Safeway Stores v Burrell* (1997) IRLR 200

13 See *Bass Leisure v Thomas* (1994) IRLR 104; also *High Table Ltd v Horst* (1997) IRLR 514

14 See *Aparau v Iceland Frozen Foods* (1996) IRLR 119

15 See *Johnson v Nottingham Police Authority* (1974) ICR 170

16 (1977) IRLR 77

17 See also *Shawkat v Nottingham City Hospital NHS Trust (No.2)* (2001) IRLR 555

18 See *Shawkat v Nottingham City Hospital NHS Trust (No.2)* (note 17)

19 See *Pfaffinger v City of Liverpool Community College* (1996) IRLR 508

20 See *AUT v Newcastle University* (1987) ICR 317

21 See *Wilcox v Hastings* (1987) IRLR 299

22 See *Jones v Aston Cabinet Co. Ltd* (1973) ICR 292

23 See *Singer Co. v Ferrier* (1980) IRLR 300

24 See *Curling v Securicor Ltd* (1992) IRLR 549

25 See *Modern Injection Moulds Ltd v Price* (1976) IRLR 172

26 See *Hindes v Supersine Ltd* (1979) IRLR 343

27 See *Taylor v Kent County Council* (1969) 2 QB 560

28 (1985) IRLR 393

29 See *Cambridge and District Co-op v Ruse* (1993) IRLR 156

30 See *Benton v Sanderson Kayser* (1989) IRLR 299

31 Section 138(6) ERA 1996

32 See *McKindley v W Hill Ltd* (1985) IRLR 492

33 Section 138(5) ERA 1996

34 See *Hempell v W H Smith & Sons Ltd* (1986) IRLR 95

35 Section 122(4) ERA 1996

36 See *Johnson v Peabody Trust* (1996) IRLR 387

37 Section 105 ERA 1996. 'Undertaking' is not defined in this context; 'position' is defined in section 235(1) ERA 1996 as meaning the following matters taken as a whole: status, the nature of the work, and the terms and conditions of employment; on 'position similar' see *Powers and Villiers v A. Clarke & Co.* (1981) IRLR 483.

38 See *Safeway Stores plc v Burrell* (1997) IRLR 200

39 See *McDowell v Eastern BRS Ltd* (1981) IRLR 482

40 (1982) IRLR 83

41 See *Hough v Leyland DAF Ltd* (1991) IRLR 194

42 See *Rolls-Royce Ltd v Price* (1993) IRLR 203

43 See *John Brown Engineering Ltd v Brown* (1997) IRLR 90

44 In *Northgate HR Ltd v Mercy* (2008) IRLR 222 the Court of Appeal ruled that a tribunal was entitled to conclude that a glaring inconsistency produced in good faith could amount to unfairness in the administration of a selection procedure.

45 See *King v Eaton Ltd* (1996) IRLR 199

46 See *King v Eaton Ltd (No.2)* (1998) IRLR 686

47 Advisory booklet on redundancy-handling (2008). It should be noted that paragraph 1 of ACAS Code of Practice on Disciplinary and Grievance Procedures states that it 'does not apply to redundancy dismissals or the non-renewal of fixed-term contracts on their expiry'.

48 See *International Paint Co. v Cameron* (1979) IRLR 62

49 (2001) IRLR 468

50 See generally ACAS advisory booklet on redundancy-handling (2008)

51 (1997) IRLR 208

52 *King v Eaton Ltd* (1996) (note 45)

53 See *De Grasse v Stockwell Tools* (1992) IRLR 269

54 See *Elkouil v Coney Island Ltd* (2002) IRLR 174

55 *Elkouil v Coney Island Ltd* (note 54)

CHAPTER 15

Unfair Dismissal and Redundancy Claims

OVERVIEW

This chapter looks at the rules about making a claim for unfair dismissal or a redundancy payment. We begin by discussing the time-limits for making a complaint to an employment tribunal and then look at the making of conciliation and compromise agreements or using arbitration as an alternative to presenting a complaint to the tribunal. We go on to examine the remedies for unfair dismissal, which consist of reinstatement, re-engagement or compensation. There is then a consideration of how levels of compensation are arrived at and the method for calculating redundancy payments. The chapter concludes by outlining the rights of employees if the employer becomes insolvent.

MAKING A CLAIM

UNFAIR DISMISSAL

Unless the 'time-limit escape clause' applies,[1] claims must normally arrive at an employment tribunal within three months of the effective date of termination. However, where employees dismissed for taking part in industrial action allege that they should have been offered re-engagement, a complaint must be lodged within six months of the date of dismissal.[2] A time-limit expires at midnight on the last day of the stipulated period even when that is a non-working day.[3] A complaint can also be presented before the effective date of termination provided it is lodged after notice has been given. This includes notice given by an employee who is alleging constructive dismissal.[4] What is or is not reasonably practicable is a question of fact and the onus is on the employee to prove that it was not reasonably practicable to claim in time. The meaning of 'reasonably practicable' lies somewhere between reasonable and reasonably capable of physically being done.[5] The tribunal will look at this issue of reasonableness against all the surrounding circumstances. Sickness may be taken into account but will be more important if it falls within the critical latter part of the three-month period rather than at the beginning.[6]

The courts have dealt with this jurisdictional point on many occasions and have taken the view that, because the unfair dismissal provisions have been in force for many years, tribunals should be fairly strict in enforcing the time-limit.[7] Nevertheless, the issue of reasonable practicability depends upon the awareness of specific grounds for complaint, not upon the right to complain at all. Thus there is nothing to prevent an employee who is time-barred from claiming on one ground from proceeding with a second complaint on another ground if it is raised within a reasonable period. According to the Court of Appeal, if employers want to protect themselves from late claims presented on the basis of newly discovered facts they should ensure that the fullest information is made available to the employee at the time of dismissal.[8]

Delaying an application through ignorance or mistaken belief

The fact that an internal appeal or criminal action is pending does not by itself provide a sufficient excuse for delaying an application.[9] The correct procedure is for employees to submit their applications and request that they be held in abeyance. It is a general principle of English law that ignorance does not afford an excuse. Nevertheless, in *Wall's Meat Co. Ltd v Khan*[10] it was decided that ignorance or mistaken belief can be grounds for holding that it was not reasonably practicable if it could be shown that the ignorance or mistaken belief was itself reasonable. Thus in *Churchill v Yeates Ltd*[11] the EAT held that it was not reasonably practicable for an employee to bring a complaint until he or she had knowledge of a fundamental fact which rendered the dismissal unfair. In this case, after the three-month period had elapsed an employee who had been dismissed on the grounds of redundancy discovered that he had been replaced. Ignorance or mistaken belief will not be reasonable if it arises from the fault of complainants in not making such inquiries as they reasonably should have in the circumstances. However, the failure by an adviser – such as a trade union official, Citizen's Advice worker or solicitor – to give correct advice about a time-limit will not necessarily prevent an employee from arguing that it was not reasonably practicable to claim in time.[12]

The correct way to calculate the period of three months beginning with the effective date of termination is to take the day before the effective date and go forward three months. If there is no corresponding date (31st or 30th) in that month, the last day of the month is taken.[13] Where an application is posted within three months but arrives after the period has expired, the question to be determined is whether the claimant could reasonably have expected the application to be delivered in time in the ordinary course of the post.[14] In relation to electronic communications, the EAT has accepted that an application is presented when it is successfully submitted online at the Employment Tribunal Service website.[15] Finally, it should be noted that the unexplained failure of an application to reach the tribunal is insufficient to satisfy the statutory test unless all reasonable steps were taken to confirm that the application was duly received.[16]

REDUNDANCY

Employees who have not received a redundancy payment will normally be entitled to make a claim only if within six months of the relevant date they have:

- given written notice to the employer that they want a payment, or

- referred a question as to their right to a payment, or its amount, to a tribunal, or

- presented a complaint of unfair dismissal to a tribunal.[17]

The written notice to the employer does not have to be in a particular form. The test is whether it is of such a character that the recipient would reasonably understand in all the circumstances that it was the employee's intention to seek a payment.[18] In this context the words 'presented' and 'referred' seem to have the same meaning – ie an application must have been received by the employment tribunal within the six-month period.[19] Nevertheless, if any of the above steps are taken outside this period but within 12 months of the relevant date, a tribunal has the discretion to award a payment if it thinks that it would be just and equitable to do so. In such a case a tribunal must have regard to the employee's reasons for failing to take any of the steps within the normal time-limit.[20]

CONCILIATION AND COMPROMISE AGREEMENTS

Copies of unfair dismissal applications and redundancy claims and subsequent correspondence are sent to an ACAS conciliation officer who has the duty to promote a settlement of the complaint:

- if requested to do so by the complainant and the employer (known as the respondent), or

- if, in the absence of any such request, the conciliation officer considers that he or she could act with a reasonable prospect of success.

In *Moore v Duport Furniture*[21] the House of Lords decided that the expression 'promote a settlement' should be given a liberal construction capable of covering whatever action by way of such promotion is appropriate in the circumstances. Where the complainant has ceased to be employed, the conciliation officer must seek to promote that person's re-employment (ie reinstatement or re-engagement) on terms that appear to be equitable. If the complainant does not wish to be re-employed, or this is not practicable, the conciliation officer must seek to promote agreement on compensation.[22] In addition, section 18(3) ETA 1996 allows conciliation officers to make their services available before a complaint has been presented if requested to do so by either a potential applicant or a respondent. However, conciliation officers have no statutory duty to explain to employees what their statutory rights are.[23]

Where appropriate, a conciliation officer is to 'have regard to the desirability of encouraging the use of other procedures available for the settlement of grievances', and anything communicated to a conciliation officer in connection with the performance of the above functions is not admissible in evidence in any proceedings before a tribunal except with the consent of the person who communicated it.[24] It should be noted that an agreement to refrain from lodging a tribunal complaint is subject to all the qualifications by which an agreement can be avoided at common law – for example, on grounds of economic duress.[25] Where a representative holds himself or herself out as having authority to reach a settlement, in the absence of any notice to the contrary, the other party is entitled to assume that the representative does in fact have that authority. In such circumstances the agreement is binding on the client whether or not the adviser had any authority to enter into it.[26] A conciliated settlement will be binding even though it is not in writing[27] and the employee will be prevented from bringing the case before a tribunal.[28]

Formerly, an agreement purporting to preclude a person from bringing an employment tribunal complaint was void unless action had been taken by a conciliation officer in accordance with the above provisions. However, an agreement to refrain from bringing certain tribunal proceedings will not be void if it satisfies the conditions governing 'compromise agreements'. These conditions are that:

- the agreement must be in writing and must relate to the particular complaint

- the employee must have received independent legal advice from a relevant independent adviser[29] as to the terms and effect of the proposed agreement and, in particular, its effect on the employee's ability to pursue his or her rights before a tribunal

- at the time the adviser gives the advice there must be in force an insurance policy covering the risk of a claim by the employee in respect of loss arising in consequence of the advice

- the agreement must identify the adviser and state that the conditions regulating compromise agreements under ERA 1996 are satisfied.[30]

According to the EAT, an employment tribunal has jurisdiction to enforce a compromise agreement relating to the terms on which employment is to terminate.[31]

CASE STUDY

David Hinton took early retirement under an agreement which included a provision purporting to compromise all claims against his employer and satisfy the conditions laid down in section 203 ERA 1996 (above). However, the Court of Appeal upheld the ET's decision that Dr Hinton was not precluded from pursuing his complaint under section 47B ERA 1996 since it had not been itemised in the agreement.

According to the Appeal Court, the requirement that in order to constitute a valid compromise an agreement must 'relate to the particular proceedings' should be construed as requiring those proceedings to be clearly identified. Although one document can be used to compromise all the proceedings, it is insufficient to use the expression 'all statutory rights'. Thus the claims to be covered by an agreement must be identified either by a generic description (for example, 'unfair dismissal') or by reference to the relevant section of the statute.[32]

ARBITRATION

ACAS has produced an arbitration scheme as an alternative to an employment tribunal hearing for the resolution of unfair dismissal claims. The central feature of the scheme is that it is 'designed to be free of legalism'.[33] The arbitrator will decide on procedural and evidential matters and appeals will be allowed against awards only where EU law or the Human Rights Act 1998 are relevant. Hearings will be conducted in an inquisitorial manner, rather than an adversarial one, and the parties must comply with any instruction given by the arbitrator. Entry to the scheme is to be entirely voluntary but the parties will opt for arbitration on the understanding that they accept the arbitrator's decision as final. The arbitrator will decide whether the dismissal was fair or unfair and, in doing so, will have regard to the ACAS Code of Practice on Disciplinary and Grievance Procedures and the ACAS Guide. Where the dismissal is found to be unfair, the arbitrator may award reinstatement, re-engagement or compensation. Hearings will take place in a location convenient to all the parties and they will be responsible for their own expenses.

THE REMEDIES FOR UNFAIR DISMISSAL

RE-EMPLOYMENT

When applicants are found to have been unfairly dismissed, tribunals must explain their power to order reinstatement or re-engagement and ask employees if they wish such an order to be made.[34] Only if such a wish is expressed can an order be made and, if no order is made, the tribunal must turn to the question of compensation.[35] Where re-employment is sought, a tribunal must first consider whether reinstatement is appropriate and, in so doing, must take into account the following matters:

- whether the complainant wishes to be reinstated
- whether it is practicable for the employer to comply with an order for reinstatement
- where the complainant caused or contributed to some extent to the dismissal, whether it would be just to order reinstatement.[36]

If reinstatement is not ordered, the tribunal must then decide whether to make an order for re-engagement, and if so, on what terms. At this stage the tribunal must take into account the following considerations:

- any wish expressed by the complainant as to the nature of the order to be made
- whether it is practicable for the employer or, as the case may be, a successor or associated employer to comply with an order for re-engagement
- where the complainant caused or contributed to some extent to the dismissal, whether it would be just to order re-engagement, and if so, on what terms.

Except in a case where the tribunal takes into account contributory fault under the last point above, if it orders re-engagement it will do so in terms that are, so far as is reasonably practicable, as favourable as an order for reinstatement.[37] However, it would seem that tribunals cannot order that employees be re-engaged on significantly more favourable terms than they would have enjoyed had they been reinstated in their former jobs.[38] According to the Court of Appeal, a tribunal could approach the question of whether it would be practicable to order re-employment in two stages. The first stage would be before any order had been made, when a provisional decision could be taken. The second stage would arise if such an order was made but not complied with.[39]

If at least seven days before the hearing the employee has expressed a wish to be re-employed but it becomes necessary to postpone or adjourn the hearing because the employer does not, without special reason, adduce reasonable evidence about the availability of the job from which the employee was dismissed, the employer will be required to pay the costs of the adjournment or postponement.[40] In addition, section 116(5) ERA 1996 states that where an employer has taken on a permanent replacement, this shall not be taken into account unless the employer shows either:

- that it was not practicable to arrange for the dismissed employee's work to be done without engaging a permanent replacement, or

- that a replacement was engaged after the lapse of a reasonable period without having heard from the dismissed employee that he or she wished to be reinstated or re-engaged, and that when the employer engaged the replacement it was no longer reasonable to arrange for the dismissed employee's work to be done except by a permanent replacement.

The practicability of reinstating employees

Practicability is a question of fact for each tribunal. In *Boots plc v Lees*[41] the EAT agreed that it was practicable to reinstate notwithstanding that the employee's ultimate superior remained convinced that he was guilty of theft. By way of contrast, in *Wood Group Heavy Industrial Turbines Ltd v Crossan*,[42] the EAT held that an employer's genuine belief that an employee was dealing in drugs made re-engagement impracticable. In addition, the following arguments have been used to prevent an order being made: that the employee was unable to perform the work; that a redundancy situation arose subsequent to the dismissal; and that other employees were hostile to the complainant's return to work. It has also been suggested by the EAT that in a small concern where a close personal relationship exists reinstatement will be appropriate only in exceptional circumstances.[43]

For these purposes reinstatement is defined as treating the complainant 'in all respects as if he had not been dismissed', and on making an order the tribunal must specify:

- any amount payable by the employer in respect of any benefit which the complainant might reasonably be expected to have had but for the dismissal, including arrears of pay, for the period between the date of termination and the date of reinstatement

- any rights and privileges, including seniority and pension rights, which must be restored to the employee
- the date by which the order must be complied with.[44]

The complainant also benefits from any improvements that have been made to the terms and conditions of employment since dismissal.[45]

The terms that a tribunal must set out for re-engagement

An order for re-engagement may be on such terms as the tribunal decides and the complainant may be re-engaged by the employer, a successor or an associated employer in comparable or suitable employment. On making such an order the tribunal must set out the terms, including: the identity of the employer, the nature of the employment and the remuneration payable, together with the matters listed above in relation to reinstatement.[46]

Redress for non-compliance with a tribunal order to re-engage

Where a person is reinstated or re-engaged as the result of a tribunal order but the terms are not fully complied with,[47] a tribunal must make an additional award of compensation of such amount as it thinks fit, having regard to the loss sustained by the complainant in consequence of the failure to comply fully with the terms of the order.[48] It is a matter for speculation how long re-employment must last for it to be said that an order has been complied with. If a complainant is not re-employed in accordance with a tribunal order, he or she is entitled to enforce the monetary element at the employment tribunal.[49] Compensation will be awarded together with an additional award unless the employer satisfies the tribunal that it was not practicable to comply with the order.[50] However, according to the Court of Appeal, a re-engagement order does not place a duty on an employer to search for a job for the dismissed employee irrespective of the vacancies that arise.[51]

The additional award will be of between 26 and 52 weeks' pay.[52] The employment tribunal has discretion as to where, within this range, the additional compensation should fall, but it must be exercised on the basis of a proper assessment of the factors involved. One factor would ordinarily be the view taken of the employer's conduct in refusing to comply with the order.[53] Conversely, employees who unreasonably prevent an order being complied with will be regarded as having failed to mitigate their loss.

AWARDS OF COMPENSATION

Compensation for unfair dismissal will usually consist of a basic award and a compensatory award. It should be noted that if an award is not paid within 42 days of the tribunal's decision being recorded, it will attract interest.

BASIC AWARD

Normally, this will be calculated in the same way as a redundancy payment and will be reduced by the amount of any redundancy payment received.[54] Where the reason or principal reason for dismissal is related to union membership or the employee's health and safety responsibilities, there is a minimum award of £4,700 in 2009 (subject to any deduction on the grounds stated below).[55] The basic award can be reduced by such proportion as the tribunal considers just and equitable on two grounds:[56]

- the complainant unreasonably refused an offer of reinstatement. Such an offer could have been made before any finding of unfairness

- any conduct of the complainant before the dismissal, or before notice was given.[57] This does not apply where the reason for dismissal was redundancy unless the dismissal was regarded as unfair by virtue of section 100(1)(a) or (b), 101A(d), 102(1) or 103 ERA 1996. In that event the reduction will apply only to that part of the award payable because of section 120 ERA 1996.

An award of two weeks' pay will be made to employees who were redundant but unable to obtain a redundancy payment in either of the following circumstances:

- they are not to be treated as dismissed by virtue of section 138 ERA 1996, which deals with the renewal of a contract or re-engagement under a new one, or

- they are not entitled to a payment because of the operation of section 141 ERA 1996, which is concerned with offers of alternative employment.[58]

COMPENSATORY AWARD

The amount of this award is that which a tribunal 'considers just and equitable in all the circumstances having regard to the loss sustained by the complainant in consequence of the dismissal insofar as that loss is attributable to action taken by the employer'.[59] This may include losses resulting from subsequent employment or unemployment if those losses can be attributed to the dismissal. In *Dench v Flynn & Partners*[60] an assistant solicitor was able to claim compensation for unemployment after a subsequent short-term job because it was attributable to the original dismissal. However, the mere fact that the employer could have dismissed fairly on another ground arising out of the same factual situation does not render it unjust or inequitable to award compensation.[61]

Section 123(3) ERA 1996 specifically mentions that an individual whose redundancy entitlement would have exceeded the basic award can be compensated for the difference, while a redundancy payment received in excess of the basic award payable goes to reduce the compensatory award. The compensatory award can be reduced in two other circumstances: where the employee's action caused or contributed to the dismissal, and where the employee failed to mitigate his or her loss. Before reducing an award on the ground that the complainant caused or contributed to the dismissal, a tribunal must be satisfied that the employee's conduct was culpable or blameworthy – ie foolish, perverse or unreasonable in the circumstances.[62] Thus there could be a finding of contributory fault in a case of constructive dismissal on the basis that there was a causal link between the employee's conduct and the employer's repudiatory breach of contract.[63] However, compensation in respect of discriminatory non-re-engagement following dismissal while taking part in industrial action will not normally be reduced on the grounds of contributory conduct.[64]

Reductions to compensatory awards

In determining whether to reduce compensation the tribunal must take into account the conduct of the complainant and not what happened to some other employee – for example, one who was treated more leniently.[65] Not all unreasonable conduct will necessarily be culpable or blameworthy: it will depend on the degree of unreasonableness. Although ill-health cases will rarely give rise to a reduction in compensation on grounds of contributory fault, it is clear that an award may be reduced under the overriding 'just and equitable' provisions.[66] Having found that an employee was to blame, a tribunal must reduce the award to some extent, although the proportion of culpability is a matter for the tribunal.[67] According to the Court of Appeal, tribunals should first assess the amount which it is just and equitable to award because this may have a very significant bearing on what reduction to make for contributory conduct.[68] The percentage amount of reduction is to be taken from the total awarded to the employee before other deductions, such as offsetting what has already been paid by the employer, because this would be fairer to the employer.[69]

Complainants are obliged to look for work but there are stages that the tribunal must go through before it can decide what amount to deduct for an employee's failure to find work.[70] These are:

- to identify what steps should have been taken by the applicant to mitigate loss
- to find the date on which such steps would have produced an alternative income
- thereafter, to reduce the amount of compensation by the amount of income which would have been earned.

The onus is on the employer to prove that there was such a failure. While acknowledging that the employee has a duty to act reasonably, the EAT has concluded that this standard is not high in view of the fact that the employer is the wrongdoer.[71]

No account is to be taken of any pressure that was exercised on the employer to dismiss the employee[72] and, according to section 155 TULRCA 1992, compensation cannot be reduced on the grounds that the complainant:

- was in breach of (or proposed to breach) a requirement that he or she: must be, or become, a member of a particular trade union or one of a number of trade unions; ceases to be, or refrains from becoming a member of any trade union or of a particular trade union or of one of a number of particular trade unions; would not take part in the activities of any trade union, of a particular trade union or of one of a number of particular trade unions; would not make use of union services

- refused, or proposed to refuse, to comply with a requirement of a kind mentioned in section 152(3)(a) TULRCA 1992

- objected, or proposed to object, to the operation of a provision of a kind mentioned in section 152(3)(b) TULRCA 1992

- accepted or failed to accept an offer made in contravention of section 145A or 145B TULRCA 1992.

Nevertheless, this section permits a distinction to be drawn between what was done by the complainant and the way in which it was done.[73]

The maximum compensatory award is £66,200 in 2009 but it should be noted that this figure is linked to the retail price index. The limit applies only after credit has been given for any payments made by the employer and any deductions have been made.[74] However, any 'excess' payments made by the employer over that which is required are deducted after the amount of the compensatory award has been fixed.[75] As regards deductions, normally an employer is to be given credit for all payments made to an employee in respect of claims for wages and other benefits (apart from pension payments received).[76] Where an employee has suffered discrimination as well as unfair dismissal, section 126 ERA 1996 prevents double compensation for the same loss.

It is the duty of tribunals to inquire into the various grounds for damages but it is the responsibility of the aggrieved person to prove the loss. The legislation aims to reimburse the employee rather than to punish the employer.[77] Hence employees who appear to have lost nothing – for example, where it can be said that irrespective of the procedural unfairness which occurred, they would have been dismissed anyway – do not qualify for a compensatory award. However, if the employee puts forward an arguable case that dismissal was not inevitable, the evidential burden shifts to the employer to show that dismissal was likely to have occurred in any event.[78] Additionally, a nil or nominal award may be thought just and equitable in a case where misconduct was discovered subsequently to the dismissal.[79]

The possible grounds (heads) of loss have been divided into the following categories:

1 *Loss incurred up to the date of the hearing*

Here attention focuses on the employee's actual loss of income, which makes it necessary to ascertain the employee's take-home pay. Thus, tax and National Insurance contributions are to be deducted, but overtime earnings and tips can be taken into account. Similarly, any sickness or incapacity benefits received may be taken into account.[80] It should also be noted that the loss sustained should be based on what the employee was entitled to, whether or not he or she was receiving it at the time of dismissal.[81] As well as lost wages, section 123(2) ERA 1996 enables an individual to claim compensation for the loss of other benefits – for example, a company car or other perks. Similarly, 'expenses reasonably incurred' are mentioned in the statute so employees will be able to recover the cost of looking for a new job or setting up their own business. However, complainants cannot be reimbursed for the cost of pursuing their unfair dismissal claims.

2 Loss flowing from the manner of dismissal

Compensation can be awarded only if the manner of dismissal has made the individual less acceptable to potential employers. There is nothing for non-economic loss – for example, hurt feelings. However, economic loss may arise where the person is not fit to take up alternative employment as early as he or she would otherwise have done (or ever); or where by virtue of stigma damage, loss of reputation or embarrassment no suitable employer was prepared to engage him or her, at any rate on terms that would not cause continuing loss.[82]

3 Loss of accrued rights

This head of loss is intended to compensate the employee for the loss of rights dependent on a period of continuous service, but because the basic award reflects lost redundancy entitlement, sums awarded on these grounds have tended to be nominal. Nevertheless, tribunals should include a sum to reflect the fact that dismissed employees lose the statutory minimum notice protection that they have built up.[83]

4 Loss of pension rights

Undoubtedly this presents the most complex problems of computation. Basically, there are two types of loss: the loss of the present pension position and the loss of the opportunity to improve one's pension position with the dismissing employer. When an employee is close to retirement, the cost of an annuity which will provide a sum equal to the likely pension can be calculated. In other cases the starting-point will be the contributions already paid into the scheme, and in addition to having their own contributions returned, employees can claim an interest in their employer's contributions, except in cases of transferred or deferred pensions. However, in assessing future loss the tribunal must take into account a number of possibilities – for example, future dismissal or resignation, early death, and the fact that a capital sum is being paid sooner than would have been expected. Although employment tribunals have been given actuarial guidelines on loss of pension rights, in each case the factors must be evaluated to see what adjustment should be made or whether the guidelines are safe to use at all.[84]

5 Future loss

Where no further employment has been secured, tribunals will have to speculate how long the employee will remain unemployed. Here the tribunal must utilise its knowledge of local market conditions as well as considering personal circumstances.[85] According to the EAT, employees who have become unfit for work wholly or partly as a result of unfair dismissal are entitled to compensation for loss of earnings, at least for a reasonable period following the dismissal, until they might reasonably have been expected to find other employment.[86] If another job has been obtained, tribunals must compare the employee's salary prospects for the future in each job and see as best they can how long it will take the employee to reach in the new position the salary equivalent to that which would have been attained had he or she remained with the original employer.[87] Where the employee is earning a higher rate of pay at the time compensation is being assessed, the tribunal should decide whether the new employment is permanent, and, if so, should calculate the loss as between the date of dismissal and the date the new job was secured.[88]

Awards and the Jobseeker's Allowance

Finally, mention must be made of Employment Protection (Recoupment of Jobseeker's Allowance and Income Support) Regulations 1996,[89] which were designed to remove the state subsidy to employers who dismiss unfairly. Such benefits had the effect of reducing the losses suffered by dismissed persons. These Regulations provide that a tribunal must not deduct from the compensation awarded any sum which represents Jobseeker's Allowance received, and the employer is instructed not to pay immediately the amount of compensation which represents loss of income up to the hearing (known as the 'prescribed element'). The National Insurance Fund can then serve the employer with a recoupment notice which will require him or her to pay the Fund from the prescribed element the amount which represents the Jobseeker's Allowance paid to the employee prior to the hearing.[90] When the amount has been refunded by the employer, the remainder of the prescribed element becomes the employee's property. It is important to note that private settlements do not fall within the scope of these Regulations.

CALCULATING A REDUNDANCY PAYMENT

The size of a redundancy payment depends on the employee's length of continuous service, his or her age and the amount of a week's pay. A week's pay is calculated in accordance with sections 220–9 ERA 1996 (see Chapter 16) and in this context means gross pay.[91] However, it does not take into account increased wage rates agreed subsequently to the employee's dismissal but backdated to a date prior to the dismissal.[92] Unless the contrary is shown, employment is presumed to have been continuous (see Chapter 16), but this only applies in relation to the dismissing employer (except when a business or undertaking has been transferred[93] or an employee has been taken into employment by an associated employer). If continuity is not preserved on a transfer, an assurance given by one employer that the obligations of another will be met will not confer jurisdiction on a tribunal to award a payment based on overall service. However, an employee may be able to show that there was a contract to the effect that he or she would retain the benefit of previous employment.[94]

Redundancy payments are calculated according to the following formula, with a maximum of 20 years' service being taken into account. Starting at the end of the employee's period of service and calculating backwards:

- one and a half weeks' pay is allowed for each year of employment in which the individual was 41 and over

- a week's pay for each year of employment in which the individual was between the ages of 22 and 40

- half a week's pay for each year of employment between the ages of 18 and 21.[95]

Thus the maximum statutory redundancy payment is £10,500 in 2009 (ie 30 x £350). However, where a tribunal decides that an employee is entitled to such a payment it can provide compensation for financial losses which are attributable to the employer's non-payment.[96] On making a payment the employer must give the employee a written statement indicating how the amount has been calculated. An employer who, without reasonable excuse, fails to do so can receive a fine not exceeding level 3 on the standard scale.[97]

EMPLOYEE RIGHTS ON INSOLVENCY

If an employer becomes insolvent or bankrupt, an employee's wages in respect of the four months beforehand, up to a maximum of £800, become a preferential debt.[98] In addition, Schedule 6 of the Insolvency Act 1986 provides that the following shall be treated as wages for these purposes: a guarantee payment; remuneration payable under suspension on medical or maternity grounds; remuneration payable during a protective award; and a payment for time off for union duties, antenatal care, or to look for work or make arrangements for training in a redundancy situation.

Section 182 ERA 1996 gives employees the right to make a written request to the Secretary of State for a payment out of the National Insurance Fund to meet certain other debts which arise out of the employer's insolvency.[99] These debts are:

- arrears of pay up to a maximum of eight weeks; this includes any of the matters treated as wages for the purposes of the Insolvency Act 1986

- wages payable during the statutory notice period. It should be noted that employees are still required to mitigate their loss

- holiday pay up to a maximum of six weeks, provided the entitlement accrued during the preceding 12 months

- a basic award of compensation for unfair dismissal

- any reasonable sum by way of reimbursement of the whole or part of any fee or premium paid by an apprentice or articled clerk.

A financial limit is imposed on the amount that can be recovered in respect of any one week[100] (£350 per week in 2009).

Before reimbursing the employee the Secretary of State must be satisfied both that the employer has become insolvent[101] and that the employee is entitled to be paid the whole or part of the debt claimed.[102] The Secretary of State is liable only to the extent to which the employee is legally entitled to make a claim against the employer. Also, a payment cannot be made unless a 'relevant officer' appointed in connection with the insolvency – for example, a liquidator, receiver or trustee in bankruptcy – has supplied a statement of the amount owed to the employee. However, this requirement may be waived if the Secretary of State is satisfied that the statement is not necessary to determine the amount owing.[103] If the Secretary of State fails to make a payment or if it is less than the amount which the employee thinks should have been made,[104] a complaint may be presented to an employment tribunal within three months of the Secretary of State's decision being communicated.[105] Where a tribunal finds that a payment ought to have been made under section 182 ERA 1996, it must make a declaration to that effect and state the amount that ought to be paid. Finally, it should be noted that when the Secretary of State makes a payment to the employee, the rights and remedies of the latter in relation to the employer's insolvency are transferred to the Secretary of State.[106]

KEY LEARNING POINTS

- Complaints of unfair dismissal must normally arrive at an employment tribunal within three months of the effective date of termination.

- Employees who have not received a redundancy payment will normally be entitled to make a claim within six months of the relevant date.

- ACAS will assist the employee and the employer by conciliating to try to reach an agreement to settle the complaint.

- Remedies for unfair dismissal include reinstatement, re-engagement or compensation.

- Compensation for unfair dismissal will consist of a basic award and a compensatory award.

- The maximum compensatory award is £66,200 in 2009 and is linked to the retail price index.

- The size of a redundancy payment depends upon the employee's age, length of service and the amount of a week's pay.

- If an employer becomes insolvent, some liabilities will pass to the Secretary of State for payment out of the National Insurance Fund.

Reinforce your understanding of this chapter by visiting www.cipd.co.uk/sss for activities, questions, weblinks and additional case studies

REFERENCES

1   Section 111(2) ERA 1996

2   Section 239(2) TULRCA 1992

3   See *Swainston v Hetton Victory Club* (1983) IRLR 164

4   Section 111(4) ERA 1996; see *Patel v Nagesan* (1995) IRLR 370

5   See *Palmer v Southend B.C.* (1984) IRLR 119

6   See *Schultz v Esso Petroleum Co. Ltd* (1999) IRLR 488

7   See *London Underground v Noel* (1999) IRLR 621

8   See *Marley Ltd v Anderson* (1996) IRLR 163

9   See *Pulmer v Southend B.C.* (note 5 above)

10   (1978) IRLR 499

11   (1983) IRLR 187; see also *Post Office v Sanhotra* (2000) IRLR 866

12   See *Marks & Spencer plc v Williams-Ryan* (2005) IRLR 562

13   See *Pruden v Cunard Ltd* (1993) IRLR 317

14   See *Consignia plc v Sealy* (2002) IRLR 624 where detailed guidance is provided

15   *Tyne & Wear Autistic Society v Smith* (2005) IRLR 336

16   See *Camden and Islington NHS Trust v Kennedy* (1996) IRLR 381

17   Section 164(1) ERA 1996

18   See *Price v Smithfield Group Ltd* (1978) IRLR 80

19   See *Secretary of State v Banks* (1983) ICR 48 and *Swainston v Hetton Victory Club* (note 3 above)

20   Section 164(2) ERA 1996

21   (1982) IRLR 31

22   Section 18(4) ETA 1996

23   See *Clarke v Redcar Borough Council* (2006) IRLR 324

24   Section 18(6) and (7) ETA 1996

25   See *Hennessy v Craigmyle Ltd* (1985) IRLR 446

26   See *Freeman v Sovereign Chicken Ltd* (1991) IRLR 408

27   See *Gilbert v Kembridge Fibres Ltd* (1984) IRLR 52

28   Section 203(2)(e) ERA 1996

29   Section 203(3A) ERA 1996 defines 'relevant independent adviser' as a qualified lawyer; an officer, official, member or employee of a trade union who has been certified to give advice by the union; an authorised advice centre worker; or others specified by the Secretary of State.

30   Section 203(2)(f) and 203(3) ERA 1996

31   See *Rock-It Cargo Ltd v Green* (1997) IRLR 582 and *Sutherland v Network Appliance* (2001) IRLR 12

32   *Hinton v University of East London* (2005) IRLR 552

33   See ACAS Arbitration Scheme (Great Britain) Order 2004, SI No.753

34   See *Constantine v Cory Ltd* (2000) IRLR 939

35   Section 112 ERA 1996

36   Section 116(1) ERA 1996

37   Section 116(4) ERA 1996

38   See *Rank Xerox v Stryczek* (1995) IRLR 568

39   See *Port of London Authority v Payne* (1994) IRLR 9

40   Section 13(2) ETA 1996

41   (1986) IRLR 485

42   (1998) IRLR 680

43   See *Enessy Co. v Minoprio* (1978) IRLR 489

44   Section 114(2) ERA 1996

45   Section 114(3) ERA 1996

46   Section 115(2) ERA 1996

47   See *Artisan Press v Strawley* (1986) IRLR 126 on the difference between not re-employing and not fully complying with an order.

48   Section 117(2) ERA 1996. See *Parry v National Westminster Bank* (2005) IRLR 193

49   See section 124(4) ERA 1996

50   Section 117(3) and (4) ERA 1996. See *Awotana v South Tyneside NHS Trust* (2005) IRLR 958

51   See *Port of London Authority v Payne* (note 39 above)

52   Section 117(3)(b) ERA 1996

53   See *Motherwell Railway Club v McQueen* (1989) ICR 419

54   Section 122(4) ERA 1996; see *Boorman v Allmakes Ltd* (1995) IRLR 553

55   Section 120 ERA 1996

56   Section 122(1) and (2) ERA 1996

57   See *RSPCA v Cruden* (1986) IRLR 83

58   Section 121 ERA 1996

59   Section 123 ERA 1996

60   (1998) IRLR 653

61   See *Devonshire v Trico-Folberth* (1989) IRLR 397

62   See *Nelson v BBC (No.2)* (1979) IRLR 304; *Morrison v ATGWU* (1989) IRLR 361

63   See *Polentarutti v Autokraft Ltd* (1991) IRLR 457

64   See *Crosville Wales Ltd v Tracey and another (No.2)* (1996) IRLR 691

65   See *Parker Foundry Ltd v Slack* (1992) IRLR 11

66   See *Slaughter v Brewer Ltd* (1990) IRLR 426

67   See *Warrilow v Walker Ltd* (1984) IRLR 304

68   See *Rao v Civil Aviation Authority* (1994) IRLR 240

69   See *Heggie v Uniroyal Englebert Tyres Ltd* (1998) IRLR 425

70   See *Savage v Saxena* (1998) IRLR 182

71   See *Fyfe v Scientific Furnishings Ltd* (1989) IRLR 331. On unreasonable refusal of an offer of re-employment and the failure to mitigate loss see *Wilding v BT plc* (2002) IRLR 524

72   Section 123(5) ERA 1996

73   See *TGWU v Howard* (1992) IRLR 170

74   Section 124(5) ERA 1996; see *Braund Ltd v Murray* (1991) IRLR 100

75   See *Digital Equipment Co Ltd v Clements (No.2)* (1998) ICR 258

76   See *Knapton v ECC Clothing Ltd* (2006) ICR 1084

77   See *Burlo v Langley* (2007) IRLR 145

78   See *Britool Ltd v Roberts* (1993) IRLR 481

79   See *Tele-trading Ltd v Jenkins* (1990) IRLR 430

80   See *Morgans v Alpha Plus Ltd* (2005) IRLR 234 and compare *Sheffield Forgemasters Ltd v Fox* (2009) IRLR 192

81   For example, the national minimum wage: see *Paggetti v Cobb* (2002) IRLR 861

82   See *Dunnachie v Hull City Council* (2004) IRLR 727

83   See *Guinness Ltd v Green* (1989) IRLR 289

84   See *Port of Tilbury v Birch* (2005) IRLR 92

85   See *Seafield Holdings Ltd v Drewett* (2006) ICR 1413

86   On compensating for career-long loss see *Kingston upon Hull City Council v Dunnachie (No.3)* (2003) IRLR 843

87   *Tradewind Airways Ltd v Fletcher* (1981) ITLR 272

88 See *Fentiman v Fluid Engineering Ltd* (1991) IRLR 150

89 SI 1996/2439; see also sections 16 and 17 ETA 1996

90 See *Homan v A1 Bacon Ltd* (1996) ICR 846

91 See *Secretary of State v Woodrow* (1983) IRLR 11; the maximum amount of a week's pay is £350 in 2009

92 See *Leyland Vehicles Ltd v Reston* (1981) IRLR 19

93 See *Lassman v Secretary of State* (1999) ICR 416 where continuity was preserved by the Transfer Regulations 1981, even though, at the time of the transfer, the employees received statutory redundancy payments

94 *Secretary od State v Globe Elastic Ltd* (1979) IRLR 327

95 Section 162(1) and (2) ERA 1996. On age discrimination see Chapter 7.

96 Section 163(5) ERA 1996

97 Section 165 ERA 1996; see *Barnsley M.B.C. v Prest* (1996) ICR 85

98 Section 386 Insolvency Act 1986

99 Insolvency is defined in section 183 ERA 1996; see *Secretary of State v Stone* (1994) ICR 761

100 See *Benson v Secretary of State* (2003) IRLR 748

101 See *Morris v Secretary of State* (1985) IRLR 297

102 See *Secretary of State v Walden* (2001) IRLR 168

103 Section 187(2) ERA 1996

104 See *Potter v Secretary of State for Employment* (1997) IRLR 21 on the ability of the Secretary of State to set off protective awards against the claims of the employees

105 Section 188 ERA 1996; the 'time-limit escape clause' applies here

106 Section 189 ERA 1996

CHAPTER 16

Continuity of Employment and Transfers of Undertakings

OVERVIEW

In this chapter we are concerned with the concepts of continuity of service, including the effect of the Transfer of Undertakings Regulations 2006 (TUPE), normal working hours and a week's pay. They are important because many statutory rights are dependent upon minimum length of service, and payments are related to statutory concepts of normal working hours and a week's pay. We begin by looking at continuity of employment and what impact different types of gaps in service have on these statutory rights. We then look briefly at normal working hours (aspects of the regulation of working time are dealt with in Chapter 10). We then examine the concept of a week's pay which is used for computing many payments under ERA 1996, such as redundancy payments and compensation for unfair dismissal. Finally we consider the TUPE Regulations 2006.

CONTINUITY OF EMPLOYMENT

Continuous employment is an important concept because many statutory rights are dependent on a minimum service qualification, and certain benefits – for example, redundancy payments and basic awards – are calculated by reference to length of service. Continuity of employment is a statutory concept[1] in accordance with sections 210–219 ERA 1996, and the courts will look to see whether there has been a break in service. In *Morris v Walsh Western UK Ltd*[2] the employer agreed to ignore a month's break in employment and treat the employee as having been continuously employed. Despite this, the EAT held that the month's gap had constituted a break in service.

Section 210(5) ERA 1996 states that employment is presumed to have been continuous unless the contrary is shown, although this is not so where there is a succession of employers.[3] Apart from redundancy payment purposes, these provisions also apply to periods of employment wholly or mainly outside Great Britain.[4] Continuity is normally assessed in relation to the particular contract on which a claim is based. However, it may be possible for an employer to deliberately subject employees to a combination of separate contracts which amount to a series of fixed-term contracts with a break in between.[5] The EAT concluded that any anomalies or avoidance of the legislation is a matter for Parliament rather than the courts (for the effect of the Fixed-term Employees/ Prevention of Less Favourable Treatment Regulations 2002 on continuity of employment see Chapter 4).

A period of continuous employment, which begins with the day on which the employee 'starts work'[6] is to be computed in months, and except insofar as is otherwise provided, a week which does not count breaks the period of continuous employment.[7] A person accrues a period of continuous service only if he or she is employed under a legal contract of employment. Thus, if for a period of time the contract is illegal, then for that period the contract cannot be relied on.[8] Where there is a dispute over continuity, employees have to establish that there was a week which counted, but in respect of subsequent weeks they can rely on the presumption contained in section 210(5) ERA 1996 that employment is continuous (unless there is evidence to the contrary).[9]

WEEKS THAT COUNT

According to section 212(1) ERA 1996, any week[10] during the whole or part of which a person has a contract of employment will count.

CASE STUDY

Sweeney v J & S Henderson Ltd (1999) IRLR 306

Mr Sweeney was originally employed on 19 June 1995. He resigned on Saturday 15 February 1997 and immediately took up employment with another employer. Within a few days he regretted his decision and applied for, and received, re-employment with his old employer, from Friday 21 February 1997. This employment lasted until 12 March 1998 when he was dismissed.

At the time there was a two-year qualification period to be entitled to make a claim for unfair dismissal. The issue was whether he had this length of service. Was the break in his employment enough to stop him having continuity of employment from February 1997 until March 1998?

The EAT held that the employment was continuous, in accordance with section 212(1) ERA 1996. This section, according to the Court, clearly contemplates that continuous employment can have gaps, provided that during the relevant weeks there is at least one day governed by the contract of employment. This was so in this case and it was not relevant how the gap was created nor what the employee did during the gap.[11]

A week counts if one of the following applies for the whole or part of that week:

- The employee is incapable of work as a consequence of sickness or injury.[12] Not more than 26 consecutive weeks can be counted under this head.[13] In this context the expression 'incapable of work' does not mean incapable of work generally, nor does it refer to the particular work provided for in the contract which has ended. According to the Court of Appeal, where the work on offer by the employer differs from that for which the employee was previously employed, the tribunal must consider whether the work offered was of a kind which the employee was willing to accept or, even if the employee was unwilling, was suited to his or her particular circumstances.[14]

- The employee is absent from work on account of a temporary cessation of work.[15] In this context the phrase 'absent from work' does not necessarily mean physical absence but means not performing in substance the contract that previously existed between the parties.[16] The words 'on account of' refer to the reason when the employer dismissed, and the fact that the unavailability of work was foreseen and the employee took another job will not prevent a tribunal holding that this provision applies. 'Cessation of work' denotes that a quantity of work has for the time being ceased to exist and was therefore no longer available to be given to the employee. Thus, when a member of a pool of casual cleaners was not allocated work under a pool arrangement, that absence was not on account of a temporary cessation of work.[17]

According to the House of Lords, 'temporary' means lasting a relatively short time and whether an interval can be so characterised is a question of fact for the employment tribunal. Where there is a succession of fixed-term contracts with intervals between them, continuity is not broken unless 'looking backwards from the date of expiry of the fixed-term contract on which the claim is based, there is to be found between one fixed-term contract and its immediate predecessor an interval that cannot be characterised as short relative to the combined duration of the two fixed-term contracts'.[18] In *Flack v Kodak Ltd*[19] the EAT held that where an employee has worked intermittently over a period of years in an irregular pattern, tribunals ought to have regard to all the circumstances and should not confine themselves to the mathematical approach of looking at each gap and immediately adjoining periods of employment. The fact that cessation is not permanent does not mean that it must be temporary for these purposes.[20]

CASE STUDY

Cornwall County Council v Prater (2006) IRLR 362

Between 1988 and 1998 Mrs Prater was employed under a succession of individual contracts to teach children who were, for a variety of reasons, unable to attend school. Work was offered to her by way of care for an individual pupil, whom she would teach at the pupil's home. There was no obligation by the Council to offer her work and she was under no contractual obligation to accept further pupils. Once she had taken on a pupil, however, she was obliged to complete the particular assignment. During the whole of the period Mrs Prater never refused any offers of work.

She became a permanent employee of the Council in 1998, but there was a dispute about whether her employment status during the period was continuous since 1988.

The EAT held that she had been employed throughout the ten-year period and that she had worked under a number of successive engagements. During each of those engagements there was a mutuality of obligation, particularly as she was obliged to complete each one, which made it a contract of employment. The gaps in between could be viewed as temporary cessations of work. Thus there was no need for an umbrella contract to ensure continuity of employment.

- The employee is absent from work in circumstances such that by arrangement or custom he or she is regarded as continuing in the employment of the employer for all or any purposes.[21] Although an arrangement must normally exist at the time the absence began, the EAT has held that the period between dismissal and voluntary reinstatement may be covered by this provision.[22] For section 212(3)(c) ERA to preserve continuity of employment by arrangement or custom there must be a mutual recognition, by the employer and the employee, that although the employee is absent from work, he or she continues to be employed by the employer. A recognition that there is some other kind of continuing relationship is not enough. Thus a child break scheme which guaranteed the employee a post similar to that which she had previously held and which had arrangements for keeping the parties in contact during the absence was held not to be an arrangement preserving continuity because the employee was required to resign her employment at the beginning of the scheme.[23]

It would appear that the cause of the absence is immaterial. Thus employees who have been loaned to a third party may be protected as well as those given leave of absence for personal reasons. In *Colley v Corkindale*[24] the EAT held that employees who worked alternate weeks were to be regarded as being absent by arrangement on their weeks off.

It should be noted that continuity of employment where employees are absent from work for family reasons is now dealt with under the Maternity and Parental Leave Regulations 1999 and the Paternity and Adoption Leave Regulations 2002 as amended (see Chapter 8).

STRIKES AND LOCK-OUTS

Days on which an employee is on strike neither count towards nor break the employee's period of continuous service.[25] By virtue of section 235(5) ERA 1996 for this purpose 'strike' means:

(a)   the cessation of work by a body of persons employed acting in combination, or

(b)   a concerted refusal or a refusal under a common understanding of any number of persons employed to continue to work for an employer in consequence of a dispute, done as a means of compelling their employer or any person or body of persons employed, or to aid other employees in compelling their employer or any person or body of persons employed, to accept or not to accept terms and conditions of or affecting employment.

Where an employee is absent from work because of a lock-out, again continuity is not broken and if the contract of employment subsists, the period of absence could be counted under section 212(1) ERA 1996.[26] 'Lock-out' means:[27]

(a)   the closing of a place of employment

(b)   the suspension of work

(c)   the refusal by an employer to continue to employ any number of persons employed by him in consequence of a dispute, done with a view to compelling those persons, or to aid another employer in compelling persons employed by him, to accept terms or conditions of or affecting employment.

It makes no difference that employees were dismissed during a strike or lock-out; as long as they were subsequently re-engaged, their period of continuous employment will be preserved. Any attempt to provide otherwise – for example, by introducing a specific term relating to previous employment – will be construed as an attempt to exclude or limit the operation of this paragraph and will be ineffective as a result of section 203 ERA 1996.[28]

CHANGE OF EMPLOYER

Usually when an employee leaves one employer and starts working for another, his or her period of continuous service will be broken. However, in certain circumstances a person will be regarded as having been employed by the new employer as from the date his or her previous employment commenced. Apart from the situation where an employer voluntarily agrees to give credit for service with a previous employer (which does not bind the Secretary of State),[29] there are six main types of case in which employment is deemed to be continuous despite a change of employer:

- if there is a transfer of a trade, undertaking, business or part of a business.[30] The words 'trade' and 'undertaking' are not defined in ERA 1996, but 'business' includes a trade or profession and any activity carried on by a body of persons, whether corporate or unincorporated.[31] In relation to business transfers the critical question is whether there has been the transfer of a 'going concern' which could be carried on without interruption or merely the disposal of assets. If the latter, continuity of employment is not maintained.

- If the transfer is a relevant transfer for the purposes of the Transfer Regulations 2006 (see below), the fact that the employees were dismissed and given redundancy payments at the time of the transfer will not necessarily affect continuity of employment.[32]

- if an Act of Parliament results in one corporate body replacing another as employer[33]

- if the employer dies and the employee is then re-employed by the personal representatives or trustees of the deceased[34]

- if there is a change in the partners, personal representatives or trustees who employ the individual[35]

- if the individual is taken into the employment of an associated employer.[36] 'Associated employer' is defined in section 231 ERA 1996 as follows: 'Any two employers are to be treated as associated if (a) one is a company of which the other (directly or indirectly) has control; or (b) both are companies of which a third person (directly or indirectly) has control.' The expression 'has control' is used in the company-law sense of controlling 51 per cent or more of the shares. However, the register of shares does not conclusively establish the identity of the possessor of control because the person registered as owner might be a nominee.[37] According to the EAT, tribunals should look at the way in which control had in fact been exercised.[38] While there must not be a gap between the employments (unless it is covered by the statute), it is not necessary that the move to an associated employer be made with the acquiescence of either employer.

- if the employee is employed by the governors of a school maintained by a local education authority or by the authority itself and he or she is transferred to another school or local education authority.[39]

A WEEK'S PAY

This concept is used for computing many payments under ERA 1996 – for example, redundancy payments and the basic award of compensation for unfair dismissal. The maximum week's pay for the purpose of calculating a redundancy payment and other awards is £350 in 2009.

Where there are normal working hours:

- if remuneration does not vary with the amount of work done, a week's pay is the gross amount payable for a week's work under the contract of employment in force on the calculation date.[40] Calculation dates are laid down in section 225 ERA 1996 and vary according to the particular statutory rights being enforced

- if the remuneration varies with the amount of work done, a week's pay is the remuneration for the number of normal working hours payable at the average hourly rate.[41] The average hourly rate is ascertained by calculating the total number of hours actually worked in the 12 calendar weeks preceding the calculation date, the total amount of remuneration paid for these hours, and then deducing the average hourly payment. The 12 calendar weeks preceding the calculation date consist of weeks during which the employee actually worked even though for some of this time he or she might have earned less than usual. However, a week in which no remuneration was required to be paid must be disregarded.[42] In *British Coal v Cheesebrough*[43] the average hourly rate was calculated by taking into account all remuneration paid in respect of all hours worked, including overtime, except that the premium element in respect of overtime was disregarded

- and they are worked at varying times and in varying amounts in different weeks – for example, in the case of shift-workers – both the average rate of remuneration and the number of hours worked in a week will have to be computed in the 12 calendar weeks preceding the calculation date. In these circumstances, a week's pay is the average weekly number of normal working hours payable at the average hourly rate of remuneration.[44]

Where there are no normal working hours, a week's pay is the average weekly remuneration received over the period of 12 calendar weeks preceding the calculation date.[45]

If an employee has not been employed for a sufficient period to enable a calculation to be made under any of the above provisions, a tribunal must decide what amount 'fairly represents a week's pay'. Section 228(2)–(3) ERA 1996 sets out some matters for consideration in this respect. Where an individual's actual rate of pay is less than the national minimum wage (see Chapter 5) then the tribunal will use the higher figure when computing basic and compensatory awards for unfair dismissal.[46]

Annualised hours contracts can present a problem here. In *Ali v Christian Salvesen Food Services Ltd*[47] the employees agreed a total number of hours per annum as part of a collective agreement. The arrangement, however, did not deal with the situation where employees left during the year, after they had worked in excess of the notional weekly hours on which their standard rate of pay was based. The Court of Appeal refused to fill the gap in the agreement so that the employees could claim for the hours actually worked.

Finally, the word 'remuneration' has not been statutorily defined for these purposes but it has been held to include any payments made on a regular basis – eg commission, bonuses and attendance allowances. The payment of commission does not, however, override the need for the amount of work done in normal working hours to vary in order for it to be taken into account. Thus, if commission is earned as a result of successful sales during normal working hours, it may not necessarily be taken into account when working out the average hourly rate. The Court of Appeal held, in *Evans v Malley Organisation Ltd*,[48] that time spent attempting unsuccessfully to sell to a client was as much work as that spent successfully selling. Remuneration did not, therefore, vary with the amount of work done, so just the basic pay was to be used in the calculation (in this case holiday entitlement under the Working Time Regulations 1998 – see Chapter 10). Payments in kind are excluded – eg free accommodation – as are payments received from a third party, such as tips. However, gratuities added to cheques and credit card vouchers are paid to the employer and may be treated as remuneration for these purposes.[49]

TRANSFERS OF UNDERTAKINGS

The Transfer of Undertakings (Protection of Employment) Regulations 2006[50] replaced the 1981 Regulations[51] and implement the Directive 2001/23/EC relating to the safeguarding of employees' rights in the event of transfers of undertakings, businesses or parts of undertakings or businesses, which had in turn amended a previous Directive on the subject. The intention of the Directive and the TUPE Regulations is to protect the contract of employment and the employment relationship of employees who are transferred from one employer to another. When a transfer takes place, it is as if the employee's contract of employment was initially agreed with the transferee employer. All rights contained in the contract of employment, except pension benefits,[52] are transferred, as are all outstanding claims and liabilities of the employer to the employees.[53] This may include non-contractual obligations such as in *DJM International Ltd v Nicholas*.[54] In this case the EAT held that liability for an alleged act of sex discrimination transferred from the transferor company to the transferee employer.

THE MEANING OF A TRANSFER OF AN UNDERTAKING

In the seminal case on the application of the original Directive the Court of Justice, in *Spijkers*,[55] defined a transfer of an undertaking as the transfer of an economic entity that retained its identity. The Court of Justice looked at the purpose of the Directive and concluded that its aim was to ensure the continuity of existing employment relationships. Thus, if the operation that is transferred is an identifiable entity before and after the transfer, then a relevant transfer is likely to have taken place. One needs to look at the situation before the transfer and identify an economic entity, then after the transfer to consider whether the economic entity has retained its identity.

The Court of Justice then gave further guidance on factors which would help in the decision as to whether a transfer had taken place. It was necessary to take all the factual circumstances of the transaction into account, including

- the type of undertaking or business in question
- the transfer or otherwise of tangible assets such as buildings and stocks
- the value of intangible assets at the date of transfer
- whether the majority of staff are taken over by the new employer
- the transfer or otherwise of customers
- the degree of similarity between activities before and after the transfer
- the duration of any interruption in those activities.

The Court stated that each of these factors was only part of the assessment. One had to examine what existed before the transfer and then examine the entity after the change in order to decide whether the operation was continued, but these factors might help that consideration.

This approach was further emphasised by the case of *Schmidt*,[56] which concerned the contracting out of a small cleaning operation at a bank. Mrs Schmidt complained about her dismissal and eventually her claim ended up in the national court (the Landsarbeitsgericht), which then referred the issue – of whether the transfer of a single person to an outside contractor could be a transfer of an undertaking – to the European Court of Justice. The bank, as well as the German and UK governments, argued that the answer should be in the negative because the cleaning operation was neither a main function nor an ancillary function of the bank and that there was not a transfer of an economic entity. The fact that it was a small operation was not held to be relevant. What mattered was that there was a stable operation which retained its identity. This was indicated by the fact that before the transfer there was a cleaning operation and, again, after the transfer this continued or was resumed.[57]

In the United Kingdom this approach by the European Court of Justice resulted in the courts' finding that contracting out of services, or outsourcing, could amount to a relevant transfer for the purposes of the Transfer Regulations.

CASE STUDY

Kenny v South Manchester College (1993) IRLR 265

The case concerned the provision of education services at a young offenders' institution. After a tendering exercise the contract was won by South Manchester College.

The question was whether the undertaking had retained its identity.

The High Court stated that 'the prisoners and young offenders who attend, say, a carpentry class next Thursday will, save those released from the institution, be likely in the main to be the same as those who attended the same class in the same classroom the day before and will doubtless be using exactly the same tools and machinery'. Thus a relevant transfer of an entity that retained its identity had taken place.

This was followed by other cases such as where the outsourcing of a local authority refuse collection contract,[58] and the moving of a hospital cleaning contract from one contractor to another,[59] were held to be relevant transfers.

It was then that the Court of Justice appeared to have second thoughts about its approach. In *Süzen*[60] the Court distinguished between the transfer of an entity and the transfer of an activity. As in the case of *Schmidt*, before the transfer there was a cleaning operation and after the transfer there was a cleaning operation. On the face of it, there was relevant transfer because the entity appeared to retain its identity, as evidenced by its continuation and resumption. The Court of Justice, however, then stated that an entity could not be reduced to the activity entrusted to it. Thus the Court distinguished between an entity that transferred and an activity that transferred. An entity, according to the Court, was

> an organised grouping of persons or assets facilitating the exercise of an economic activity which pursues a specific objective.

There has, therefore, to be something else, other than the activity taking place, which needs to transfer, such as assets or 'an organised grouping' of people. Without these, there appeared to be only the transfer of an activity. This was not enough to provide the protection of the Directive.

It is from this point that many of the problems concerning the applicability of the Directive and the Regulations arose. *Süzen* set limits on the applicability of the Directive, but there has been confusion as to where these limits apply and the real difference between an entity and an activity. Both the *Schmidt* and the *Süzen* cases concerned the transfer of cleaning contracts, but in one the Court held that an entity transferred, and in the second held that the cleaning contract only amounted to an activity and was therefore not protected by the Directive.

TUPE REGULATIONS 2006

The Government decided to try to remove this uncertainty with the introduction of the 2006 TUPE Regulations.

Regulation 3(1)(a) of the 2006 TUPE Regulations states that the Regulations apply, firstly, to a transfer of an undertaking, business or part of an undertaking or business situated immediately before the transfer in the United Kingdom where there is a transfer of an economic entity that retains its identity (the *Spijkers* test), and, secondly, to a service provision change. An economic entity is defined in Regulation 3(2) as 'an organised grouping of resources which has the objective of pursuing an economic activity, whether or not that activity is central or ancillary' (the *Süzen* test).

Regulation 3(1)(b) provides that the Regulations also apply to a service provision change. These are relevant to outsourcing situations and are meant to ensure a wide coverage of the Regulations. A service provision change takes place when a person (client) first contracts out some part of its activities to a contractor; when such a contract is taken over by another contractor (so-called second-generation transfers); and when the client takes back the activity in-house from a contractor. Whereas, however, a relevant transfer consists of an 'organised grouping of resources', a service provision change requires there to be 'an organised grouping of employees, which has, as its principal purpose, the carrying out of activities concerned'.[61]

The issue of where the business or undertaking is situated is important, especially with cross-border transfers. The Regulations were held to apply, for example, when a company transferred part of its business from the UK to Israel.[62]

WHO IS TO BE TRANSFERRED?

Regulation 4(1) of the 2006 Regulations provides that except where an objection is made, a relevant transfer shall not operate to terminate any contract of employment of any person employed by the transferor and assigned to the 'organised grouping of resources or employees that is subject to the relevant transfer'. Although Regulation 2(1) states that temporary assignments are excluded the European Court of Justice has held that the Directive can apply to the transfer of a temporary agency workforce from one agency to another.[63]

One problem that has occurred is in deciding who is assigned to the part transferred, when only part of an organisation is transferred to a new employer. If, for example, a business decides to contract out its non-core activities and only retain those parts of the business that are concerned with its primary activities, or if only a part of the business is sold off, there are likely to be a number of employees, such as those in Human Resources, who work in the parts remaining, but whose jobs consisted of servicing those parts transferred. This may be the entire content of their jobs or only a part. If such staff remain with the transferor organisation, they may be faced with the loss of their jobs or, at the very least, a significant change in their job activities. The question then is whether these support staff have the right to transfer also.

It was in the case of *Botzen*[64] that the European Court of Justice first devised the assignment test to deal with such situations. The Advocate General in the case proposed a test for deciding who should be transferred if only a part of a business was sold off:

> A basic working test, it seems to me, is to ask whether, if that part of the business had been separately owned before the transfer, the worker would have been employed by the owners of that part or the owners of the remaining part.

The Advocate General did admit that employees could be involved in work other than for the part transferred, but only on a *de minimis* basis.

Some people, of course, would not have been employed in either part if they were separately owned. It may have been because the whole was a certain size that they were employed. This may be especially true of HR departments in that bigger organisations may perhaps have the capacity to employ more specialists whereas a smaller organisation might demand more generalist abilities.

CASE STUDY

Kimberley Group Housing Ltd v Hambley (2008) IRLR 682

This case concerned a contract from the Home Office to provide accommodation and other services for asylum-seekers while their asylum applications were being processed. In 2006 the contractor lost the contact and it was taken over by two new contractors, both of whom denied that the TUPE Regulations applied. Some of the employees of the original contractor had lost their jobs and they claimed unfair dismissal.

The EAT agreed that a service provision had taken place within the provisions of the 2006 TUPE Regulations. The issue then was to which of the two new contractors the dismissed employees should have transferred. The employment tribunal had held that the liabilities under the contracts of employment should be split between the two contractors.

The EAT did not agree. It held that the principle was that if the employee was assigned to the part transferred, then the contract of employment passes to the transferee. There is no exhaustive list of factors which can conclusively determine this issue and it would have to be resolved as a matter of fact. In this case the great majority of the activities of the employees had passed to one contractor, Kimberley Housing, so the contracts of employment were transferred to them solely.

Regulation 4(3) also provides that it is only persons employed immediately before the transfer, or who would have been had they not been unfairly dismissed, who are protected, as well as being assigned to such an organised grouping.[65]

CONTRACT VARIATIONS

An important aspect of the 2006 Regulations is added flexibility, perhaps mostly for employers. This is true when the issue of the ability to vary contracts of employment during or after the transfer is considered. The whole issue of making changes and reorganising the business either before or after a transfer is one that is important to many employers. Quite apart from the issue of bringing in a workforce with different terms and conditions, there is often a need to reorganise the business to cope with any such transfers. The 2006 TUPE Regulations provide that it is not possible to vary a contract of employment if the sole or main reason was the transfer or any other reason that was not an economic, technical or organisational reason entailing changes in the workforce (ETO reason; Regulation 4(4)). The employer and employee are able, therefore, to agree a variation if it is changed for an ETO reason or 'a reason unconnected to the transfer'.

EMPLOYEE CHOICE

The original Directive was silent on the subject of whether an individual employee can decide that he or she does not wish to transfer. Initially it was left to the European Court of Justice to decide. In *Daddy's Dance Hall*[66] the Court suggested that employees had no choice in the matter. Whether the individuals wished it or not, there was a public policy reason for not allowing employees to opt out, because the alternative would normally be that they would be worse off by opting out. This position was considerably softened in *Katsikas*[67] when the Court of Justice held that to stop someone objecting to the transfer of his or her employment would undermine the fundamental rights of the employee, who must be free to choose his employer and cannot be obliged to work for an employer whom he or she has not freely chosen to do. It followed, therefore, that the Directive does not oblige employees to transfer provided that they choose freely not to continue the employment relationship. It was then left to the Member State to 'decide the fate of the contract of employment or employment relationship with the transferor'.

The problem for such an employee in the UK is that he or she is left in a sort of employment nether region with no claims against the transferor or the transferee. Regulation 4(7) of the 2006 Regulations repeats the current position that an employee is not transferred if he or she objects to being so transferred. The outcome is contained in Regulation 4(8) where the employee is then in a 'no man's land'; he or she has not been transferred, but the transferor cannot be treated as having dismissed the employee. *Capita Health Solutions Ltd v McLean*[68] concerned an occupational health nurse working for the BBC. Her function was transferred to a contractor and she intimated that she was unhappy with the prospect of being transferred. In the event she agreed to continue working for the contractor for six weeks after the transfer date, although her pay etc was provided by the BBC. At the end of this secondment the question was whether or not the contract of employment had transferred, even though she was unhappy at the prospect. The EAT held that an objecting employee cannot then be employed by the transferee, no matter what agreements have been reached. If Mrs McLean had objected, then at best she was working under a new temporary contract with the transferee. She could not be said to have objected and then taken up temporary work for the transferee. She had not therefore objected, but had, in effect, agreed to transfer for six weeks. It is sometimes possible to object to a transfer after it has taken place. In *New ISG Ltd v Vernon*[69] employees did not know the identity of the transferee until after the transfer had taken place. They then objected and the High Court held that they were valid because of a fundamental principle that allows an employee to choose his or her own employer.

INSOLVENCY

Measures to deal with insolvency situations were absent from the original Directive and the problems resulting from this were recognised by the European Court of Justice at an early stage. The main problem perceived was that the obligation, imposed by the original Directive, for the transferee enterprise to take over all the debts in relation to the insolvent organisation's employees and, indeed, to transfer all those employees at their current terms and conditions, would act as an disincentive to the 'rescue' of such enterprises.

The 2001 Directive incorporated much greater flexibility and in Article 5(1) excluded any transfers where the transfer is the subject of bankruptcy proceedings with a view to liquidation of the assets of the transferor. Article 5(2) of the Directive also gives Member States the option of excluding transfers of liabilities in other types of insolvency proceedings as well as giving them the option of agreed changes to terms and conditions of employees which are 'designed to safeguard employment opportunities by ensuring the survival of the undertaking, business or part of the undertaking or business'.

The TUPE Regulations 2006 take advantage of both of these options in Regulations 8 and 9. Relevant insolvency proceedings for this purpose in the Regulations repeat the definition stated in the Directive – namely, that they are 'insolvency proceedings which have been opened in relation to the transferor not with a view to the liquidation of the assets of the transferor and which are under the supervision of an insolvency practitioner' (Regulation 8(6)).

The outcome is that those elements which the government would normally be responsible for under its statutory obligations towards the employees of insolvent employers do not transfer. The debts owed to employees by the transferor, to the limits of its statutory obligations, will be guaranteed by the Secretary of State. This, of course, includes some arrears of pay, notice periods, holiday pay and any basic award for unfair dismissal compensation.[70] Other debts owed to employees will transfer.

In addition to this subsidy there is provision in Regulation 9 for the employer and employee representatives to agreeing 'permitted variations' to their contracts of employment. Permitted variations are those which are not due to ETO reasons entailing a change in the workforce and are designed to safeguard employment opportunities by ensuring the survival of the undertaking (Regulation 9(7)). It is interesting that the phrase 'employment opportunities' is used, rather than just 'employment'. This suggests that the justification for any variations can be argued widely on the basis that the business is rescued or safeguarded and this will safeguard employment opportunities in the future.

INFORMATION AND CONSULTATION

Regulations 13 to 15 TUPE Regulations 2006 contain the obligations to inform and consult employees (see Chapter 17).

Regulations 11 and 12 of the TUPE Regulations 2006 concern the notification of employee liability information and now provide a statutory duty for the transferor to pass on to the transferee certain information. This includes the identity and age of the employee; his or her terms and conditions of employment (as required by section 1 of the Employment Rights Act 1996); disciplinary or grievance action over the previous two years and any details of any claims, cases or action brought in the last two years and any future actions that the transferor might have reasonable grounds to believe are possible. The 2006 Regulations provide for compensation to be paid to the transferee, with a normal minimum of £500 per employee. Whether such compensation is sufficient detriment remains to be seen.

PUBLIC SECTOR

The Government has decided that 'employees in public sector organisations should be treated no less favourably than those in private sector organisations when they are part of an organised grouping of resources that is transferred between employers'. The chosen methods of implementing this policy are to be the application of the Statement of Practice on *Staff Transfers in the Public Sector*,[71] by applying any case-specific legislation when necessary and by the use of section 38 of the Employment Relations Act 1999.

There are a number of outcomes in the public sector. These are

- that all contracting-out exercises with the private and voluntary sector and all transfers between different parts of the public sector will be treated as if the Transfer Regulations apply, unless there are exceptional reasons for not doing so

- that second-generation transfers – ie when there is a change of contractor dealing with an outsourced public service – and transfers back into the public sector are to be treated as being covered by the Regulations

- that there should be appropriate arrangements for the protection of occupational pensions, redundancy and severance payments to staff affected by these situations.

The Statement of Practice represents a willingness to generally apply the Transfer Regulations throughout the public sector with the result that they will still be applied even if there is no change of employer, such as transfers of functions within the civil service.

PENSIONS

The 2006 Regulations repeat the provisions of the Directive in Regulation 10(1) by excluding occupational pension schemes, but state that any other provisions which do not relate to old age, invalidity or survivors' pensions should not be treated as part of the scheme (Regulation 10(2)). Despite this, the objective in the public sector is to offer 'broadly comparable' pensions. This is the objective set out in an annex to the Cabinet Statement of Practice.[72] Other workers are to be offered less with provisions for contributions of at least 6 per cent of pensionable pay from the employer.[73]

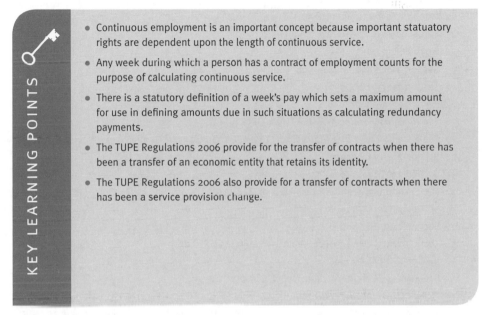

KEY LEARNING POINTS

- Continuous employment is an important concept because important statuatory rights are dependent upon the length of continuous service.

- Any week during which a person has a contract of employment counts for the purpose of calculating continuous service.

- There is a statutory definition of a week's pay which sets a maximum amount for use in defining amounts due in such situations as calculating redundancy payments.

- The TUPE Regulations 2006 provide for the transfer of contracts when there has been a transfer of an economic entity that retains its identity.

- The TUPE Regulations 2006 also provide for a transfer of contracts when there has been a service provision change.

Reinforce your understanding of this chapter by visiting www.cipd.co.uk/sss for activities, questions, weblinks and additional case studies

REFERENCES

1 See *Collison v BBC* (1998) IRLR 239

2 (1997) IRLR 562

3 See *Secretary of State v Cohen* (1987) IRLR 169

4 See section 215 ERA 1996 and *Weston v Vega Space Ltd* (1989) IRLR 509

5 See *Booth v United States of America* (1999) IRLR 16; on fixed-term contracts see Chapter 5

6 See *General of the Salvation Army v Dewsbury* (1984) IRLR 222

7 Section 210(4) ERA 1996

8 See *Hyland v J. Barker Ltd* (1985) IRLR 403

9 See *Nicoll v Nocorrode Ltd* (1981) IRLR 163

10 'Week' means a week ending with Saturday; see section 235(1) ERA 1996

11 (1999) IRLR 306

12 Section 212(3)(a) ERA 1996

13 Section 212(4) ERA 1996

14 See *Pearson v Kent C.C.* (1993) IRLR 165

15 Section 212(3)(b) ERA 1996

16 See *Stephens & Son v Fish* (1989) ICR 324

17 *Byrne v City of Birmingham D.C.* (1987) IRLR 191

18 *Ford v Warwickshire C.C.* (1983) IRLR 126

19 (1986) IRLR 255

20 See *Sillars v Charrington Ltd* (1989) IRLR 152 on seasonal work

21 Section 212(3)(c) ERA 1996

22 *Ingram v Foxon* (1985) IRLR 5

23 *Curr v Marks & Spencer plc* (2003) IRLR 75

24 (1995) ICR 965

25 Section 216(1) and (2) ERA 1996

26 Section 216(3) ERA 1996

27 Section 235(4) ERA 1996

28 See *Hanson v Fashion Industries* (1980) IRLR 393

29 See *Secretary of State v Globe Elastic Thread Co. Ltd* (1979) IRLR 327

30 Section 218(2) ERA 1996

31 Section 235(1) ERA 1996

32 See *Secretary of State v Lassman* (2000) IRLR 411

33 Section 218(3) ERA 1996

34 Section 218(4) ERA 1996

35 Section 218(5) ERA 1996; see *Jeetle v Elster* (1985) IRLR 227

36 Section 218(6) ERA 1996

37 See *Payne v Secretary of State* (1989) IRLR 352

38 *Tice v Cartwright* (1999) ICR 769

39 Section 218(7) ERA 1996; see also section 218(8)–(10) on certain types of employment
in the health service

40 Section 221(2) ERA 1996; see *Keywest Club v Choudhury* (1988) IRLR 51

41 Section 221(3) ERA 1996

42 Section 225 ERA 1996; see *Secretary of State v Crane* (1988) IRLR 238

43 (1990) IRLR 148

44 Section 221 ERA 1996

45 Section 224 ERA 1996

46 *Paggetti v Cobb* (2002) IRLR 861

47 (1997) IRLR 17

48 (2003) IRLR 156

49 See *Nerva v UK* (2002) IRLR 815

50 SI 2006/246

51 SI 1981/1796

52 See *Adams v Lancashire County Council* (1996) IRLR 154

53 Regulation 5(1) Transfer Regulations 1981

54 (1996) IRLR 76

55 Case 24/85 *JMA Spijkers v Gebroeders Benedik Abbatoir CV* (1986) ECR 1119

56 Case 392/92 *Schmidt v Spar- und Leihkasse der Früheren Ämter Bordesholm, Kiel und
Cronshagen* (1995) IRLR 302

57 See also *Dudley Bower Building Services Ltd v Lowe* (2003) IRLR 260

58 *Wren v Eastbourne Borough Council* (1993) IRLR 425

59 *Dines v Initial Health Care Services and Pall Mall Services Group Ltd* (1994) IRLR 336

60 Case 13/95 *Süzen v Zehnucker Gebäudereinigung* (1997) IRLR 255 ECJ

61 Regulation 2(1) provides that references to an 'organised grouping of employees' includes a single employee; nor does it apply to single specific events or tasks of a short-term duration, Regulation 3(3)(ii).

62 *Holis Metal Industries Ltd v GMB and Newell Ltd* (2008) IRLR 187

63 Case C-458/05 *Jouini v Princess Personal Service GmbH* (2007) IRLR 1005

64 *Arie Botzen and others v Rotterdamsche Droogdok Maatschappij BV* Case 186/83 (1986) 2 CMLR 50 ECJ

65 *Litster v Forth Dry Dock and Engineering Ltd* (1989) IRLR 161

66 Case 324/86 *Foreningen af Arbejdsledere i Danmark v Daddy's Dance Hall A/S* (1985) IRLR 315

67 Case 132/91 *Katsikas v Konstantidis* (1993) IRLR 179

68 *Capita Health Solutions Ld v McLean* (2008) IRLR 595

69 *New ISG Ltd v Vernon* (2008) IRLR 115

70 See, for example, Part XII of the Employment Rights Act 1996

71 Issued by the Cabinet Office, January 2000

72 *Staff Transfers from Central Government: A fair deal for staff pensions*, HM Treasury, 1999

73 The Transfer of Employment (Pension Protection) Regulations 2005, SI 2005/649

CHAPTER 17

Information and Consultation

OVERVIEW

Some of the current mandatory requirements for employers to consult their employees in the United Kingdom are as a result of European Union measures. The European Union has had a policy of trying to introduce a comprehensive and harmonised approach to consultation for a number of years and there are a number of levels at which this policy works. These are at the EU level itself, at a transnational level amongst employers who operate at this level, and at the national level within Member States of the Community. This has resulted in a number of measures which have required, and will require, employers, who may not previously have had one, to set up a formal information and consultation process with their employees. This includes European Works Councils at transnational level and the Information and Consultation Directive at the national level.

TRANSNATIONAL INFORMATION AND CONSULTATION

The measures considered here are those concerned with the establishment of European Works Councils and those dealing with the information and consultation requirements in a European Company (SE).

THE EUROPEAN WORKS COUNCIL DIRECTIVE

The European Works Council Directive (EWC Directive) was finally adopted after some 14 years of debate. It was originally adopted under the Agreement on Social Policy 1992 and so did not bind the United Kingdom. After the 1997 general election, and a willingness of the United Kingdom to accept the Social Policy Agreement, the Council adopted an extension Directive with a requirement for it to be transposed into UK national law by 15 December 1999.[1] The purpose of the Directive was to improve the right to information and to consultation of employees in Community-scale undertakings and Community-scale groups of undertakings.[2]

A Community-scale undertaking is one that has at least 1,000 employees within the Member States and at least 150 employees in each of at least two Member

States. A Community-scale group of undertakings is one where a group of undertakings has at least 1,000 employees within the Member States with at least two group undertakings in different Member States employing at least 150 employees.[3] The EWC Directive was transposed into national law by the Transnational Information and Consultation of Employees Regulations 1999 (TICE Regulations), which came into effect on 15 January 2000.[4]

Consultation is defined in the TICE Regulations as meaning the exchange of views and the establishment of a dialogue in the context of an EWC or in the context of an information and consultation procedure.[5] The central management of an undertaking is responsible for creating the conditions and the means necessary for setting up an EWC, where the central management is situated in the United Kingdom; where it is situated outside the country, but has its representative agent based in the United Kingdom; or, if neither of these, where it has its biggest group of employees in the United Kingdom.

The number of UK employees is to be calculated by taking an average over a two-year period, with provision for counting some part-timers as a half number. The number of employees in undertakings in other Member States is to be calculated in accordance with whatever formula that State has adopted in its law implementing the EWC Directive. Employee representatives are entitled to information on these calculations so that they can decide whether the employer qualifies. If the information given to them is incomplete or inadequate, they may present a complaint to the Central Arbitration Committee (CAC).

If central management does not act on its own initiative, the whole process of establishing an EWC can be started with a request from 100 employees, or their representatives, in two undertakings in two Member States. If there is a dispute as to whether a valid request has been made, this can be referred to the CAC for a decision.

The first stage is the establishment of a special negotiating body (SNB), whose task is to negotiate, with central management, a written agreement covering 'the scope, composition, functions and terms of office' of an EWC or the arrangements for implementing an information and consultation procedure. The SNB must consist of at least one representative from each Member State and there is a weighting formula to increase representation from bigger units in different States. The UK representatives are to be elected by a ballot of UK employees and any complaints about the ballot are to be made to the CAC. Where there is already an elected body in existence with whom consultation takes place, that body can nominate representatives from its membership.

The two parties are to negotiate in 'a spirit of co-operation with a view to reaching an agreement'. They may negotiate an agreement to set up an EWC or to establish an information and consultation procedure. The EWC agreement must include agreement on

- the undertakings which are covered by the agreement
- the composition of the EWC

- the functions and procedures for information and consultation
- the venue, frequency and duration of meetings
- the financial and material resources to be allocated to the EWC
- the duration of the agreement and the procedure for re-negotiation.

If the parties decide to establish an information and consultation procedure instead of an EWC, then this agreement must specify a method by which the information and consultation representatives[6] 'are to enjoy the right to meet and discuss the information conveyed to them'.

The information conveyed to the representatives must relate in particular to 'transnational questions which significantly affect the interests of employees'. If negotiations do not start within six months of a valid request by employees or fail to finish within three years from the date of that request, the Regulations provide for a default agreement, which is contained in the Schedule. These provide for an EWC of between 3 and 30 members, with at least one member from each Member State where there are undertakings. This representation is weighted according to the relative size of the undertakings in different States. The rules cover the election or appointment of UK delegates and provide that the EWC should meet at least once per annum.

Complaints about the failure of the negotiating process, either because of lack of agreement or a failure to start the process, or because of a failure to keep to the agreement, are to be referred directly to the EAT. The EAT may order the defaulter to remedy the failure and impose a fine of up to £75,000. Central management will have a defence if they are able to show that the failure resulted 'from a reason beyond the central management's control or that it has some other reasonable excuse for its failure'.

One concern related to statutory rights to information is the revealing by management of 'confidential' information. Regulation 24 TICE Regulations provides that central management is not required to disclose any information or document which, 'according to objective criteria', would seriously prejudice or harm the functioning of the undertaking concerned. It is interesting to speculate as to what this actually means. Would the sale of a subsidiary undertaking in one Member State be such information, if it would prejudice the price received, even though it might have important effects for employees? There is an obligation for a representative, or an adviser to a representative, not to disclose confidential information unless it is a protected disclosure under section 43A ERA 1996 (whistleblowing). The Central Arbitration Committee has the responsibility of settling disputes about confidentiality and can order information to be disclosed by management or order a representative not to disclose information.

Information and consultation representatives, members of EWCs, SNBs and candidates for relevant elections have certain rights. These are:

- the right to reasonable time off with pay during working hours
- protection against unfair dismissal – dismissal as a result of performing any of

the functions or duties related to any of these bodies will make the dismissal automatically unfair

- the right not to be subject to detriment as a result of performing any of the duties or functions related to the bodies.

Complaints about any infringement of these rights are to be made to an employment tribunal.

THE COMPANY STATUTE

The European Company Statute gives a company operating in more than one Member State the option of establishing itself as a 'European company' (*Societas Europaea* or SE) operating under EU rules rather than under a variety of national rules as at present. An SE can be established by the merger or formation of companies with a presence in at least two different Member States.

One concern in establishing this procedure was that companies previously based in countries with strong requirements for information and consultation might be able to avoid these requirements by establishing themselves as an SE, especially if they were merging with companies from countries with weak consultation requirements. As part of this agreement, therefore, there is a Directive[7] establishing rules for information, consultation and, possibly, participation of workers employed by the SE.

- *Information* is defined as informing the representatives of the employees in a manner and with a content which allows the employees' representatives to undertake an in-depth assessment of the possible impact and, where appropriate, prepare consultations with the competent organ of the SE.[8]

- *Consultation* is defined as the establishment of dialogue and exchange of views between the body representative of the employees and the competent organ of the SE, at a time, in a manner and with a content which allows the employees' representatives, on the basis of information provided, to express an opinion on measures envisaged by the competent organ which may be taken into account in the decision-making process within the SE.[9]

When the SE is created there must be a special negotiating body to discuss the arrangements for employee involvement. In the absence of any agreement there will be standard rules established by the Directive that must be followed. These require information and consultation on matters such as

- the structure, economic and financial situation
- the probable development of the business and of production and sales
- the situation and probable trend of employment and investment
- substantial changes concerning organisation, introduction of new working methods or production processes
- transfers of production, mergers, cut-backs or closures of undertakings, establishments or important parts thereof
- collective redundancies.

There are also provisions for employee participation for those SEs which include companies from countries where there are such rules. Participation can include the right to elect or appoint, or oppose the election or appointment, of members of the supervisory or administrative board.

In 2003 the European Co-operative Society Statute (SCE) was also adopted.[10] This provided similar rules for dialogue and consultation for any newly formed SCEs.

INFORMATION AND CONSULTATION REQUIREMENTS IN THE UNITED KINGDOM

Apart from the consultation requirements related to European Works Councils and the European Company there are a number of other areas where there are mandatory rules on consultation with employees. Those considered here relate to collective redundancies, transfers of undertakings, and health and safety.

COLLECTIVE REDUNDANCIES

Employers proposing to dismiss as redundant 20 or more employees at one establishment within a period of 90 days or less must consult appropriate representatives of employees affected by the proposed dismissals or who may be affected by measures taken in connection with those dismissals.[11] Those volunteering to take redundancy in a redundancy situation can count towards this total, so, as in *Optare Group plc v TGWU*,[12] when there are 17 people made compulsorily redundant together with a further three who took voluntary redundancy, then that is enough to trigger the process. The consultation must begin 'in good time' and in any event:

- where the employer is proposing to dismiss 100 or more employees, at least 90 days, and

- otherwise, at least 30 days before the first of the dismissals takes effect.[13]

'Appropriate representatives' are representatives of trade unions recognised for the purposes of collective bargaining. If there are no such representatives, the employer may choose to consult either employee representatives who have been elected or appointed by the affected employees for the purpose of this consultation or existing employee representatives who may have been elected or appointed by the employees for another purpose.[14] Employers have a responsibility for ensuring that elections for employee representatives are fair and may determine the number of representatives to be elected.[15] If the affected employees fail to elect or appoint representatives, employers may fulfil their obligations by giving them the appropriate information.[16] Conversely, if there is a complaint that an employer has failed in its duty with regard to the election of employee representatives, it is for that employer to show that it has satisfied the requirements in section 188 TULRCA 1992.[17] According to section 188(5A) TULRCA 1992, employers must allow appropriate representatives access to the employees whom it is proposed to dismiss and must provide the representatives with appropriate accommodation and facilities.[18]

REDUNDANCY WHERE NO JOBS ARE ACTUALLY LOST

In this context, redundancy is defined as 'dismissal for a reason not related to the individual concerned or for a number of reasons all of which are not so related'. This might include, for example, dismissals resulting from a refusal to accept a change in terms and conditions of employment. It will also be presumed that a dismissal is by reason of redundancy unless the contrary is proved.[19] In *GMB v Man Truck & Bus UK Ltd*[20] a new company was formed by the merger of two independent businesses. In order to harmonise the terms and conditions of the employees of the two businesses, the company wrote to all the employees terminating their contracts of employment on a particular day. They also wrote to all the employees offering to re-employ them from the same day, but on the new harmonised terms and conditions. The EAT held that these were not 'technical' dismissals but genuine dismissals for reasons of redundancy, as defined in section 195 TULRCA 1992 (see Chapters 12 and 13). Similarly, if an employer is proposing to redeploy staff and putting them on what is in reality a different contract of employment, then this may amount to a proposal to terminate the existing contracts.[21]

It is important to note that the employees covered need not be employed for any minimum number of hours per week. However, those who work under a contract for a fixed term of three months or less will be excluded unless the employment lasted for more than three months.[22]

Defining 'establishment'

'Establishment' is not defined by the statute and the EAT has ruled that this is a question for the tribunal acting as an industrial jury using its common sense on the particular facts of the case. In *Bakers' Union v Clark's of Hove Ltd*[23] it was accepted that separate premises could be regarded as one establishment if there was common management and accounting. The ECJ has indicated that the word 'establishment' must be understood as designating the unit to which the workers made redundant are assigned to carry out their duties. It is not essential for that unit to be endowed with a management that can independently effect collective dismissals.[24]

THE CONSULTATION PROCEDURE

The consultation required must include consultation about ways of:

- avoiding the dismissals,
- reducing the numbers to be dismissed, and
- mitigating the consequences of the dismissals,

and must be undertaken 'with a view to reaching agreement with the appropriate representatives'.

An employer is required to consult on each of the three aspects individually. It is not enough just to consult on ways of reducing the numbers of employees to be dismissed and mitigating the consequences of dismissals, without consulting on ways of avoiding the dismissals. In such a case the employer would not have met the statutory requirements.[25] The obligation to consult over avoiding redundancies almost inevitably means consulting over the reasons for the dismissals.[26]

It is important to note that Article 2 of the Collective Redundancies Directive[27] requires consultation where an employer is 'contemplating' collective redundancies. The meaning of the word 'contemplating' has been the subject of a number of cases such as in *Scotch Premier Meat Ltd v Burns*,[28] where an employer decided on two options, which were either the sale of the business as a going concern or its closure and sale as a development site. The latter option would have led to all the employees' being dismissed as redundant. The meeting at which these options were decided upon was held to be the occasion when the employer was contemplating (and proposing) redundancies. In *MSF v Refuge Assurance plc*[29] the court held that it was not possible to construe the word 'proposing' as the same as the word 'contemplating'. The word 'proposing' relates to a state of mind which is much more certain and further along the decision-making process than 'contemplates'. The situation was clarified by the European Court of Justice in *Junk v Kühnel*.[30] The Court held that 'contemplating' meant a situation where no decision had yet been taken on whether there would be redundancies. Contracts of employment can therefore only be terminated after the period of consultation. The Directive requires the employer to effectively negotiate – and to allow the termination of the contracts of employment before that negotiation takes place would be to compromise those negotiations.

CASE STUDY

Leicestershire County Council v UNISON (2005) IRLR 920

In accordance with a national agreement, the Council had carried out a job evaluation exercise covering about 9,000 jobs. As a result of the exercise there were a number of jobs which were due to be downgraded and some others which would have various payments lowered or removed. The Officers decided that the best way to deal with this was to give notice terminating the contracts of those affected and then sumultaneously offer new contracts on the new terms.

On 18 November an Officer of the Council presented a report to the Employment Committee with this recommendation. The formal decision to proceed was taken by the Committee on 12 December. On 18 December a notice was sent to the local Branch Secretary of UNISON and, thereafter, there was total failure to consult on these staff.

The EAT held that the proposal to dismiss employees as redundant took place in mid-November, even though it was a month later before the decision was taken by the politicians on the Employment Committee. 'Proposing to dismiss' was less than a decision that dismissals are to be made and more than a possibility that they might occur. This proposal was consistent with the decision in *Junk* and proposing to dismiss could be construed as proposing to give notice of dismissal, as in this case.

What employers must disclose in writing

The employer must disclose in writing the following matters at the beginning of the consultation period, although a lack of information should not be allowed to delay the start of consultation.[31]

(a) the reason for the proposals

(b) the number and description of employees whom it is proposed to dismiss

(c) the total number of employees of any such description employed by the employer at that establishment

(d) the proposed method of selecting the employees who may be dismissed

(e) the proposed method of carrying out the dismissals, with due regard to any agreed procedure, including the period over which the dismissals are to take effect

(f) the proposed method of calculating the redundancy payment if this differs from the statutory sum.

This information must be delivered to each of the appropriate representatives, or sent by post to an address notified by them or, in the case of union representatives, to the union head office. In *E Green Ltd v ASTMS and AUEW*[32] it was held that items (d) and (e) had not been complied with when the method of selecting employees who might be dismissed was given as 'to be in consultation with union representatives'.

'Special circumstances' permitting employers to depart from consultation requirements

If there are 'special circumstances' which render it not reasonably practicable for the employer to comply with the above-mentioned provisions, an employer must take 'all such steps towards compliance' as are reasonably practicable in the circumstances. 'Special circumstances' mean circumstances which are uncommon or out of the ordinary, so insolvency by itself will not provide an excuse, as it may well be foreseeable.[33] However, that the employer has continued trading in the face of adverse economic pointers in the genuine and reasonable expectation that redundancies would be avoided can justify non-compliance.[34] Additionally, a pending application for government financial aid, the withdrawal of a prospective purchaser from negotiations combined with a bank's immediate appointment of a receiver, and the need for confidentiality in negotiating a sale, have all constituted 'special circumstances'. By way of contrast, the following have not been accepted as being 'special':

• the alarm and chaos caused by the disclosure of information about the proposed redundancies

• a genuine belief that the union had not been recognised: in *Wilson & Bros Ltd v USDAW*[35] it was held that such a belief must be reasonable

• the fact that the employer had been informed by the relevant government department that there was no duty to consult in the particular case.[36]

Section 188(7) TULRCA 1992 also states that where the decision leading to the proposed dismissals is that of a person controlling the employer, a failure on the part of that person to provide the employer with information will not constitute 'special circumstances'. In addition, if the employer has invited any of the employees who may be dismissed to elect employee representatives, and this invitation was issued long enough before the time when consultation must begin to allow them to elect representatives by that time, the employer is not in breach of the statute if he or she complies with the consultation requirements as soon as reasonably practicable after the election of the representatives.[37]

PROTECTIVE AWARDS

Where the employer has failed to comply with any of the requirements of section 188 TULRCA 1992, employee representatives can complain of any failure relating to them and the union can complain where there is a failure relating to its representatives. In any other case, employees who have been or may be dismissed as redundant can complain. Claims can be made to an employment tribunal before the proposed dismissal takes effect or within three months of its doing so.[38] Employers wishing to argue that there were 'special circumstances' justifying non-compliance must prove that these circumstances existed and that they took all such steps towards compliance as were reasonably practicable. If a complaint is well-founded, the tribunal must make a declaration to that effect and may also make a protective award. A protective award refers to the wages payable for a protected period to employees who have been dismissed or whom it is proposed to dismiss. The protected period begins with the date on which the first of the dismissals to which the complaint relates takes effect (ie the proposed date of dismissal)[39] or the date of the award (whichever is the earlier) and will be of such length as the tribunal determines 'to be just and equitable in all the circumstances having regard to the seriousness of the employer's default'. The protected period is a maximum of 90 days.[40]

One object of an award is to compensate employees for their employer's failure to consult with the union even where compliance with the statute would have made no difference.[41] A consequence of focusing on the loss of days of consultation rather than the loss or potential loss of remuneration during the relevant period is that it becomes possible to make a protective award in favour of employees who have suffered no pecuniary damage – for example, where alternative employment was immediately secured.[42] The rate of remuneration payable under a protective award is a week's pay for each week of the protected period, with proportionate reductions being made in respect of periods less than a week.[43]

Where protected awards will not apply

If during the protected period employees are fairly dismissed for a reason other than redundancy, or if they unreasonably resign, then their entitlement to remuneration under the protective award ceases on the day the contract is terminated. Similarly, employees who unreasonably refuse an offer of employment on the previous terms and conditions or an offer of suitable alternative employment will not be entitled to any remuneration under a protective award in respect of any period during which, but for that refusal, they would have been employed.[44] Employees who are of a description to which a protective award relates may complain to a tribunal, within three months unless the 'time-limit escape clause' applies, that their employer has failed, wholly or in part, to pay the remuneration under that award. If the complaint is well-founded, the employer will be ordered to pay the amount due to the complainant.[45] The three-month period runs from the last day of the protected period to which the award relates. This is a problem for many applicants because the order for the award will often not be obtained until some considerable time has passed. In such cases the tribunal is likely to accept that it was 'not reasonably practicable' to present the complaint in time.[46]

Finally, section 198 TULRCA 1992 enables the parties to a collective agreement to apply to the Secretary of State for an exemption order in respect of the consultation provisions.

NOTIFICATION

An employer proposing to dismiss as redundant 100 or more employees at one establishment within a period of 90 days, or more than 20 employees within 30 days, must notify the Secretary of State in writing of the proposal within 90 or 30 days respectively.[47] There is thus no obligation to notify if fewer than 20 employees are to be dismissed. In addition, the employer must give a copy of the notice to appropriate representatives. The written notice must be in such form and contain such particulars as the Secretary of State may direct, but it is expressly provided that where there are representatives to be consulted under section 188 TULRCA 1992 the employer must identify them and state when consultation began.[48] At any time after receiving a notice under this section the Secretary of State may require the employer to give further information.[49]

If there are special circumstances rendering it not reasonably practicable for an employer to comply with the requirements of section 193 TULRCA 1992, the employer must take all such steps as are reasonably practicable in the circumstances. Again, where the decision leading to the proposed dismissals is that of a person controlling the employer, a failure on the part of that person to provide the employer with information will not constitute 'special circumstances'.[50] Employers who fail to give notice in accordance with this section may be prosecuted and suffer a fine not exceeding level 5 on the standard scale.[51]

TRANSFERS OF UNDERTAKINGS

The purpose of the Acquired Rights Directive[52] and the Transfer Regulations[53] is contained in Article 3(1) of the Directive. Article 3(1) states that the transferor's rights and obligations arising from a contract of employment or from an employment relationship existing on the date of the transfer shall be transferred to the transferee employer. It is as if the contract of employment was originally made between the transferee and the employee (see Chapter 16).

Regulations 13 and 14 of the Transfer Regulations are concerned with the duty to inform and consult employee representatives, and Regulation 15 with the consequences of failing to do so. Information should be provided 'long enough before a relevant transfer to enable the employer of any affected employees to consult all the persons who are appropriate representatives of any of those affected employees'. The High Court, in *Institution of Professional & Civil Servants v Secretary of State for Defence*,[54] decided that the words 'long enough before' a transfer to enable consultation to take place meant as soon as measures are envisaged and if possible long enough before the transfer. The Court held that the words did not mean as soon as measures are envisaged and in any event long enough before the transfer. This case concerned the introduction of private management into the Royal dockyards at Rosyth and Devonport – a measure that was opposed by the trade unions. Before consultation could take place there had to be some definite plans or proposals by the employer around which consultation could take place.

The information to be provided should consist of:

- the fact that a relevant transfer is to take place
- approximately when it is to take place
- the reasons for it
- the legal, economic and social implications for the affected employees
- the measures that are envisaged to take place in connection with the transfer, in relation to the affected employees or the fact that there are no such measures envisaged.

The rules concerning the election of employee representatives are contained in Regulation 14 Transfer Regulations. These are identical to those rules concerning the appointment of appropriate representatives for the purposes of consultation in collective redundancies (see above). The representatives are the independent trade union which is recognised by the employer. If there is no such trade union, then there are employee representatives to be elected or appointed by the affected employees, whether for the purpose of these consultations or for some other purpose.

It is, of course, both the transferor and the transferee that must consult, and there is an obligation upon the transferee to provide the transferor with information about their plans, so that the transferor can carry out their duty to consult. The 2006 version of the Transfer Regulations introduced joint liability between the transferor and the transferee for any compensation awarded as a result of a failure to inform or consult (Regulations 15(8) and 15(9)). This is because if the transferor did not retain some liability, there would be no incentive for him or her to inform or consult at all. An example of this occurred in *Alamo Group (Europe) LN v Tucker*.[55] Here the transferor, which was a company in administration, failed to inform or consult employees about the transfer. The EAT held that the liability to consult transferred and that the transferee was therefore liable to pay compensation for the transferor's lack of activity. The transferee, according to the court, could protect themselves by providing warranties and indemnities in the contract of transfer. In those cases where there was no relationship between the transferor and the transferee, such as in transfers between contractors, there is a defence in the Regulations that consultation was not 'reasonably practicable'.

Where the employer actually envisages taking measures in relation to any of the affected employees, then the employer must consult the appropriate representatives 'with a view to seeking their agreement to the measures to be taken'. In the course of these consultations the employer will consider the representations made by the appropriate representatives, and if any of those representations are rejected, the employer must state the reasons for so doing.

There is a special circumstances defence for the employer if it renders it not reasonably practicable to perform the duty to consult and inform. In such a case the employer must take all such steps as are reasonable in the circumstances. There is also a defence for the employer if the employees fail to elect representatives. In such a case the duty to consult is fulfilled if the employer gives each employee the necessary information.

Complaints to an employment tribunal may be made for a breach of the rules concerning consultation. If the complaint is well-founded the employment tribunal may make an award of up to a maximum of 13 weeks' pay to each affected employee. As with protective awards for failure to consult in collective redundancy situations, awards for failure to inform and consult here should contain a punitive element designed to punish the employer as well as to compensate the employee.[56]

HEALTH AND SAFETY

The European Council Directive on the introduction of measures to encourage improvements in the safety and health of workers[57] has specific requirements both for providing workers with information and for the consultation and participation of workers. Article 10 ensures that workers receive information from the employer about the safety and health risks of their jobs, or their workplaces, as well as information about what protective and preventive measures are to be taken. Article 11 of the Directive provides that employers shall consult workers and/or their representatives 'and allow them to take part in discussions' on all questions relating to safety and health at work. Protection is also offered to the workers or workers' representatives who take part in this process, including the right to time off work with pay for the purpose of carrying out their duties.

The Health and Safety (Consultation with Employees) Regulations 1996 (HSCE Regulations) were introduced to ensure that the information and consultation requirements of the SRSC Regulations were extended to those workplaces where there was no trade union recognised for collective bargaining purposes.

Regulation 5 requires employers to make available to those employees or representatives such information as is necessary to enable them to participate fully and effectively in the consultation. Representatives of employee safety must also be given information to enable them to carry out their functions.[58] In addition, inspectors are obliged, in circumstances in which it is necessary to do so for the purpose of assisting in keeping employees adequately informed about health, safety and welfare matters, to give employees or their representatives factual information relating to an employer's premises, as well as information with respect to any action which they have taken or propose to take in connection with those premises. Such information must be conveyed to the employer, and inspectors can also give a written statement of their observations to anyone likely to be a party to any civil proceedings arising out of any accident, etc.[59]

The words 'instruction' and 'training' suggest that employees should be taught to understand the duties imposed by legislation. Indeed, Regulation 13 of the MHSW Regulations stipulates that in entrusting tasks to their employees, employers must take into account their capabilities in relation to health and safety. In particular, employers have a duty to ensure that their employees are provided with adequate health and safety training when recruited or if they are exposed to new or increased risks. As regards supervision, it would seem to follow that if the employer's efforts do not persuade an employee to adopt safe working practices, disciplinary or other action may have to be taken.

SAFETY REPRESENTATIVES

Section 2(4) HASAWA 1974 provides for the appointment by recognised trade unions of safety representatives from amongst the employees.[60] Where such representatives are appointed, employers have a duty to consult them with a view to the making and maintenance of arrangements that will enable the employer and employees to co-operate effectively in promoting and developing measures to ensure the health and safety at work of the employees, and in checking the effectiveness of such measures.[61] In particular, employers must consult union safety representatives in good time with regard to:

- the introduction of any measure which may substantially affect the health and safety of the employees represented

- the arrangements for appointing or nominating competent persons in accordance with Regulations 7(1) and 8(1)b of MHSW 1999

- any health and safety information that the employer must provide to the employees represented

- the planning and organisation of any health and safety training the employer is required to provide for the employees represented

- the health and safety consequences for the employees represented of the planning and introduction of new technologies.[62]

Employers' duty to consult

Union safety representatives may be elected or appointed. If there are employees who are not covered by union safety representatives under the SRSC Regulations, the employers must consult the employees directly or 'representatives of employee safety', who have been elected by employees, about the matters listed above. In either case employers must make available such information within their knowledge as is necessary to enable full and effective participation in the consultation.[63] Where employers consult representatives of employee safety, they must inform the employees represented of the names of the representatives and the groups they represent.[64] Similarly, if employers discontinue consultation with a representative of employee safety, they must inform the employees in the group concerned of that fact.[65]

Trade union safety representatives

The SRSC Regulations stipulate that if an employer has received written notification from a recognised independent trade union of the names of the people appointed as union safety representatives, such persons have the functions set out in Regulation 4 of the SRSC Regulations (below). So far as is reasonably practicable, union safety representatives will either have been employed by their employer throughout the preceding two years or have had at least two years' experience in similar employment.[66] Employees cease to be union safety representatives for the purpose of these regulations when:

- the trade union which appointed them notifies the employer in writing that their appointment has been terminated
- they cease to be employed at the workplace[67]
- they resign.

Functions of union safety representatives

Apart from representing all employees (not only trade union members) in consultation with the employer under section 2(6) HASAWA 1974, union safety representatives are given the following functions by Regulation 4(1) SRSC Regulations:

- to investigate potential hazards and dangerous occurrences at the workplace (whether or not they are drawn to their attention by the employees they represent) and to examine the causes of accidents at the workplace
- to investigate complaints by any employee they represent relating to that employee's health, safety or welfare at work
- to make representations to the employer on general matters affecting the health, safety or welfare at work of the employees at the workplace
- to carry out inspections in accordance with Regulations 5, 6 and 7 SRSC Regulations
- to represent the employees they are appointed to represent in consultation at the workplace with inspectors from the enforcing authorities

- to receive information from inspectors in accordance with section 28(8) of HASAWA 1974

- to attend meetings of safety committees where they attend in their capacity as safety representatives in connection with any of the above functions.

Functions of representatives of employee safety

By way of contrast, representatives of employee safety have only the following functions:[68]

- to make representations to the employer on potential hazards and dangerous occurrences at the workplace which affect, or could affect, the group of employees represented

- to make representations to the employer on general matters affecting the health and safety at work of the group represented and, in particular, on such matters as he or she is consulted about by the employer under Regulation 3 of the HSCE Regulations 1996, and

- to represent the group of employees in consultations at the workplace with inspectors appointed under section 19 HASAWA 1974.

Further points to note are:

- None of these functions imposes a duty on safety representatives, although they will be liable for the actions they take as ordinary employees.

- Employers who consult representatives of employee safety have a duty to ensure that those representatives are provided with such training in respect of their functions as is reasonable in all the circumstances. The employer must also meet any reasonable costs associated with such training, including travel and subsistence costs.[69]

Regulation 5 SRSC Regulations entitles safety representatives to inspect the workplace at least every three months, but they must give reasonable notice in writing of their intention to do so. Of course, inspections may take place more frequently if the employer agrees. Additional inspections may be made if there has been a substantial change in the conditions of work or new information has been published by the HSC or HSE relevant to the hazards of the workplace. Inspections may also be conducted where there has been a notifiable accident or dangerous occurrence or a notifiable disease[70] contracted, for the purpose of determining the cause. The employer must provide reasonable facilities and assistance for the purpose of carrying out an inspection, including facilities for independent investigation by the union representatives and private discussion with the employees. However, there is nothing to prevent the employers or their representatives from being present during an inspection.

Time off for safety representatives

According to Regulation 4(2) of the Safety Representatives and Safety Committee Regulations 1977[71] (SRSC Regulations) and Regulation 7(1)(b) of the Health and Safety (Consultation with Employees) Regulations 1996 (HSCE Regulations) a trade union safety representative or a representative of employee safety[72] is entitled to time off, with normal or average pay,[73] during working hours to perform his or her functions and to undergo such training as may be reasonable in the circumstances. In relation to trade union safety representatives elected or appointed under the SSRC Regulations, regard has to be had for the provisions of an approved code of practice. In *White v Pressed Steel Fisher*[74] the EAT held that if employers provide an adequate in-house course it is not necessarily reasonable for them to be required to grant paid time off for safety representatives to attend a union course. The Code recommends that as soon as possible after their appointment union safety representatives should be permitted time off with pay for basic training approved by the TUC or the independent union which appointed the representatives. Further training, similarly approved, should be undertaken where the safety representative has special responsibilities or where such training is necessary to meet changes in circumstances or relevant legislation. Aggrieved safety representatives or representatives of employee safety can complain to an employment tribunal that their employer has failed to permit them to take time off or that they have not been paid in accordance with the Regulations. If the complaint is well-founded, the tribunal must make a declaration and may make an award of compensation.[75]

SAFETY COMMITTEES

Where at least two union safety representatives submit a written request, employers must establish a safety committee, but before doing so they must consult the union safety representatives who made the request and the representatives of recognised trade unions. Such a committee must be formed within three months of the request being made, and a notice must be posted stating the composition of the committee and the workplaces covered.[76] Under section 2(7) HASAWA 1974 the function of safety committees is to keep under review the measures taken to ensure the health and safety at work of employees.

It should be noted that the Code of Practice advises employers, recognised unions and union safety representatives to make full and proper use of existing industrial relations machinery to reach the degree of agreement necessary to achieve the purpose of the SRSC Regulations and to resolve any differences. However, where an employee suffers a detriment as a result of health and safety activities, a complaint may be brought under section 100 ERA 1996 (if the individual was dismissed) or section 44 ERA 1996. The remedies available for infringement of section 44 mirror those available for detriment on trade union grounds (see Chapter 18). In *Shillito v Van Leer*,[77] for example, an employee who was a safety representative for one production line became involved, in a belligerent way, in safety issues affecting another production line, for which the employee was not a representative. The employee was disciplined and given a formal warning. A complaint to the tribunal about suffering a detriment failed because the person involved was not a safety representative in the area concerned. In *Goodwin v Cabletel*[78] a construction manager who had responsibility for health and safety matters on site was unhappy with one subcontractor and took an aggressive approach. The manager's employer, however, wished to be more conciliatory. The construction manager was demoted and claimed constructive dismissal. The EAT subsequently confirmed that protection extended to the way duties were carried out.

THE INFORMATION AND CONSULTATION DIRECTIVE

Directive 2002/14/EC of the European Parliament and of the Council establishing a general framework for informing and consulting employees in the European Community[79] was finally unanimously adopted by the Council of Ministers in December 2001 after some years of debate. It is the first EU Directive to introduce a generalised requirement to provide information and to consult with employees or their representatives. All other information and consultation measures have been concerned with specific situations, such as collective redundancies, transfers of undertakings or in situations where companies have a European Works Council.

The Directive applies to all undertakings with 50 or more employees. This represents less than 3 per cent of all EU companies, but about 50 per cent of all employees.

In the preamble to the Directive the European Commission provides the justification for the measure. Some of the reasons given are that:

- the existence of current legal frameworks at national and Community level concerning the involvement of employees have not always prevented serious decisions, that affect employees, from being taken and made public without adequate consultation[80]

- there is a need to strengthen dialogue in order to promote trust within undertakings. The result of this will be an improvement in risk anticipation, making work organisation more flexible and facilitate employee access to training within the undertaking. It will also make employees more flexible in their approach and involve them in the operation and future of the undertaking as well as increasing its competitiveness[81]

- timely information and consultation is a prerequisite for successful restructuring and adaptation of undertakings to the needs of the global economy, especially through the new forms of organisation at work[82]

- the existing legal frameworks for employee information and consultation are inadequate, because they 'adopt an excessively *a posteriori* approach to the process of change, neglect the economic aspects of decisions taken and do not contribute either to genuine anticipation of employment developments within the undertaking or to risk prevention'.[83]

Article 2 of the Directive defines information and consultation:

- *Information* means transmission by the employer to the employees' representatives of data to help them acquaint themselves with the subject matter and to examine it.

- *Consultation* means the exchange of views and establishment of dialogue between the employer and the employees' representatives.

THE INFORMATION AND CONSULTATION REGULATIONS 2004

The Information and Consultation with Employees Regulations 2004[84] came into effect in April 2005. They apply to all undertakings with 50 or more employees.

There is a complex procedure:

(i)　Employees may request to negotiate an information and consultation agreement. At least 10 per cent of the employees must make this request (in one request or a number) subject to a maximum figure of 2,500 employees. The request may be sent to the employer or to the CAC. If sent to the latter, then the CAC will verify the number of employees making the request (Regulation 7).

(ii)　Where a valid request is made by less than 40 per cent of the employees and there are already one or more existing agreements, then instead of starting negotiations, the employer may hold a ballot to seek the endorsement of employees for the request. In order for it to be endorsed, at least 40 per cent of the employees employed must have voted for it and also a majority of those who vote in the ballot (Regulations 8–9).

 CASE STUDY

Stewart v Moray Council (2006) IRLR 592

Mr Stewart, an employee of Moray Council, submitted a request to the Council of behalf of 500 employees, asking for negotiations on an information and consultation agreement. The Council had a number of agreements with trade unions and took the view that there were existing agreements and that they would therefore hold a ballot to seek employee endorsement of the request.

The rules in Regulation 8(1) provide that the pre-existing agreement must (a) be in writing; (b) cover all employees; (c) have been approved by the employees; and (d) set out how the employer is to give information to the employees or their representatives and seek their views on such information.

Mr Stewart complained that the agreements did not cover all employees, only those in trade unions; similarly, he argued that the existing agreements had been approved only by those employees who were trade union members.

The Employment Appeal Tribunal approved the approach of the Central Arbitration Committee. The CAC had held that the agreements did cover all employees and that it could not be accepted that the agreements only covered those who were members of the trade unions. The agreements related to negotiation and consultation for all employees. Nor, according to the CAC, could it be held that the agreements had not been approved by the employees. The CAC did, however, hold that one of the conditions was not met. This related to the setting out of how the employer was going to give information and seek the views of representatives. A provision that stated that the joint negotiating committee would be a forum for discussion and/or consultation on a range of matters not subject to national bargaining was not sufficiently detailed. As a result the collective agreements did not fulfil the criteria for pre-existing agreements and the Council was ordered to initiate negotiations.

(iii) Negotiations may start also as a result of the employer's initiative by issuing a notice to his or her employees (Regulation 11).

(iv) Regulations 14 and 15 provide for the election or appointment of the employee negotiating representatives.

STANDARD INFORMATION AND CONSULTATION PROVISIONS

Where the employer fails to initiate negotiations, the standard information and consultation provisions will apply. This will take place from a date which is either six months from when the original employee request was made or when the information and consultation representatives are elected (whichever is the sooner) (Regulation 18(1)). Where there are negotiations but no agreement is reached within six months, the standard provisions will apply from that date. There is then considerable pressure upon employers to take action and come to an agreement if they wish any sort of arrangement other than the standard provisions to be agreed. Failure to follow the procedures can result in significant fines such as the penalty of £55,000 imposed on Macmillan Publishers where the employer, according to the EAT, ignored the provisions of the Regulations at almost every stage.[85] In this case the employer had argued that they had an existing consultation agreement in place. This argument failed because the agreement did not cover all employees and because the employer did not follow the necessary procedures.[86]

It is likely also that the standard provisions will set the minimum standard for negotiations, because they will take effect if no agreement is reached. It is open to the employer and the employee representatives to reach an agreement that is different from the standard provisions at any time after they have come into effect (Regulation 18(2)).

In accord with the standard provisions the employer must provide the information and consultation representatives with information on (Regulation 20(1)):

● the recent and probable near future development of the undertaking's activities and economic situation

● the situation, structure and probable development of employment within the undertaking and any anticipatory measures envisaged – in particular, where there is a threat to employment within the undertaking, and

● decisions which are likely to lead to substantial changes in work organisation or contractual relations, including those concerned with collective redundancies and transfers of undertakings (where there are specific requirements to inform and consult – see above).

The information must be given in good time, so that the representatives have time to carry out a study and prepare for the consultation, which must be carried out on the basis of the information supplied by the employer. The employer must ensure that the representatives are able to meet and consult with the relevant level of management. Management must provide a reasoned response (Regulation

20(4)). All parties have a duty 'to work in a spirit of co-operation' (Regulation 21).

CONFIDENTIALITY

This has always been an important concern of employers, and the question of what is confidential and what is not is an interesting one. There are two aspects to confidentiality. One is imposing an obligation upon the parties to maintain a confidence. The second is the decision over what material is so confidential that it cannot be revealed at all.

In dealing with the first of these, according to Article 6 of the Directive, Member States may provide that employee representatives, and any experts who assist them, may not reveal information to employees or third parties if provided in confidence 'in the legitimate interest of the undertaking or establishment', unless that other party is bound by a duty of confidentiality. This obligation may continue after the expiry of a term of office.

Member States may also provide that the employer need not provide information or consult when the nature of the information or consultation is such that 'according to objective criteria' it would seriously harm the functioning of the undertaking or establishment or would be prejudicial to it.

Member States shall provide for judicial review of situations where the employer requires confidentiality or does not provide information or consult in accordance with the above. This is the case with the TICE Regulations implementing the European Works Council Directive. The independent body is the Central Arbitration Committee. Regulation 25 provides that revealing confidential information (unless it is done as a 'whistleblower' under section 43A ERA 1996) is a breach of a statutory duty owed to the employer. The employer may also withhold information that he or she believes is 'such that, according to objective criteria, the disclosure of the information or document would seriously harm the functioning of, or be prejudicial to, the undertaking' (Regulation 26). Any dispute as to whether something was this confidential will be settled by the CAC. Part VIII provides for protection and the right to time off for information and consultation representatives.

It is likely that HRM practitioners will play a central role in introducing and administering the new information and consultation procedures. The CIPD itself supported the principle of legislation on the subject, but called for the regulations to be as flexible as possible so that organisations may develop arrangements that are best suited to their circumstances.[87]

- Community-scale undertakings with at least 1,000 employees within the EU and at least 150 employees in two Member States must establish a European Works Council.

- A company that establishes itself as a 'Societas Europaea' is required to negotiate an information and consultation procedure with representatives of employees.

- Mandatory requirements to consult, in the United Kingdom, include matters in relation to health and safety, transfers of undertakings and collective redundancies.

- The Information and Consultation Directive will require the establishment of information and consultation procedures in all UK organisations employing 50 or more people.

Reinforce your understanding of this chapter by visiting www.cipd.co.uk/sss for activities, questions, weblinks and additional case studies

REFERENCES

1   Council Directive 97/74/EC OJ L 010/22

2   Article 1(1) EWC Directive

3   Article 2(a) and (c) EWC Directive

4   SI 1999/3323; the Regulations are some 57 pages long, so what follows can only be regarded as a summary of the main points.

5   Regulation 2 TICE Regulations 1999

6   Defined in Regulation 2 TICE Regulations as a person who represents employees in the context of an information and consultation procedure

7   Directive 2001/86/EC

8   Article 2(i)

9   Article 2(j)

10   Directive 2003/72/EC

11   Section 188(1) TULRCA 1992 as amended by the Collective Redundancies and Transfers of Undertakings (Protection of Employment) (Amendment) Regulations 1999, SI 1999/1925

12   (2007) IRLR 931

13   Section 188(1A) TULRCA 1992

14   Section 188(1B) TULRCA 1992

15   Section 188A TULRCA 1992

16   Section 188(7B) TULRCA 1992

17   Section 189(1B) TULRCA 1992

18   On time off for employee representatives, see Chapter 11

19   Section 195 TULRCA 1992

20   (2000) IRLR 636

21   *Hardy v Tourism South East* (2005) IRLR 243

22   Section 282(1) TULRCA 1992

23   (1978) IRLR 366

24   *Rockfon A/S v Specialarbejderforbundet i Danmark acting for Nielsen and others* (1996) IRLR 168

25 See *Middlesborough B.C. v TGWU* (2002) IRLR 332

26 *UK Coal Mining Ltd v National Union of Mineworkers* (2008) IRLR 4

27 Directive 98/59

28 (2000) IRLR 639

29 (2002) IRLR 324

30 Case C-188/03 (2005) IRLR 310

31 Section 188(4) TULRCA 1992 and *GMB and Amiens v Beloit Walmsley Ltd* (2004) IRLR 18

32 (1984) IRLR 135

33 See *GMB v Rankin* (1992) IRLR 514

34 See *APAC v Kirwin* (1978) IRLR 318

35 (1978) IRLR 20

36 See *UCATT v Rooke & Son Ltd* (1978) IRLR 204

37 Section 188(7A) TULRCA 1992

38 Section 189(1) and (5) TULRCA 1992

39 See *E Green Ltd v ASTMS and AUEW* (1984) IRLR 435

40 Section 189(4) TULRCA 1992 as amended by the CRTUPEA Regulations 1999

41 See *Sovereign Distribution v TGWU* (1989) IRLR 334

42 See *Spillers-French Ltd v USDAW* (1979) IRLR 339

43 Section 190(2) TULRCA 1992

44 Section 191(1–3) TULRCA 1992

45 Section 192 TULRCA 1992

46 See *Howlett Marine Services Ltd v Bowlam* (2001) IRLR 201

47 Section 193 TULRCA 1992

48 Section 193(4) and (6) TULRCA 1992

49 Section 193(5) TULRCA 1992

50 See section 193(7) TULRCA 1992

51 Section 194 TULRCA 1992

52 Now Directive 2001/23/EC

53 Transfer of Undertakings (Protection of Employment) Regulations 2006

54 (1987) IRLR 373

55 (2003) IRLR 266

56 *Sweetin v Coral Racing* (2006) IRLR 252

57 Directive 89/391/EC

58 For exceptions see Regulation 5(3) HSCE Regulations 1996

59 Section 28(8)(b) HASAWA 1974

60 In this context 'recognition' means recognition for the purposes of collective bargaining.
    See Regulation 2 SRSC Regulations and *Cleveland C.C. v Springett* (1985) IRLR 131

61 Section 2(6) HASAWA 1974

62 Regulation 4A SRSC Regulations

63 Regulation 5(2) of HSCE 1996. 'Representatives of employee safety' are defined in
    Regulation 4(1)(b) HSCE Regulations 1996

64 Regulation 4(2) HSCE Regulations 1996

65 Regulation 4(3) HSCE Regulations 1996

66 Regulation 3(4) HSCE Regulations 1996

67 Defined by Regulation 2(1) SRSC Regulations

68 Regulation 6 HSCE Regulations 1996

69 See Regulation 7(1)(a) HSCE Regulations 1996

70 For definitions see Regulations 6(3) SRSC Regulations

71 SI 1977/500

72 See Chapter 12

73 See the Schedule to the SRSC Regulations 1977 and the HSCE Regulations 1996

74 (1980) IRLR 176

75 Regulation 11 SRSC Regulations and Schedule 2 HSCE Regulations 1996

76 Regulation 9 SRSC Regulations. See also the Guidance notes on safety committees

77 (1997) IRLR 495

78 (1997) IRLR 665

79 OJ L80/29 23.3.02

80 Preamble para (6)

81 Preamble para (7)

82 Preamble para (9)

83 Preamble para (13)

84 SI 2004/3426

85 *Amicus v Macmillan Publishers Ltd* (2007) IRLR 885

86 *Amicus v Macmillan Publishers Ltd* (2007) IRLR 378

87 CIPD (2001). Response of the CIPD to the government's consultation on implementation of the EU Directive on information and consultation

CHAPTER 18

Trade Unions and Collective Bargaining

OVERVIEW

The general and specific duties of ACAS, the functions of the Central Arbitration Committee (CAC) and the role of the Certification Officer were all outlined in Chapter 1. In this chapter we first consider the legal definition of an employers' association and a trade union, and describe the mechanism by which a union can obtain a certificate of independence. We also consider the question of recognition, including the statutory right to recognition of trade unions, and the duty placed upon employers to disclose information for the purpose of collective bargaining. Finally, we consider what protection trade unionists receive to stop them being discriminated against by employers.

EMPLOYERS' ASSOCIATIONS

According to section 122 TULRCA 1992 an employers' association is an organisation that consists either:

- wholly or mainly of employers or individual proprietors whose principal purposes include the regulation of relations between employers and workers (or trade unions), or

- wholly or mainly of constituent or affiliated organisations with these purposes or representatives of such organisations,

and in either case is an organisation of which the principal purposes include the regulation of relations between employers and workers (or trade unions) or between constituent and affiliated organisations.[1]

Thus whether a trade association is or is not to be legally regarded as an employers' association will depend on its particular objectives. The Certification Officer is responsible for maintaining a list of employers' associations containing the names of those organisations that are entitled to have their names entered on it.[2] Whether listed or not, employers' associations are granted immunity in respect of the doctrine of restraint of trade, although the immunity of incorporated associations is only in connection with the regulation of relations between employers (or employers' associations) and workers (or trade unions).[3] Like trade unions, employers' associations are required to keep accounting records, to make annual returns and to have their accounts audited.[4] Part 1 Chapter 3 of TULRCA 1992 deals with the administrative provisions relating to employers' associations and trade unions.

TRADE UNIONS AND CERTIFICATES OF INDEPENDENCE

A trade union is an organisation, whether permanent or temporary, which consists either:

- wholly or mainly of workers whose principal purposes include the regulation of relations between workers and employers (or employers' associations), or

- wholly or mainly of constituent or affiliated organisations with those purposes, or representatives of such organisations,

and in either case is an organisation whose principal purposes include the regulation of relations between workers and employers (or employers' associations) or include the regulation of relations between its constituent or affiliated organisations.[5]

This definition covers not only individual and confederated unions and the TUC, but also the union side of a joint negotiating committee. Section 10 TULRCA 1992 states that a trade union 'shall not be, or be treated as if it were, a body corporate', yet it is capable of making contracts, suing and being sued in its own name, and being prosecuted. However, in *EETPU v Times Newspapers*[6] it was held that the union could not sue for libel because it did not have the necessary legal personality to be protected by an action for defamation. All property belonging to a trade union must be vested in trustees, and any judgment, order or award is enforceable against the property held in trust.[7] Trade unions are protected against the doctrine of restraint of trade, in respect of both their purposes and their rules[8] (on immunity from certain actions in tort see Chapter 19).

'LISTED' TRADE UNIONS

The Certification Officer maintains a list of trade unions, and a trade union which submits the appropriate fee, a copy of its rules, a list of officers, the address of its head office and the name under which it is known may apply for inclusion on this list.[9] A listed union is entitled to a certificate stating that its name is included on the list and such listing is a prerequisite for obtaining a certificate of independence. The Certification Officer makes copies of the lists of trade unions and employers' associations available for public inspection and must remove the name of an organisation if requested to do so by that organisation or if he or she is satisfied that the organisation has ceased to exist.[10] Any organisation that is aggrieved by the refusal of the Certification Officer to enter its name on the relevant list, or by a decision to remove its name, may appeal to the EAT on a question of fact or law.[11]

CERTIFICATION OF INDEPENDENCE FOR UNIONS

A trade union whose name is on the relevant list can apply to the Certification Officer for a certificate that it is independent. The Certification Officer is responsible for keeping a record of all applications and must decide whether the applicant union is independent or not.[12] Section 5 TULRCA 1992 deems a trade union to be independent if:

- it is not under the domination or control of an employer or a group of employers or of one or more employers' associations, and

- it is not liable to interference by an employer or any such group or association, arising out of the provision of financial or material support or by any other means whatsoever, tending towards such control.

A certificate constitutes conclusive evidence for all purposes that the union is independent. If a question arises in any proceedings as to whether a trade union is independent and there is no certificate in force and no refusal, withdrawal or cancellation of a certificate recorded, the body before whom the issue arose cannot decide the matter but may refer it to the Certification Officer.[13]

CASE STUDY

Monk Staff Association v CO and ASTMS (1980) IRLR 431

This staff association applied for a certificate of independence. The application, and two subsequent ones, were rejected because the Certification Officer concluded that it was not independent. Factors that influenced the decision were that all the association's officers and members were employed by the company, and because the company still decided individual salaries, it had the power to influence officers of the association; the association was also dependent upon company facilities.

In the EAT it was confirmed that the following matters should be considered:

- the union's history (was it originally the employer's creation?)
- its organisation and structure (is it likely to be controlled by senior members of management?)
- its finances (to what extent is it subsidised by the employer?)
- the extent of employer-provided facilities (are there free premises, etc?)
- its collective bargaining record.

Here there had been significant changes since the Certification Officer investigated the matter, including the appointment of an independent consultant/negotiator. In this case it was also held, on appeal against the Certification Officer's decision, that the question of independence should be decided on all the evidence available and not confined to the material that was before the Certification Officer.

As regards 'liable to interference', the Court of Appeal ruled that the Certification Officer is not required to assess the likelihood of interference by the employer. The Certification Officer's interpretation of the words as meaning 'vulnerable to interference' was the correct one – ie the degree of risk is irrelevant so long as it is recognisable and not insignificant. Thus in (the quite separate) *GCSF v Certification Officer*[14] the Government Communications Staff Federation was denied a certificate because its continued existence depended on the approval of the GCHQ director.

Employer control of or domination over a union

Over the years, certain criteria have evolved for assessing whether a union is under the domination or control of an employer.

Finally, it is worth documenting the major advantages that accrue to independent trade unions:

- If recognised, they have the right to appoint safety representatives (see Chapter 9).

- If recognised, their representatives are entitled to receive information for collective bargaining purposes (see below).

- If recognised, their representatives may be consulted in respect of redundancies and transfers of undertakings (see Chapter 16).

- If recognised, their officials can take time off for union activities (see Chapter 10).

- Employees cannot have action taken against them because they seek to join, have joined, or have taken part in the activities of such a union. Interim relief is available to members who have been dismissed.

RECOGNITION

An independent trade union must be recognised by the employer in order to enjoy a number of statutory rights. The same definition applies in respect of each of these rights – namely, 'Recognition in relation to a trade union means the recognition of the union by an employer, or two or more associated employers, to any extent for the purpose of collective bargaining.'[15]

Collective bargaining means negotiations relating to or connected with one or more of the matters specified in section 178(2) TULRCA 1992.[16] Although the question of recognition is one of fact for a court or employment tribunal to decide, it would appear that there must be an express or implied agreement between the union and the employer (but see statutory rights to recognition below) to negotiate on one or more of the matters listed in section 178(2) TULRCA 1992. For agreement to be implied there must be clear and unequivocal conduct over a period of time.[17] Thus although recognition has been inferred from consultations on discipline and facilities for union representatives despite the absence of formal agreement,[18] a discussion on wages which took place on a particular occasion was held to be insufficient to establish recognition, particularly when the employer's attitude was one of refusing to bargain.[19] Neither the fact that the union has a right of representation on a national body responsible for negotiating pay[20] nor the fact that the employers' association to which the employer belongs recognises the union will, by itself, constitute recognition by the employer.[21]

STATUTORY RECOGNITION PROCEDURES

The rules regarding the statutory right of trade unions[22] to recognition for collective bargaining purposes are contained in Schedule A1 of TULRCA 1992. In this the meaning given to 'collective bargaining' by section 178(1) TULRCA 1992 (see above) does not apply. Unless otherwise agreed by the parties, collective bargaining that is the result of the statutory recognition procedure relates to negotiations on pay, hours and holidays only.[23]

REQUEST FOR RECOGNITION

A union seeking recognition must make a request for recognition to the employer. The request must be in writing, identify the union and the bargaining unit and state that it is made under this Schedule.[24] The basic rules concerning the parties are:

- The union must have a certificate of independence (see section 6 TULRCA 1992).[25]

- The employer, including associated employers, must employ at least 21 workers on the day of the request, or have employed an average of 21 workers in the 13 weeks ending on the day of the request.[26]

The parties agree[27]

- If, before the end of a 10-day period, starting on the day the employer received the request, the parties agree on a bargaining unit and that the union is to be recognised for collective bargaining purposes on behalf of that unit, then the matter is complete.

- If, before the end of the first period of 10 working days the employers inform the union that they do not accept the request but are willing to negotiate, then negotiations may continue into a second period. This second period lasts for 20 working days, starting on the day after the first period ends, or longer if both parties agree.

Negotiations fail[28]

- If, before the end of the first period of 10 days the employers fail to respond or inform the union that they do not accept the request (and show no willingness to negotiate), then the union may apply to the Central Arbitration Committee (CAC) to decide two important issues. These are:
  - whether the proposed bargaining unit is appropriate or some other bargaining unit is appropriate
  - whether the union has the support of a majority of the workers constituting the bargaining unit.

- If the employers refuse the request for recognition or no agreement is reached by the end of the second period of 20 working days, then the union may apply to the CAC to decide the two issues described above.

- If the employers inform the union that they intend to request ACAS to assist in the negotiations and this proposal is rejected by the union or the union fails to respond, the application to the CAC must be delayed.

APPROPRIATE BARGAINING UNIT[29]

If the CAC accepts an application from a trade union, it is obliged to help the parties reach an agreement, within the appropriate period, on what the appropriate bargaining unit is. In deciding whether a bargaining unit is appropriate the CAC must consider the trade union's proposal first. If it thinks that the proposed unit is appropriate, then that will be enough. Employers' proposals can be considered but only in respect of whether the trade union's proposal is appropriate or not. They need only be considered further if the trade union proposal is not considered appropriate.[30]

The appropriate period is 20 working days, beginning with the day after that on which the CAC accepts the application, or a longer period, if the CAC specifies, with reasons. If there is no agreement within the appropriate period, then the CAC has 10 working days, or a longer period, if the CAC specifies, beginning with the day after the end of the appropriate period, to make a decision.

In making the decision the CAC must take into consideration the need for the bargaining unit to be compatible with effective management and, provided they do not conflict with this consideration, with:

- the views of the employer and the union
- existing national and local bargaining units
- the desirability of avoiding small, fragmented bargaining units within an undertaking
- the characteristics of workers falling within the proposed bargaining unit and of any other employees the CAC considers relevant
- the location of the workers.

It is possible for a bargaining unit to consist of more than one employer. If the reality is that technically separate employers were really one and the same employer, it might be possible to join them into one bargaining unit. Indications of this might be standard contracts of employment, interchangeability of employees and a unitary management in parts of the two organisations.[31]

Although it is possible for an employer to seek judicial review of a decision concerning appropriate bargaining units reached by the CAC, the courts will be reluctant to intervene unless the panel has made an error of law or has acted irrationally, such as failing to take into account relevant matters or taking into account irrelevant material.[32]

BALLOTS FOR UNION RECOGNITION[33]

Once the appropriate bargaining unit has been decided upon by agreement between the parties or by CAC decision, the CAC must decide whether the union is likely to have the support of a majority of the workers in the unit. The CAC can only proceed if it is satisfied that the union is likely to have support.

If the union shows that a majority of the workers in the unit are members of the union, the CAC must issue a declaration that the union is recognised for collective bargaining purposes. In *Fullarton Computer Industries Ltd v CAC*,[34] for example, a slender majority of 51.3 per cent of employees who were trade union members was sufficient for there not to be a ballot called.

If one of three qualifying conditions is fulfilled, the CAC will hold a ballot rather than make a declaration. The three qualifying conditions are:

- the CAC is satisfied that a ballot is in the interests of good industrial relations

- a significant number of union members within the bargaining unit inform the CAC that they do not want the union to conduct collective bargaining on their behalf

- membership evidence is produced which leads the CAC to doubt whether a significant number of union members want the union to represent them. This evidence is about the circumstances in which employees became members and evidence about the length of time for which union members have belonged.

The CAC will appoint a qualified independent person to conduct the ballot within a period of 20 working days, starting the day after the appointment.[35] If it gives reasons, the CAC may specify a longer period. The ballot can be conducted at a workplace, or workplaces, or by post. In deciding which method to select, the CAC must take into account:

- the likelihood of unfairness or malpractice if the ballot is conducted at a workplace

- costs and practicality

- any other matters it thinks appropriate.

As soon as practicable the CAC must inform the parties of its decisions. Once the employers are informed, they must comply with three duties:

- to co-operate with the union and the independent person in connection with the ballot

- to give the union access to the workers so that they can inform them of the ballot and seek support. The Code of Practice on Access to Workers during Recognition and Derecognition Ballots[36] recommends that consideration should be given to establishing an agreement, preferably in writing, on access arrangements. Such an agreement should include the union's programme for where, when and how it will access workers, together with a mechanism for resolving any disputes that might arise

- to provide the CAC, within 10 working days, with the names and home addresses of the workers concerned, together with the names and addresses of any workers who join or leave after this.

The CAC will pass this information to the independent person who is conducting the ballot. This person will send out material provided by the union to the workers concerned, at the union's expense. If the CAC is satisfied that the employer has failed to comply with any of the three duties, it may order the employer to take steps to do so, or it may declare that the union is recognised for collective bargaining purposes. The costs incurred in the ballot will be shared equally between the employer and the union.

As soon as practicable the CAC will inform the parties of the result of the ballot. It will issue a declaration that the union is recognised if:

- a majority of those voting support recognition, and

- at least 40 per cent of the workers constituting the bargaining unit supported recognition.

CASE STUDY

R v Central Arbitration Committee (2005) IRLR 641

Two trade unions sought recognition on behalf of a group of workers. The employer refused the request and so the unions made an application under the statutory recognition procedure.

The CAC arranged a secret ballot and appointed a qualified independent person to conduct it. The result of the ballot was that a majority of those voting supported recognition, but the numbers in favour fell short of the 40 per cent total by four votes.

The unions complained that not all workers had received ballot papers. After an enquiry by the CAC it was concluded that five workers who would have voted in favour of recognition had not been given sufficient opportunity to vote. The CAC ordered the ballot to be re-run.

The employer challenged this and stated that the CAC did not have the power to go behind the result of the ballot. The Court of Appeal, however, concluded that the CAC did have jurisdiction to investigate and, if necessary, to annul the result. The CAC had control over all the other stages and Parliament could not have intended that the CAC would be deprived of the power to investigate, and act upon, a ballot that might have been unreliable.

THE CONSEQUENCES OF RECOGNITION[37]

Following the declaration from the CAC the parties may negotiate, within a certain period, about the way in which they will conduct collective bargaining. The negotiating period is 30 working days from when the parties were notified of the declaration. The parties may agree to a longer period.

If no agreement is reached, the employer or the union may ask the CAC for assistance. There is then an agreement period of 20 working days, or longer if the CAC decides (with the agreement of the parties), in which the CAC will try to help the parties reach an agreement. If no agreement is reached, the CAC may specify the method by which they are to conduct collective bargaining. The CAC is obliged to take into account the method specified in The Trade Union Recognition (Method of Collective Bargaining) Order 2000.[38] This method recommends that the employer and the union establish a joint negotiating body to discuss and negotiate pay, hours and holidays of the workers in the bargaining unit. There should be at least three employer and three union representatives on this body and each side will take turns in chairing the body for 12 months at a time.

This agreement will be a legally enforceable contract between the parties. It may be varied by the parties agreeing, but it will remain a legally enforceable agreement. The only remedy available for breach of this agreement will be that of specific performance, by which the court will order an employer to carry out the terms of the agreement. The CAC may stop the whole process prior to issuing its ruling at the joint request of the parties.

General provisions

The CAC will not accept an application:

- if it is satisfied that there is already a union recognised on behalf of any of the workers in the bargaining unit

CASE STUDY

R v Central Arbitration Committee (2006) IRLR 53

The National Union of Journalists (NUJ) had a significant number of members among the sports division of Mirror Group Newspapers. The union had a meeting with the management to discuss recognition and became hopeful that an agreement could be reached whereby they could show that they had the support of the majority of the journalists concerned.

In the meantime the employers were also approached by a breakaway union called the British Association of Journalists (BAJ), which had, at most, just one member working in the sports division. The BAJ was an independent union, but was not affiliated to the TUC. The result was that the employers recognised the BAJ exclusive bargaining rights to represent its journalists in the sports division.

The NUJ submitted an application to the CAC for statutory recognition. The employer opposed the application on the grounds that there was another trade union already recognised for collective bargaining purposes, even though at that stage there had been no negotiations on pay or conditions. The union argued that because this negotiation had not taken place, the collective agreement was 'not yet in force'.

The Court of Appeal held that the agreement was in force, within the natural meaning of those words. Thus the NUJ was unable to progress its claim for recognition.

- if it decides that members of the union constitute at least 10 per cent of the workers and there is *prima facie* evidence that a majority of the workers are likely to favour recognition; the CAC will decide whether this is so within 10 working days of receiving the application
- if the employer alleges that they are below the 21-employee threshold (see above); in this case they may have up to 10 working days in which to produce

the evidence; the CAC will consider the views of the union before making a decision

- where there is more than one union involved, if the CAC is not yet satisfied that the unions 'will co-operate with each other in a manner likely to secure stable and effective bargaining' or will make, if the employer so wishes, joint negotiating arrangements

- where there is another application within a period of three years for substantially the same bargaining unit by the same union.

Voluntary recognition

If the parties reach a voluntary agreement on recognition, they may still apply to the CAC to specify the method by which collective bargaining is to be carried out.[39] The CAC will accept the application, provided the employee threshold has been met (see above) and it is clear that the parties have either not agreed a method or have failed to implement a method to which they have agreed. There is an agreement period of 20 working days, or longer if both the parties agree, in which the CAC will help them to reach an agreement. If no agreement is reached, the CAC may specify the method to be used. The same rules about legally enforceable contracts and the remedy of specific performance apply (see above).

CHANGES AFFECTING THE BARGAINING UNIT[40]

There will be situations where the original bargaining unit becomes inappropriate. If either the employer or the trade union believes that this has happened, they may apply to the CAC to make a decision as to what the appropriate bargaining unit should be. For such an application to be admissible, the reason must be that there has been:

- a change in the organisation or structure of the business carried on by the employer

- a change in the activities pursued by the employer in the course of the employer's business

- a substantial change in the number of workers employed in the original unit.

If the parties cannot agree on new arrangements, the CAC is empowered to issue a declaration on the changes to be made.

Employers may also give notice to the union, with a copy to the CAC, that they believe that the original bargaining unit has ceased to exist. If the CAC accepts this, it may make a declaration ending the bargaining arrangements or may make a decision on a more appropriate bargaining unit.

DE-RECOGNITION[41]

This applies where the CAC has issued declarations on recognition and/or the method to be used for collective bargaining purposes. The process is the reverse of that for recognition, albeit with different initiators and a different question in the application to the CAC. The relevant date is the expiry of a three-year period after the date of the CAC's declaration or the parties' agreement.

PROTECTION AGAINST DETRIMENT AND DISMISSAL[42]

Detriment

A worker has the right not to be subject to any detriment by any act, or any deliberate failure to act, by the employer if the act or failure takes place on any of the following grounds:

- the worker acted with a view to obtaining or preventing recognition of a union
- the worker indicated that he or she supported or did not support recognition of a union
- the worker acted with a view to securing or preventing the ending of bargaining arrangements
- the worker indicated that he or she supported or did not support the ending of bargaining arrangements
- the worker influenced or sought to influence the way in which votes were to be cast by other workers in a ballot
- the worker influenced or sought to influence other workers to vote or abstain in the ballot
- the worker voted in such a ballot
- the worker proposed to do, failed to do, or proposed to decline to do, any of the above.

The worker is not protected, however, if the ground is an unreasonable act or omission by the worker.

The only remedy available to a worker is complaint to an employment tribunal, normally within three months of the act, or failure to act, which constitutes the detriment. The tribunal may issue a declaration and award compensation 'such as the tribunal considers just and equitable in all the circumstances having regard to the infringement complained of and to any loss sustained by the complainant which is attributable to the act or failure'.

Workers have a duty to mitigate their loss, and there will be a reduction in compensation if the worker contributed to the act or failure. Compensation for ending a contract is subject to the limits on compensation for unfair dismissal specified in the ERA 1996.

Dismissal

For the purposes of Part X of the ERA 1996, which is concerned with the right not to be unfairly dismissed (see Chapter 12), the dismissal of an employee shall be regarded as unfair if it takes place for any of the reasons listed above (under *Detriment*). This applies only to employees rather than those covered by the wider definition of 'worker', as in section 296(1) TULRCA 1992, but includes those on fixed-term contracts.

The dismissal of an employee for redundancy shall also be unfair if it is shown to be for one of the reasons listed above or if it is shown that there are others in a similar position and the same circumstances who were not dismissed for reasons of redundancy.

DISCLOSURE OF INFORMATION FOR COLLECTIVE BARGAINING

For the purposes of all the stages of collective bargaining between employers and representatives of recognised independent trade unions, employers have a duty to disclose to those representatives, on request, all such information relating to their undertakings as is in their possession or that of any associated employer which is both:[43]

- information without which the union representatives would be to a material extent impeded in carrying on such collective bargaining, and

- information which it would be in accordance with good industrial relations practice that they should disclose.

An employer can insist that a request for information must be made in writing, and likewise the information itself must be in written form, if that is the wish of the union representatives.[44] According to section 181(1) TULRCA 1992, a 'representative' is an 'official or other person authorised by the trade union to carry on such collective bargaining'. However, an 'undertaking' is not defined for these purposes.

UNIONS' RIGHT TO INFORMATION ON MATTERS NOT COVERED BY COLLECTIVE BARGAINING

The phrase 'of all the stages' means that information can be sought in order to prepare a claim, although it must relate to matters in respect of which the union is recognised. In *R v CAC ex parte BTP Tioxide*[45] the High Court held that the CAC had misdirected itself in concluding that the union was entitled to information relating to a job evaluation scheme in respect of which it had no bargaining rights but only the right to represent its members in re-evaluation appeals:

> There is no obstacle under the Act to an agreement which recognises the union's right to collective bargaining, that it is negotiating, in respect of one aspect of terms and conditions of employment and also recognises a right to some form of dealings with employers which does not answer to the description of collective bargaining, about another aspect.

In essence, for information to be disclosed under these provisions it must be both relevant and important. Although each case must be judged on its merits, unions may be entitled to information about groups not covered for collective bargaining purposes. Thus in Award 80/40 the CAC held that information about a productivity scheme for management not covered by the union was relevant and important to negotiations over a scheme for technical staff because of the similarity of the work of some employees within both groups.

'GOOD PRACTICE' AND THE ACAS CODE

In determining what constitutes 'good industrial relations practice' attention must be paid to the ACAS Code of Practice,[46] although other evidence is not to be excluded.[47] Thus unions may seek to demonstrate good practice by referring to the approaches taken by comparable employers. To decide what information is relevant, negotiators are advised to take account of the subject matter of the negotiations and the issues raised during them, the level at which negotiations take place, the size of the company, and its type of business.[48] There is no list of items that should be disclosed in all circumstances, but the following examples of information which could be relevant in certain situations are given as a guide:[49]

- pay and benefits
- conditions of service
- manpower
- performance
- finance.

This is not an exhaustive list and other items may be relevant in particular negotiations. The underlying philosophy of the code is that employers and unions should endeavour to reach a joint understanding on how the disclosure provisions can be implemented most effectively: 'In particular, the parties should endeavour to reach an understanding on what information could most appropriately be provided on a regular basis.'[50]

The duty to disclose is subject to the exceptions detailed in section 182 TULRCA 1992. Employers are not required to disclose:

(a) any information the disclosure of which would be against the interests of national security

(b) any information which could not be disclosed without contravening other legislation

(c) any information which has been communicated to the employer in confidence

(d) any information relating specifically to an individual unless he or she has consented to its disclosure

(e) any information the disclosure of which would cause substantial injury to the employer's undertaking for reasons other than its effect on collective bargaining

(f) information obtained by the employer for the purpose of bringing or defending any legal proceedings.

WHERE DISCLOSURE MAY LEAD TO 'SUBSTANTIAL INJURY'

Although (c) applies to standard form tenders headed 'In confidence',[51] it should be noted that it does not protect an employer who discloses information in confidence to lay union representatives and restricts them from communicating it to union members and full-time officials. Where a union seeks disclosure about individual salaries without the consent of the individuals concerned, in order to avoid the impact of (d) it must be clear that the information relates to the posts involved and not to the individuals who fill them. As regards (e), paragraph 14 of the Code offers some examples of information which, if disclosed in particular circumstances, might cause substantial injury. This would cover such matters as cost information on individual products, detailed analysis of proposed investment, marketing or pricing policies, price quotas, and the make-up of tender prices. Further guidance is offered in paragraph 15:

> … substantial injury may occur if, for example, certain customers would be lost to competitors, or suppliers would refuse to supply necessary materials, or the ability to raise funds to finance the company would be seriously impaired as a result of disclosing certain information. The burden of establishing a claim that disclosure of certain information would cause substantial injury lies with the employer.

By virtue of section 182(2) TULRCA 1992 employers are not obliged to produce, allow inspection of, or copy, any document other than a document conveying or confirming the information disclosed, and are not required to compile any information where to do so would involve an amount of work or expenditure out of reasonable proportion to the value of the information in the conduct of collective bargaining.

REDRESS TO UNIONS FOR FAILURE TO DISCLOSE

A union which feels that its representatives have not received the information to which they are entitled can complain in writing to the CAC, and if the CAC is of the opinion that the complaint is 'reasonably likely to be settled by conciliation', it must refer it to ACAS. Where no reference to ACAS is made or no settlement or withdrawal is achieved, the CAC must hear the complaint, make a declaration stating whether it is well-founded, wholly or in part, and give reasons for its finding. If the complaint is upheld, the declaration will specify the information in respect of which the CAC believed the complaint to be well-founded, the date on which the employer refused or failed to disclose information, and the period within which the employer ought to disclose the information specified.[52]

At any time after the expiry of this period the union may present a 'further complaint' that the employer has failed to disclose the required information. Again, the CAC must hear and determine the complaint and declare whether it holds it to be well-founded.[53] On or after presenting the further complaint the union may submit a claim that the employees' contracts should be amended to include the terms and conditions detailed in the claim – eg for more pay. However, no such claim can be lodged, or if presented it will be treated as withdrawn, if the relevant information is disclosed at any time before the CAC has adjudicated on the further complaint. If the further complaint is well-founded, the CAC may, after hearing the parties, award the terms and conditions detailed in the claim or others which it considers appropriate. Such an award will relate only to matters in respect of which the trade union is recognised. The terms and conditions awarded take effect as part of the contracts of employment of the employees covered, except insofar as they are superseded or varied by:

- a subsequent award under these provisions
- a collective agreement between the employer and the union
- an individual agreement, express or implied, effecting an improvement in the terms and conditions laid down in the award.[54]

It should be observed that these statutory provisions do not enable a union to force the disclosure of information.

THE LEGAL ENFORCEABILITY OF COLLECTIVE AGREEMENTS

In this section we are concerned with the legal enforceability of collective agreements between employers and trade unions and not the effect of such agreements on individual contracts of employment. It is important to remember that the legal status of the arrangements made between the employer and the union has no bearing on the relationship between the employer and his or her workers. The mechanisms by which the terms of a collective agreement may be enforced between the parties to a contract of employment have been described in Chapter 2.

A collective agreement is statutorily defined as any agreement or arrangement made by or on behalf of one or more trade unions[55] and one or more employers, or employers' associations, which relates to one or more of the matters mentioned in section 178(2) TULRCA 1992.[56] A collective agreement is conclusively presumed not to have been intended by the parties to be a legally enforceable contract unless the agreement is in writing and contains a provision which states that the parties intend the agreement to be a legally enforceable contract,[57] or the agreement has been specified by the CAC as a result of the statutory recognition procedures. Equally, the parties may declare that one or more parts only of an agreement are intended to be legally enforceable.[58] Nevertheless, it should not be assumed that a collective agreement which declares the parties' intention to create legal relations is necessarily legally binding, because agreements exist which are too vague or uncertain to be enforced as contracts.

DISCRIMINATION ON THE GROUNDS OF TRADE UNION MEMBERSHIP OR ACTIVITIES

UNLAWFUL REFUSAL OF EMPLOYMENT

Section 137(1) TULRCA 1992 makes it unlawful to refuse employment to people because:

- they are or are not members of a trade union

- they refuse to accept a requirement that they become a member or cease to be a member, or a requirement that they suffer deductions if they fail to join.[59]

Section 138 makes it unlawful for an agency which finds employment for workers, or supplies employers with workers, to refuse its services to people because they are or are not union members or are unwilling to accept a condition or requirement of the type mentioned in section 137(1)(b). The provisions relating to advertisements also apply to such agencies.

COMPLAINTS ABOUT UNLAWFUL REFUSAL OF EMPLOYMENT

A complaint about the infringement of these provisions must normally be presented to an employment tribunal within three months of the date of the conduct complained about. Provision is made for conciliation, but if a complaint is upheld, the tribunal must make a declaration to that effect and may make such of the following remedies as it considers just and equitable:[60]

- an order obliging the respondent to pay compensation, which is to be assessed on the same basis as damages for breach of statutory duty and may include damages for injury to feelings

- a recommendation that the respondent takes such action as the tribunal thinks practicable to obviate or reduce the effect on the complainant of the conduct to which the claim relates. If such a recommendation is not complied with, any award of compensation can be increased, although the total award cannot exceed the amount stipulated in section 124 ERA 1996 (£66,200 in 2009).

SUBJECT TO DETRIMENT SHORT OF DISMISSAL

Section 146 TULRCA 1992 gives employees the right not to be subjected to any detriment as an individual by any act, or any deliberate failure to act, by an employer if the act or failure takes place for the sole or main purpose of:

- preventing or deterring them from being or seeking to become members of an independent trade union, or penalising them for doing so

- preventing or deterring them from taking part in the activities of an independent trade union or from making use of trade union services at any appropriate time, or penalising them for doing so

- compelling them to become members of any trade union or of a particular trade union or of one of a number of particular trade unions

- enforcing a requirement that in the event of their failure to become, or their ceasing to remain, members of any trade union or a particular trade union or one of a number of particular trade unions, they must make one or more payments. For this purpose, any deduction from remuneration which is attributable to the employee's failure to become, or his or her ceasing to be, a trade union member will be treated as a detriment.

As regards the requirement that the action must be taken against an employee as an individual, the Court of Appeal has offered the following guidance: 'If an employee is selected for discrimination because of some characteristic which he shares with others, such as membership of a particular trade union, then the action is ... taken against him as an individual.'[61] Thus de-recognition of an individual shop steward by an employer can be action taken against the shop steward as an individual, rather than action taken against the trade union.[62]

The word 'purpose' connotes an object that the employer seeks to achieve, and the purpose of an action must not be confused with its effect. Thus when a full-time union official was turned down for promotion, the Court of Appeal accepted that section 146 had not been infringed because the employer's purpose had been to ensure that only those with sufficient managerial experience were promoted.[63] By way of contrast, when a full-time branch secretary was offered promotion without the usual salary increase, it was held that the employer's purpose was to deter the individual from engaging in union activities.[64] It is clear that employees have the right to join any independent trade union of their choice.[65] Thus in *Carlson*'s case[66] the EAT decided that the denial of a car-park permit to a member of a non-recognised independent trade union constituted a form of penalisation outlawed by the section. In this context 'penalising' was held to mean 'subjecting to a disadvantage'. For the purposes of this section and section 152 (see below), 'trade union services' are those made available by virtue of union membership, and 'making use' includes consenting to the raising of a matter by the union on the member's behalf.[67]

DISMISSALS RELATING TO TRADE UNION MEMBERSHIP

According to section 152(1) TULRCA 1992 a dismissal is unfair if the reason for it (or if more than one, the principal reason) was that the employee:

- was or proposed to become a member of an independent trade union
- had taken (or proposed to take) part in the activities of an independent trade union or had used (or proposed to use) union services at an appropriate time
- was not a member of any trade union or of a particular trade union, or had refused or proposed to refuse to become or to remain a member
- had failed to accept an offer in contravention of section 145A or B (see above).

Section 152(3) TULRCA 1992 states that dismissals are to be treated as falling within the third bullet-point above if one of the reasons for them was that employees:

- refused (or proposed to refuse) to comply with a requirement that in the event of their failure to become, or their ceasing to remain, a trade union member they must make some kind of payment

- objected, or proposed to object, to the operation of a provision under which their employer was entitled to deduct sums from their remuneration if they failed to become or remain a trade union member.

It would seem that if an employee is dismissed because of her or his proposal to leave an independent trade union, that will be unfair, even though the proposal is conditional on something occurring or not occurring.[68]

The usual qualifying period for claiming unfair dismissal does not apply if the reason, or principal reason, for dismissal was one of those specified in section 152 TULRCA 1992.[69] This being so, the burden is on employees to prove that their dismissal related to trade union membership. However, where the question of jurisdiction does not arise, the only burden on the employee is to produce some evidence that casts doubt upon the employer's reason.[70]

Where employees allege that their dismissals were unfair by virtue of section 152 TULRCA 1992, they can seek 'interim relief'.[71] This is available where employees present their claims within seven days of the effective date of termination and, where sections 152(1)(a) or (b) TULRCA 1992 are relied on, they submit written certificates signed by an authorised union official which state that there appears to be reasonable grounds for supposing that the reason for dismissal was the one alleged in the complaints. The tribunal must hear such an application as soon as practicable,[72] and if it thinks it 'likely' (ie there is a pretty good chance) that the complainant will be found to have been unfairly dismissed by virtue of section 152 TULRCA 1992, it must ask whether the employer is willing to reinstate or (if not) to re-engage the employee pending the determination of the complaint. If the employer is willing to reinstate or the employee is willing to accept re-engagement, the tribunal should make an order to that effect. Where the employer fails to attend the hearing or is unwilling to re-employ, the tribunal must make an order for the continuation of the employee's contract of employment. In essence, such an order amounts to suspension on full pay.[73]

Where there has been pressure to dismiss on the grounds of non-membership of a trade union, section 160 TULRCA 1992 enables the person who applied the pressure to be joined (by either the employer or the employee) – ie be brought in as a party to the unfair dismissal proceedings. A request that a person be joined must be acceded to if it is made before the hearing but can be refused if it is made after that time. No such request can be entertained after a remedy has been awarded, and the tribunal is empowered to apportion compensation in a 'just and equitable' manner.

- The Certification Officer decides if a trade union is entitled to a certificate of independence.

- An independent trade union must be recognised by an employer in order to enjoy a number of statutory rights, such as the right to the disclosure of information for collective bargaining purposes.

- The statutory recognition procedures apply to firms with 21 or more employees on the day an independent trade union requests recognition.

- Establishing the bargaining unit is a necessary prerequisite for the recognition procedure. The CAC will assist and take into account, among other factors, the need for bargaining units to be compatible with effective management and the desirability of avoiding small fragmented units within an undertaking.

- Employers have a duty to disclose to trade unions recognised for collective bargaining purposes such information without which the union representatives would be to a material extent impeded in carrying on collective bargaining with them.

- A collective agreement is conclusively presumed not to be a legally enforceable contract unless it is in writing and contains a provision that the parties intend it to be a legally enforceable contract.

- It is unlawful to refuse employment to a person because he or she is or is not a member of a trade union.

- Employees have the right not to be dismissed or subjected to a detriment for the purposes of preventing them from becoming a member or taking part in the activities of or using the services of a trade union or, conversely, for not wanting to be a member or take part in union activities.

Reinforce your understanding of this chapter by visiting www.cipd.co.uk/sss for activities, questions, weblinks and additional case studies

REFERENCES

1 The words 'employee', 'employer' and 'worker' are defined in sections 295–6 TULRCA 1992; the expression 'associated employer' is defined in section 297 TULRCA 1992.

2 Section 123 TULRCA 1992

3 Section 128 TULRCA 1992

4 Section 131 TULRCA 1992

5 Section 1 TULRCA 1992

6 (1980) 1 All ER 1097

7 Sections 12 and 13 TULRCA 1992

8 Section 11 TULRCA 1992

9 Section 3 TULRCA 1992

10 Section 4 TULRCA 1992

11 Section 9(1) TULRCA 1992

12 Section 6(2) and (5) TULRCA 1992

13 Section 8 TULRCA 1992

14 (1993) IRLR 260

15 Section 178(3) TULRCA 1992

16   Section 178(1) TULRCA 1992

17   See *NUGSAT v Albury Bros* (1978) IRLR 504

18   See *J. Wilson and Albury Bros v USDAW* (1978) IRLR 20

19   See *NUGSAT v Albury Bros* (note 17)

20   See *Cleveland County Council v Springett* (1985) IRLR 131

21   See *NUGSAT v Albury Bros* (note 17)

22   All references in this section to a trade union should also be taken as references to more than one union if there is more than one union involved in the application for recognition.

23   Schedule A1 para 3(3) TULRCA 1992; see also *UNIFI v Union Bank of Nigeria* (2001) IRLR 712, which held that pay includes matters related to the group pension scheme.

24   Schedule A1 para 8 TULRCA 1992

25   Schedule A1 para 6 TULRCA 1992

26   Schedule A1 para 7 TULRCA 1992 The meaning of 'worker' is defined in section 296(1)(b) TULRCA 1992; see *R v CAC* (2003) IRLR 460

27   Schedule A1 para 10 TULRCA 1992

28   Schedule A1 para 12 TULRCA 1992

29   Schedule A1 para 18 TULRCA 1992

30   (2001) IRLR 752

31   See *Graphical, Paper and Media Union v Derry Print Ltd* (2002) IRLR 380

32   *R v CAC and Communication Workers Union* (2008) IRLR 425

33   Schedule A1 paras 20–29 TULRCA 1992

34   (2001) IRLR 752

35   See the Recognition and Derecognition Ballots (Qualified Persons Order) 2000, SI 2000/1306, which describes those who are qualified persons

36   Introduced in 2000 and revised in 2005 by SI 2005/2421

37   Schedule A1 paras 30–31 TULRCA 1992

38   SI 2000/1300

39   Schedule A1 paras 58–63 TULRCA 1992

40   Schedule A1 Part III TULRCA 1992

41   Schedule A1 Part IV TULRCA 1992

32   Schedule A1 Part VIII TULRCA 1992

43   Section 181(1) and (2) TULRCA 1992

44   Section 181(3) and (5) TULRCA 1992

45   (1982) IRLR 61

46   Disclosure of Information to Trade Unions for Collective Bargaining Purposes, ACAS, 1997

47   Section 181(4) TULRCA 1992

48   Code of Practice paragraph 10

49   Code of Practice paragraph 11

50   Code of Practice paragraph 22

51   See *CSU v CAC* (1980) IRLR 274

52   Section 183 TULRCA 1992

53 Section 184 TULRCA 1992

54 Section 185(5) TULRCA 1992

55 See *Edinburgh Council v Brown* (1999) IRLR 208, where an agreement between the employer and the joint consultative committee constituted a collective agreement

56 Section 178(1) TULRCA 1992

57 Section 179(1) TULRCA 1992

58 Section 179(3) TULRCA 199

59 According to Section 285 TULRCA 1992, these provisions do not apply if the employee ordinarily works outside Great Britain

60 Section 140 TULRCA 1992

61 *Ridgway v NCB* (1987) IRLR 80

62 See *Farnsworth Ltd v McCoid* (1998) IRLR 626

63 *Gallagher v Department of Transport* (1994) IRLR 231

64 See *Southwark London Borough Council v Whillier* (2001) ICR 142

65 See *Ridgway v NCB* (note 61)

66 *Carlson v Post Office* (1981) IRLR 158

67 Sections 146 (2A) and 152*(2A) TULRCA 1992

68 See *Crosville Motor Services Ltd v Ashfield* (1986) IRLR 475

69 Section 154(1) TULRCA 1992. An employee wishing to complain must first submit a statement of grievance to the employer.

70 See *Maund v Penwith D.C.* (1984) IRLR 24

71 Section 161 TULRCA 1992

72 Section 162 TULRCA 1992

73 See section 164 TULRCA 1992

CHAPTER 19

Trade Unions and Industrial Action

OVERVIEW

Industrial action is likely to constitute a breach of an individual's contract of employment. In this chapter we shall be concentrating on the liability more of those who organise industrial action than of those who participate in it. In this respect we shall be examining the nature of the common-law liabilities and the extent to which statutory provisions can be used to negate their effect. We begin with an examination of the economic torts and then consider the protection offered by statute for action that takes place in contemplation or furtherance of a trade dispute. This is followed by a consideration of the statutory hurdles that have to be overcome before lawful action can take place. We shall be focusing mainly on the civil law, but it will also be necessary to deal with the possibility of criminal prosecutions.

THE 'ECONOMIC' TORTS

INDUCING A BREACH OF CONTRACT

There are two forms of inducement: direct and indirect.

Direct inducement may occur when a union official puts direct pressure on an employer to breach a commercial contract. Thus if A induces B to break the contract of supply with C and C suffers loss as a result, C could sue B for breaking the contract (but is unlikely to in the circumstances), or could sue A if the following matters are shown:

- that A knew of the contract which would be broken or was 'recklessly indifferent' as to its existence
- that A's conduct was intentional; here, once sufficient knowledge has been established, the intention to produce a breach will be presumed
- that there was clear evidence of inducement; in this context 'inducement' means pressure, persuasion or procuration and must be distinguished from the giving of advice, information or a warning.[1]

Indirect inducement is when A induces union members to break their contracts of employment so that B is forced to break the contract with C. C can sue A if the requirements of knowledge, intention and inducement are met and the use of unlawful means is proved. It makes no difference that A believed that the functions performed by the members were voluntary rather than contractual.[2] For the purposes of all the economic torts, unlawful means may be either tortious – eg breaking a contract or inducing a breach of statutory duty – or criminal acts – eg the use of violence.

Thus the essential difference between direct and indirect inducement is one of causation. Where the person immediately responsible for bringing the pressure to bear was the defendant or someone for whose acts he or she was legally responsible, the inducement is direct. If it was a third party responding to the defendant's inducement or persuasion but exercising his or her choice (and not being a person for whom the defendant was legally responsible), the inducement is indirect.[3]

Section 219(1)(a) TULRCA 1992 provides that an act done in contemplation or furtherance of a trade dispute – the so-called 'golden formula' (see below) – will not be actionable in tort on the ground only that it induces another to break a contract. In *Norbrook Ltd v King*[4] it was pointed out that the effect of the phrase 'on the ground only' is that the use of unlawful means to induce a breach of contract deprives the user of statutory protection. However, it is clear that section 219 does not provide immunity against prosecution in respect of acts which are in themselves criminal.[5]

INTIMIDATION

This tort is committed where C suffers as a result of action taken by B in response to an unlawful threat made to B by A. In this situation C or B can sue A at common law, whether the threat is of tortious or criminal conduct.[6] However, section 219(1)(b) TULRCA 1992 states that an act done in contemplation or furtherance of a trade dispute shall not be actionable in tort on the ground only that it consists of a person 'threatening that a contract (whether one to which he is a party or not) will be broken or its performance interfered with, or that he will induce another person to break a contract or interfere with its performance'.

CONSPIRACY

Again, this tort could take one of two forms:

- a combination to injure with illegitimate objectives. This is where two or more persons combine in order to harm the plaintiff by use of means which are lawful in themselves but with a predominant purpose other than that of advancing their own legitimate interests. Thus if those combining can show a genuine trade union reason behind their action (for example, protecting jobs), the conspiracy will not be actionable despite any loss caused to an employer[7]

- a situation in which people combine in order to harm the plaintiff by using unlawful means. In this way a tort is committed irrespective of the purpose of the combination. The use of unlawful means eliminates the justification of self-interest.

Because almost all strikes involve combinations of workers inflicting loss on employers, section 219(2) TULRCA 1992 provides that a combination to do any act in contemplation or furtherance of a trade dispute is not actionable in tort if the act is one which, if done by one person alone, would not be actionable.

INTERFERENCE WITH BUSINESS BY UNLAWFUL MEANS

This tort was developed to take account of the practice of inserting *force majeure* clauses into commercial contracts. The effect of such a clause is to exempt a party from liability where a breach of contract would otherwise have arisen as a result of industrial action. The Court of Appeal has stated that to succeed in establishing the tort of wrongful interference with contractual rights, five conditions must be fulfilled. These are:

- It must be shown that the defendant persuaded or procured or induced a third party to break its contract with the plaintiff.

- It must be shown that the defendant when so acting had knowledge of that contract.

- The defendant must be shown to have had the intent to persuade or induce a breach of that contract. According to the Court of Appeal, a specific subjective intention to interfere with a contract is required. Recklessness is not enough.[8]

- The plaintiff must show that it suffered more than nominal damage.

- If justification is put forward as a defence, the plaintiff must be able to rebut this.[9]

Statutory immunity is provided by section 219(1)(a) TULRCA 1992, which states that so long as the 'golden formula' applies, an act is not to be actionable in tort on the ground only that it 'interferes or induces any other person to interfere' with the performance of a contract. In *Hadmor Productions v Hamilton*[10] the House of Lords held that inducing, or threatening to induce, a breach of contract could not be regarded as unlawful means for the purpose of establishing liability for interference with the business of a third person.

INDUCING A BREACH OF STATUTORY DUTY

In *Meade v Haringey L.B.C.*[11] two Court of Appeal judges expressed the opinion that persons inducing a public body to act in breach of its statutory duty would be committing a tort for which there would be no statutory immunity. If this view were adopted, it would be relatively easy to restrain action taken by workers in the public sector.

ECONOMIC DURESS

If the financial consequences to an employer of not acceding to the request of a trade union or another person are catastrophic, it could be argued that there was such coercion of the employer's will as to vitiate consent to any agreements made with, or payments made to, the union (or person) applying the pressure. Contracts made in these circumstances will be voidable and it will be possible to claim restitution of money paid under them. The rationale is that the employer's apparent consent was induced by pressure exercised by that other party which the law does not regard as legitimate. In *Universe Tankships Inc of Monrovia v ITWF*[12] the House of Lords accepted that sections 219 and 244 TULRCA 1992 afforded an indication of where public policy requires the line to be drawn between the kind of commercial pressure by a trade union which ought to be treated as legitimised and the kind that amounts to economic duress. The events which gave rise to this case occurred in 1978 and it is safe to say that subsequent legislation will have encouraged the judiciary to take a narrower view of what is regarded as legitimate pressure.

THE 'GOLDEN FORMULA'

We have observed that statutory immunity in tort for various types of industrial action depends on that action taking place in contemplation or furtherance of a trade dispute. Although we shall be outlining later the requirement to conduct a ballot before industrial action (see below), it should be noted that so long as the action taken is in contemplation or furtherance of a trade dispute the TULRCA 1992 immunities apply irrespective of whether or not the action is in breach of a disputes procedure. However, if the 'golden formula' does not apply, it will be relatively easy for an employer to show that one of the economic torts is being committed, and to obtain an interim injunction on that basis.

THE MEANING OF 'TRADE DISPUTE'

Section 244 TULRCA 1992 defines a trade dispute as a dispute between workers and their employer which relates wholly or mainly to one or more of the following:

- terms and conditions of employment, or the physical conditions in which any workers are required to work.[13] These are not confined to contractual terms and conditions, and the House of Lords has held that a dispute about the reasonableness of an employer's instruction may be covered[14]

- engagement or non-engagement, or termination or suspension of employment, or the duties of employment of one or more workers. This might include a dispute about a proposal to transfer an undertaking and its employees.[15] However, if the reason or one of the reasons for calling industrial action is 'the fact or belief that the employer has dismissed one or more employees in circumstances such that by virtue of section 237 TULRCA 1992 (dismissal in connection with unofficial industrial action) they have no right to complain of unfair dismissal', the immunity provided by section 219 TULRCA 1992 is lost[16]

- allocation of work or the duties of employment as between workers or groups of workers

- matters of discipline

- the membership or non-membership of a trade union on the part of a worker. Nevertheless, there will be no immunity from liability in tort where the purpose of the industrial action is to enforce union membership or persuade employers to insert recognition or consultation requirements in contracts for the supply of goods or services[17]

- facilities for officials of trade unions

- the machinery for negotiation or consultation and other procedures relating to any of the foregoing matters, including the recognition by employers or employers' associations of the right of a trade union to represent workers in any such negotiation, or consultation, or in the carrying out of such procedures.

In *University College London Hospital NHS Trust v Unison*[18] the union gained an overwhelming majority in favour of strike action in support of a demand for employment guarantees associated with the building of a new hospital under the Private Finance Initiative. This would have involved the transfer of some workers to a new employer. The Court of Appeal held that the dispute was about terms and conditions which would apply to workers not currently employed by the NHS Trust and that such a dispute about future employment with a new employer was outside the provisions of section 244. Subsequently the European Court of Human Rights has ruled that in these circumstances the UK did not exceed the margin of appreciation accorded to it in regulating trade union action.[19]

Clearly, where there is a dispute between a union and an employer there is a dispute between those workers on whose behalf the union was acting and that employer.[20] In addition, section 244(2) TULRCA 1992 provides that in certain circumstances a dispute between a Minister of the Crown and any workers is to be treated as a dispute between those workers and their employers.[21]

A 'worker' is defined to cover only those employed by the employer in dispute.[22] However, the 'golden formula' will not apply if the dispute concerns a former employee unless either the employment was terminated in connection with the dispute or the termination was one of the circumstances giving rise to the dispute. A realistic view of who is an employer was taken in *Examite Ltd v Whittaker*[23] where it was stated that 'the Act applies to employers whatever particular hat these particular employers may wear from time to time.'

A trade dispute can exist even though it relates to matters occurring outside the UK:

> so long as the person or persons whose actions in the UK are said to be in contemplation or furtherance of a trade dispute relating to matters

occurring outside the UK are likely to be affected in respect of one or more of the matters specified in section 244(1) TULRCA by the outcome of that dispute.[24]

It is also stated that an act, threat or demand done or made by a person or organisation against another which, if resisted, would have led to a trade dispute with that other, 'shall, notwithstanding that because that other submits to the act or threat or accedes to the demand no dispute arises, be treated as being done or made in contemplation or furtherance of a trade dispute'.[25]

CONTEMPLATION OR FURTHERANCE

The word 'contemplation' refers to something imminent or likely to occur, so the 'golden formula' cannot be invoked if the action was taken too far in advance of any dispute. 'Furtherance' assumes the existence of a dispute and an act will not be protected if it is not for the purpose of promoting the interests of a party to the dispute (for example, if it is in pursuit of a personal vendetta) or occurs after its conclusion.[26] In *MacShane and Ashton v Express Newspapers*[27] the House of Lords held that while the existence of a trade dispute had to be determined objectively, the test for deciding whether an act is in furtherance of such a dispute is a subjective one: 'If the person doing the act honestly thinks at the time he does it that it may help one of the parties to the dispute to achieve their objective and does it for that reason, he is protected.' Apparently there is no requirement that a union should act exclusively in furtherance of a trade dispute; it is sufficient if the furtherance of a trade dispute is one of its purposes. Indeed, the presence of an improper motive is relevant only where it is so overriding that it negates any genuine intention to advance the trade dispute.[28]

SECONDARY ACTION

In this book 'primary action' refers to action taken directly against the employer in dispute and 'secondary action' is that taken against the employer's suppliers and customers. Section 244 defines secondary action as being an inducement to break or interfere with a contract of employment or a contract for personal services, or a threat to do so, where the employer under that contract is not party to the dispute. For these purposes an employer is not to be regarded as a party to a dispute between another employer and its workers. Similarly, where more than one employer is in dispute, the dispute between each employer and its workers is to be treated as a separate dispute.[29]

The protection afforded against certain tort liabilities by section 219 TULRCA 1992 will not be available unless the secondary action satisfies the requirements of section 224. These can be met only if the secondary action is taken in the course of such attendance as is declared lawful by section 220 TULRCA 1992:

- by a worker employed (or last employed) by the employer who is party to the dispute, or

- by a union official whose attendance is lawful by virtue of section 220(1)(6) TULRCA 1992 (on peaceful picketing and section 220 TULRCA 1992, see below).

UNION RESPONSIBILITY FOR THE ACTS OF ITS MEMBERS AND OFFICIALS

Trade unions are to be treated in law as ordinary persons. This means that they get the benefit of the immunities conferred by section 219 TULRCA 1992 but can be sued if they are responsible for unlawful industrial action. However, a union will be held liable for the torts mentioned in section 20(1) TULRCA 1992 only if the acts in question were authorised or endorsed by the union.[30] Where other torts are committed, the ordinary principles of vicarious liability apply.[31] Irrespective of union rules, acts are to be regarded as authorised or endorsed if there was authorisation or endorsement by:[32]

- any person empowered by the rules to do, authorise or endorse acts of the kind in question

- the principal executive committee or the president or general secretary, or

- any other committee of the union or any other official of the union (whether employed by it or not).

In this context 'rules' means the 'written rules of the union and any other written provisions forming part of the contract between a member and other members'. 'President' and 'general secretary' are defined to include, where there is no such office in the union, the person who holds the 'nearest equivalent' office.[33] For these purposes any group of persons constituted in accordance with the rules of the union is a committee of the union and 'an act shall be taken to have been done, authorised or endorsed by an official if it was done, etc,' by any member of a group whose purposes include organising or co-ordinating industrial action.[34] These provisions apply irrespective of anything in the union rules that prevents particular officials or committees from calling industrial action.

HOW UNIONS MAY REPUDIATE MEMBERS' AND OFFICIALS' ACTS

A union can avoid liability for the actions of union committees and officials if those actions are repudiated by the principal executive committee or the president or general secretary 'as soon as reasonably practicable after coming to the knowledge of any of them'. However, a repudiation will be effective only if:

- written notice of the repudiation is given to the official or committee in question without delay, and

- the union has done its best to give individual written notice of the fact and date of repudiation without delay to every member who the union has reason to believe is taking part, or might otherwise take part, in the industrial action. The notice to members must contain the following statement: 'Your union has repudiated any call for industrial action to which this notice relates and will give no support to such action. If you are dismissed while taking unofficial industrial action, you will have no right to complain of unfair dismissal.' This notice must also be given to the employer of every such member.[35]

An act shall not be treated as repudiated if the union's principal executive committee, president or general secretary subsequently behaves in a manner inconsistent with that repudiation. Additionally, if a request is made to any of these bodies within three months by a person who is party to a commercial contract that has been, or may be, interfered with and who has not been given notice of the repudiation, that body must immediately confirm the repudiation in writing.[36] Finally, in any injunction proceedings arising out of this section, the courts are empowered to require unions to take such steps as are considered appropriate for ensuring that:

- there is no inducement of persons to take part in industrial action, and

- no person engages in any conduct after the grant of the injunction by virtue of having been induced before it was granted to take part in industrial action.[37]

BALLOTS AND NOTICE OF INDUSTRIAL ACTION[38]

Trade unions and their officials can benefit from immunity provided by section 219 TULRCA 1992 only if the union has authorised or endorsed the industrial action, having gained majority support in a ballot of the members concerned not more than four weeks before the start of the action.[39] It is the Court of Appeal's view that once industrial action has begun it should continue 'without substantial interruption' if reliance is to be placed on the result of the original ballot. Whether the original action has come to an end is a matter of fact and degree.[40]

For section 219 TULRCA 1992 immunity to be available, the following requirements must be met:

(i)   Trade unions must take such steps as are reasonably necessary to ensure that at least seven days before the start of the ballot a written notice is received by 'every person who it is reasonable for the union to believe ... will be the employer of persons who will be entitled to vote in the ballot'. This notice must

- state that the union intends to hold a ballot

- specify the date which the union reasonably believes will be the opening day of the ballot

- provide the employer with a list of the categories of employees concerned and their workplaces, together with the total number of employees concerned, the number in each category and at each workplace. Additionally, at least three days before the opening of the ballot, the union must take such steps as are reasonably necessary to ensure that the same employer receives a sample voting paper.[41]

(ii)   Entitlement to vote must be given equally to those, and only those, who the union reasonably believes will be called upon to take strike or other industrial action.[42] In *London Underground v RMT*[43] the Court of Appeal accepted that a union could call for newly recruited members to take part in industrial action even though they had not been balloted.

(iii) There must be a separate ballot at each workplace unless the ballot is limited to all the members of a union who

- according to the union's reasonable belief have an occupation of a particular kind or have any of a number of particular kinds of occupation, and

- are employed by a particular employer, or by any number of particular employers, with whom the union is in dispute.[44]

(iv)   So far as is reasonably practicable, all members entitled to vote must be sent a voting paper at his or her registered address, and be given a convenient opportunity to vote by post.[45]

(v)   The voting paper must

- state the name of the independent scrutineer appointed to carry out the functions described above[46]

- specify the address to which, and the date by which, it is to be returned

- be marked with a number which is one of a series of consecutive whole numbers

- contain the following statement:

If you take part in a strike or other industrial action you may be in breach of your contract of employment. However, if you are dismissed for taking part in a strike or other industrial action which is called officially and is otherwise lawful, the dismissal will be unfair if it takes place fewer than eight weeks after you started taking part in the action, and depending on the circumstances may be unfair if it takes place later.

- invite a 'yes' or 'no' answer to the question whether members are prepared to participate in a strike or other industrial action. According to the Court of Appeal, the questions on the ballot paper must be framed so that members can draw a distinction between their willingness to take strike action and their willingness to take action short of a strike.[47] In *Connex South Eastern Ltd v NURMTW*[48] employees voted for strike action and the employer was notified by the union that they proposed to start a ban on overtime and rest-day working. The employer claimed that this discontinuous action was not strike action and was therefore unlawful. The Court of Appeal held that the action was lawful because strike action was not restricted to stoppages of all work, but could include stoppages on particular days and at particular hours. However, section 229(2A) TULRCA 1992 now states that overtime bans and call-out bans are forms of industrial action short of a strike. Each question has to be voted on individually and the majority in respect of each question considered separately[49]

- identify the person(s) authorised to call industrial action and that person must be one of those specified in section 20(2) TULRCA 1992 (see above).

(vi) Industrial action will not be regarded as having the support of a ballot if a member who was likely to be induced into taking part in the action was not accorded the right to vote.[50]

(vii) As soon as is reasonably practicable after the ballot, the union must take such steps as are reasonably necessary to ensure that all those entitled to vote and every relevant employer are informed of the number of votes cast, the numbers voting 'yes' and those voting 'no', and the number of spoiled ballot papers.[51] If there is a failure to inform one or more relevant employers, the ballot and subsequent action will still be valid in relation to the other employers who were informed correctly.[52]

(viii) Trade unions must take all reasonably necessary steps to ensure that the employer of those to be called upon to take industrial action receives written notice of the action. This notice must be received after the employer has been informed of the ballot result and at least seven days prior to the date on which the action is to commence. The notice must contain

- a list of the categories of employees concerned and their workplaces, together with the total number of employees concerned, the number in each category and at each workplace[53]

- a statement of whether the industrial action is intended to be continuous or discontinuous[54]

- where there is continuous action, the date on which it is intended to start; where the action is discontinuous, the dates on which it is intended to take place. The ballot will cease to be effective after a period of four weeks, or up to eight weeks if the union and the employer agree[55]

- a statement that the notice is given for the purposes of section 234A TULRCA 1992.

If there are accidental and minor failures to comply with all the balloting requirements, these may be ignored as long as they are unlikely to affect the ballot outcome.[56]

Where industrial action ceases to be authorised or endorsed (other than in compliance with a court order or undertaking), and is subsequently re-authorised or re-endorsed, the union must give another notice to the employer before the industrial action is resumed.

Finally, where a member has been (or is likely to be) induced by the union to take part in any industrial action which does not satisfy the ballot requirements of Part V TULRCA 1992, he or she can apply to the High Court for an order requiring the union to stop authorising or endorsing the industrial action without the support of a valid ballot.[57] It should be noted that although a court can order the union to ensure that there is no further inducement, it has no power to compel the union to conduct a valid ballot.

DAMAGES

Section 22(2) TULRCA 1992 limits the amount of damages that can be awarded 'in any proceedings in tort' against a trade union which is deemed liable for industrial action.[58] The words 'in any proceedings' are crucial, since separate proceedings may be brought by all those who have suffered from the industrial action. The limits set are:

- £10,000, if the union has fewer than 5,000 members
- £50,000, if the union has 5,000 or more members but fewer than 25,000
- £125,000 if the union has 25,000 or more members but fewer than 100,000
- £250,000 if the union has 100,000 or more members.

It should be noted that interest on such damages may be available.[59] Finally, it should be noted that damages, costs or expenses cannot be recovered from certain 'protected property'. This includes union provident funds and political funds, which cannot be used for financing industrial action.[60]

INJUNCTIONS

If an employer is suffering economic harm as a result of unlawful industrial action, the logical remedy is to seek an injunction so as to prevent further loss being incurred. An injunction may be sought against a trade union or some other person, although section 236 TULRCA 1992 prevents a court from compelling an employee to do any work. The general principle that if damages would provide an adequate remedy an injunction must be refused will not apply in this context: 'Where it is clear that the defendants were acting unlawfully, it would require wholly exceptional circumstances to be a proper exercise of discretion to allow such conduct to continue.'[61]

There are two basic types of injunction that should be mentioned:

- In situations of extreme urgency an *interim injunction* can be sought. This is a temporary measure which endures until a named day and can be obtained on the basis of sworn statements submitted by the applicant alone. If the respondent is absent, this is known as an *ex parte* (one-sided) injunction.

- According to section 221 TULRCA 1992, a court shall not grant an application if the party against whom the injunction is sought claims (or in the court's opinion might claim) that the act was done in contemplation or furtherance of a trade dispute unless all reasonable steps have been taken to give that party notice of the application and an opportunity of being heard.

- A *permanent injunction* is one which is granted at the end of the trial.

Before granting an interim injunction, a judge will have to consider the following questions:

- Is there a serious question to be tried?

- Does the balance of convenience lie with the plaintiff? In *NWL v Nelson*[62] Lord Diplock argued that judges should not blind themselves to the practical realities by pretending that an injunction merely preserves the status quo until the trial is heard: 'It is the nature of industrial action that it can be promoted effectively only so long as it is possible to strike while the iron is hot; once postponed, it is unlikely that it can be revived ... The grant or refusal of an interim injunction generally disposes finally of the action.' In such a case the court has to balance the risk of doing an injustice to either party and evaluate the public interest.[63]

- Where the party against whom the injunction is sought claims that the action was in contemplation of furtherance of a trade dispute, is there a likelihood of the defendant's establishing a defence to the action under section 219 or 220 TULRCA 1992?[64] It has been held by the House of Lords that the effect of section 221(2) TULRCA 1992 is that in exercising its discretion a court should put into the balance of convenience the degree of likelihood of the defendant's succeeding in establishing a trade dispute defence.[65] Thus in *Heath Computing v Meek*[66] no injunction was granted because there was a 'substantial probability' that the defendants would establish that they were acting in contemplation or furtherance of a trade dispute. By way of contrast, in *RJB Mining v NUM*[67] an interim injunction was granted because it was at least arguable that the union was in breach of section 227 TULRCA 1992 by omitting to ballot all of its members who might be involved in the industrial action. However, that it is likely that a trade dispute defence would be established should not be regarded as an overriding or paramount factor precluding the granting of an injunction. There may be cases where the consequences to the plaintiff or to others may be so serious that the court feels it necessary to grant this form of remedy. In the *Duport Steels* case[68] the Law Lords confirmed that there is a residual discretion to grant an injunction notwithstanding the likelihood of a trade dispute defence succeeding at trial. Nevertheless, the opinion was expressed that it required an exceptional case in which the consequences of the threatened act might be disastrous.

- What good will be done to the plaintiff by the grant of the injunction sought? In *Hadmor Productions v Hamilton*[69] the House of Lords held that the High Court judge had been entitled to attach great weight to the view that an injunction would not have been of practical use to the plaintiff. It is not sufficient ground for granting an injunction to argue that if the defendants had no intention of engaging in unlawful conduct the injunction would do them no harm![70]

CASE STUDY

Gate Gourmet supply in-flight catering to airlines and recognised the Transport and General Workers Union (TGWU) for the majority of non-manual employees at its Heathrow South premises. The company agreed a package of staff reductions and changes in working practices with the union, but this was rejected in a membership ballot. Before mediation talks started, employees stopped work and held a sit-in without a ballot. This was alleged to be a response to the hiring of seasonal workers. Following the dismissal of 622 workers, there was picketing at two of the company's sites, and the employer maintained that there was intimidation and harassment of the remaining employees.

The High Court granted an interlocutory injunction on the basis that there was a good arguable case that tortious acts contrary to section 20 TULRCA 1992 had occurred which had been authorised or endorsed by the union. Because the TGWU had not repudiated the unlawful activity, it was right that the injunction should be directed at the union. Despite the right to peaceful assembly's being guaranteed by Article 11 of the European Convention on Human Rights, the balance of convenience lay firmly in favour of expressly prohibiting any activity which went beyond peaceful approaches being made to the employees.[71]

Failure by union officials to comply with an injunction may amount to contempt of court, for which the union is vicariously liable. Indeed, it would appear that a delay in complying with a court order cannot be justified by reference to the union's internal constitution.[72] Where there is deliberate defiance of a court order, a substantial fine may be imposed.[73] In this context it should be observed that section 15 TULRCA 1992 makes it unlawful for a union to use its property to indemnify an individual on whom a penalty has been imposed for contempt or a criminal offence. Additionally, where it is alleged that a union's trustees have unlawfully applied union property or complied with an unlawful direction given under the union rules, a member can seek a High Court order to remove the trustees, recover the property or appoint a receiver.[74]

INDUSTRIAL ACTION THAT AFFECTS THE SUPPLY OF GOODS OR SERVICES TO AN INDIVIDUAL

Section 235A TULRCA 1992 gives an individual the right to apply to the High Court for an order if:

- a trade union or other person has done, or is likely to do, an unlawful act to induce a person to take part in or continue with industrial action, and
- an effect, or likely effect, of the industrial action is, or will be, to prevent or delay the supply of goods or services, or to reduce the quality of goods or services supplied to the claimant.

For these purposes an act is unlawful if it is actionable in tort by anyone, or if it could form the basis of an application by a union member under section 62 TULRCA 1992 (see above). It is immaterial whether or not the individual concerned is entitled to be supplied with the goods or services in question.

PICKETING

CIVIL LAW ASPECTS

According to section 220 TULRCA 1992, it shall be lawful for a person in contemplation or furtherance of a trade dispute to attend:

- at or near their own place of work, or
- if they are an official of a trade union, at or near the place of work of a member of that union whom they are accompanying and whom they represent

for the purpose only of peacefully obtaining or communicating information, or peacefully persuading any person to work or abstain from working.

'Place of work' is not statutorily defined but it would seem to refer to a person's principal place of work or base.[75] As regards the words 'at or near', the Court of Appeal has confirmed that a geographical approach should be taken and that the matter will be one of fact and degree in each case.[76] If people normally work at more than one place or at a place where it is impracticable to picket, their place of work is any of their employer's premises from which they work or from which their work is administered.[77] Unemployed workers whose last employment was terminated in connection with a trade dispute, or whose dismissal was one of the circumstances giving rise to a trade dispute, are entitled to picket at their former place of work. It should be observed that section 220 TULRCA 1992 does not necessarily provide employees with a place that they can effectively picket – for example, if their place of work is closed down. A trade union official who has been elected or appointed to represent some of the members is to be regarded for the purposes of picketing as representing only those members; otherwise, a union official is regarded as representing all the union's members.[78]

Section 220 TULRCA 1992 protects mere attendance only for one of the designated purposes. If an act is done in the course of picketing which is not lawful by virtue of section 220, then section 219 TULRCA 1992 will not prevent an action in tort from being brought. Thus pickets acting within the scope of section 220 TULRCA 1992 may be liable for conspiracy to use unlawful means if they are accompanied by pickets who are not so acting. Equally, a person who is not picketing at a permitted place may be sued for trespass to the highway as well as all the economic torts. This is so even if the employer at the premises picketed has accepted the work of the primary employer in dispute. Peaceful picketing at one's own place of work may also result in civil liability – for example, if it is in support of workers in dispute with another employer.

Mass picketing and intimidation

In *Thomas v NUM (South Wales)*[79] Mr Justice Scott refused to distinguish between 'so-called pickets who are stationed close to the gates of the colliery and the rest, so-called demonstrators, who stand near by'. The judge held that whether the presence or conduct of pickets represents a tortious interference with the right of those who wish to go to work depends on the particular circumstances of the case. In his view, where feelings run high, substantial numbers of pickets are almost bound to have an intimidatory effect on those going to work. Thus while picketing *per se* is not a common-law nuisance, mass picketing is – ie picketing so as by sheer weight of numbers to block the entrance to premises or prevent the entry of vehicles or people.[80]

Injunctions to stop unlawful picketing

An employer whose contracts are interfered with by picketing which falls outside section 220 TULRCA 1992 may bring an action for damages against those responsible and ask a court to make an order stopping the unlawful picketing. An injunction will normally be sought against the person or union on whose instructions or advice the picketing is taking place, but it will also restrict the activities of any others who act on behalf of that person or union (see above on a union's responsibility for the acts of its officials). While the police are not obliged to help an employer identify pickets, a court can ask the police to assist its officers in enforcing injunctions.

THE IMPACT OF THE CRIMINAL LAW

The immunity provided by the civil law cannot protect a picket who commits a criminal offence, and even peaceful picketing can lead to criminal proceedings if it is not lawful by virtue of section 220 TULRCA 1992:

> The criminal law protects the right of every person to go about his lawful daily business free from interference by others. No one is under any obligation to stop when a picket asks him to do so, or if he does stop, to comply with the picket's request – for example, not to go into work. Everyone has the right, if he wants to do so, to cross a picket line to go into his place of work or to deliver or collect goods. A picket may exercise peaceful persuasion, but if he goes beyond that and tries by means other than peaceful persuasion to deter another person from exercising those rights, he may commit a criminal offence.[81]

Paragraph 43 of the Department for Employment (now the Department for Business, Enterprise and Regulatory Reform, BERR) Code of Practice on Picketing lists a range of criminal offences that may be committed by pickets:

- using threatening, abusive or insulting words or behaviour, or disorderly behaviour within the sight or hearing of any person ... likely to be caused harassment, alarm or distress by such conduct

- using threatening, abusive or insulting words or behaviour towards any person with intent to cause fear of violence or to provoke violence

- using or threatening unlawful violence

- obstructing the highway or the entrance to premises or to seek physically to bar the passage of vehicles or persons, etc

- being in possession of an offensive weapon

- intentionally or recklessly damaging property
- engaging in violent, disorderly or unruly behaviour or taking any action which is likely to lead to a breach of the peace
- obstructing a police officer in the execution of his duty.[82]

The police may limit picket numbers

Although it is not the function of the police to take a view of the merits of a particular trade dispute, the law gives them the discretion to take whatever measures may reasonably be considered necessary to ensure that picketing remains peaceful and orderly. Thus the police are entitled to limit the number of pickets at any one place where they have reasonable cause to fear disorder.[83] Having identified the main causes of violence and disorder on the picket line as excessive numbers, the Code of Practice exhorts pickets and their organisers to ensure that 'in general the number of pickets does not exceed six at any entrance to, or exit from a workplace; frequently a smaller number will be appropriate'.[84] The code also has paragraphs dealing with the functions of a picket organiser and the safeguarding of essential supplies and services.[85]

Trespass: liability under civil and criminal law

Apart from the law relating to picketing, the criminal law does not generally play an important role in regulating industrial conflict. However, if employees occupy their employer's premises they become trespassers under the civil law and the employer may invoke a specified procedure to regain possession. Of the statutory provisions which could give rise to criminal liability, the most important today are probably sections 240–1 TULRCA 1992. According to section 240:

> A person commits an offence who wilfully and maliciously breaks a contract of service or hiring, knowing or having reasonable cause to believe that the probable consequence of his so doing, either alone or in combination with others, will be (a) to endanger human life, or cause serious bodily injury, or (b) to expose valuable property whether real or personal to destruction or serious injury.

Establishing guilt

Anyone found guilty of such an offence is liable to pay a fine not exceeding level 2 on the standard scale or to be imprisoned for up to three months, or both. This provision is less likely to form the basis of a prosecution than an action for an injunction to prevent a breach of it by someone who expects that serious injury will result from industrial action.

Section 241 TULRCA 1992 states that:

> A person commits an offence who, with a view to compelling another person to abstain from doing or to do any act which that person has a legal right to do or abstain from doing, wrongfully and without legal authority:

(a) uses violence to or intimidates such other person or his wife or children, or injures his property, or

(b) persistently follows such other person about from place to place, or

(c) hides any tools, clothes or property owned or used by such other person, or deprives him of or hinders him in the use thereof, or

(d) watches or besets the house or other place where such other person resides, or works, or carries on business, or happens to be, or the approach to such house or place, or

(e) follows such other person with two or more other persons in a disorderly manner in or through any street or road.

A person found guilty of this offence is liable to imprisonment for a term not exceeding six months or a fine not exceeding level 5 on the standard scale, or both.

To establish guilt under this section it must be proved that the conduct relied on was wrongful and that the intention with which it was done was, at least in part, to compel others from doing specified acts which they had a legal right to do. In *Galt v Philp*[86] it was held that employees who locked and barricaded the entrance to the premises where they were employed so as to prevent others from working were guilty of 'besetting' within (d) above.

KEY LEARNING POINTS

- The economic torts considered here are inducing a breach of contract, intimidation, conspiracy, interference with business by unlawful means and inducing a breach of statutory duty.

- Statutory immunity from these torts depends on the action's taking place in contemplation or furtherance of a trade dispute. This is known as the 'golden formula'.

- A union will be held liable for the actions of its committees and officials unless those actions are repudiated by the principal executive committee, the president or the general secretary, and the union has done its best to inform the officials, and those taking part in the industrial action, of its repudiation.

- Trade unions and officials can claim immunity only if the union has authorised and endorsed the industrial action after a ballot of members has shown a majority in support of that action.

- Trade unions must take all reasonably necessary steps to ensure that the employer of those to be called upon to take part in industrial action receives written notice of both a ballot and any proposed action. The union must also provide information about the number and categories of employees concerned and their workplaces.

- Remedies available for unlawful action are damages, and interim and permanent injunctions.

- Picketing is lawful in contemplation or furtherance of a trade dispute if it takes place near the employee's own place of work, or if the picket is an official of the union accompanying a member, with the intention of peacefully persuading someone to work or abstain from working.

Reinforce your understanding of this chapter by visiting www.cipd.co.uk/sss for activities, questions, weblinks and additional case studies

REFERENCES

1 See *Camellia Tanker Ltd v ITWF* (1976) IRLR 183

2 See *Metropolitan Borough of Solihull v NUT* (1985) IRLR 211

3 See *Middlebrook Mushrooms Ltd v TGWU* (1993) IRLR 232

4 (1984) IRLR 200

5 See *Galt v Philp* (1984) IRLR 156

6 See *Messenger News Group v NGA* (1984) IRLR 397

7 See *Crofter Harris Tweed Co. v Veitch* (1942) AC 435

8 *Mainstream Properties Ltd v Young* (2005) IRLR 964

9 See *Timeplan Education Group Ltd v NUT* (1997) IRLR 457

10 (1982) IRLR 103

11 (1979) ICR 494; see also *Barretts & Baird Ltd v IPCS* (1987) IRLR 3

12 (1982) IRLR 200; see also *Dimskal Shipping Co. v ITWF* (1992) IRLR 78

13 See *British Telecommunications v CWU* (2004) IRLR 58

14 See *P v NAS-UWT* (2003) IRLR 307

15 See *Westminster City Council v Unison* (2001) IRLR 524

16 Section 223 TULRCA 1992; see Chapter 14 on dismissal during industrial action

17 Sections 222 and 225 respectively TULRCA 1992

18 (1999) IRLR 31

19 See *Unison v UK* (2002) IRLR 497

20 *ABP v TGWU* (1989) IRLR 399

21 See *London Borough of Wandsworth v NAS-UWT* (1993) IRLR 344

22 Section 244(5) TULRCA 1992

23 (1977) IRLR 312; compare *Dimbleby & Sons v NUJ* (1984) IRLR 161

24 Section 244(3) TULRCA 1992

25 Section 244(4) TULRCA 1992

26 See *Huntley v Thornton* (1957) 1 WLR 321; also *Stratford v Lindley* (1965) AC 307

27 (1980) IRLR 35

28 See *ABP v TGWU* (1989) IRLR 305

29 Section 224(4) TULRCA 1992

30 See *Gate Gourmet Ltd v TGWU* (2005) IRLR 881

31 See *News Group v SOGAT* (1986) IRLR 227

32 Section 20(2) TULRCA 1992

33 Section 119 TULRCA 1992

34 Section 20(3)(b) TULRCA 1992

35 Sections 21(1)–(3) TULRCA 1992. See *Balfour Kilpatrick v Acheson* (2003) IRLR 683

36 Section 21(5) and (6) TULRCA 1992

37 Section 20(6) TULRCA 1992

38 See Code of Practice on Industrial Action Ballots and Notice to Employers 2005

39 This can be extended to eight weeks with agreement by the employer; section 234 TULRCA 1992; see also *RJB Mining v NUM* (1997) IRLR 621

40 *Post Office v UCW* (1990) IRLR 143

41 Section 226A TULRCA 1992

42 Section 227 TULRCA 1992; see *RMT v Midland Mainline Ltd* (2001) IRLR 813

43 (1995) IRLR 636

44 Section 228A TULRCA 1992

45 Section 230(2) TULRCA 1992. See *P v NAS-UWT* (note 14)

46 See sections 226B and 231B TULRCA 1992

47 *Post Office v UCW* (note 40)

48 (1999) IRLR 249

49 See *West Midlands Travel v TGWU* (1994) IRLR 578

50 Section 232A TULRCA 1992; see *P v NAS-UWT* (note 14)

51 See sections 231 and 231A TULRCA 1992

52 Section 226(3A)

53 Section 234A TULRCA 1992

54 See *Connex South Eastern Ltd v NURMTW* (1999) IRLR 249

55 See section 234(1) TULRCA 1992

56 Section 232B TULRCA 1992. See *P v NAS-UWT* (note 14)

57 Section 62 TULRCA 1992

58 For exceptions see section 22(1) TULRCA 1992

59 See *Boxfoldia Ltd v NGA* (1988) IRLR 383; on aggravated and exemplary damages, see *Messenger News Group v NGA* (note 6)

60 Section 23 TULRCA 1992

61 *Express Newspapers v Keys* (1980) IRLR 247 per Griffiths J

62 (1979) IRLR 478

63 *ABP v TGWU* (note 28)

64 See section 221(2) TULRCA 1992

65 See *NWL v Nelson* (1979) IRLR 478

66 (1980) IRLR 437

67 See note 34

68 *Duport Steels Ltd v Sirs* (1980) IRLR 112

69 See note 10

70 See *Shipping Company Uniform Inc v ITWF* (1985) IRLR 71

71 *Gate Gourmet Ltd v TGWU* (note 30)

72 See *Kent Free Press v NGA* (1987) IRLR 267

73 See *Read Transport v NUM (South Wales)* (1985) IRLR 67

74 Section 16 TULRCA 1992

75 See *Union Traffic v TGWU* (1989) IRLR 127

76 See *Rayware Ltd v TGWU* (1989) IRLR 134

77 See section 220(2) TULRCA 1992

78 See section 220(4) TULRCA 1992

79 (1985) IRLR 136

80 See also *News Group v SOGAT* (note 31), where the torts of nuisance and intimidation were committed

81 Department of Employment Code of Practice on Picketing, paragraph 42

82 See also the Public Order Act 1986 for the offences of disorderly conduct, riot, violent disorder, affray and threatening behaviour

83 See *Moss v McLachlan* (1985) IRLR 76

84 Department of Employment Code, paragraph 51; see *Thomas v NUM (South Wales)* (1985) IRLR 136

85 Department of Employment Code, paragraphs 54–57 and 62–64

86 See note 5

Index

The CIPD would like to thank the following members of the CIPD Publishing editorial board for their help and advice:
Caroline Hook, Huddersfield University Business School
Edwina Hollings, Staffordshire University Business School
Pauline Dibben, Sheffield University Business School
Simon Gurevitz, University of Westminster Business School
Barbara Maiden, University of Wolverhampton Business School
Wendy Yellowley and Marilyn Farmer, Buckinghamshire New University School of Business and Management